THE 19TH CENTURY.

A History.

BY

ROBERT MACKENZIE.

CHAUTAUQUA EDITION.

CHICAGO:
FAIRBANKS, PALMER & CO.
1881.

CONTENTS.

Book First.

CHAPTER I.—THE OPENING OF THE CENTURY.

CHAPTER II.—NAPOLEON BONAPARTE.

Book Second.

CHAPTER IV.—THE REDRESS OF WRONGS—II.

CHAPTER V.—CHARTISM.

CHAPTER VI.—OUR WARS.

CHAPTER VII.—THE VICTORIES OF PEACE—I.

CHAPTER VIII.—THE VICTORIES OF PEACE—II

CONTENTS.

Book Third.

CHAPTER II.—FRANCE: THE SECOND EMPIRE.

CHAPTER III.—PRUSSIA.

CHAPTER IV.—AUSTRIA.

CHAPTER V.—ITALY.

CHAPTER VI.—RUSSIA.

CHAPTER VII.—TURKEY.

CHAPTER VIII.—THE UNITED STATES OF AMERICA.

CHAPTER IX.—THE PAPACY.

CHAPTER X.—THE PROGRESS OF LIBERTY IN EUROPE.

THE

NINETEENTH CENTURY.

---◆---

𝕭𝖔𝖔𝖐 𝕱𝖎𝖗𝖘𝖙.

CHAPTER I.

THE OPENING OF THE CENTURY.

AT the opening of the Nineteenth Century all Europe was occupied with war. The European people then numbered one hundred and seventy million, and of these, four million were set apart, by their own choice or the decree of their governments, to the business of fighting. They were withdrawn from the occupations of peace, and maintained at enormous cost, expressly to harm their fellow-men. The interests of peace withered in the storm; the energies of all nations, the fruits of all industries were poured forth in the effort to destroy. From the utmost North to the shores of the Mediterranean, from the confines of Asia to the Atlantic, men toiled to burn each other's cities, to waste each other's fields, to destroy each other's lives. In some lands there was heard the shout of victory, in some the wail of defeat. In all lands the ruinous waste of war had produced bitter poverty; grief and fear were in every home. This had lasted already for ten years, and was yet to last for fifteen years more. It was not to cease till millions of men had perished.

Peace, it has been said, is the dream of the wise, but war is the history of man. It has been even so. It need not surprise us to find the men of Europe enduring unutterable miseries, sustained only by the hope that they would be able to inflict yet greater miseries upon their neighbors—for Europe has spent the larger portion of her time in fighting. But yet the wars which occupied the early years of the century do excite our wonder. They were gigantic beyond example. They wasted life and treasure with a profusion to which Europe, with her bloody experience of centuries, knows no parallel. They were so prolonged that before the close men were fighting in the quarrel who had been unborn when it broke out. Whence came these monstrous wars, and what were the questions which the men of this time sought, by methods so coarse, to solve?

It was in France—always the most unquiet member of the European family—that these huge and mournful disorders originated. France contained then a population of twenty-five million, and she had long been the victim of misgovernment so base and cruel that it had now become intolerable.*

In course of ages liberty had become wholly extinct in France. The king held in his hands the unquestioned right to dispose, at his will, of the lives and property of the people. He was the sole legislator; his own pleasure was his only rule. He levied taxes, asking no consent of those who had to pay. He waged war to avenge personal slights, to gain personal ends; and thousands of his subjects laid down their lives that his frivolous antipathies might find gratification. He sent men to prison without any crime being laid to their charge, and kept them there, without trial, till they died. Within the walls of his capital stood the Bastile—a prison vast and grim

---

* It is not, however, to be supposed that the condition of the French people was worse than that of the other Continental nations. On the contrary, De Tocqueville shows that it was better.

—the slow growth of ages of despotism. The king's order filled those gloomy towers and dungeons with prisoners, many of whom never knew wherefore this dreadful fate had befallen them. An Englishman was once found who had suffered thirty years of captivity, and it could not, by any diligence of inquiry, be discovered what he had done, or whom he had offended. Nor was it enough that the king avenged himself upon his own enemies. An agreeable courtier was requited with a gift of *lettres de cachet* already signed by the king, but with a blank left for the name of the victim. The rich man could purchase for money the power to destroy those whom he hated.

During sixty years of the eighteenth century the king of France was Louis XV.—one of the meanest and basest of human creatures. It was the belief of this unworthy person that France was his, and that she and her twenty-five million of people were of no value, otherwise than as they ministered to his enjoyment. No one about him ever, in all his long life, suggested another view of the subject. The great nobles went daily to see him dressed and undressed*—regaling him the while with the obscene gossip which he loved so well to hear. The king "had not an hour in the day for attention to important matters." He wasted the resources of France upon his filthy pleasures. His mistresses made him sign drafts on the treasury for such amounts as they desired. Even to this most debased of men it became evident that a change was near. Voltaire and the others, he said, were ruining the monarchy; but it was consolation enough to believe that it would last out his time. Under Louis XV. France ripened apace for her doom.

Next to the throne stood the noble families, numbering one hundred and fifty thousand persons. All positions of dignity were held by members of these families. The superior clergy

* Several of the great nobles shared the daily honor of handing to their sovereign his shirt, or reverentially denuding him of that garment.

were nobles; the officers of the army, the judges, the ambassadors—all were noble. They enjoyed exemption from most
of the taxation which pressed so heavily upon their inferiors.
They possessed strange powers to oppress, which they mercilessly exercised. For the most part they were poor—ages of
extravagance having wasted their substance; and they were
known to the people only by the unsparing severity of their
exactions. With revolution about to burst forth, that was not
a desirable introduction. They lived in utter idleness. "They
absolutely did nothing," said Edmund Burke. "Their very
look wearied me. They could only die of war or of ennui."

Beyond the nobles were the French people. A gulf impassable separated them from the awful splendours of the
aristocracy. They might grow rich, but they could not rise
out of the original degradation of their origin; they could
never cease to be despised.

Three-fourths of the French people lived in the country,
and earned their living by lowly peasant toil. Their lot was
hard—harder than we in this happier time are able fully to
understand. The laws had not been made with any thought
of their interests. The laws were made and administered by
men who regarded the people of France as born for the uses
of the higher class.

The tax-gatherer was everywhere, and among the simple
peasantry he could work his cruel will without fear of detection
or rebuke. The great lords preserved game for their lordly
sport.* Droves of wild boars, herds of deer ranged the country, trampling the crops into ruin. The peasant who slew one
of these invaders expiated his offence by imprisonment. The
weeding and hoeing of crops were forbidden, as tending to disturb the young partridges. Limitations were imposed upon the
use of manures, lest the flavor of the game should be injuriously

* For thirty leagues around Paris game was strictly protected for the use of the
royal family.

affected. Now and then the ruined peasantry in their despair demanded, "with a great cry," the abolition of all sorts of game; but their cry was unheeded. Men were bound to grind their corn only at the seigneur's mill; to press their grapes only in his press; to bake their bread only in his oven. Hand-mills were forbidden; but sometimes the great lord sold for money to the wretched peasant permission to crush his handful of wheat between two stones. Services the most intolerable were exacted, or exemption from them obtained by payment. When the lady of the seigneur was ill, it became the duty of the peasants to beat the marshes all night and terrify the frogs into silence, lest the great lady should be disturbed by their clamour. This obligation was, in course of ages, commuted into an annual payment. Many seigneurs had their principal revenue from such exactions.

It pleased the government of France to encourage manufactures and commerce, and to overburden agriculture. In some cases the poor cultivator paid to the tax-gatherer five-eighths of the produce of his ground. In many cases cultivation ceased —utterly crushed out by intolerable taxation. Everywhere the pressure of taxation and the oppression of the nobles kept the farmer hopelessly poor, and cultivation rude and unproductive.*

Justice was vilely administered. The judges were ignorant, and dependent on the seigneurs. Men were not ashamed to sit as judges in a cause in which they were interested. Bribes were essential to the satisfactory issue of litigation. Indeed, it grew to be an accepted truth that it was folly to appeal to a court of law without some better support than the mere justice of a cause.

* Smollett speaks of the French farmers as he saw them in 1765—" Without cattle to furnish manure, without horses to execute the plans of agriculture; their farm-houses mean, their furniture wretched, their apparel beggarly; themselves and their beasts the images of famine.'' French agriculture at the breaking out of the revolution was not beyond that of the tenth century. The plough used was that of Virgil's time. But even then the habit of economy was firmly rooted. The peasant was said to starve himself, hoard his money, and buy land.

The roads near the great cities of France were perhaps the finest in Europe. The traveler remarked with grateful wonder upon their unexpected smoothness. Alas! he knew little of the sufferings by which it had been gained. Roads were made by the forced labor of the country people; and the labor was so mercilessly imposed that many persons sank and died under the intolerable severity.

It was a savage age in which these things were inflicted and endured. Men not yet old had seen the torture to which Damiens was subjected for attempting to murder the king. The wretched man's flesh was torn from his bones by red-hot pincers, and molten lead was poured into his wounds. Almost to the close of the century criminals endured the torture of the wheel. The limbs were broken by blows of a heavy iron bar, and then the mangled body was hung across the edge of an upright wheel, till the poor remains of life ebbed in agony away. With all these horrors the men and women of France were familiar from their youth. When they rose to avenge the wrongs which made their lives bitter, it was not probable that they would use milder expedients than those in the practice of which their superiors had so amply instructed them.

1757 A.D.

The time came at length when the cruel wrongs which had been patiently borne for centuries ceased to be longer tolerable. France had enjoyed an unusually lengthened repose. The exhaustion produced by the mad wars of Louis XIV. had been the defence of the country against the repetition upon any great scale of similar iniquities. France had given herself, with energy unknown before, to the pursuits of peace; and her vast resources were being developed with a rapidity which, tried by the standard of the time, was altogether satisfactory. Her commerce was flourishing; her manufactures prospered and extended. She had founded colonies, and her commercial marine approached in extent to that of England herself. Her cities were becoming large; her middle classes were becoming wealthy and intelligent. The education of her merchants was superior to that of the nobles, who yet looked with unconcealed and offensive disdain upon the wisest and wealthiest of the classes beneath them.

The silent pressure of opinion would gradually have wrested from the nobles a redress of grievances which the altered circumstances of the country rendered unendurable. But, strangely enough, the protest against the blind tyranny of ages found voice first among the nobility themselves.

Among the younger nobles there sprang up a sentimental love of liberty and detestation of tyranny. Those speculations regarding equality which are so frequently the solace of the poor, were at this time in France the occupation of the privileged classes. The heroes of ancient Greece and Rome were objects of passionate admiration to the young nobility of France. Count Segur recalled, fifty years after, the thunders of applause with which the courtiers in the theatre at Versailles received the lines of Voltaire: "I am the son of Brutus, and bear graven on my heart the love of liberty and horror of kings." The influence of England, too, became powerful among the higher classes of France. Montesquieu had already taught to his countrymen the superiority of English institutions. The perception of this superiority was expressed in a manner sufficiently fanciful. A rage for English fashions sprang up, and for a time possessed society. The fantastic dresses of the old court were replaced by the simpler costumes of the islanders.* French gardens were remodelled after English designs. English horses and horse-races, English gigs, English grooms, and the English mode of riding, were indispensable to a man of fashion. The export of English goods to France rose from £90,000 to £830,000. It was justly held that this

---

* Count Segur was troubled by the reign of frock-coats, which, as he foretold, wou d be found to indicate a dangerous passion for equality. So strong was the reaction in favor of simplicity that men now buttoned their coats to conceal the stars and other decorations which they had formerly been proud to exhibit.

2

grotesque passion expressed French admiration of the liberty
and independence which the English form of government
secured to the people.

The literary influences of the time were singularly powerful
and vehemently hostile to the old order of things. In the
later years of Louis XV. the men of letters combined to produce an Encyclopædia which should instruct mankind in
regard to nearly every object of human thought. It was a
vast enterprise carried out with extraordinary ability. The
Encyclopædia became at once a great power in France. It
claimed a huge enlargement of human liberty in thought and
action; it execrated the cruel despotisms under which the
world groaned; it advocated representation and self-government. Every educated Frenchman read the Encyclopædia,
to learn there how he had been robbed of his birthright by
the government whose duty it was to protect him.

The writings of Voltaire exercised a prodigious influence
upon French thought. His reproduction of ancient heroes
who had defied tyrants stirred the French heart to its depths.
Voltaire had spent three years in England, whose institutions
he learned to admire. In innumerable writings he expressed
his abhorrence of tyranny. He expressed, with especial energy
his abhorrence of the tyranny of priests—unhappily for France
including the Christian religion itself in his condemnation.*
His words reached the hearts of the upper classes in France
with unexampled authority. He became a power which it is
not easy for us now to comprehend. A few weeks be-
1778   fore his death he revisited Paris from his retirement at
A.D.
        Ferney. He was now a man of eighty, bent, shrivelled
recalling by his antique dress the manners of an extinct genera-

---

* The primary object of Voltaire's attack was Christianity as represented by the
Roman Catholic Church of his day. His error lay in confounding two things so dis-
similar as the Church and the Christianity of the New Testament, and in indiscrimi-
nately denouncing both. Christianity, as Voltaire saw it around him, was not
deserving of better treatment than it received at his hands.

tion; the deep piercing eye alone asserting his old supremacy. The learned, and the noble, and the beautiful worshipped at the shrine of the withered unbeliever, who had uttered so vividly their protest against the evils of the time.

The writings of Rousseau were still more widely read, and exercised a more powerful influence over the growth of opinion and the course of public affairs.* In 1753 Rousseau had written on the "Origin of Inequality among Men." His discussions of that and kindred topics so attracted the public mind, that fiction, and poetry, and the drama occupied now a subordinate place. Political and economical questions alone were regarded. Even assemblies of the merely fashionable were invaded by this passion, which, with the rapidity of growth customary in France, soon absorbed the attention of all classes. The new tendency fed itself by a close study of the policy of the government and its results. When Necker, in 1781, published his Report on National Finance, the demand for copies was so large that for some time it could not be supplied. A few years before, the proceedings of the government commanded little attention; now, a watchfulness which, under existing circumstances, was full of peril attended every step.

While the public mind was becoming conscious of the miseries which oppressed society, and yearning vaguely for deliverance, word came to Paris that the American colonies of England were in revolt. The enthusiasm which the news enkindled was intense. The attempt to reject arbitrary power and establish popular government, awakened deep sympathy among the adherents of one of the most despotic governments in Europe. The younger nobles sought eagerly to join the insurgents. Count Segur was refused permission to do so, but went in defiance of prohibition; Lafayette was arrested in the attempt. The king was most reluctant to aid the revolted

* "It was Rousseau alone who inoculated the French with the doctrine of the sovereignty of the people, and its extremest consequences."—MALLET DUPAN.

colonists; but the popular sentiment was too strong, and he had at last to declare war against England. The American deputies—Franklin and his companions—were received with boundless delight. It presents a striking contrast—the rustic plainness of apparel and speech, the massive good sense and simple honesty of the republicans, as they moved amid the splendours of Versailles, and the frivolous elegance of the courtiers. Out of the alliance between France and America there sprang a quickened perception of the evils of despotism and an enormous increase of the national burdens.

Ages of misgovernment and profligate waste had brought French finance to a crisis. For many years there had been a constant excess of expenditure, until, on the eve of the revolution, the debt of France amounted to £244,000,000. The interest on this debt and the expenses of government were £26,400,000, while the revenue for the year was only £18,800,000. Every device had been tried to increase the revenue, ending still in disappointment and dismissal of the unsuccessful minister. Even the embarrassment deepened. Once for a brief season the decay of the monarchy seemed to be stayed.

1783
A.D.

The king, groping after a capable financier, lighted, happily as it appeared, on M. de Calonne. Calonne was a compliant, agreeable man, too frivolous to concern himself deeply about the crisis whose approach he was yet acute enough to perceive. His confidence brought sunshine back to the gloomy court. He paid the debts of the princes; he purchased new palaces for the queen; he pleased the courtiers by magnificent *fêtes;* he began the construction of great docks at Cherbourg. Once more the treasury was full and money abundant. Even the Baron de Talleyrand was satisfied that Calonne had saved the state, and only expressed surprise that he had been able to do it so quickly.

He had gained the confidence of the bankers, and prevailed

on them to lend money,—that was all; and when that resource was exhausted, as it quickly was, deepened gloom fell upon the penniless government.

When Calonne could no longer borrow, he intimated that the nation was supporting itself by artifices whose efficacy had ceased. He proposed to the king to summon the notables,— the chief men of all ranks, whom it was customary in time of peril to convene. To this august assembly he would propose that the nobles and the clergy should yield to the service of the state their special exemption from taxation. Thus would the exchequer be replenished, and the *tiers état* relieved from a sense of wrong. The poor king was so charmed with the idea that he lost the sleep of a whole night for very pleasure. The assembly met; the awful aspect of national finance was fully disclosed; the noble and reverend senators were invited to make sacrifices for the public good. 1787 A. D. They responded with a shout of indignation against the minister who made such a request. Calonne was dismissed. After much profitless talk, the notables were sent home, having achieved nothing. The deficiency was undiminished: there was only a deeper conviction of its gravity in the public mind.

Meanwhile, Paris was devoured by a thirst for political discussion. For some years the national accounts had been published and all men could see to what a pass the country had been brought by the misgovernment of its kings. The middle class discussed the errors of their government and the wrongs of the people, dwelling much upon the insignificance to which the citizens had been reduced that the king and the nobles might be great. The poor men heard the echo of the discussions which occupied the ranks above them, and they learned to trace to their kings the poverty which made their lives so bitter. The fever in the minds of men was expressed by an issue of pamphlets, which reached a weekly average of nearly one hundred. The cost of printing increased twofold by the unwonted demand. These writings were hawked about the streets and eagerly bought. They were read aloud to little groups of ill-fed workingmen, whose upturned faces, eager, hungry, stern, reflected with ominous fidelity the fierce suggestions which were addressed to them. In every coffee-house an orator, mounted on chair or table, discoursed to as many people as could crowd within hearing about the miseries which government imposed upon them. As the steadily-deepening antagonism between government and people advanced, every step was vehemently discussed, and excitement swelled day by day into wilder excesses.

It was no longer believed by any one that the king and nobles could save the state. The nation itself must do that. A meeting of the States-general was demanded and readily ordered by the compliant king.

In the month of May, 1789, there came to Versailles, gathered by universal suffrage from all parts of France, twelve hundred men, whose wisdom was to undo the mischiefs which king and nobles had wrought, and restore the sinking fortunes of France. As the chosen twelve hundred walked in procession to hear mass before entering on their duties, a vast crowd, thrilled by the hopes of a new era, looked on with wonder and joy. The clergy walked foremost, superbly clad in violet robes; the nobles followed in black, with gold vests, and white plumes in their hats; last of all came the *tiers état* in simple black, unglorified by the gay colors of their superiors, but numerous as all the others put together.

When the assembly met, the three orders went each to a separate chamber. It was the wish of the clergy and nobles to vote apart from the commons, whose purposes they could thus bridle; but it was the determination of the commons that the voting should be in one chamber, because thus their superior numbers secured them absolute

May 2,
1789
A. D.

predominance. Their demand was resisted, and eight weeks were spent in idleness. The public, waiting eagerly for the expected regeneration, execrated the stubbornness of the clergy and nobles. At length the commons declared themselves the National Assembly,* and intimated their intention to proceed alone to save the country. The poor king, tremblingly anxious to please all, first exhorted the three orders to meet together; then he ordained them to meet separately; finally, he commanded the clergy and nobles to yield to the wishes of the commons, in which he was reluctantly obeyed. The commons had won their first great victory, and for a brief season Paris rejoiced. The revolution, it was said, was virtually accomplished without costing a single drop of blood!

But the secret advisers of the king were unable to accept their defeat. They failed to discover that a nation was against them, and hoped by overawing or dissolving the insubordinate assembly to restore the endangered supremacy. In July, thirty thousand soldiers, with one hundred pieces of cannon, were encamped between Paris and Versailles; for the court had no wiser thought than the forcible trampling out of disaffection. The assembly requested the king to withdraw the troops, but his majesty refused. Soon the march of regiments through Paris alarmed the already agitated citizens. The city burst into uncontrollable excitement: the shops were closed; business was suspended; the population was in the streets discussing the crisis which had arisen. The wildest rumors were eagerly believed. A great massacre, it was said, was planned by government; cannon were pointed on the city; even now red-hot shot was being prepared in the Bastile. Paris was to be blockaded and starved. The only safety of the people was to take up arms, and oppose by force the designs of their oppressors.

*It was believed that this important step was taken by the advice of Jefferson, one of the American deputies, whose great talents inevitably gained for him commanding influence.

Under the influence of alarms such as these, a patriot army sprang at once into existence. Forty thousand men enlisted in one day. Pikes and sword-blades were forged; scythe-blades were fastened to poles; ancient fire-arms were dragged from their retirement;—but still the supply of arms was inadequate. It was known that in the' Hôtel des Invalides were arms enough, slightly guarded. Thither hastened the patriot hordes. Ready entrance was gained, and an ample supply of muskets with some cannon rewarded the daring of the invaders.

A greater enterprise was now to be attempted. The Bastile was to the Parisians an expressive symbol of that July 14, despotism under which they and their fathers had 1789 groaned. A sudden impulse of the mob, now flushed A. D. with the first consciousness of strength, decreed the fall of that hated fortress. It seemed hopeless for a mob to attempt the overthrow of the famous citadel, with its ponderous draw-bridges, its massive walls, its lofty towers, its artillery which could inflict injuries so terrible upon the undefended besiegers. But the garrison was feeble in number and irresolute in spirit. Both governor and garrison quailed before the countless multitude of their assailants. The Bastile was surrendered after a slight resistance, and many of its defenders were pitilessly massacred.

For many days the fallen fortress was visited by crowds of curious and horrified citizens. They pierced its dark staircases and mysterious passages; they entered its awful cells, which reminded them of graves; they shuddered at the heavy chain in each dungeon, and the great stone which served as bed and as chair. Strange instruments of torture were found, among which was particularly noted an iron suit of armour, so fashioned as to grasp every part of the victims's body and utterly forbid movement. What nameless agonies of forgotten men had that armour once infolded! But all these devilish engines had been long unused, for the rule of Louis XVI. was mild. There was not found so much as one political prisoner in the Bastile, and only seven prisoners of any description. The National Assembly decreed that the Bastile should be razed to the ground for its hateful recollections.

While these vast changes were in progress in Paris, King Louis at Versailles still suffered himself to dream of restoring tranquility by the help of his army. Even while listening to the sound of cannon fired upon the Bastile, it was not supposed that the disorders which had arisen were of a very alarming character. But in the middle of the night a courtier entered the king's chamber and told him that Paris was in arms and the Bastile taken. The dismayed monarch sat long in silence. "Why, this is a revolt!" he said at length. "Sire," replied the courtier, "it is a revolution!" Next morning the humbled monarch announced to the assembly that his troops would be withdrawn from Paris and Versailles. The unequal combat between the court and the people had fairly opened, and already the result to the former was defeat never to be retrieved.

Even at this early stage of the revolution, with the fierce excitement yet in its infancy, the atrocities committed by the mob of Paris was such as only the most debased savages can be guilty of. The heads of their victims were cut off and borne in triumph along the streets. Occasionally the heart of a victim was plucked out and exhibited to the crowd. Pieces of human flesh were mingled with the wine which the frantic savages quaffed to the confusion of tyrants. Dotted over France stood the pleasant homes of the old nobility. The relations between the seigneurs and the peasants who lived beside them had not been kindly. The seigneur was known mainly by his exactions. He had lorded it haughtily over his poor neighbours, caring nothing for their hopeless toil, their obscure suffering. But their hour had come at length. They burst upon the château of their lord; they slaughtered its inmates with unheard-of torture; the house itself they plun-

dered and burned. The rural districts became at once unin-
habitable, and the nobles fled in terror out of France.

The assembly in angry haste abolished the unjust laws which
had for ages oppressed the French people. During the
hours of a single evening sitting, the whole fabric of
feudal privilege was thrown to the ground. Henceforth
the burden of taxation was to lie equitably on all classes;
personal servitude, the exclusive right to hunt and shoot, the
criminal jurisdiction of the nobles, the sale of public offices,—all
were instantly swept away, amidst transports of delight possible
only in France. The abolition of tithes for support of the clergy
followed immediately. Municipal government and universal
suffrage were set up. The service of the state was no longer
reserved for a favoured class; all offices, civil and military,
were now open to all Frenchmen. The evil which had slowly
crystallized during centuries into wicked laws was effaced at a
stroke by the indignant representatives of the sufferers.

The revolution had been very glorious, but it began to prove
very costly. The people of Paris were too much elated to return to vulgar toil. They wandered about the streets, engaged
in heated debate upon the rights of man and the iniquities of
kings and nobles. And soon they found that as they earned
no money so they could buy no food. The municipality had to
feed the idle people. Bailly, the mayor of Paris, whom his
thankless constituents ultimately hanged, often did not know at
midnight how the city was to be fed next day.

And thus also the revenue fell off by the decay of commerce,
till it was smaller by one-third than it had been before. The
deficit yawned wider and more devouring than it had done when
the notables were summoned to close the awful gulf. But
measures were possible now of which the notables dared not to
have dreamed. The possessions of the church, amounting to
one-third of all the soil of France, were seized. Henceforth

Aug.
1789
A. D.

the priests were to be paid their painfully reduced salaries by the state.*

The meek Louis was swept almost unresistingly along by the torrent which surged around. A crowd of women, pressed by want, marched out to Versailles, and brought the king and his family back with them to Paris,—away from the splendours of Versailles, which no French monarch has since enjoyed. He tried to escape with his wife and children from the thick-ening horrors which beset him. He got as far as Varennes, where he was to meet an escort which would secure his safety. But, alas! the poor king stopped to wait at one end of the little town, while the horses and escort were waiting at the other. Alarm was raised, and the king was taken back to his palace. An English traveller saw him shortly after at the Tuileries: "The king as plump as ease can make him; the dauphin, working with his little hoe and rake, a good-natured looking boy of five or six, guarded by two grenadiers."

The amazing events which followed each other in so swift succession in France were watched with profound interest in other lands. By many they were hailed with exultation as the dawn of a brighter era for mankind.† There was hope for all oppressed states when France, most oppressed of all, had so quickly and so thoroughly vindicated her liberties. The lower class—too much oppressed in all countries—began to cherish extravagant hopes. Inequality was to be effaced; poverty and suffering were to be things of the past. Mr. Fox spoke the sentiment of many Englishmen when he pronounced the new

---

* The church held property valued at £80,000,000, and yielding an annual revenue of over £8,000,000.

† "Bliss was it in that dawn to be alive,
But to be young was very heaven! O times
In which the meagre, stale, forbidding ways
Of custom, law, and statute, took at once
The attraction of a country in romance!
Not favoured spots alone, but the whole earth
The beauty wore of promise."—WORDSWORTH.

constitution of France the most glorious edifice of liberty which had been erected on the basis of human integrity in any age or country.

The kings and nobles of Europe looked on these transactions with a different eye. The overthrow of their orders in France was an inexpressible shock to their long-established beliefs about themselves. In every court the opinion still prevailed that the king ruled by divine right, and that any invasion of his authority was an act of profane violence.

The relations of France with the neighbouring powers could not but be troubled. The audacious temper of the revolutionary government was certain to lead to offences which monarchs, outraged by the violence offered to one of their own order, would be swift to resent. And so it proved. The Emperor of Austria—brother-in-law to King Louis—and the King of Prussia openly asserted their right to maintain the French throne by force of arms. The emigrant nobles gathered on German soil,* and intrigued, as it was natural they should, against the revolutionary government. The irritated French demanded redress of these grievances, but got none. They were eager for war. The fierce energy which the revolution had evoked could not otherwise find due scope. War with Austria and Prussia was declared in April, 1792.

England remained for some time neutral. But as the excitement of the French became more ungovernable, they followed a course which made every government their enemy. Perceiving that similar revolutions in other countries were the surest guarantee for the success of their own, they laboured to awaken discontent and promote everywhere the establishment of republican institutions. They offered assistance to any people so disposed. They announced hostility to any people who adhered to their prince and nobility. These measures caused reasonable anxiety in England. The English govern-

* They and their families numbered over one hundred thousand persons.

ment, with a higher intelligence than Germany evinced, emphatically disavowed any claim to dictate to the French, and demanded only that Erance should keep within her own frontiers, and leave to other nations that freedom which she asserted for herself. An angry correspondence passed between the governments, terminating when the execution of the king rendered war inevitable. England closed diplomatic Feb. relations with her excited neighbour; impatient and 1793 reckless France declared war against England. Russia A.D. made common cause with England, so soon as she heard of the execution of the king.

In the summer months of 1792 the Duke of Brunswick was marching towards Paris with a vast force* of Prussians and Austrians. In his train swarmed emigrant nobles burning for revenge,—eager to contribute to the restoration of the old abuses which they had found so pleasant. The French were making ready to fight, but their enthusiasm was not yet fully enkindled, and their preparations were backward. They were busy celebrating the triumphs they had won,—planting trees of liberty—listening to fervid expositions of the rights of man— marching in great procession to impress their sentiments upon the legislature. As they were thus occupied, the Duke of Brunswick, moving on towards Paris, issued for the instruction of men a declaration of the objects which he proposed to gain. He was to put an end to the anarchy which prevailed in France, —he was to defend the church and the throne,—he was to restore to the king the liberty and dignity which he had lost, and inflict signal vengeance upon all who dared to insult or wrong his majesty. In a word, he would snatch from the rejoicing Frenchmen the liberty which they had just achieved, and restore the ancient, lately overthrown tyranny which their souls loathed.

So, then, it was plain that king and nobles were in their

* One hundred and forty thousand men.

hearts opposed to liberty, and allied with foreigners to suppress it. All Frenchmen now were brothers, leagued to resist the avowed enemies of human freedom. The foolish proclamation evoked a deep and indignant defiance, and men rushed to arms. But with a powerful enemy approaching their gates, was a traitor to the great cause to occupy the throne? The proclamation sealed the fate of the monarchy. A cry arose for the dethronement of the king. One party wished it to be accomplished in a formal and orderly way, by decree of the assembly; another preferred that it should be achieved by the uprising of an outraged people. The advocates of insurrection gave prompt decision in favour of their own views. Thirty Aug. 10, thousand men, with 'a suitable artillery, stormed the 1792 Tuileries, and massacred the Swiss guards. The king A.D. with his wife and children sought refuge in the National Assembly, whence they were transferred to a prison.

Meanwhile, the Duke of Brunswick was moving on. By the 30th August he was before Verdun, the last fortification which barred his road to Paris. The rage and fear of the excited people made them cruel. The king and his friends were the cause of this invasion. On them it was surely fitting that vengeance for the woes of the nation should fall. Danton, with a fierce energy and boundless audacity of speech, which roused a fury unknown before in the Parisian heart, urged the necessity of putting the royalists in fear. They must paralyze by terror those who still favored monarchy. Not otherwise could the machinations of wicked persons be baffled, and the country saved.

Verdun fell almost at the first breath of bombardment, and on the night of the 1st September, it was known in Paris that the progress of the enemy was unopposed. The prisons were full of royalists, in whose interest France was enduring the miseries of invasion. The mob crowded around the prisons, clamouring fiercely for the blood of the unhappy inmates. A mock tribunal was extemporized. The victims were hurridly interrogated, almost invariably condemned, and then thrust forth into the armed crowd—resembling fiends rather than men —who swarmed in the court-yard. Men who had never even in thought sinned against their country—men whose lives had been devoted to the relief of the poor and suffering, passed un-pitied through the fatal gateway to a death of horror. Women, young and beautiful—women in helpless, unoffending age, were hewn to pieces by savages. Eleven hundred persons were thus slaughtered. When all was over, the murderers were duly paid for their service by the municipality of Paris. By atrocities such as these the maddened Parisians sought to lay upon the royal-ists the restraint of fear.

The French army of defence, under Dumouriez, encountered the Prussians at Valmy. After a slight engagement, in Sept. 28, which the French fought with unexpected spirit, the 1792 Duke of Brunswick fell back, discouraged, and France A.D. was delivered from her danger.

And now that the invader was driven away, what was to be done with the discrowned king whom he had come to restore, and who was known to have plotted, or allowed others to plot, for the overthrow of the revolution? The Prussian in-vasion sealed the ruin not merely of the throne, but of Louis and his family.

The king had been for four months a prisoner, entertaining the most gloomy anticipations regarding his fate, reading much of a history sadly resembling his own—that of Charles I. of England. He was brought to the bar of the Convention, charged with offences against the republic. By a narrow majority he was doomed to die. Two days after he was led forth. From his prison to the place of execution was a journey of an hour, between double rows of armed men, amid countless hostile faces, without one look or word of sympathy. On the scaffold

he sought to address the people.   But his voice was drowned
by the beating of drums; the executioners seized their strug-
Jan. 21,   gling victim, and bound him to the plank.   The axe
1793   fell, and the sorrows of poor King Louis were ended.
A. D.   " The kings threaten us," said Danton; " we hurl at
their feet as gage of battle the head of a king."

The internal history of France during a period of two years
from the fall of the monarchy, is perhaps the most appalling
record which the annals of the human family present.   There
was much suffering among the people, and the pressure of
hunger helped to make them fierce.   They were agitated by
fears for the success of the revolution, which, if it gave them
scant supply of bread, had undeniably freed them from the
intolerable oppression of their superiors.   A diseased suspicion
filled their minds.   They believed that they lived on "a volcano
of conspiracies."   Every man against whom a word or even a
look of disapproval was alleged, was an ally of the discarded
system, and therefore a traitor.   This continued suspicion, acting on a national character formed under cruel oppression and
prone to extremes, produced results at which successive generations of men will shudder so long as history endures.   A fury,
incomprehensible and almost incredible—a thirst of blood absolutely insatiable, possessed the minds of the people.   There were
eight or ten thousand suspected persons crowed into the
horrible prisons of Paris.   Every afternoon carts laden with
unhappy men and women, condemed for imaginary offences,
passed along the streets to the place of death.   The daily average
at first was low, not exceeding eight or ten.   A little later it
stood at forty or fifty.   Towards the close of the Reign of
Terror it ranged sometimes as high as eighty.   In the provinces
scenes equally dreadful were constantly enacted.   It was
reckoned that not fewer than a million of persons were murdered by the infuriated French people before the merciful

reaction occurred which terminated the unutterable horrors of the time.

All the great parties possessed themselves of supreme power—now the Girondists, now the Communists, now the Jacobins. Each, as it fell, suffered without pity the agonies which it had inflicted. When the Girondists were overthrown, their leaders were conveyed together to the guillotine. They numbered twenty-one persons, and the execution occupied thirty-eight minutes. The doomed men sang patriot songs as they waited their fate—the strain becoming ever feebler as man after man was snatched away, till it ceased when the last survivor was bound to the plank.

For two years France had suffered Robespierre to work his own fiendish will in the slaughter of thousands of unoffending persons. But the inevitable reaction came at length, July 27, and the murderer with his chief accomplices were 1794 hurried to the scaffold. And then it was found that men were wearied with the horrid work of which they A. D. had seen so much. The prisons were gradually emptied. Two months after Robespierre's death there was not one suspected person in the prisons. The guillotine ceased to have its daily victims, and the public mind was set free from that burden of terror under which it had so long been crushed

CHAPTER II.

NAPOLEON BONAPARTE.

THE island of Corsica, in the Mediterranean, over which the Genoese exercised an ineffective and decaying sovereignty, had for many years been coveted by the government of France. At length the shadowy rights of the Genoese were purchased for a large sum, and French troops landed to enter on possession. But the high-spirited islanders indignantly refused to acknowledge the shameful bargain by which they had been sold to a foreign power. They rose in arms, and for many months, under incredible hardships, maintained a heroic resistance. But 1769 A. D. at length they were crushed by the overwhelming power of France, and were forced to reconcile themselves as they best could to the hated yoke.

In due time they had their revenge—the strangest, the most signal which a wronged people ever enjoyed. They furnished to France a despot who poured out her blood and treasure during twenty long years to serve the ends of his own ambition; who led her to depths of humiliation and misery unknown before in modern Europe.

Napoleon Bonaparte was born in Corsica shortly before 1768 A. D. that island was subdued by the French. When he became Emperor of France, it was a painful reflection that he had been born a foreigner. With that marvelous excellence in falsehood which distinguished his whole career, he changed the date of his birth, and gave it to be believed that he had been born after the conquest. His father was a lawyer of small income and large family, whose life, ending prematurely, was a continuous struggle with insufficient means. Napoleon's own inclination destined him for a military career, and while a child of eleven, he began his training in the school of Brienne. When the revolution broke out he was found on the popular side. He received his commission, and greatly distinguished himself at the siege of Toulon, the successful issue of which was indeed mainly owing to his genius. Not long afterwards he was intrusted with the defence of the Convention against a formidable insurrection of the National Guard. His eminent skill and success in this task gave him fame, and opened for him his wonderful career. He was immediately appointed to the command of the army of Italy. Napoleon put himself at the head of forty thousand ill-clad and imperfectly fed men, who were contending in a somewhat 1796 A. D. heartless manner against superior forces of Sardinians and Austrians, and were making no progress in the enterprise. In four weeks he so defeated the Sardinians that they hastened to conclude with him a humiliating peace. In less than two years he defeated the Austrians in eighteen pitched battles, destroyed their armies by slaughter or surrender, and laid firm hold of their Italian territory. When he assumed command, Austria was preparing with a large a my to cross the Rhine and invade France. The success of Napoleon in Italy utterly baffled this project, and Austria was fain to accept a peace whose terms were dictated by the conqueror. The Pope raised a considerable army, and embarked in warlike operations, which ended in instant defeat, and the punishment of his ill-judged boldness by exactions which the finances of his holiness were not very well prepared to meet. A number of small potentates in the north of Italy were effaced, and their territories were grouped into a republic under the fostering care of France. Venice fell, surrendering to the youthful conqueror her ancient but sorely decayed glories. Napoleon had completed the conquest of Italy, and returned to Paris, a young man of twenty-nine, with the first military reputation in Europe.

When the early fervours of his reception in Paris had passed, it became obvious to Napoleon himself that he must find some field for new exploits, and to the Directory that they must remove from the capital so formidable a rival in the public regard. Already the idea of an invasion of England was freely discussed; already Napoleon announced it as indispensable to the welfare of mankind that the English monarchy should be abolished. But the time for gravely meditating this arduous enterprise had not yet come. Napoleon, who emulated the glory of Alexander, resolved upon the conquest of Egypt, from which the Indian possessions of England could be threatened. The Directory entertained no lively hope of accomplishing so large an undertaking; but the shame of defeat would fall upon their rival, and meantime they were delivered from the presence of a soldier whose success was too brilliant for their tranquility.

Napoleon possessed himself easily of Alexandria, and intimated to the Egyptians that he had come to punish
July
1798
A. D.
their tyrants and restore the true religion of Mohammed. After a trying march across the desert, he fought and destroyed the Egyptian army within view of the Pyramids, from the summit of which, as he reminded his soldiers, forty centuries contemplated their achievements. Lower Egypt was in his power, and Napoleon governed it with wisdom and justice.

But all the while an enemy—sleepless, terrible, inflexibly devoted to his overthrow—was ranging the seas in quest of Napoleon. An English fleet under Admiral Nelson commanded the Mediterranean, but a gale of wind had blown it off the coast, and the French squadron accomplished in peace its voyage eastward. Nelson's pursuit was vehement, but, for a time, fruitless. Once he was, unknowingly, so near that the sound of his guns was heard in the French ships. Twice he sailed past them in the eagerness of his search. At length he found them anchored in the Bay of Aboukir. Elated Aug. 1, by the approach of battle, he told his officers that to- 1798 morrow he should have gained a peerage or a place in A. D. Westminster Abbey. His victory was so complete that the splendid French fleet was almost literally annihilated.

Ruinous as this blow must prove to the hopes of Napoleon in the East, he still allowed himself to entertain vast projects of Oriental conquest. He marched into Syria, stormed Jaffa, and massacred by cannon-shot four thousand prisoners of whom he could not conveniently dispose otherwise. Then he advanced to the siege of Acre; but here the English antici- pated him: Sir Sidney Smith, with two ships of the line, expected his coming. The siege was pressed with extraordin- ary energy during a period of two months; but the defence was too obstinate, and Napoleon retired baffled from the ruined walls of the ancient city, on whose conquest, as he him- self remarked, the fate of the East depended. Long afterwards, when he reviewed the events of his life in the enforced leisure of St. Helena, he said that Sir Sidney's defence of Acre had made him miss his destiny.

Reduced as his forces now were, it could no longer serve any purpose of Napoleon to continue in the East, Aug. 22, shut out from the more inviting arena of European 1799 warfare. He embarked almost secretly, braved the A. D. peril of capture by the English ships, and landed safely in France.

During his absence disaster had overtaken the young re- public. Italy had been torn from her grasp. Her armies everywhere had been defeated. Russia, Austria, and England, were leagued for her overthrow. Large armies stood ready to invade her soil. Royalist insurrections weakened her at home. Fierce dissensions raged in the capital. The Directory, under whose rule these disasters had come so thickly, had incurred the contempt of the people. An urgent desire prevailed that a man of capacity should assume the government, and displace the incapables, whose rule brought only shame. All eyes were turned to the conqueror of Italy and Egypt, whose authority over the public mind was undiminished by the failure of his Eastern enterprise. His grenadiers drove the legislative body from its hall, and Napoleon, under the title of first consul, became the supreme ruler of France, with powers which, in his hands, quickly became despotism as absolute as ever France had endured before.

One of the first public acts of Napoleon was to address a letter to the King of England, with proposals for peace between the countries. The English government decisively rejected his overtures, and chose to continue the strife. France, it was held, had declared war against all established governments; her success meant the overthrow of social order, the destruction of religious liberty and even of personal freedom. She was so faithless that treaties would not bind her. England avowed the huge and lawless design of continuing the war till France should give security, by the restoration of the Bourbons, or otherwise, that she had laid aside those principles on which her revolution was founded. It is not probable that Napoleon was sincere in professing a desire for peace; it is certain that he expressed his gratification when England so peremptorily refused to listen to him. He was possessed of an unparalleled talent for war, and his sure path to greatness led through the carnage and agony of battle-fields.

Dec. 25, 1799 A. D.

The vast power of Russia was at that time wielded by the lunatic Emperor Paul. Napoleon's first care was to detach him from the hostile alliance, and he did so at no greater cost than a few civil words and polite attentions. Austria and England remained his foes. The burden of the fighting fell chiefly on Austria, for England as yet did little more than contribute money to sustain the military powers of the Continent in their resistance to France. The French army in Germany was commanded by Moreau, and fought successfully against the Austrians, although without results of special brilliancy. In Italy, Napoleon took command in person of the sorely discouraged and ill-supplied troops who, during his absence in Egypt, had been driven out of the peninsula. He advanced into Lombardy, and at Marengo the opposing forces met. It was yet the day of small armies. The troops who fought that memorable battle numbered only thirty thousand on each side.

The Austrians took Napoleon somewhat by surprise, while his troops were yet much scattered. At first the French gave way before the attack of their foes. After many hours of fighting, victory seemed to remain with the Austrians, whose commander, an old man of eighty, [June 14, 1800 A.D.] yielding to fatigue, and regarding his work as done, retired from the field. Napoleon asked General Desaix what he thought of the situation. "The battle," said that officer, "is completely lost; but it is only four o'clock, and there is time to gain another." The retreating French were rallied for a fresh effort. The Austrians, called to fight where they expected only to pursue, were advancing to the attack, when the French cavalry, concealed from view by thick foliage, burst suddenly upon their flank. This charge decided the battle, and the Austrians, after bravely fighting for twelve hours, fled in utter disorder from the field. Napoleon regained by this decisive victory all that had been lost in Italy during his absence. The Austrian general owned his defeat by a convention in which he yielded all the fortresses held by the Austrians in Lombardy and Piedmont to the conqueror.

A few months later the French army, under Moreau, fought the Austrians in the forest of Hohenlinden, and in-flicted upon them a crushing defeat. The way to Vienna was now open, and a humiliating peace, which Austria was forced to accept, alone averted disasters yet more extreme.

Dec. 3, 1800 A.D.

The position of England at the close of this campaign was sufficiently alarming. Of her two great allies, Russia had become hostile, and Austria, humbled by the victorious arms of Napoleon, had made peace with the conqueror. Prussia, availing herself of the unfreinded condition of England, had taken forcible possession of Hanover. Italy, Holland, and Spain were in abject subservience to Napoleon. And, finally, the northern powers, Russia, Denmark, and Sweden, entered into a league to suppress the right of search which England valued so highly, and forcibly to establish the doctrine that the goods of an enemy, if under a neutral flag, must be safe from capture. Thus England, in this time of uni-versal war, had no friend but Austria, and she was helpless. But England was true to herself. She promptly despatched to Copenhagen a powerful fleet, of which Lord Nelson, nominally second, was really chief. A battle was fought off the harbour of Copenhagen. Of all the engagements in which Nelson had taken a part,—and they were over a hundred,—he considered this the most terrible. It resulted in the utter defeat of the Danes, and the ruin of their splendid fleet. Thus one limb was struck from the Northern Confederacy. A few days before, the Emperor Paul, who had recently given more decided evidences of insanity, was strangled by some of his nobles, who were of opinion that the empire required a change of policy. His son Alexander hastened to make peace with England, and thus our great danger passed harmlessly away.

Dec. 16.

April 2, 1801 A.D.

Mar. 23.

But now a brief respite was to be enjoyed by the European

powers from the bloody occupation to which for so many years they had given themselves. It was not the expectation—perhaps it was not even the desire—of the governments, that a lasting peace could yet be attained, but it suited the interests of all that at this stage of the war a breathing-time should be afforded, It was true that England, by whom the first overtures were made, had not yet gained any of the ends which she had proposed to herself by the war. But the government frankly admitted that it seemed hopeless to reduce the power of France, and asserted the desirableness of at least attempting to live in peace with their neighbour. The negotiations were attended with considerable difficulty. But the wish to have some interval of peace was strong both in England and France, and at last an agreement was arrived at. The other European powers effected quickly an adjustment _{Oct,} of differences. For the first and the last time in his public life, Napoleon found himself without any war upon his hands. The Peace of Amiens, destined to give Europe but a few months of uncertain rest, was hailed with delight in all lands.

Napoleon, although nominally first consul, was in the full exercise of absolute power, and already surrounded himself with the observances of royalty. As a soldier he had no rival. He was still a young man, only thirty-three years of age; he could boast the double conquest of Italy, the conquest of Egypt, the defeat of Austria. Already the Corsican lawyer's son held the destinies of Europe in his hands. The glory which he had gained for them made him supreme in the hearts of Frenchmen. But his greatness was not merely that of the successful soldier. He governed with clemency and wisdom, and returning prosperity obtained for him the joyful submission of a people wearied out by the cruelty and weakness of revolutionary governments. During the months of peace which succeeded the treaty of Amiens, he gave much thought to the reconstruction of institutions which the revolution had overthrown. Napoleon did not allow religious considerations to exercise any considerable influence over his own life; but he regarded religion as an indispensable instrument of government, which he would have been constrained to invent had he not found it already in existence. The Roman Catholic religion was now restored, to the joy of the devout peasantry, but grievously to the dissatisfaction of the Parisians and the soldiery. The Sabbath became again the weekly day of rest. Education was promoted, although as yet only in its higher forms; for Napoleon was not sufficiently enlightened to desire that the masses of the French people should receive education. Improved methods of levying taxation were instituted, in place of the system established during the revolution, which was in the highest degree unequal and oppressive. To occupy the attention of the Parisians, and to prevent a too searching discussion of the policy of the first consul, extensive improvements of the capital were originated. In the provinces canals and roads were formed. The families banished by the revolution were permitted to return, and such of their possessions as had not been sold to meet the necessities of the state were restored. Throughout France the laws differed excessively. In one day's journey the traveller encountered several varieties of law. Napoleon formed the grand design of framing a uniform system of law for France. His beneficent conception was in due course of years given effect to, he himself taking no inconsiderable share in the labor involved.

Vast changes had occurred in England and France as the result of nine years of incessant war. The English fleet had been doubled in strength, and now consisted of eight hundred vessels, carrying one hundred and twenty thousand fighting men; a naval force such as the world had never seen. On the other hand, the navy of France, blighted by the overwhelming strength of England, had dwindled by one-half, and was destined to yet greater decay. On land, the fighting strength of Britain had grown from eighty thousand men to nearly half a million; while the French forces had swelled out from two hundred and seventy thousand to about a million of armed men. England was now spending sixty million sterling, and France twenty-two million. The old debt of France had been disowned, and she had not yet had time to contract any larger obligation then fifty-five million. The debt of England had been doubled, rising during those unhappy years from two hundred and forty-four million to the enormous sum of four hundred and eighty-four million. The trade of England had greatly increased— bringing power to bear these prodigious burdens. The imports and exports together had grown from forty million to seventy million. On the other hand, the foreign trade of France was almost literally extinct. Her flag had been chased from the sea by the terrible and now unresisted ships of England.

The reconciliation between Napoleon and England was too superficial to be enduring. Difficulties arose out of the continued aggressions of France on the Continent. The English newspapers spoke evil of Napoleon, and he vainly demanded the suppression of the offending journals. He gathered forces on the shores of the Channel, as if he meditated early invasion. England, on her part, delayed to evacuate Egypt and Malta, of which Napoleon vehemently complained. In the temper of both countries these troubles could have but one ending. After twenty months of peace, England broke off diplomatic relations, and the European people turned them again, without reluctance, to the familiar work of mutual destruction, from which they were not to rest again till twelve bloody years had passed.

May
1803
A. D.

England had now to brace herself for a prolonged and perilous conflict. Her purpose was so to weaken France as to

remove what she deemed a menace to the welfare and independence of all European nations.' Napoleon hoped so to
humble England as to destroy the main obstacle which barred
his path to universal dominion. Neutrality seemed no longer
to be dreamed of. In the general madness, every European
power fell into its place, on the one side or the other, and
every people drank deeply of the miseries of war. A coalition
of all governments hostile to France was at once framed.
England and Russia were already in perfect accord. Sweden
was controlled by Russia. Austria was slow to avow hostility;
but her wounds were so deep and so recent that she could safely
be reckoned upon. On the other hand, Spain leagued with
Napoleon. Holland, Italy, Switzerland, and many of the
small German states, were under his control. Prussia followed
a timid and ungenerous course. Tempted by the possession of
Hanover, she cultivated the friendship of Napoleon, and awoke
from her dream of aggrandizement only to sink in ruin under
the blows of the conqueror whom she had humbled herself to
serve.

Napoleon's first enterprise was a sufficiently arduous one.
He prepared to invade England. He had undoubtedly persuaded himself that this undertaking was practicable, and he
made his preparations on a scale which almost rendered it so.
He assembled on the shores of the Channel one hundred and
fifty thousand men in the highest state of discipline and equipment, with two thousand vessels for their transport. But
England, with a powerful fleet, held command of the Channel,
and rendered hopeless the attempt to convey an army across.
Napoleon, with the help of his Spanish allies, brought together
sixty ships of the line; but even with that immense force he
shunned a sea-fight. He schemed rather to decoy the English
ships into distant seas, so that the passage of his troops might
be unobstructed. His own fleets were ordered to the West
Indies, with secret instructions to return immediately to Europe.

Nelson fell into the snare, and gave chase across the Atlantic. When he discovered the stratagem, he sent his swiftest ship to England to intimate the danger which impended. His warning was received in time, and a strong squadron, under Sir Robert Calder, was ready to meet the returning allies. A battle ensued, not memorable otherwise than by its results. These were in the highest degree momentous. The allies sustained a defeat, and instead of pressing on to the Channel, they took shelter in Ferrol. Had they dared all and sailed onward, a French army would probably have landed in England. Their retreat made the invasion at once and for ever impossible.

Three months later, Nelson met the combined fleets off Cape Trafalgar, and inflicted upon them a defeat which was well-nigh annihilating. This great triumph placed beyond challenge the naval supremacy of Britain, for it did not leave afloat any power fit to encounter her in battle. But the death of Nelson, perhaps the best-loved of all their heroes, changed into mourning the joy which this final assurance of their safety from all invaders naturally kindled in the hearts of the British people. Oct. 21, 1805 A. D.

Napoleon* knew so soon as he heard of the retreat of his fleet that all his combinations were baffled, and that England was now beyond his reach. He indulged himself in a free expression of the boundless rage which the feeble conduct of his admiral inspired. And then, without the delay even of an hour, he turned him to a field where the most brilliant successes of his life awaited him. On the instant, he designed the campaign of Austerlitz. With a promptitude unexampled in the movements of so large bodies of men, his army moved from the shores of the Channel to confront his enemies on the Rhine.

Austria had now committed herself to another war with France. Near the valley of the Danube, around the fortress of

*He was now Emperor of the French. He assumed the imperial dignity, in virtue of an Act of the Senate (1804), confirmed by a practically unanimous vote of the people.

Ulm, with no enemy near them, lay eighty thousand Austrian soldiers, meditating hostile action against French territory. In absolute secrecy, and with amazing swiftness, Napoleon provided for the converging of one hundred and eighty thousand Frenchmen around the supine and unsuspecting Austrians. In six weeks from the abandonment of his project of invasion the Austrians were surrounded, and every avenue by which they might regain a position of safety was securely barred by an overwhelming force directed by the matchless skill of Napoleon himself. The Austrian general, Mack, appalled by the sudden calamity which had fallen upon him, hastened to surrender.

The road to Vienna was once more open, and Napoleon lost no time in entering the capital of his foe. He supplied the wants of his army from the vast stores accumulated there. But his situation was full of peril, and admitted of no repose. A Russian army, strengthened by the remnants of the ruined Austrian force, was marching against him; and Prussia, offended by an indignity which he had offered, was arming suspiciously, although as yet she withheld any declaration of her purposes. Napoleon took up his position at Austerlitz, and artfully contrived to impress his enemies with the belief that he knew the dangers of his position, and was seeking a way to withdraw. Under this fatal delusion the Emperor Alexander directed his troops to march across the front of the French army in order to turn its right flank. Napoleon, at the head of an army almost equal in number and greatly more experienced, looked calmly on while the Russians involved themselves in this fearful peril, and foretold the ruin which he saw was now inevitable. Restraining the impatience of his troops, he waited till the cross-march had made irretraceable progress. Dec. 2, And then the masses of his eager veterans, issuing from 1805 the mist which veiled the field, were launched against A. D. the disordered Russians. Although taken unawares the allies fought stubbornly; but in the end their overthrow was complete, and they were driven from the field, weakened by a loss of thirty thousand men in killed, wounded and prisoners. The dispirited emperors, deeming further resistance hopeless, hastened to negotiate for an armistice.

William Pitt had laboured to form a league of European powers to curb the dangerous ambition of Napoleon. Already the edifice which he had just completed lay in ruins before him. Broken by the toils and anxieties of his position, his health sank under the defeat of Austerlitz, and the great minister died a few weeks after the battle.

Prussia had at length determined to avenge the indignities to which Napoleon had subjected her, and had fixed the 15th December for the opening of hostilities. But when her envoy reached Vienna, on his way to intimate this warlike purpose to Napoleon, he found that the battle of Austerlitz had been fought. He prudently said nothing of war; nay, he arranged a treaty with Napoleon. It suited the conqueror's purpose for the moment, but he well understood and utterly despised the cowardly policy of the Prussian government. The destruction of Prussia now waited merely the convenience of the conqueror.

The treaty remained in force only for a few months. Napoleon's conduct to Prussia was studiously and intolerably insulting. The Prussian people, galled by the indignities which were heaped upon their country, clamoured for war. The government yielded to the pressure, and Prussia, without allies and with most imperfect preparation, rashly flung herself into a conflict with the giant power of Napoleon.

A few weeks sufficed to accomplish her overthrow. Her armies, miserably commanded, were surprised by the French at Jena and Auerstadt, and hopelessly defeated, their retreat being changed into rout by the hot pursuit of the French. The country was rapidly overrun. Eighty thousand prisoners were taken, and every fortress in

Oct. 14,
1806
A. D.

the country surrendered. Within one month from the breaking out of war the French entered Berlin, and Prussia lay
helpless at the feet of her conqueror. The severities which he
inflicted upon the unhappy people seemed to be dictated by
unreasoning hatred rather than considerations of policy. He
levied enormous contributions. He carried off the relics which
the affection of the Prussians had placed on the tomb of the
great Frederick. He declared that he would make the
Prussian nobility so poor that they would have to beg their
bread. The civil authorities were required to take an oath of
fidelity to the French emperor as the source of their power.
Prussia disappeared from among the great powers, and it was
evident that Napoleon contemplated her speedy annexation to
France.

There now remained only Russia and England to dispute
the will of Napoleon. England, rendered finally safe from his
assaults by the destruction of every fleet but her own, was
relentless in her determination to reduce his intolerable power.
But England, great as her strength was, had as yet taken no
effective part in the war elsewhere than at sea. Russia alone
had now to withstand the undivided force of the conqueror.

Napoleon marched one hundred thousand men to encounter
the Russians, who advanced to the Vistula to meet him. So bitter
had the hostility of the warring powers become, that even
Feb. 8, the severities of a northern winter did not impose a sus-
1807
A. D. pension of operations. Beside the town of Eylau, on
fields thickly covered with snow, the two armies met
and fought during all the daylight hours of that winter day.
The slaughter was unusually horrible even in that age of blood.
Fifty thousand men, dead and wounded, lay among the snow.
The resistance of the Russians had been so stubborn that the
enthusiasm of the French troops and the skill of their chief
barely averted a defeat, which would have been well-nigh
ruinous. Napoleon was saved from disaster only by the undue

caution of the Russian commander, who chose to retreat after the battle contrary to the wish of his generals, who were eager to pursue the advantage they had gained.

Four months later the armies met again at Friedland, and once more Napoleon encountered a resistance more June 14, determined than he had ever experienced from the 1807 armies of Southern Europe. But this time he was vic- A. D. torious, and the Russians, weakened by terrible slaughter, retired from the field.

Alexander, left alone by the other great powers, who had a deeper interest in the struggle than he had, and disheartened by the losses of this campaign, immediately opened negotiations for peace. He deeply resented the refusal of England to aid him in his hour of danger. He felt that the safety of his own empire was more to him than the defence of other states which were able to do nothing for themselves. A week after the battle, the two emperors met on a great raft moored for their reception in the river Niemen. The imperial robbers laid there the foundations of the most gigantic scheme of plunder known to history. But their designs were baffled by succeeding events, and need not detain us here.

Napoleon was now supreme in Europe. Nothing in romance approaches the facts of his amazing career. He was yet only thirty-nine years of age; twelve years ago he was an unemployed officer of artillery, without influence or friends; now he made or unmade kings, and regulated at his pleasure the destiny of nations, no man daring to question what he did. His extraordinary power to fascinate gained for him an ascendency over the Emperor Alexander, which for a time was absolute. Austria was silently restoring her shattered strength, but as yet was too much broken to oppose her will to that of her conqueror. Prussia, shorn of nearly half her population and territory, and laid under crushing exactions, could only nurse in secret her purposes of revenge. Many of the smaller German

4

states, Italy, and Holland were, for all warlike purposes, virtually French territory. The fleets of Denmark, Spain, and
Portugal were at the command of this irresistible soldier.
England alone maintained invincible hostility against the despotism which had now overspread the rest of Europe.

Already the daring idea was entertained by Napoleon of
surrounding himself with tributary thrones occupied by his
own relations. He began with Naples. The Bourbons everywhere were his natural enemies, and he availed himself of very
slight pretexts to announce that the dynasty of Naples was
incompatible with the peace of Europe and the honour of his
crown, and that it had ceased to exist. His sister's husband,
Murat, the son of an innkeeper, became King of Naples. His
brother, the gentle Louis, was placed upon the throne of Holland. Joseph reluctantly accepted the throne of Spain, his
occupation of which brought only disaster to himself and to
Napoleon. Jerome was made King of Westphalia. Lucien
would have had a crown also, but his too loyal and pronounced
republicanism offended his imperial brother. The principality
of Lucca was bestowed upon his eldest sister, Eliza. Pauline
received the principality of Guastalla. His adopted son, Eugene,
married the daughter of the King of Bavaria. Josephine's
niece became Princess of Baden. Bernadotte, one of his mar-
shals, the son of a lawyer, accepted the crown of Sweden.
Napoleon impressed it upon all these subsidiary monarchs that
their first duty was to him, their next to France. After discharging these claims, they might consider the welfare of the
people over whom they ruled. Napoleon's mother lived to
witness his fall. She never believed in the permanency of those
splendours by which her son had surrounded himself. She
stored up what money she became possessed of, foretelling that
the kings and queens of her family would one day have need
of it.

Napoleon could no longer hope to reach England with the

sword, but he could strike at that on which her life depended—her commerce. He declared the British Islands in a state of blockade, and rigorously forbade commercial intercourse between England and those Continental states over which his control extended. England replied by declaring those states under blockade, and their ships liable to capture. It is in the power of governments to impede, but not to arrest the movements of commerce. Smuggling was a capital offence, and its penalty was so sternly inflicted that a man was shot in Hamburg because a little sugar was found in his house. But men smuggled on a huge scale in defiance of law; and both governments sold for money permission to break the law, thereby earning large profits. From this sale of licenses Napoleon had amassed the enormous sum of sixteen million sterling, which was not entered in the public accounts, but was ultimately used for his military expenses.

During the whole of his career Spain and Portugal had obsequiously obeyed the commands of Napoleon and placed their resources at his disposal. The fleet of Spain shared with that of France in the destruction inflicted by Nelson at Trafalgar. The flower of her army fought in his Polish campaign, and shed their blood among the snows of Eylau to serve the purposes of his ambition. Portugal, at his demand, placed herself in an attitude of hostility toward her ancient ally England, and was driven so far as to confiscate the property of English citizens who were resident in the country. But even this extreme of subserviency failed to conciliate the selfish and imperious conqueror. It seemed to him that his frontier on the Spanish side required to be thoroughly assured, and that this could not be done otherwise than by placing a French prince on the throne of Spain. In utter disregard of all obligation, and without the decency of even a pretext of quarrel, he overran the Peninsula with his soldiers. The King of Portugal

withdrew to Brazil to wait for happier times. The King of
Spain was forced by threats to resign his crow:., which Napoleon placed upon the head of his brother Joseph. It proved
an unhappy gift, and Napoleon lived to acknowledge that the
seizure of the Peninsula was a fatal mistake. When he was
soon to be engaged in a deadly struggle with Northern Europe,
he had made the Spaniards his enemies, and prepared for
England a field most advantageous on which to fight out a
strife which could have no termination now but the ruin of
either of the combatants.

The Spaniards offered what resistance they could, but that
availed little against the hosts which Napoleon poured into the
country. At this time, however, the great contest entered
upon a new phase. England, heretofore, had expressed her
hostility to Napoleon chiefly at sea, or by money contributions
to the military powers. Now, at length, she resolved to take
a more prominent place in the strife, and the Peninsula was
the chosen theatre of her operations. Her earliest effort was
on a modest scale. A little army of ten thousand men was
landed in Portugal. It was under command of Sir Arthur
Wellesley, destined in six years of arduous war to drive the
French from the Peninsula, and to earn a military reputation
second only to that of Napoleon himself.

Portugal was wrested from the invaders without serious difficulty. The First battle was fought in Vimiera. The
French massed, as their practice was, in dense columns,
attacked the English position. Sir Arthur had formed
the opinion that English troops in line could withstand
the terrible columns which hitherto had cleft their way through
all that opposed them. He had judged wisely. At Vimiera,
and onwards to Waterloo, the thin English lines threw back
with great slaughter the formidable columns of the French.
After the battle, Marshal Junot offered to evacuate Portugal.
The English accepted his proposals, and agreed to convey
back to France the defeated troops of their enemy.

Aug. 21,
1808
A. D.

The British army, raised to thirty thousand men, and now transferred to the command of Sir John Moore,* set out from Lisbon and marched into Spain. It was a bold measure, and one of doubtful prudence. Napoleon himself was present in Spain, and he had three hundred thousand men scattered over the country. He commenced a concentration of these troops and a rapid approach to the enemy. Sir John, warned of his peril, turned, and by a disastrous and demoralizing retreat, made for his ships. At Corunna he fought and defeated one wing of the pursuing force, himself falling in the battle. The troops, grievously reduced in numbers, were at once embarked for England. There was absolute dismay when the shattered remnants of this splendid expedition were seen by the English people, and again the opinion was loudly urged that resistance to Napoleon, excepting on the sea, was a vain sacrifice of brave men's lives.

Oct., 1808 A. D.

Jan. 16, 1809 A. D.

So deep was the hatred cherished by Austria, that she suffered herself to be hurried into a premature renewal of hostilities, which resulted in swift and terrible disaster. Her military preparations were sadly defective; her finances were in utter confusion. But the French army was occupied in Spain; and England, it was known, would provide with funds any government which was willing to war against France. Borne up by a vehement popular desire to avenge the wrongs which the empire had endured, Austria once more took the field.

Napoleon was urging the pursuit of the English towards Corunna, when tidings reached him which sufficiently revealed the purposes of Austria. He turned back, on the instant, to direct the greater operations of which

Jan. 1, 1809 A. D.

* Sir Arthur Wellesley had been recalled to England. People who were incapable of judging of the circumstances highly disapproved of the convention by which the French had been sent home. Government ordered an inquiry, the result of which freed Sir Arthur from all blame. So strong, however, and so unreasoning was the public sentiment, that Sir Arthur did not regain employment without high influence and considerable difficulty.

Germany was now to become the field. The concentration of
his troops was conducted with such energy, that in three
months he had three hundred thousand men ready to strike at
Austria. Never had his success been so dazzling in the rapidity
with which it was gained and the vastness of the results which
it yielded. In little more than a month from the opening of
the campaign, Vienna had again fallen into his power. The
tenacious Austrians fought on; and at Aspern inflicted a defeat
which, if sustained by a commander of inferior skill, must
have proved disastrous. But Napoleon extricated himself from
the perils which surrounded him, and at Wagram regained the
advantage he had lost. In a campaign of a hundred days,
unhappy Austria was once more beaten to the ground, and a
treaty was signed by which one-fifth of the territory and population of the empire was handed over to France. Enormous
pecuniary exactions still further weakened the fallen foe.
Austria submitted to extreme humiliations. She became bound
to reduce her army to one hundred and fifty thousand men.
And that no element of bitterness might be awanting, the
ancient ramparts of Vienna the favourite walk of the citizens—
were in utter wantonness destroyed by the orders of Napoleon.

When the war with Austria was beginning, Lord Wellington arrived at Lisbon to command the English army of
April, twenty thousand men, and England now put her hand in
1809 good earnest to the work of rescuing the Peninsula from
A. D. the grasp of Napoleon. It was a giant undertaking, to
expel from the country they had seized three hundred thousand
of the best troops in the world, ably led and amply supplied.
Years were required for its accomplishment. The means employed seemed wholly inadequate, the British force in the Peninsula having at no time exceeded fifty thousand men. To this
was added a large force of Portuguese and Spaniards, equipped
mainly by England, not always reliable when brought to face

the enemy. The genius of Wellington bestowed upon these apparently insufficient means an efficacy not naturally their own. In his hands they achieved an unbroken series of victories in battle, and the final expulsion of the French from the Peninsula, of which they had so lawlessly possessed themselves.

Wellington's earliest care was to provide for his troops a position in which they could find a safe retreat if the fortune of war should turn against him. At Torres Vedras, on the Portuguese coast, he formed three great lines of fortification, which he knew his army could make good against any assailant; and where, at the very worst, he could embark, if that extreme necessity should arise. From the sure basis of these impregnable defences he would extend his operations as his strength permitted.

Wellington had advanced to the Spanish frontier, when the vast forces which Napoleon had directed against him counselled a retreat. At Busaco he waited for the French in a strong position, and having there inflicted upon them a bloody repulse, he continued his retreat to the lines of Torres Vedras. Thither Massena followed him. The French general searched eagerly for some point so weak that he might hope to force an entrance, but there was none. He _Oct. 1810 A. D._ waited for several weeks, expecting that supplies would fail, and that Wellington must come forth and give battle. But the English ships maintained abundance in the camp. Massena himself, obliged to depend upon a wasted country, began to feel straightened. At length the inevitable retreat began. It is memorable as the first step in a backward movement, which was not interrupted till the last invader was driven from the Peninsula, and the victorious British stood upon the soil of France.

During the next campaign Wellington achieved considerable, although not rapid, progress; and at its close Portugal was delivered, and the French possession of Spain somewhat shaken. Wellington was now able to _1812 A. D._

enter Spain, and in quick succession he assailed and captured the great frontier fortresses of Ciudad Rodrigo and Badajoz. At Salamanca he utterly defeated the French, who retired precipitately from the field with heavy loss. A few days after, the English army entered Madrid, awakening the rapturous joy of the people, who had long groaned under the lawless and merciless exactions of the French. Napoleon had still an enormous preponderance of force in Spain, but the difficulty of supply compelled their dispersion, and the compact English army, handled with consummate skill, already sufficed to shake to its foundations the rule of France in the Peninsula.

The peace which Napoleon concluded at Tilsit with the Emperor Alexander had now lasted for five years. Latterly it was not anticipated that this concord could be permanent, and for a considerable time preparations had been silently making to renew the strife. In the spring of 1812 the estrangement which had been growing between the emperors ripened into a declaration of war. With the exception of England, which he could not reach, Napoleon had no enemy now but Russia. All other hostile powers had been overthrown. The time seemed to have come when it was possible to accomplish the ruin of the only power which could dispute his sway over the European continent. Napoleon resolved upon the invasion and conquest of Russia. There was scarcely another capital in Europe which had not heard the tramp of his victorious legions, and Moscow was no longer to enjoy this exemption.

It was a stupendous enterprise to which the audacious ambition of the emperor now impelled him; but Napoleon had at his disposal a force which seemed equal to any undertaking. He had one million and a quarter of armed men obedient to his will. After leaving ample forces at home and for the defence of Spain, he had over half a million of men available for his operations against Russia. The composition of this enormous army illustrates the almost universal dominion to which he had attained. Scarcely half the number were native

French; the remainder were Austrians, Germans, Italians, Poles, and Swiss. Never had it been permitted to man to wield such power. But already the axe was laid to its root, and its fall was near.

On the 24th of June, 1812, the French army crossed the river Niemen and entered Russian territory. No such force had ever been seen before—so vast in its numbers, so perfect in its equipment, directed by skill so consummate. The emperor watched the march of his legions in the pride of a strength which he might well deem irresistible. No presage of approaching doom tempered his confidence that a crowning triumph was within his grasp. Could he have foreseen that nearly every man of that countless multitude was about to find a grave in the land he came to conquer, even his iron soul must have been shaken.

The policy of the Russians was to retire before the irresistible force of Napoleon, laying waste the country as they went. At an early period in the campaign it became evident that Napoleon had brought into those thinly-peopled wilds a host of men so great that it was beyond his power to feed them. It was impossible to carry supplies for such multitudes, and the wasted country through which their march led yielded nothing adequate to their enormous wants. Almost from the beginning the soldiers were put on half-rations. Water was scanty and bad; the heat of the weather was intense. Large numbers of the hungry soldiers strayed on marauding expeditions, and were lost. The mortality soon became excessive, and the army left ghastly traces of its presence in the carcasses of horses and the unburied bodies of men scattered thickly along the line of march. Before they reached Moscow, one-half of the men had sunk under the hardships of the journey.

Encouraged by the losses of their enemy, the Russians determined to abide the issue of a great battle before yielding Moscow. They took up a strong position at Borodino, and

there awaited the French attack.   The Battle which ensued
was distiguished over all the bloody cncounters of that time
by its enormous slaughter.   At its close, one hundred
thousand men lay dead or mangled on the field.   The
result was indecisive, both armies continuing to hold
their original positions.   But the Russians retreated
next day, and left Moscow open to the invaders.

Sept.7,
1812
A. D.

The French army greviously weakened by battle and by
hardship, entered Moscow with the rapturous joy of men
whose dangers were over and their triumph assured. But their
rejoicing quickly experienced a disastrous eclipse.   To their
dismay they found Moscow utterly abandoned by its inhabitants
—silent as the city of the dead.   Still worse remained.   The
heroic people had resolved to destroy their ancient capital
rather than suffer it to be polluted by the occupation of the
French army.   Arrangements had been made to set fire to
buildings in every quarter, and care had been taken to remove
every appliance which could aid the extinction of the flames.
The invaders, helpless and appalled, watched the unresisted
progress of the fire; and even Napoleon admitted that this
ushered in a long train of disaster.

The emperor shrank from owning the utter failure of his
enterprise.   He lingered among the ruins of Moscow during
five or six precious weeks, which might almost have sufficed
to place his army beyond the perils of a Russian winter.   At
length the retreat was begun, and the great tide of conquest rolled backward.* The Russian army, in renewed
strength, and amply supplied, hung upon the flanks and rear
of their enemy, and inflicted severe loss by their unwearying
attacks.   Soon the snow began to fall, and a Russian winter
of exceptional severity set in.   The retreat was henceforth
attended by horrors unsurpassed in human history.   At one
time the unsheltered wretches were subjected to cold thirty

Oct. 19.

*The army was now reduced to one hundred thousand men.

degrees under zero. Thousands perished daily of hunger and cold. The river Berezina had to be passed under fire of the Russian artillery. So terrible was the disaster which befell them there, that when thaw came the Russians buried twelve thousand bodies of Frenchmen found in the river. At last the agonies of this awful retreat came to an end. ^{Dec. 18,} Six hundred thousand fighting men had entered Russia; ¹⁸¹² eighty thousand recrossed the Niemen. Of these, a large ^{A.D.} proportion had been late reinforcements. But very few who had been with the expedition from the beginning returned to their homes. Nearly all had perished, or remained prisoners in the hands of the enemy. The miseries of this expedition stand alone in their appalling magnitude.

The political results of the Moscow campaign were necessarily of extreme importance. Napoleon was the abhorred oppressor of Germany; but his power had been such that resistance was hopeless, and Germany had to suffer the humiliation of sending troops to fight under the banner of the tyrant. But with the destruction of the French army hope dawned upon the suffering and degradation of years. Prussia, without loss of time, under the influence of a vehement popular impulse, entered into an engagement with Russia to aid her in the war with France. Austria followed—not inconsiderably strengthened in her disposition by an offer of ten million sterling from England. Sweden sent an army under Napoleon's old marshal, Bernadotte, to join the allies. The emperor was not yet wholly without friends. Denmark adhered to him in his days of adversity, as did several of the smaller German states. But the balance was now hopelessly against him.

Napoleon returned to Paris, and, with a candour unusual in his career, revealed the magnitude of the disaster which had fallen upon him. The confidence with which unparalleled success had inspired the French people was too strong to yield

at once even to this unparalleled calamity. When the first
paroxysm of dismay had exhausted itself, a belief in the genius
and good fortune of the emperor was found to have survived.
Napoleon applied himself with his wonted energy to the creation of a fresh army to replace that which had perished amid
the Russian snows. The waste of life during these many years
of war was now pressing hard upon the population of France.
The military age was reduced to seventeen, and the standard
of height to five feet one inch. Imperfectly grown boys, unfit
to endure the fatigues of war, filled the ranks, and speedily
crowded the hospitals. So vigorous, however, were the emperor's measures, and so well did his people support him, that
in April he had two hundred thousand men ready to meet the
Russians and Prussians on the Elbe.

In the campaign which followed, victory revisited the imperial standard. In the battles of Lutzen and Bautzen,
1813 the advantage remained with the French sufficiently to
A.D. make it desirable for the allies to seek an armistice,
which Napoleon granted.

But this gleam of hope was delusive. In the next campaign
he sustained, at Leipsic, a defeat which made his retreat to the
Rhine indispensable, and Germany was delivered.

And now France had to endure the miseries of invasion,
which she had so long and so ruthlessly inflicted upon others.
On the south-west, Wellington, with a hundred thousand veteran troops, who had come victorious out of every battle, stood
ready to enter French territory. On the north-east, the allies,
numbering almost a million of fighting men, were ready to fall
upon her. Napoleon, with forces utterly inadequate to quell
the storm which his ambition had raised, struggled heroically
but vainly to defend his throne against the overwhelming
strength of his enemies. The allies forced their way to Paris.
With slight resistance the capital yielded to their summons.
The fickle Parisians received them with delight. Napoleon

was promptly abandoned by the courtiers who had lately lived
in his smile. He abdicated the throne after an unsuccessful attempt to commit suicide. The allied sover- 1814
eigns behaved generously to their fallen foe. He was A.D.
allowed to retain the title of emperor; the island of Elba was
assigned as his residence, and a sum of £100,000 as his yearly
income. Four hundred French soldiers were given him as a
body-guard. He set out at once for his new home. He had
to travel towards the coast in disguise to escape the fury of the
people, who were eager now to have the blood of him who
had so long been their idol.

Napoleon lived for nine or ten months in his little kingdom,
—an islet sixty miles in circumference. He visited every corner of his dominions; laid out new roads; built several new
palaces; imposed new taxes, to the discontent of his subjects;
had a supply of water brought into his capital; took possession
of an adjoining island, still smaller than his own. Soon these
pursuits ceased to interest a mind accustomed to a sphere of
activity so vastly higher. Then he turned his attention to the
recruiting of his little army. It may be supposed that Napoleon would scarcely pause to consider the proportion which his
income bore to his expenditure, and he quickly ran himself into
pecuniary difficulties. All the while he spoke of his political
career as closed. He spoke freely of the public affairs of
Europe, but always with the tone of an unconcerned spectator.
For him now there were no interests but his family, his house,
his cows, his poultry. The disguise was skilfully assumed, for
Napoleon was unequalled as a dissembler. But ordinary
credulity could scarcely trust in the permanence of a change
so violent.

Meantime Louis XVIII. was on the throne of France, the
fickle Parisians having hailed the restoration of the Bourbons
with enthusiastic loyalty. At Vienna an august congress of
royal and highly distinguished persons sat down to dispose

of the enormous territories which had been redeemed from the grasp of Napoleon. The avaricious monarchs wrangled over the distribution of their vast spoils, and at one period there was imminent danger that their differences would fall to be arranged by the sword. But while their debates were in progress, tidings were received which suspended all disputes. Napoleon had left Elba, and was again in France.

The emperor had unostentatiously increased his army to a thousand men, and his fleet to seven small ships. A conspiracy had been formed in France to obtain the support of the soldiers, by whom the reign of peace was regarded unfavorably. When the time was fully ripe, Napoleon invited his principal subjects to a ball, over which his mother and sister presided. Meanwhile his troops were embarked, and Napoleon, quietly disengaging himself from his guests, went on board one of the ships. The little fleet at once put to sea, and steered for the French coast.

The restored government of the Bourbons melted into air before the awful figure of the returning emperor. The King and those who remained faithful to him withdrew in haste from Paris. The army everywhere pronounced for the chief who had so often led them to victory and plunder. Some of those whom Napoleon had raised to eminence, and who had accepted office from the king, hesitated to cancel their new allegiance. But Napoleon's personal ascendency over the men who had served him was irresistible. Marshal Soult, who was War Minister to King Louis, after some decent hesitation, lent his sword to his old chief. Marshal Ney left Paris to take command against Napoleon, assuring the king that he would bring back the disturber in an iron cage. No sooner had he come within the range of Napoleon's influence than he yielded to the charm, and his army followed him. The civil population of France did not desire the renewal of strife; but the army was wholly with the emperor, and the destinies of France were in the hands of the army. Napoleon returned to the Tuileries, and resumed at once his old occupation of gathering men together to fight his battles and be slain in the interests of his ambition.

The allied monarchs prepared to renew their efforts to crush this destroyer of the peace of Europe. They bound themselves to furnish unitedly about a million of armed men, and never to rest from their efforts while Napoleon was on the throne of France. The troops, but recently arrived at their homes, were at once ordered to retrace their steps towards the French frontier. In a few months an overwhelming force would tread the soil of France. But the only troops immediately available to resist Napoleon were the English and Prussian armies in Belgium, commanded by the Duke of Wellington and Marshal Blucher. In numbers, these forces amounted to nearly two hundred thousand men, scattered over a wide territory, for it was uncertain where the attack of Napoleon would fall. The French army was one hundred and thirty thousand strong,— excellent in material and equipment. Napoleon's plan was to concentrate his own troops, and attack the widely-dispersed allies in detail. He burst upon the Prussians—imperfectly prepared to receive him—at Ligny, and drove ^{June 16,} them back with a loss nearly double his own. At the ^{1815 A.D.} same time Marshal Ney attacked the English at Quatre Bras. The English also were caught before they had time to bring up their forces, but they fought with their accustomed courage. Reinforcements arrived during the battle, and, after a desperate conflict, Ney retired baffled. Next day, Wellington drew back his army in such a direction as to approach the Prussians, and took up his position near the village of Waterloo.

It was Napoleon's design to break the English by the attacks of his superior force before the Prussians came up. It was Wellington's design to hold his position till the arrival of the Prussians. The united armies would greatly outnumber their

enemies. Napoleon had eighty thousand soldiers present on
the field,—veterans on whom he could rely. Wellington had
sixty-seven thousand, of whom only twenty-four thousand were
British; the rest were Belgians, Hanoverians, and others of
doubtful quality. The fate of the campaign depended on
Wellington's ability to make good his defence against the
superior force which now came against him.

The Prussians were long delayed by the difficulties of their
march, and the battle had to be fought by the British army
alone. Wellington had chosen his position on the crest of a
range of gentle heights, with two strongly-held farmhouses
in his front. The French occupied a corresponding eminence
on the other side of a little valley. For eight hours the battle
raged. Napoleon strove to break the English line of defence.
In close succession, furious attacks were directed against the
outnumbered English. The splendid French cavalry rode
round the English squares, and up to the very muzzles of the
muskets. A powerful artillery maintained a withering fire.
Massive columns of infantry—strong enough, it seemed, to
cleave their bloody path through every obstacle—ascended the
slope. But it was all in vain. The English held the ridge, and
repulsed every assault with terrible slaughter. At length the
cannons of the advancing Prussians were heard. Napoleon
moved forward, for a last attack, the splendid soldiers of his
Guard—every man a veteran who had seen at least twelve
campaigns. They too were driven back. And then the whole
English line moved from its position, and advanced upon the
shattered enemy. The Prussians, in great force, appeared on
the field, and took up the pursuit. The French army fled in
hopeless rout, and now indeed the rod of the oppressor was
broken. Napoleon himself had to ply his spurs to keep from
capture. He rode on during all the hours of that midsummer
night, with such thoughts as may be imagined.

He hurried to Paris, where he arrived almost alone. Irretrievable as all men knew his ruin to be, he demanded that his ministers should find him money and three hundred thousand men to continue the war. While men were still to be found in that France which he had so cruelly wasted, he had no better wish for them than that they should feed with their lives the devouring fire which his ambition had kindled. But all Frenchmen were sick of this murderous and now hopeless fighting. Napoleon had to abdicate his throne, and then he had to surrender himself to an English ship-of-war. He wrote to the Prince Regent that he had closed his political career, and now came, like Themistocles, to throw himself on the hospitality of the British people. But the British people could accept no such trust. The government intimated that they could not again leave him opportunity to disturb the peace of Europe. He was told that his place of residence during the remainder of his life was to be St. Helena, an island in the South Atlantic, remote from any inhabited land. He declared that he would not go there, and pointed to a refuge in suicide. But he accepted his fate. The early portion of his residence in St. Helena was not heroic. It was full of angry negotiations with the governor, and vehement complaints against all the conditions and circumstances by which he was surrounded. Then he was smitten by the disease of which his father had died, and of which he himself had long expected to die,— cancer of the stomach. He suffered much pain; he was subject to deep and prolonged depression of mind. And _{May 5, 1821 A.D.} then the conqueror died. Thus darkly closed a career, the most brilliant in its success, the most influential to produce vast and enduring change of human affairs, which has ever been permitted to man.

A Bourbon was again upon the throne of France, and Europe was at peace. It was well nigh a quarter of a century since the distracted nations had known rest. Men almost in middle age had no recollections excepting of war. Millions of

5

lives had been squandered; treasure beyond computation had
been wasted; the progress of mankind had been absolutely
arrested. A huge inheritance of debt was bequeathed, to
press upon the resources of future generations and diminish
their enjoyments. But vast as these evils were, the compen-
sations were not inadequate. The energy and patience begot-
ten in the long years of trial survived to gain in the coming
time those victories of peace for which the next half-century
is so renowned. In the great upheaval the old European despotisms were shaken to their foundations, and the people
began to assert their claim, not merely to justice, but to power.
And the miseries of twenty-three years of fighting seemed to
have awakened so strong a repugnance to war, that ever since
the nations have resorted with lessened frequency to that most
ill-chosen of all methods for reaching the adjustment of a
difference.

The influence which Napoleon exerted upon the course of
human affairs is without parallel in history. Never before had
any man inflicted upon his fellows miseries so appalling; never
before did one man's hand scatter seeds destined to produce a
harvest of political change so vast and so beneficent. Assuming, as he did, the control of a people who had flung aside their
government, it was a necessity of his position, not merely to
defer to democratic influences at home, but also, as opportunity
offered, to extend their dominion among foreign states. It was
he who roused Italy from her sleep of centuries, and led her
towards that free and united national life which she at length
enjoys. It was he who, by destroying the innumerable petty
states of Germany, inspired that dream of unity which it has
required more than half a century to fulfill. He was the
dreaded apostle of democracy. When Washington died, Napoleon invited his soldiers to mourn the man who had fought for
liberty and equality. It was his intention, had he effected a
landing in England, to proclaim the sovereignty of the people.
By the institutions which he created, by the doctrines which he

was obliged to profess, by the very violences of which he was guilty, he communicated to the human mind an impulse which it can never lose. And even when he became utterly and shamelessly despotic—when he laid intolerable burdens upon the people, when he squandered their lives, when he trampled on the life of nations—even then his influence was favourable to popular rights. For the hatred which his despotism evoked, and the vast combination of forces which it rendered necessary, united the people, and taught them to know their own strength. For a time the kings who had conquered him were irresistible. But his career had created and strengthened impulses in presence of which kings are powerless. Napoleon, himself one of the most selfish and remorseless of despots, made the overthrow of despotism and the final triumph of liberal principles inevitable in all European countries.

CHAPTER III.

THE conquests of Napoleon had marvellously disordered the territorial arrangements of Europe.
When the revolution began there were between
three and four hundred sovereign powers on the
Continent. There were a few great and powerful states, and
a multitude of very small ones—each with its miniature court,
and its petty army, and its despotic code of laws emanating
from the will of the prince, and conflicting vexatiously with
the codes enacted by surrounding princes. In Africa, it is said,
the traveller meets a new language in every sixty miles of his
progress. In Europe he had to encounter within a similar
range the annoyances resulting from a change of sovereign
and a change of law. Over some of the fairest portions of the
Continent there still prevailed that same inconvenient and
wasteful method of government which existed in England in
the days when there were seven kingdoms on her soil.

Italy was one of the countries thus unfortunately circumstanced. Italy had once been firmly compacted under the
strong rule of ancient Rome; but when Rome fell, every bar-
barian chief possessed himself of what he could, and Italy sank
into a multitude of petty states. Charlemagne for a space
recombined the fragments, or most of them, under his own
rule. The tribune Rienzi dreamed of uniting Italy in a great
federal republic, of which Rome should be the head. But the

eighteenth century closed upon Italy still disintegrated and powerless for her own defence. Piedmont and Naples were independent kingdoms. Venice, the oldest state in Europe, although grievously decayed, still maintained her precarious existence. Austria ruled in Lombardy. The Pope exercised paternal sway over two million miserably governed subjects. Genoa was ruled by an aristocracy. There were several duchies; and some of the free cities which sprang up so vigorously in the twelfth century now swelled out into little states. There was no federation. The petty monarchs could enter into treaties to unite their toy armies for mutual defence, but there was no organization for that purpose, and Italy was practically at the mercy of any strong invader.

Germany was composed of nearly three hundred independent powers; there were princes civil and princes ecclesiastical; there were electors; there were free towns; there were some kings of secondary importance; there were also the great Austrian and Prussian monarchies. Over this constituency the King of Austria exercised the authority of emperor, representing in a shadowy way the old Cæsars, whose dignities he was supposed to have inherited. Each of the petty states might be required to contribute troops for the defence of the empire. But it was only from the more considerable members of the federation that help could be obtained. The revenues of the smaller states could do little more than support the outlays of the sovereign, with his train of unprofitable and burdensome dependants.

Austria had for centuries predominated in Central Europe. Her population numbered twenty-five million. In addition to her German territory, she possessed Flanders, Lombardy, Hungary and the Tyrol.

Prussia had as yet scarcely been admitted to the rank of a first-class power. Her population was only eight million. But her military organization was effective; the victories which she gained under the great Frederick had given her confidence in her own prowess; strong national impulses pointed to aggrandizement at the cost of her weaker neighbours.

The national existence of Poland had recently been subverted by the arms of Russia, Austria and Prussia, and her territory divided among the conquerors. She had not relinquished her earnest desire for unity and independence, nor for many years was she to desist from heroic efforts to regain them.

Holland was leading a quiet existence under a republican form of government. She had long ceased to attempt a prominent part in European politics. The days were past when Holland contested the maritime supremacy of England. Peacefully and unostentatiously she now sought greatness in the more profitable paths of commercial enterprise. Her artisans were exceptionally industrious and ingenious. The labour of her careful peasantry was overcoming the difficulties of an uncongenial climate and an unproductive soil, and drew abundantly from those discouraging plains the elements of solid and generally diffused material well-being. Her neighbour Belgium, after centuries of vicissitude, was prospering beside her under the rule of Austria.

Switzerland was a federation of twenty-two little republics. Her whole population was only two million. For two centuries she had cherished her independence, and from a position of well-established neutrality looked serenely down upon the contests which desolated her neighbours.

Over states thus circumstanced the tide of French invasion rolled for nearly a quarter of a century. What were the changes produced on the political arrangements of the multitudinous and, for the most part, fragile sovereignties thus rudely dealt with ?

Italy underwent political changes of the most sweeping and, in their results, of the most beneficial character. Napoleon contemplated from a very early period the combination of all the Italian states into one. He began with the creation of a strong republic in the north, overcoming the objections of the petty states by the declaration that he was laying the foundation of a united Italy. He became the chief of that republic, and in due time the neighbouring states were forcibly absorbed. Even the territories of the Pope shared the common lot. In the end Napoleon reigned as king over the larger portion of the peninsula; and his brother-in-law, as king of Naples, governed nearly all the rest. The dream of Italian unity was for a brief space almost fulfilled.

Unoffending Holland was erected into a monarchy, and Louis Bonaparte became its king. When Louis, unable to submit longer to the despotic harshness of his brother, resigned his crown, Holland was at once annexed to France. Belgium also was overrun in the early years of the revolution, and held to the close as a French possession.

In Germany Napoleon took advantage of internal jealousies to break off from the empire states with a population of sixteen million, and to combine them anew into the Confederation of the Rhine, under his own protection, and available for his own purposes. He reduced the number of German governments from three hundred down to thirty. Prussia has been despoiled of half her territory—portions of which Napoleon bestowed upon his German allies; some he retained, and some he erected into the Kingdom of Westphalia, for the benefit of his brother Jerome. Austria had been plundered in like manner after the campaign of Wagram, and the spoils similarly disposed of. That part of Poland which belonged to Prussia was taken away from her, and, under the title of the Grand Duchy of Warsaw, was bestowed upon the King of Saxony.

Switzerland had been subjugated while Napoleon was still first consul. He forcibly imposed on her a new constitution, and held her in a tributary position, guaranteeing, however, her independence against all others.

The great monarchs who had overthrown Napoleon had
now to bring order out of the territorial confusion which he
had created, and to make restitution to a crowd of dethroned
princes.   It was a work of unexampled difficulty: on its wise
performance hung the welfare of generations.   Unhappily
the monarchs who then held the destinies of Europe in their
hands did not rise to the greatness of their opportunity.   It
was not a reconstruction of Europe which they sat down to
accomplish, with a wise regard to the wants of the European
people.   They met to satisfy the demands of a horde of bereaved princes.   They met in the spirit of a supreme regard
to personal interests.   Their avowed object was to restore to
Europe as nearly as possible the political arrangements which
existed before the war.   They took no account of the vast
changes which the war had caused.   They were blind to the
new impulses which had risen to unsuspected strength, and
were henceforth to shape out the destinies of Europe.   On
every petty throne they would reseat the petty despot who
had occupied it before.   Certain weak states which lay near
France were strengthened, the better to withstand the encroachments which that unquiet power might be expected to
attempt when her strength returned.   Otherwise the worn-
out system of the eighteenth century was to be faithfully
reproduced.   A reconstruction of Europe on this principle
could not be lasting; but it cost Europe many years and much
blood to undo it.

Absolute monarchy was about to enter upon a period of
swift, almost of sudden decay.   But its splendours were yet
untarnished.   Indeed, absolute power never seemed so far beyond reach of decay as when four or five men sat down in
Vienna* to regulate the political destinies of the European
people—no other thought than that of submission presenting

*The sovereigns of Russia, Austria and Prussia, and the representatives of Great
Britian, were supreme in the congress. France, Spain, Portugal, Sweden, and the
Pope were also represented. A crowd of smaller potentates hovered around, and
sought to impress their views upon the members of the congress.

itself to any of the victims of their arrangements. The success of their arms had made the allied monarchs supreme in Europe. Neither they themselves nor the European people questioned their right to dispose of territories and races according to their own pleasure.

They had at the outset to deal with France, and they did so justly. France was at one stroke divested of territories which held a population of thirty-two million—the enormous gains of Napoleon's unscrupulous aggressions. All that France had unlawfully acquired she was now compelled to relinquish. It was the design of the allies that she should resume the identical dimensions of 1792; and this substantially was affected, although several unimportant modifications in the direction both of increase and diminution left her to a small extent a gainer.

Italy awoke from her dream of unity. Lombardy was given back to Austria. Venice, humbled and indignant, was added to the gift. The pope resumed his temporal sovereignty. The Bourbons quickly regained the throne of Naples. The dukes swarmed back to their paltry thrones. Genoa was handed over to Piedmont, amid the vehement but unheeded remonstrances of the people thus transferred. Italy was once more a mass of incohering fragments. But the desire for unity, although frustrated for half a century, was already enkindled in strength sufficient to compel fulfi'ment.

Germany, too, received back her innumerable sovereignties. Only, they were knit together in a league, of which Austria and Prussia were the supreme directors. The states forming this confederation were bound to afford mutual support against foreign attack. Austria, as the most powerful member of the union, naturally looked to be its head. But the rising strength and ambition of Prussia involved a perilous competition for the coveted supremacy.

Holland and Belgium were crushed together into a kingdom.

Hanover, for the possession of which Prussia sinned and
suffered so greviously, was restored to England. Norway was
annexed to Sweden. Switzerland had a constitution bestowed
upon her by royal hands, and having meekly accepted it,
resumed her independence. The old partition of Poland was
confirmed with some modifications in the interest of Russia,
and a people numbering fifteen million were formally handed
over to Russia, Austria, and Prussia. The poor King of
Saxony had a hard fate. He had adhered too faithfully to the
falling emperor, and thus in the congress he had few friends.
Prussia claimed the whole of his territory. Ultimately she
consented to accept something less than the half of her demand.

England came with credit and dignity out of this ignoble
contest over the spoils of the war. She gave back to France
and her allies all the colonies which she had taken, with some
inconsiderable exceptions. She asked nothing for herself but
the glory of having contributed to the deliverance of Europe.

At length the settlement was complete. The monarchs
were able to cherish the pleasing conviction that they had
created a perfect and enduring political equilibrium. The
European powers were now so happily balanced that permanent tranquility would gladden the tormented nations. Alas!
they omitted from their calculations one most vital factor: they
took no thought of the European people. Their ingeniously
devised system was abhorred by the people who were required
to live under it. For half a century to come many of the
nations had to give their energies to the overthrow of the
balance which the Congress of Vienna established.

Book Second.

CHAPTER I.

SOCIAL CONDITION OF GREAT BRITAIN.

THE light which falls upon the condition of the British people during the earlier years of the century serves mainly to discover sights of woe. England rendered illustrious to all ages the splendid fighting capabilities of her people. She vindicated for herself a foremost place among the European nations, because she proved that she was just, wise, and energetic beyond the others. But her glories were bought with a great price. The social condition of her people had fallen very low, and the war suspended all effort for its elevation.

When she first engaged in the war, Great Britain had a population of fourteen million. Notwithstanding the lavish expenditure of life, she had grown steadily, till in 1815 she numbered twenty million. While the war lasted, the condition of the people was not intolerable. Out of four or five million adult males, one million were in the closing years of the war withdrawn from the competition for employment, and dedicated to the business of fighting. Agriculture and our rapidly growing manufactures employed the others, at a rate of wages which ordinarily furnished a decent maintenance. The unskilled labourer earned eleven shillings in Scotland, and thirteen to fifteen shillings in England. Carpenters, masons, and brick-layers received seventeen to eighteen shillings in Scotland, and twenty-two to twenty-five shillings in England. Even the hand-loom weaver enjoyed tolerable comfort. He earned thirteen to seventeen shillings in Scotland. At Bolton, where the work called for greater skill and delicacy, a diligent weaver received twenty-two to twenty-five shillings in requital of his weekly labour.

During the commercial agitations which followed the close of the war, the wages of the trades connected with building suffered little. Those operatives who had to do with spinning and weaving were less fortunate. The demand which the war created for their products ceased. The power-loom had recently entered upon its career, and the poor hand-loom weaver was called to take the first step in his downward progress. His wages sank about one-half. The reward of his daily toil of sixteen or eighteen hours ranged from ninepence to one shilling and fourpence, and often he was unable to obtain the privilege of working even at these miserable rates. Long years of suffering followed to those whose fortunes were embarked in this sinking ship. The hungry weavers invoked the help of Parliament. They begged to be sent to Canada. They proposed that the terrible power-loom should be restrained by law; and when that was denied them, they rose in their despair and lawlessly overthrew the machines which were devouring the bread of their children. They craved that a legal minimum of wages should be fixed, adequate for the maintenance of a family. Unfortunately it was beyond human power to grant their prayer. A better weaver than they had arisen. The hand-loom had to be put away among the rubbish of the past, and the poor workman had to endure a life of ever-deepening want till he died.

The war brought much prosperity to those who had to do with land, and to the mercantile classes. Rents advanced till at the close of the war they had more than doubled. The land-owning class rose to a height of splendour hitherto unexampled. Nor had the farmers less reason to be satisfied. Their grain enjoyed a monopoly, and the prices which they obtained enabled them to become rich. Many lucrative contracts were enjoyed by the merchants. The manufactures of the country were in excellent request, and the foundations of many large fortunes were then laid.

But although the wages of labour remained high throughout the years of war, the purchasing power of the labourer diminished. At the close of the war, a working-man could not acquire one-half of the commodities which his labour yielded to him twenty years before. Prices of food and clothing rose, under war influences, to an extreme point. Wheat, which in 1792 was so low as forty-seven shillings per quarter, rose in 1801 to one hundred and eighty shillings. During some weeks of that year the quartern loaf sold at one shilling and tenpence. Throughout the war wheat averaged eighty-four shillings per quarter. We had then no foreign grain to relieve us in our straits. Government occasionally reinforced our too scanty supplies by a measure which not even the necessities of the time can vindicate. The grain-ships of neutral powers were stopped on the high seas, and a forcible sale of their cargoes exacted.

The law-makers of that time were gentlemen who owned land and let it out for rent to the men who tilled it. During the war there could be no serious incursion of foreign grain, for millions of the men who ought to have been peaceably ploughing and reaping were expending their energies in the slaughter of one another. But with peace there might come wheat from abroad, and a consequent decline in rents. In order that the farmer should continue to pay his accustomed rent, it was needful that wheat should continue extravagantly dear. The operation of natural laws would now have given the people cheaper food, but this would have been calamitous to the land-owner,

and must be prevented. So in the year 1815 a new corn law
was passed, the object of which was to make the poor man's
bread dear that the rich man's rental might be high. No foreign grain was to be imported, until wheat in the home markets
had been for six months at or over eighty shillings per quarter.
The object of this arrangement was to keep the price of wheat
steady at a point not far from ninety shillings, a price which
could not fail to satisfy the land-owner and the farmer, however it might fare with the consumer of their wares. For
thirty years this corn law * was a blight and a curse to the
British people. Practically it came very nearly to this, that if
our own fields did not produce grain enough to supply our
wants, we were obliged to content ourselves without it. In
other words, poor people had to go on short allowance, and
many of them had to die. Famines were of frequent occurrence. It is told of Paisley, during a time of scarcity, that the
town was often utterly without grain or meal, and that when a
dealer was fortunate enough to secure a small supply, the hungry people crowded in eager competition to his shop. In Edinburgh, under the prevalence of scarcity, one in every eight of
the population was maintained by the charity of others; and a
proclamation of the magistrates regulated the amount of bread
which each family was expected to consume. The careful
authorities prohibited the sale of bread until it had been
twenty-four hours out of the oven, that the waste in cutting
might be diminished.

When bread was dear work was often scarce, and the misery
endured was dreadful. And men explained it all by saying
that the country was over-peopled. They perversely shut out
the boundless supplies of food which the world was longing to
send them, and then bemoaned the deficiency. Philosophers
speculated upon measures for restraining the increase of the
population; and they looked forward with hopeless despondency upon the constant growth of a population for whom

* Modified, not beneficially, into the sliding scale of 1828.

already there was not sufficiency of food. It seemed to many observers as if nature, like some poor men, was bringing into the world a larger number of children than she had the means to rear.

It was not corn alone which the legislators of that time rejected. The law was yet more peremptory in its exclusion of beef. Corn was admitted on some terms; cattle, living or dead, were admitted on none. It was a prevailing belief of theorists that to be safe a country should produce the whole of its own food, and of agriculturists that the shutting out of foreign competition was an arrangement which yielded financial results highly satisfactory to the land-owner and the farmer. Between theorist and practical monopolist, an increasing population ran no inconsiderable risk of perishing from want.

Taxation was monstrous, for expenditure had long been boundless. Towards the close of the war we had a million of armed men in our pay, and we hired poor foreign governments, by huge payments, to equip their subjects for the same bloody work in which we ourselves were engaged. When the war began we had been spending twenty million sterling, and our debt was two hundred and sixty-eight million; at its close we were spending one hundred and seven million, and our debt had grown to the amazing sum of eight hundred million. During the brief interval of peace between the war with our revolted colonies in America and the war with France, our expenditure was little over twenty shillings for each of the population; now it is at the rate of £2, 7s. But in 1814 it had risen to £6 for each person in the country—a rate of government expenditure unknown upon the earth excepting then. Our gifts to foreign powers, during the years from 1793 to 1815, were sixty-eight million, including a sum of two hundred thousand pounds which we generously bestowed on the restored King Louis, that he might with becoming dignity seat himself upon the throne of his fathers.

When peace returned, our expenditure fell to fifty-two million, which was at the rate of £2, 12s. for each person. It was a welcome relief from the load which men had borne so long. But public finance was as yet imperfectly comprehended, and taxation was so imposed as to produce the maximum of evil. Bread was taxed, not to yield revenue, but avowedly to increase rental. Sugar and tea were so taxed that during the forty years which intervened between 1791 and 1831, while population had grown from fourteen million to twenty-two million, the consumption of sugar had grown no more than from two hundred and ninety ounces to three hundred and fifty-eight ounces for each individual, and tea no more than from twenty-four to twenty-six ounces. The rate of consumption of tobacco had slightly lessened. The building of houses was so discouraged that the consumption of bricks and glass was actually declining. A heavy tax on malt made beer so costly that, during the thirty years which followed 1791, the use of that beverage had fallen off by fifty per cent. This was no calamity had the fact stood alone; but a more deadly stimulant took the place of the comparatively inoffensive beer. Between 1821 and 1831 the consumption of spirits had more than doubled. There was a tax on windows, which yielded a million and a quarter annually, and which caused the building up of windows, and a consequent shutting out of the sunlight, to the serious diminution of human comfort and health.* Paper was taxed from three halfpence to threepence per pound. This article was made to yield a revenue three times larger than the wages of all the workpeople employed in its manufacture. Newspapers were taxed fourpence each copy, partly to yield revenue, but still more to render them too costly for the use of poor people.† Salt was taxed to the extent of forty times its cost. One of the cheapest

* This very injurious tax was not abolished till 1851.
† The newspaper is the natural enemy of despotic government, and was treated as such in England. Down to 1765 the duty imposed was only one penny; but as newspapers grew in influence the restraining tax was increased from time to time, until in 1815 it reached the maximum of fourpence.

and most indispensable articles was thus made so expensive that the poor could with difficulty obtain it. On the coast, people habitually used the water of the untaxed ocean for the purposes of their simple cookery. It was estimated that a poor weaver, in that hard time, paid nearly half his income to government in direct and indirect taxation. The prudent man who insured his house against fire, or his goods at sea against shipwreck, suffered the discouragement of a tax which ranged from one shilling and threepence to five shillings per cent. He who desired to promote his business by an advertisement in the newspapers, was charged three shillings and sixpence for the privilege. From the medicines of the sick Briton government wrung an annual sum of fifty thousand pounds.*

The criminal laws were savage, and they were administered in a spirit appropriately relentless. The feeling of the time was so entirely in favour of severity, that Edmund Burke said he could obtain the assent of the House of Commons to any bill imposing the punishment of death. Every class strove to have the offences which injured itself subjected to the extreme penalty. Our law recognized two hundred and twenty-three capital offences. Nor were these mainly the legacy of the dark ages, for one hundred and fifty-six of them bore no remoter date than the reign of the Georges. It seems, at first, that there can scarcely be two hundred and twenty-three human actions worthy even of the mildest censure.† But our

* Sidney Smith did not caricature when he wrote: "The schoolboy whips his taxed top; the beardless youth manages his taxed horse with a taxed bridle on a taxed road; and the dying Englishman, pouring his medicines which has paid seven per cent. into a spoon which has paid fifteen per cent., flings himself back upon his chintz bed, which has paid twenty-two per cent., and expires in the arms of an apothecary, who has paid a license of one hundred pounds for the privilege of putting him to death. His whole property is then immediately taxed from two to ten per cent. Large fees are demanded for burying him in the chancel; his virtues are handed down to posterity on taxed marble; and he is gathered to his fathers—to be taxed no more."

† Sir Samuel Romilly asserted that there was no other country in the world " where so many and so large a variety of actions were punishable with loss of life."

stern fathers found that number worthy of death. If a man
injured Westminster Bridge, he was hanged. If he appeared
disguised on a public road, he was hanged. If he cut down
young trees; if he shot at rabbits; if he stole property valued
at five shillings; if he stole anything at all from a bleachfield;
if he wrote a threatening letter to extort money; if he returned prematurely from transportation,—for any of these
offences he was immediately hanged. The criminal class has
become, in recent times, a most painful embarrassment. Our
fathers experienced no similar difficulty. They solved the
problem by putting to death, with little discrimination, every
rogue, great or small, on whom they could lay their hands.
Judge Heath avowed from the bench the theory which seemed
to govern the criminal policy of the time. There was no hope,
he said, of regenerating a felon in this life. His continued
existence would merely diffuse a corrupting influence. It was
better for his own sake, as well as for society, that he should
be hanged. In 1816 there were, at one time, fifty-eight persons under sentence of death. One of these was a child ten
years of age. The hanging of little groups of men was of
constant occurrence. Somewhat earlier it had been even worse.
"A fortnight ago, " wrote Charles Wesley in 1776, I "preached
a condemned sermon to about twenty criminals; and every
one of them, I had good grounds to believe, died penitent.
-Twenty more must die next week. "   Men who were not old
when the battle of Waterloo was fought were familiar with the
nameless atrocities which it had been customary to inflict on
traitors. Within their recollection, men who resisted the government were cut to pieces by the common executioner, and
their dishonoured heads were exposed on Temple Bar to the
derision or pity of passers-by. It seemed, indeed, as if society
were reluctant to abandon these horrid practices. So late as
1820, when Thistlewood and his companions were executed
for a poor, blundering conspiracy which they were supposed

to have formed, the executioner first hanged and then beheaded the unfortunate men.

The prison accommodation provided by the state was well fitted to reconcile criminals even to the gloomiest of all methods of deliverance. It was in 1773 that John Howard began his noble and fruitful researches among the prisons of England, but many years passed before remedies were found for the evils which he revealed. In Howard's time the jailer received no salary; nay, he often paid a considerable annual sum for the situation which he filled.* He was remunerated by fees extracted at his own pleasure, and often by brutal violence, from the wretches who had fallen into his power. It was his privilege to sell their food to the prisoners, and to supply, at an extortionate price, the straw which served them for beds, unless they were content to sleep on the damp floor. To be acquitted of the charge on which he had been arrested did not imply that the prisoner was to regain his liberty. The payment of certain fees was an indispensable preliminary to the opening of the prison doors; and many who had been declared innocent of crime were detained for years, because they were unable to satisfy the exactions of their jailers.

The prisoners supported themselves by such forms of handicraft as best suited them. John Bunyan, during his occupancy of that "den" from which heavenly light streamed out upon the world, was diligent in the production of cotton laces. Facilities were given for the sale of these manufactures. The prisoners were allowed to stand outside the gate, chained by the ankle, and offer their wares to those who passed. Howard saw this done; and no doubt, a century before, the people of Bedford often saw John Bunyan similarly occupied. And then the prisoners were allowed to beg. If on the level of the street, they projected from the window a spoon fastened to a stick; If on a higher level, a stocking, suspended by a string,

* The jailer of Northampton, for example, paid forty pounds a year for his place.

offered itself to the charitable passer-by.   The grated openings
of·the prison were crowded by miserable wretches, who
assailed with their piteous tale all who would listen to them.

The rooms in which the prisoners lived were small, dark,
damp, and ordinarily crowded.   No bed was provided; there
was no ventilation; vermin swarmed; prison fevers from time
to time swept off the unhappy captives.   No provision was
made for separation of the sexes.   The child arrested for some
petty offence was at once introduced to the society of old and
hardened offenders, and subjected to its inevitable contamina-
tion.*

In the early period of English history the trouble of poverty
and mendicancy prevailed to a grievous extent.   The legislators of that time had no thought of removing the causes of
these maladies, or of extending relief to the sufferers.   Theirs
was the simpler device of forcible suppression.   A man might
be poor, but he must endure his poverty at home.   In the
fourteenth century begging was an offence, and especially begging beyond the district in which the mendicant had been born.
The English poor were a restless people then.   It was deemed
that they had never settled down after the wanderings of the
Crusades; but, perhaps, it is a juster inference that their home-
life was not attractive or satisfying.   As they wandered they
supported themselves by begging—enforcing their petitions
by such an amount of ьhreat as might suffice to obtain for
them a favourable hearing.   The law for some centuries gave

* Lord Cockburn's description of Edinburgh prison,—the Heart of Midlothian,—
which was used till near the close of the war, is applicable to British prisons generally.   "A most atroctous jail it was, the very breath of which almost struck down
any stranger who entered its dismal door.   It was very small; the entire hole being
filled with little dark cells; heavy manacles the only security; airless, waterless,
drainless; a living grave.   One week of that dirty, fetid, cruel torture-house was a
severer punishment than a year of our worst modern prison."   The prisons of France,
at that time, were in advance of ours, and the food supplied was adequate.   But gen
erally on the Continent torture was habitually practiced.   In the prisons of Hanover
a machine was used to tear off the hair of the offending wretches.

its energies to the suppression of this practice, not looking at all to the merciful alternative of relieving the deserving poor. In the time of Henry VIII. it was enacted that the "sturdy beggar" should be well whipped for his first offence, and have his ears cropped for the second. In the event of his proving so obdurate as to sin a third time, he was to be put to death as a felon.* But the attempt to make men endure hunger in silence did not prosper. In the sixteenth century we find the dawn of a legislative provision for the impotent poor. At first the funds were to be raised by an appeal to those who were able to contribute, the clergy being directed to " exhort gently " those who were disinclined to the duty. This arrangement, as it might have been expected, proved disappointing; and a few years later power to enforce payment was given by an act of Queen Elizabeth. The regulations instituted by the wise government of that time continued in force till the year 1834.

Toward the close of the eighteenth century a change came over the spirit in which the poor law had been administered. There set in with much energy a reaction against old severities, and a dangerous relaxation of strictness. It was not wholly or mainly an enhanced tenderness of feeling towards the poor which produced this reaction. It came to be understood that the poor were suffering, and were in consequence discontented. To avert the probable results of their dissatisfaction, an act was passed enlarging the powers of magistrates, and ordaining that relief should be given   1782 in such a manner as would make the condition of the   A. D. paupers more comfortable. This law was construed with dangerous liberality. The able-bodied laborer who sought relief was no longer obliged to enter the poorhouse; money was given to him at his own home; insufficient wages were supplemented from the rates. The lowest class of persons

---

* That the authorities were in earnest is made plain by the circumstance that during the whole of this reign the yearly average of persons hanged for vagrancy was two thousand.

obtained relief with such unwholesome facility that the condition of pauper became more desirable than that of self-supporting labourer. The cost of the system became intolerable.
In 1801, four million sterling was expended in relief of the
poor of England and Wales. In 1818, the amount had grown
to nearly eight million. There were parishes in which the
owners and farmers offered to give up their land, which could
no longer be cultivated to a profit under the scourge of an
intolerable poor-rate, and where the assembled paupers refused
to accept the land of the parish, because " they liked the present
. system better." The paupers were the chief support of the
beer-shops. The old law had worked fairly well during
many generations; but the utter demoralization of the labouring class in the rural districts of England was now resulting
from the altered spirit in which it was administered.

The size which our great cities had attained was inconsiderable in comparison with their present dimensions. London itself, instead of the monstrous city of nearly four million which
we know it to be, held only one million of inhabitants. Manchester and Salford had a population of 110,000; Liverpool, of
100,000; Birmingham, of 85,000; Glasgow, of 100,000; Edinburgh and Leith, of 100,000; Dundee, of 33,000. There was
no drainage, and the filth of the city lay festering on the streets,
poisoning the unhappy people. The citizen who ventured
forth of a winter night, supplemented by a lantern the feeble
light of the scattered oil-lamps. Gas as yet was little known,
except for indoor uses. Only in 1807 had it been tried in the
streets of London. It was vehemently opposed with the prediction of ruin to existing interests, which has been urged against ·
every beneficial change. Whale-fishing, it was said, would be
destroyed; thousands of sailors, carpenters, and rope-makers
would be ruined. But parliament gave London leave to light
her streets, and soon the cheerful blaze chased away the foul

creatures who were wont, in the darkness, to plunder and to kill.*

It has been boasted that while the Continental governments forced their subjects to take up arms, Great Britain was able to maintain her enormous forces by voluntary enlistment. This, however, is only true in part. The ranks of the militia were filled by conscription, and means were successfully used to induce the men of this service to enlist as soldiers. And in manning the navy, voluntary enlistment was largely supplemented by the efforts of the press-gang.† Any seaman who could be stolen from the merchant service was carried on board a ship-of-war, and compelled to fight. A band of men armed with this formidable power lurked in every sea-port, ready to seize the sailor returning from his voyage.

Military and naval discipline was maintained by a savage use of the lash. When we inflict two or three dozen strokes upon a criminal, we deem the punishment sufficiently sharp. Long ago a soldier or sailor was doomed, often for a slight offence, to such punishments as five hundred lashes. The men who applied the torture were changed at short intervals, lest the punishment should be at all mitigated by their fatigue. The doctor stood by to say how much the victim could bear without dying. When that point was reached, he was taken down and carried to the hospital, to be brought back for the balance of his punishment when his wounds were healed.‡ Immediately after Waterloo, when the House of Commons was

---

* Like many of the appliances which render modern life agreeable, the lighting of streets is comparatively of recent origin. Before 1683, London, then a city of half a million inhabitants, had no artificial light whatever for her streets. In that year an oil-lantern was placed before every tenth door on the nights when the moon did not shine. The disorders which darkness invited among such a population was frightful.

† An institution which had long been a terror to the people. Dr. Johnson's favourite black servant was seized by the press-gang, and the doctor was under the painful necessity of being indebted for his deliverance to the intervention of the hateful John Wilkes.

‡ In 1811 the London *Examiner* reported a case exceptionally horrible. A soldier was sentenced by court-martial to one thousand lashes, of which seven hundred and fifty were actually inflicted. The *Examiner* copied from a country paper an article which mentioned, in connection with this atrocity, that flogging was not practised in the French army:—" Bonaparte's soldiers cannot form any notion of that most

voting large sums to the Duke of Wellington and the other heroes of the war, it was proposed that the punishment of a soldier or sailor should be limited to a hundred lashes. Lord Palmerston resisted the proposal. The English, he said, owing to the freedom of their constitution and their higher feeling of personal independence, required more punishment than other nations did. His views prevailed, and the motion was rejected without a division. The brave men who fought our battles continued to be subjected to all the brutalities which their officers chose to inflict, till the advancing humanity of the age interposed for their rescue. In 1846 a soldier was flogged so that he died. Immediately after, punishment by flogging was limited to fifty lashes. Twenty years later, the House of Commons resolved, by a small majority, that flogging in time of peace should be wholly abolished. Since then the punishment of flogging has been inflicted only on three occasions.

The men who are slain in battle form but an inconsiderable proportion of those who lose their lives in war. In the Crimean war two thousand six hundred British soldiers were killed, while eighteen thousand died in hospital of wounds and disease. During the first seven months of that war the men died of disease at the rate of sixty per cent. per annum. So miserably, at first, were the wounded cared for, that operations which, under more favourable circumstances, would have involved no risk, nearly always proved fatal. The hospital was a position immeasurably more dangerous than the battle-field. Nor are the special risks of the soldier limited to the period of actual warfare. The Life Guards in their barracks in London experience a mortality twice as large as that of civilians of the same age.

heartrending of all exhibitions on this side hell—an English military flogging. " Governments prosecuted the conductors of the *Examiner* for libel, but the jury returned a verdict of not guilty. The editor of the country newspaper which originated the offending article was less fortunate. A jury of squires, resolute to uphold the government, found him guilty, and he was sentenced to eighteen months' imprisonment.

Until her sad experience in the Crimea, England had not bestowed much thought upon the care of her wounded. She had accepted as inevitable the terrible ravages of disease among the brave men whom she gathered around her standard. Each of her regiments had its surgeons, and each of her wounded soldiers was ministered to in course of time. But the power to inflict wounds is immeasurably in advance of the power to heal. The sufferers had often to lie for days in their anguish before it was possible to relieve them. Multitudes perished from neglect. Multitudes perished from disease engendered by crowded hospitals. If England had lost only those soldiers who were slain or received fatal wounds in battle, her wars would have been fought out at a cost comparatively trifling.

Slavery still existed throughout the world to an enormous extent. The great mass of the Russian peasants were serfs. There were nine millon slaves in Hungary. The peasantry of Austria and Prussia were nearly all slaves. America had put down the slave-trade,* but she still owned slaves, and had not begun to question the propriety of doing so. During the first seven years of the century English ships conveyed annually across the Atlantic forty thousand Africans, one-half of whom perished at sea or soon after landing. The British Parliament had expressed its approval of the traffic in twenty-six acts, and was not roused to its suppression until after twenty years of agitation. The Genius of universal emancipation, it was poetically said, forbade the presence of a slave in England; but slaves lived and suffered in her colonies. The whip was still freely used on her West India plantations. It was eight years after Waterloo till the flogging of women was put a stop to by a government order, and the planters resented so highly this limitation of their rights that they spoke of asserting their independence of the mother country. Slavery

*In 1808.

existed in Scotland down to the very last year of the eighteenth century. The colliers and salters were slaves, bound to their service for life, bought and sold with the works at which they laboured.

Women and children worked in coal-pits. They dragged about little waggons by a chain fastened round the waist, they crawling like brutes on hands and feet in the darkness of the mine. Children of six were habitually employed. Their hours of labour were fourteen to sixteen daily. The horrors among which they lived induced disease and early death. Law did not seem to reach to the depths of a coal-pit, and the hapless children were often mutilated, and occasionally killed, with perfect impunity by the brutalized miners among whom they laboured. There was no machinery to drag the coals to the surface, and women climbed long wooden stairs with baskets of coal upon their backs.

People used to employ little boys, and sometimes little girls, of five or six to sweep their chimneys. Chimneys were built narrower in those days than now, and the child was compelled to crawl into them, often driven by blows to the horrid work. Sometimes the chimney was not sufficiently cooled, and the child was burned. Often he stuck fast in a narrow flue, and was extricated with difficulty, Occasionally he was taken out dead. Parliament refused for some time to suppress these atrocities, even after a machine could be got for fifteen shillings which swept chimneys better than a climbing-boy did.*

In the early years of the century the manufacturing skill which has since made Great Britain so famous was still in its infancy. The machines on which our manufacturing supremacy depended were already in existence, but they were not yet in

---

* The barbarous practice of cleaning chimneys by making boys climb was unknown, excepting in England, where it originated about the beginning of the eighteenth century. By the time the boy was sixteen he was ordinarily too big for this occupation, and he found himself helpless, without a trade, and very frequently with enfeebled health. This method of cleaning chimneys was not suppressed till 1840.

extended use. Arkwright's spinning-frame was invented in 1769; Crompton's spinning-mule in 1775; Cartwright's power-loom in 1787; Eli Whitney's cotton-gin in 1793. Thus closely were the great inventions grouped, the consequences of which fashioned the destinies of half the world. The manufacture of cotton already felt the impulse of these new powers, and was beginning to assert its ascendency over the industries hitherto practised in the country. The woolen trade lay prostrate under disabling legislation. An act passed in the days of Edward VI., and still in force, grievously limited the woolen manufacturers in their use of machinery. Down to 1807 the manufacture of wool was conducted by appliances scarcely superior to those which had been introduced by the Romans. So lately did the passion for mechanical improvement find any place in this important industry.

A glance at the history of the linen manufacture—one of the very oldest of our industries—reminds us how very recently we have issued from a mechanical stagnation which has lasted from the dawn of human history; how amazingly swift have been the steps which have carried us to our present mechanical eminence. Three methods of spinning have been practised by men; three processes by which flax has been converted into the form from which it can be woven into cloth. The earliest of these was the spindle and distaff, a surprisingly rude agency, in which the human hand did much and mechanical appliance very little. The yard which made the cloth in which the old Pharaohs were rolled when they lapsed into mummyhood was spun in this manner. Homer's ladies industriously plied the same artless mechanism. The virtuous woman of Solomon's time laid her hands to the spindle, and her hands held the distaff. During all the heroic ages of our own history, and its prosaic ages as well, this was our only method of changing flax into yarn. When Richard of the Lion Heart was chasing, or vainly trying to chase, pagans from the sacred soil of Palestine,

the virtuous women of England laid their hands to the spindle.
When George III. went to war to suppress the revolution in
America, there was still in use in all the homes in England the
same rude contrivance by which the fibres of the primeval
world had been spun. Only towards the close of the eighteenth
century did mechanical progress make its lowly beginning.
We adopted the spinning-wheel. For a period of fifty years
this wheel, which was regarded as a marvellous triumph of
inventive genius, was in use by all industrious females. And
then, a few years after Waterloo, came the spinning-frame,
driven by water or by steam, from before the presence of
which the quaint old wheel followed the distaff, and disappeared for ever.

During a war of twenty-five years a marked improvement of
the appliances for mutual slaughter was a probable result of the
constant thought which must have been directed to the efficacy
of such agencies. But no such improvement took place. The
weapons with which all the tremendous battles of that war
were fought, and all its tremendous devastations accomplished,
were very rude. The musket was fired by a spark produced
by the striking of a piece of flint upon a surface of steel.* The
interior of the barrel was smooth, and the whole fabric was so
inartistically constructed that aim was scarcely possible. The
bullets flew wildly over the field, hitting in the most unexpected
places. Of all the shots which we fired in the Peninsula, only
one in six hundred harmed a Frenchman. It was calculated
that before the slaughter of an enemy could be achieved, a
weight of lead equal to the weight of his body was expended.
The bayonet could be trusted to in British hands; but its influence was chiefly moral. Only once or twice were the French
induced to abide the actual touch of that terrible weapon.

In the tower of London there are breech-loading muskets of

* The percussion-cap was invented in 1815, just as the value of the invention was
happily diminished by the return of peace.

Under the stimulous of a war demand, manufacturing works were multipied rapidly. Ere the change had attracted much notice, large numbers of children were massed together in attendance on machinery. At first no limit was laid upon their hours of labour. A nation long engrossed in war is apt to be wanting in tender thought for the weak and helpless. Little children had to work just as long as the exigencies of their masters' trade demanded. In course of years a process of physical deterioration was seen to be at work among the factory population, and an inquiry into its causes was ordered by the House of Commons. Evils the most gigantic and full of danger to the community were disclosed.

1832 A.D.

Children of six, it was found, were often put to work in factories. The hours of labour ranged from thirteen to fifteen daily, and might rise even higher in an unusually good state of trade. The children often fell asleep at their work, and sustained injuries by falling against the machinery. The overseer beat them severely to make them keep awake. The appetite was injured by excessive fatigue, and a tendency to the use of stimulants resulted. The children could not be instructed on Sundays because of their utter exhaustion. All the ills that flesh is heir to came down upon the devoted heads of the wretched little labourers. They were stunted in size, pallid, and emaciated. They were scrofulous and consumptive. They had an aptness to catch every type of disease, and disease among them was exceptionally fatal. The foundations were being rapidly laid of a population feeble, short-lived, ignorant, and in all respects debased. Already the recruiting sergeant complained that men suitable for his purposes could not be found in the manufacturing districts.

Intelligence travelled by a process so slow that it amuses us now to hear of it, although it is but as yesterday since no one dreamed of anything better. When the battle of Waterloo was fought, and the despatches three days after reached London, they were printed in newspapers, and the newspapers were loaded into mail-coaches. By day and night these coaches rolled along at their pace of seven or eight miles an hour. At all cross-roads messengers were waiting to get a newspaper, or a word of tidings from the guard. In every little town, as the hour approached for the arrival of the mail, the citizens hovered about their streets, waiting restlessly for the expected news. In due time the coach rattled into the market-place, hung with branches, the now familiar token that a battle had been fought and a victory gained. Eager groups gathered. The guard, as he handed out his mail bags, told of the decisive victory which had crowned and completed our efforts. And then the coachman cracked his whip, the guard's horn gave forth once more its notes of triumph, and the coach rolled away, bearing the thrilling news into other districts. Thus was intelligence conveyed during the first thirty or forty years of the century.

M en traveled by the same mail-coaches which carried their news. It was not very long since there had been no way of performing a journey but by mounting on a horse's back—well armed as need was—and trotting along thirty or forty miles daily.* England for many centuries was contented with little traveling, and therefore without roads. It was only as the eighteenth century advanced that she applied herself in earnest to the construction of tolerable highways. Her system of coach traveling struggled into existence as the roads improved. In 1774 Edmund Burke, having occasion to address the electors of Bristol, traveled from London on that errand in little over twenty-four hours; but this was deemed almost an incredible speed. Towards the close of the century Lord Campbell

* In 1796, when Mr. Simeon of Cambridge came to Scotland on a preaching tour, he bought a horse at Stirling, and rode him not only throughout his Highland journey, but actually home to Cambridge. This horse enhanced the discomforts inseparable from the enterprise by occasionally taking a fit, and suddenly tumbling to the earth.

accomplished the journey from Edinburgh to London in three days and three nights. But judicious friends warned him of the dangers of this enterprise, and told him that several persons who had been so rash as to attempt it had actually died from the mere rapidity of the motion!

On sea men traveled in little trading ships whose movements were grotesquely uncertain. The adventurous citizen who set forth upon a voyage of a few hundred miles, might be hurried by a favourable gale to his destination at a pace which rivaled that of steam; or he might lie motionless for many days longing for wind. The voyage from Leith to London has been known to occupy six weeks. The Atlantic might be crossed in one month, or it might require three. The use of steam in navigation was at hand, but it had not yet come. In 1801 it was offered by Fulton to Napoleon, and if the emperor had received the suggestion he might have landed in England. Happily he referred it to a commission of wise persons, and as such persons always regard novelties with suspicion, the application of steam to navigation was put down as an obvious absurdity.

The journeys which poor people had occasion to undertake were ordinarily accomplished on foot. Of necessity they were few in number, and the distance traversed was small. Each little community sat apart from its fellows, following its own customs, cherishing its own prejudices, feeding on its own traditions, speaking in a dialect which men from a distance failed to understand. A stranger was *ipso facto* an enemy. There were villages in England, at the beginning of the century, in which the inhabitants incited their dogs to attack any stranger whose curiosity led him to visit them.

Five hundred years ago the Great Plague swept over England with such deadly power that one-half of the population perished. After the panic had passed away, and the currents of business began to resume their interrupted course, there was found to be a scarcity of labourers. Farms "were like to be abandoned. Sheep and cattle strayed through the fields and corn, and there were none left who could drive them." Fields were untilled; crops rotted on the ground. It was found too—at least the employers constantly said so—that those labourers who survived presumed upon the monopoly which death had conferred upon them, and became audacious in their demand for higher wages. But the time was yet centuries away when the demands of labour could be listened to. The government was moved to correct the insolence of the masses. An act was passed commanding that working-people should, under pain of imprisonment, serve the first who asked them, and be contented with the wages which were customary before the plague. Another act was passed, by which it was made criminal for working-people to enter into any combination the object of which was to raise wages or reduce the hours of labour.*

The act which prohibits combinations remained in force till 1824. Down to so recent a period the interests of the British working-man were regulated by a law passed in 1350, soon after the battle of Bannockburn. Its avowed object was to repress him, and keep him back from asserting his right to the market value of his labour. Although this law was long felt to be oppressive, the working-classes did not have sufficient influence upon the course of legislation to procure its earlier repeal. No better evidence could be found that the government of the country was guided by a regard to the interests of certain classes, rather than a regard to the general good.

They were a hospitable people the men who flourished during the earlier years of the century, but their exercise of

---

* This act was long regarded as essential to the national welfare. In the reign of Edward VI. the penalty for a third transgression was the cropping of one of the offender's ears.

7

this excellent virtue was not according to knowledge. When they received their friends, it was deemed indispensable that every friend should mark his appreciation of the good fare which he enjoyed by becoming intoxicated. The host claimed it as his due that every guest should drink till he could drink no longer. The supreme crowning evidence that an entertainment had been successful was not given till the guests dropped one by one from their chairs, to slumber peacefully on the floor till the servants removed them.

A general coarseness of manners prevailed. Profane swearing was the constant practice of gentlemen. They swore at each other because an oath added emphasis to their assertions. They swore at inferiors because their commands would not otherwise receive prompt obedience. The chaplain cursed the sailors because it made them listen more attentively to his admonitions. Ladies swore, orally and in their letters. Lord Braxfield offered to a lady at whom he swore, because she played badly at whist, the sufficient apology that he had mistaken her for his wife. Erskine, the model of a forensic orator, swore at the bar. Lord Thurlow swore upon the bench. The king swore incessantly. When his majesty desired to express approval of the weather, of a handsome horse, of a dinner which he had enjoyed, this "first gentleman in Europe" supported his royal asseveration by a profane oath. Society clothed itself with cursing as with a garment.

Books of the grossest indecency were exhibited for sale side by side with Bibles and prayer-books. Indecent songs were sold without restraint on the streets of London, and sung at social gatherings by the wives of respectable tradesmen without sense of impropriety. Sir Walter Scott relates that he once lent to a very old lady the works of a female novelist of some reputation in her day. The old lady returned the volumes with the remark that they were much too coarse for her perusal now, although she remembered hearing them in her youth read aloud to admiring audiences of fashionable ladies and gentlemen.*

The educational condition of the English people was alarmingly defective. The existing means of education were utterly inadequate to the wants of the nation. At the beginning of the century there were no more than 3363 schools, public and private, in all England.† In 1818 it was found that more than one-half of the children were growing up without education. A few years after it was noticed that of all the persons who came to be married, one-third of the men and one-half of the women could not sign the register. In the manufacturing districts it was still worse. Forty per cent. of the men and sixty-five per cent. of the women were positively unable to write their own names. The weaving population, in the collapse of their fortunes which occurred after the close of the war, lost the power to bestow education on their children. And, besides, child labor had grown to be an important source of revenue to poor parents. What hope did the child have to be educated when the dissipated and the poor could earn money by his labor from the time he was six years of age? England had fallen into an abyss of ignorance, her rescue from which is a bright page in the annals of the succeeding generation.

In the darker ages of the world's history, justice was a thing of difficult attainment. The patient search and sagacious

---

* Many causes have conspired to bring about the remarkable improvement which has taken place in the moral tone of British society. Among these, the influence exerted upon public morals by the pure domestic life of Queen Victoria and Prince Albert fills no inconsiderable place. The intellectual ability recognized in the Queen and her husband, and their manifest devotion to the public good, added largely to the authority which their high station conferred upon them, and disposed the nation to be guided by their example. The Queen and Prince lived conspicuously blameless lives in the earnest and effective discharge of the family and public duties which their position imposed. Their example confirmed and powerfully reinforced the influences which at that time ushered in a higher moral tone than had distinguished previous reigns. The service thus rendered to the nation was valuable beyond all estimate.

† Fifty years later they numbered forty-five thousand.

tracing out of evidences of guilt from a mass of trivial circumstances, by which, as by the unerring vision of Heaven, the
criminal is revealed, was far beyond the untrained intellect of
the time.   How was guilt to be ascertained?   Our ancestors,
unable to achieve the discovery by their own efforts, referred
it to the judgment of Heaven.   The suspected man was appointed to meet his accuser in single combat, and the right
was held to be on his side who was so fortunate as to cleave
the head of his antagonist, or pierce him through with his lance.

The Normans introduced trial by combat into England.
For centuries it enjoyed formal sanction as a recognized method
of judicial settlement in certain classes of legal proceeding. As
ages wore on, the uncertainties of the process became slowly
manifest, and better methods of administering justice were
established.*   But the duel was not therefore abandoned.   It
expressed, conveniently, the love of fighting which the English
mind has never been able to put far away.   It served the purpose of wounded vanity or personal hatred.   The governments
of Europe strove vainly to suppress these private wars.   The
ferocity of a half-civilized people refused, in defiance of law,
to forego the privilege of slaughtering an enemy.

Long before the opening of the century it was a capital
offence to kill in a duel.   But public feeling was so tolerant of
duelling that juries would not, under ordinary circumstances,
convict the murderer.   In 1808, Major Campbell, a successful
duellist, was hanged, but it was for special enormities by which
his crime was distinguished.   The ordinary duelist was, upon
the whole, upheld by public opinion in his defiance of the law.

During the earlier years of the century duelling was famil-
liarly practised.   Outside the domain of law, questions con-

---

* The ordeal of battle was claimed by a criminal so recently as 1817, and was not
formally abolished till then. Society has discontinued the combat as a mode of settling individual differences, but retains it for the settlement of differences between
communities. Growing enlightenment will, in time, discredit this foolish and brutal
practice, as it has done the other.

stantly arose which it was deemed by the imperfect civilization of the time could not be settled otherwise than by the blood of either disputant.   These questions were, for the most part, utterly trivial.   In 1804 Lord Camelford, nephew of the Earl of Chatham, challenged his intimate friend, Mr. Best, for having spoken disrespectfully of him.   He was satisfied that he had been misinformed, but persevered in his challenge, and was so wounded that he died in great agony.   About the same time, Colonel Montgomery fell by the bullet of a friend with whom he had a quarrel concerning the merits of their favorite dogs.   In 1822, Sir Alexander Boswell published in an obscure Glasgow newspaper a song by which his relative, Mr. James Stuart of Dunearn, considered himself aggrieved.   Mr. Stuart challenged him, and wounded him to death.   Most of the leading politicians of the time waged private war.   Fox, Pitt, Castlereagh, Canning, O'Connell, and Wellington, had all attempted the slaughter of a foe.   So recently as 1840 two members of Parliament, Mr. Horsman and Mr. Bradshaw, had a hostile meeting, and after exchanging harmless shots, mutually offered and accepted explanations.   The ferocious passions which had so long supported this wicked usage were now dying out, and duelling in its decay had seldom a more respectable motive than the fear of being esteemed a coward. To meet this childish sentiment, the war office, in 1844, issued a formal declaration that it was suitable to the character of honorable men to offer and accept explanations and apologies for wrong committed.*

Small-pox was still the scourge of the people.   One-tenth of all deaths was caused by this disease.   Undrained fields gen-

---

*For this important declaration, which irretrievably discredited duelling in its last stronghold, the army, the country was indebted to Prince Albert, then a young man of twenty-five.   A fatal duel had been fought between two soldiers—Colonel Fawcett and Lieutenant Monroe.   The Prince took up the question, and his communications with the Duke of Wellington resulted in the Amended Articles issued by the War Office.

erated intermittent fevers which destroyed many lives, and pressed heavily on the vitality of the rural population. In the cities, the filth of the streets and of the dwellings of the poor produced undue mortality. The death-rate of London about the middle of last century had been as high as one in every twenty-four. Epidemics were frequent and desolating. Med· ical science, whose era of progress was yet in the future, could do little to limit the ravages of disease. But yet the sanitary condition of the people was better than that of their fathers had been. The average duration of human life was steadily lengthening. In 1780, one Englishman died in every forty of the population. In 1800 the death-rate had fallen to one in forty·eight. As the century wore on, the improvement continued, and in 1820 the deaths were only one in fifty-seven. Especially marked was the economy of life among the young, on whose immature strength the evil sanitary conditions of the time pressed most severely. At the beginning of the century, the deaths in London exceeded the births, and the growth of the metropolis depended wholly on immigration from the provinces. After 1810, these conditions were reversed, and the births exceeded the deaths.

CHAPTER II.

DURING many years the chosen occupation of the British people had been to rescue Europe from the despotism which Napoleon sought to establish. It was an enterprise which taxed their resources and pressed heavily upon their welfare. But they were able to persuade themselves that it was an enterprise to which honour and safety alike impelled them. Napoleon was the great enemy of Europe, and his overthrow must be effected before good in any solid or enduring form could be enjoyed by the European people. In this belief a generation of Englishmen had been educated. The war engrossed their thoughts to the exclusion, for the time, of domestic interests. To interfere with the pursuit of the common foe, by any complaint of individual wrong or assertion of individual right, was an impropriety which no well-conditioned citizen was expected to commit.

The necessity of reform in our system of representation had been recognized long ago. Lord Chatham advocated reform fifty years before the battle of Waterloo. It formed the subject of public discussion among the people of Scotland about the same time. William Pitt followed in the footsteps of his father, and during the ten years which preceded the French revolution introduced several measures of a reforming character.*

* Pitt does not, however, take rank as an advanced reformer. He proposed, mainly, a redistribution of seats. Members were to be taken from decayed con-

103

In 1776 John Wilkes proposed a measure which embraced all the leading changes afterwards enacted by the Reform Bill. In 1791 Sir James Mackintosh, urging the claim of the people to a share in their own government, went so far as to say that while the grievances of England did not yet justify a change by violence, they were in rapid progress to that state in which they would both justify and produce it. A very general concurrence of opinion warranted the hope that some beneficial change in the representative system could not long be delayed.

The need, in truth, was very urgent. The people of England had little influence and no authority over their government. It was said that they lived under a representative system, but the system had become so corrupt there was scarcely a shred of honest representation left in it. Two-thirds of the House of Commons were appointed by peers, or other influential persons. Every great nobleman had a number of seats at his unquestioned disposal. The Duke of Norfolk owned eleven members; Lord Lonsdale owned nine; the Duke of Rutland owned six. Seventy members were returned by thirty-five places where there were scarcely any voters at all. Old Sarum had two members, but not one solitary inhabitant; Gatton enjoyed the services of two members, while her electors were seven in number. The right to appoint these two members had been valued at £100,000. The revenue officers, who cast their votes as the government directed them, controlled seventy elections. Three hundred members, it was estimated. were returned by one hundred and sixty persons. All this time Leeds, Birmingham, and Manchester were unrepresented. Seats were openly offered for sale down to the very eve of the Reform Bill. Hastings had been so often sold for £6000 that her market price was perfectly established. Sudbury publicly advertised herself for sale. Generally the purchaser was expected to belong to the same political party with the

stituencies and bestowed on the growing communities, pecuniary compensation being given to the disfranchised. Besides this, ninety-nine thousand householders were to receive the franchise.

majority of his constituents; but this was not indispensable. A man was once purchasing the representation of a place called Petersfield, and the price, which was being adjusted in pounds, was raised to guineas because he was on the wrong side of politics. The members who bought their seats sold their votes, and thus made their outlay reproductive. At one period George III. supplied money, almost openly, to buy seats and bribe members. Till 1784 the polling might continue for six weeks. In that year its duration was reduced to fifteen days. Throughout that awful period violence and drunkenness prevailed without restraint. The unhappy constituency which was the victim of a contested election could scarcely have suffered more if it had been subjected to bombardment.

The political condition of Scotland was yet more lamentable. The people were utterly excluded from any part in the representation. The election was transacted in a room, or it might be in a church, and awakened no interest whatever in the public mind. The inhabitants were often apprised by the ringing of the city bells that an election had taken place. The county voters in 1830 did not number over two thousand. The county of Bute had at one time only a single voter who resided in the county. At an election this momentous person took the chair, proposed and seconded his own return, recorded his vote in his own favour, and solemnly announced that he was unanimously elected. The government of the day, or the landed gentlemen, regulated every election with absolute and unquestioned authority.

In the burghs of Scotland the town councils appointed delegates, by whom the members were chosen. These bodies nominated their successors, so that the people did not enjoy even an apparent connection with the appointment of members. Edinburgh alone had a member for herself; the other burghs being united for the purposes of the election into groups of four or five. Even in Edinburgh, with a population exceeding 100,000, thirty-three persons, virtually self-elected, held in their hands

the appointment of the representative.   They ordinarily discharged their trust at the bidding of government; and their
sons and brothers, it was remarked, were the happy recipients
of an unusual proportion of government patronage.   The
burgh constituencies of Scotland did not contain quite fifteen
hundred electors.

The occurrence of the French revolution was a powerful
reinforcement to those who sought to remedy the intolerable
abuses of our political system.   The easy vindication of their
liberties by a people so oppressed as the French inspired the
minds of reformers in England with a sure hope of success.
The general feeling approved warmly of what the French had
done.   The moderate English press constantly expressed its
approbation.   The frequent allusions on the stage to the triumph
of liberty in France never failed to call forth the hearty applause of the audience.   Pitt himself looked on with approval,
and wished success to the patriots of France.   Charles Fox
hailed the movement as the dawn of European regeneration.
To Sheridan it appeared that the French were "virtuously
engaged in obtaining the rights of man."   The rejoicing
Liberals of England were persuaded that the battle of human
liberty had been victoriously fought in Paris.

But their joy was not enduring.   There came, in swift and
dark succession, the unimagined atrocities of these new allies of
freedom; the wanton invasion by the French republic of the
rights of other nations; and the triumphant despotism of
Napoleon.   The sentiment of England experienced a sudden
revulsion.   France combined against herself the abhorrence of
all classes of politicians—from those on the one extreme who
feared the undue power of the populace to those on the other
whose apprehension pointed wholly to the excessive authority
of the government.   A passionate hatred to change took
possession of English minds.   "This is no time," said Pitt,
"to make experiments."   The cause of reform, tainted by an

alliance with the national foe, was abandoned by most of its former friends. England, resigning herself to the evils of her political lot, gave her undivided attention to the overthrow of the Emperor Napoleon.

With peace there came relief from that bloody and profitless labour which for nearly a quarter of a century had engrossed the mind ~~and barred the progress~~ of the British people. With peace came instantly the long-banished thought of their own internal concerns. The shout of triumph with which the rejoicing people hailed their splendid but dear-bought victory had scarcely passed into silence when they seemed to awaken to a bitter sense of wrong and pain. The change from war to peace brought the usual commercial dislocations. The war expenditure suddenly ceased. The country was exhausted by the fathomless extravagance and waste of prolonged war; and when the feverish excitement of the contest was over the exhaustion made itself felt at once. An unfavorable season added untold bitterness to the inevitable trial. The harvest of 1816 was so poor that wheat rose to one hundred and six shillings per quarter. Employment was scarce, and wages in many occupations were low. Depression pervaded nearly all industries. Factories were closed, iron-furnaces were blown out, coal-pits were shut up. Idle and hungry men wandered over the country, vainly seeking for employment. Hunger persuades men to evil, and the sufferers of those days were no wiser than other sufferers have been. Incendiary fires lighted up the evening sky. Bands of lawless persons attacked factories and destroyed the machinery, which, as they supposed, lessened the demand for human labour. In cities riots of huge dimensions were of constant occurrence. Once the mob in Glasgow were strong enough and fierce enough to maintain a fight of two day with the soldiers.

It was in those days of misery and violence that the demand for reform in our system of Parliamentary representation first became formidable. Prominent among those who created and directed public opinion on this subject was William Cobbett. His writings were read beside every cottage hearth in England, and exercised an authority immediate and powerful. Cobbett never ceased to urge that misgovernment was the source of all the misery which the people endured, and that Parliamentary reform was its natural and its only cure. His words sank deep into the public heart. Clubs to promote reform sprang up all over the country, and before the end of 1816 the demand even for universal suffrage was loud and urgent.

The great work of the next sixteen years was this agitation for reform of the representative system. Had governments of greater wisdom or of inferior strength been in office, much evil would have been spared. But the right of the people to interfere in politics had been for many years disused,* and a government, powerful by right of triumph over the greatest of all military despotisms, was not prepared to suffer its revival. The contest was a singularly bitter one. The government had no foundation in national choice; the relations between rulers and people were not friendly, but hostile. The people looked upon the government as a power high above them, of opposing interests, oppressive, contemptuous, cruel. The government believed that the new impulse which had seized the masses threatened danger to the institutions of the country; that every popular leader was a traitor; that every demand for political privileges was seditious. They spurned the thought of concession, and prepared to carry out inflexibly to its bitter end the policy of forcible suppression.

In this unhappy spirit the greatest of our domestic battles was fought. Many of the years across which the contest stretched were years of acute national suffering, for it was long before the country recovered from the exhaustion of the war. The resumption of specie payments in 1819 intensified the

* At a trial for libel in 1811 the judge (Baron Wood) explicitly denied the existence of such a right. "The right to discuss the acts of our legislature," he said, "would be a large permission indeed."

general distress. Money became very scarce; exports fell away; prices of nearly all commodities sank about one-half. Widespread ruin passed over the mercantile class; and England, it was said, "exhibited all the appearances of a dying nation."

The feeling deepened rapidly among a suffering people that they were ruined by misgovernment; that their welfare was deliberately sacrificed to promote the interests of the privileged classes; that there was no safety for them but in gaining for themselves a share in the government. Among the working population of the cities, especially, reform became now the absorbing interest. They were unused to agitate,* and at the outset they were not happy in their leaders. They pledged themselves to abstain from the purchase of articles which contributed to the revenue. An ominous passion for military drill sprang up among the artisans. The unrepresented towns began to appoint representatives, who should claim a place in that House from which they were wrongfully excluded. Huge meetings, expressing themselves by monster petitions, were continually held; and unhappily these constitutional methods of influencing the legislature were emphasized by occasional riots.

The government was resolute to extinguish, by military force, the discontent of the people. The Manchester reformers held a meeting of sixty thousand persons, with no design but to petition for Parliamentary reform. A strong military force was provided by the authorities—infantry, cavalry, and artillery. The proceedings had scarcely begun when a large body of mounted yeomanry dashed at a rapid trot among the defenceless multitude. Many persons—men, women, and little children—were carried from the field killed or injured. The thanks of the prince-regent were promptly offered to the magistrates who had directed this wicked and

1819
A.D.

---

* So utterly were the people excluded from any part in politics, that for twenty years there had not been in Edinburgh any public meeting of a political character.

cowardly slaughter. The chairman and others who promoted the meeting were put on their trial for sedition, and sentenced to various terms of imprisonment. In further prosecution of the mode of treatment which was thus applied, Parliament was now induced to pass the six acts proposed by the Tory government. Henceforth Englishmen were not to assemble in larger numbers than fifty, unless a magistrate convened them; and the exciting privilege of carrying a flag on such occasions was expressly denied them. The magistrates had large powers given to search houses suspected to contain weapons. Military exercises were forbidden. Newspapers were fettered with certain arrangements as to stamps, which, it was held, would restrain their unwarrantable boldness in discussing the measures of government. The liberties of Englishmen were now at the discretion of Lord Castlereagh and Lord Sidmouth.

The Whig chiefs represented in Parliament the movement which was rapidly taking possession of the country. Their management of the cause at the outset was timid even to weakness. They aimed to mediate between the extreme Liberals and the Tories—between that party which was making "unlimited demands" and that other party which replied with "a total and peremptory denial." How unevenly at this time they held the balance may be judged from Lord John Russell's proposal of 1819. It was nothing greater than that the franchise of any constituency convicted of bribery should be handed over to some populous town. Even this morsel of reform was denied. The Whigs were obliged to accept the disfranchisement of one very rotten burgh and the transfer of its franchise.

Deep among the masses of the British people was already a demand for universal suffrage and vote by ballot. Among the governing class was a settled conviction that any demand by the people for a share in the government was deserving of punishment as a crime. It was evident that a satisfactory measure of reform was not near. Many years passed before it was wrung from the reluctant hands of those who had it in their power to give or to withhold. The people never relaxed their effort to gain reform. Their patience and forbearance under the cruel frustration of their wishes argued fitness for the privileges from which they were debarred. They learned to put trust in the moderate counsels of Earl Grey, Lord John Russell, and the Whig party, and they ceased to think of force. The wishes of a people without representation in Parliament gathered weight slowly, but quite inevitably.

In the summer months of 1830 the despotism of the restored house of Bourbon made itself unendurable by the French people. The Parisians, after three days of fighting, expelled their king, and reasserted the liberties of which he had sought to rob them. Again, as forty years before, French example exercised a powerful influence in England. For fifteen years the English people had been vainly striving for a little reform in their system of government. In three days the French had struck to the earth a tyrannical government, and vindicated their right to be governed as they chose. The impression produced in England was deep and universal. Public meetings to express approval of this new revolution were held everywhere; and the desire for immediate reform now passed into a determination.

A few weeks before the expelled King of France came to find his refuge in the old palace of Holyrood, George IV., the worn-out voluptuary, passed unlamented away, and a general election consequent upon the accession of his brother, was ordered. The new Parliament was of a greatly more reforming spirit than its predecessor. The prolonged struggle of the people was visibly approaching a victorious close.

At the very outset Earl Grey made it plain that the question of immediate reform was to be made the engrossing business of the session. The Duke of Wellington, on the part of the ministry, intimated, with the calm resolution which never failed him, that in his opinion the country possessed a legislature which answered every good purpose, and that he would resist any proposal of change. But within a few days the government saw reasons for resigning, and a ministry pledged to reform, with Earl Grey as prime minister, was appointed.

It was not, however, to be permitted to this Parliament to inaugurate the era which was about to open. The ministry having sustained a defeat, appealed once more to the country, and a new Parliament was returned, pledged to support to the utmost the great measure which now absorbed the thought of the British people.

The Reform Bill was carried in the House of Commons by great majorities. But victory was not yet secured. The House of Lords, appropriately commanded by the Duke of Wellington, in its antagonism to popular rights, threw out the Bill. Earl Grey demanded from the King power to create peers in sufficient number to overbear the resistance offered by the House of Lords. The timid monarch refused and the ministry resigned.

Popular excitement was unbounded. Petitions rained upon the House of Commons, demanding that the House should refuse to vote supplies. A run upon the bank was commenced. Enormous meetings in all parts of the country resolved to pay no taxes till the Bill should pass. Plans were laid for arming large bodies of men in the northern counties and marching on London. There were serious discussions of barricades and street-fighting. The duke was reported to have said that "there was a way to make the people quiet." It was believed that he meant to suppress reform by violence, and the dragoons were seen by the eye of imagination, if not in actual fact, grinding their sabres as for the work of immediate battle.

Meantime, while this fierce excitement was raging over the

land, a feeble effort was made to form a Tory administration with a view to some acceptable compromise. The hopeless attempt was quickly abandoned, and Earl Grey returned to office with power to add to the House of Lords such a number of new peers as would effectually quell the resistance of the obstructive dignitaries. Their lordships did not wait to be thus diluted. The Duke of Wellington and a hundred other peers, majestically sullen, quitted the House and ceased from troubling. Amid rejoicing such as political victory 1832 never awakened in England before, the great measure A. D. passed which inaugurated, for all the coming generations, government of the people, by the people, and for the people.*

* The Reform Act bestowed the privilege of the franchise in towns upon occupants who paid a rental of ten pounds: in counties, upon those who paid a rental of forty pounds. In England, fifty-six burghs with a population under two thousand, and returning one hundred and eleven members, were disfranchised; thirty burghs with a population under four thousand, and returning each two members, were reduced to one member. Twenty new burghs received each one member; twenty-two received each two members; the county members were raised from ninety-four to one hundred and fifty-nine. Scotland received an addition of eight burgh members.

8

CHAPTER III.

THE Reform Bill of 1832 is undoubtedly, for the British people, the greatest political feat of the nineteenth century. It has been called by its enemies a revolution; and it was so. Two methods of government have been practised among men. The oldest and the most widely prevalent has been government by an individual or a class, very naturally with a supreme regard to the interests of that individual or that class. The other, which is of later origin, and until recently was confined for the most part to the Anglo-Saxon family, is government by the people themselves, and for their own interests. The Reform Bill marks for Great Britain the vast transition from the old method to the new. Inasmuch as self-government educates and ennobles, inasmuch as the government of another humiliates and debases, the revolution which raised the British to the rank of a self-governing people may well be ranked as one of the most beneficent in their history.

And what have been its fruits? A period longer than the lifetime of a generation has passed since the great transition was accomplished. At that serene distance we should be able to estimate with calmness and impartiality the results which the change has yielded to us. A very slight examination reveals the fact that the legislation which followed the Reform Bill differs in spirit and intention from that which went before

114

as widely as it is possible for one thing to differ from another. The ruling idea of legislation before 1832 was Protection,—special privilege bestowed upon some special class or interest at the expense of other classes or interests. Every one was protected. The landlord and farmer were protected by laws which shut out foreign grain and foreign cattle, and levied a heavy duty on foreign wool and timber. The shipowner was protected by a law which forbade the entrance of goods unless they were conveyed in British ships, or imposed heavy additional duties on those which foreign ships were allowed to bring. The manufacturer was protected by heavy duties on silks, woolens, and linens, on paper, on glass, on iron,—indeed on nearly every manufactured article which foreigners could send. Liberal grants from the public funds encouraged him to export his products to foreign markets. For his benefit the export of English wool was prevented. He was further protected by a law which forbade the emigration of artisans; by another law which forbade the exportation of machinery; and by yet another law which forbade the combination of workmen, lest the price of labour should be advanced. Every one was raised up on some special platform of artificial privilege and superiority—every one but the working-man, who, having no voice in Parliament, was regarded as the common prey of those who had.

The ruling idea of legislation since 1832 has been that legislation has no favourites; that all men are equal in the eye of the law; that all men are entitled to protection of life and property, and that no man is entitled to more. Before 1832, legislation occupied itself with the creation of special advantages for the benefit of favoured classes at the expense of those who were less favoured; after 1832, legislation occupied itself with the overthrow of all those iniquitous preferences. I propose now to give some account of the undoing of those numerous wrongs which during many generations had pressed heavily upon the welfare of the British people. During the next forty years this benificent process forms by much the larger portion of their political history.

The influences of the reforming spirit were growing in power during all the years which followed the close of the war. They were strong enough to gain some important successes even before that crowning triumph which made all others easy.

First in the long roll of wicked or foolish laws now to be abolished, there fell the old laws which had been enacted five hundred years ago, for the purpose of keeping the working-classes in a position of convenient subordination to their employers. The working-classes would bear the injustice no longer, and it was plain to all men that relief must be given. The exportation of machinery was now permitted. Artisans were no longer bound like serfs to British soil, but were free to carry their labour elsewhere if they desired. Above all, combinations of workmen to obtain better wages, or for any other reasonable purpose, were no longer forbidden. Hitherto workmen combined in secret, now they did so openly; and the troubled but in the end beneficent era of trades-unions began.

1824
A.D.

In the days of Charles II., when the people lay under continual fear that the Roman Catholics would regain their lost ascendancy, an act was passed which provided that no man could hold a seat in Parliament, or any office under the crown, until he had repudiated the doctrine of transubstantiation, and partaken of the sacrament according to the rites of the Church of England. This Test Act, aimed at the Catholics, fell with equal weight on Protestant dissenters; but they, sharing the common dread, were contented to suffer bereavement of their own privileges if only they might disable the common foe. In 1790, Charles Fox had vainly sought the repeal of this law. It was the prevailing feeling of that time, that men who

did not conform to the church which the nation had established, ought to be contented with bare toleration. Lord John
Russell now moved the repeal of the Test Act. Mr.
Peel and Mr. Huskisson opposed the change, but with   1828
out success. In the House of Lords the measure had   A.D.
an easy victory. One of the bishops, however, contrived to
have the words " on the true faith of a Christian " attached to
the declaration which was required of a member of Parliament.
These words continued the exclusion of the Jews from the
House of Commons, and the Jews, few in number although
wealthy, had to wait twenty-three years before the injustice
done to them was repaired.

During the eighteenth century the Irish Parliament, composed of Protestants of an exceedingly bitter type, had heaped
upon the unhappy Catholics of Ireland an accumulation of the
most wicked laws which have ever been expressed in the
English tongue. A Catholic could not sit in Parliament, could
not hold any office under the crown, could not vote at an
election, could not be a solicitor, or a physician, or a sheriff, or
a gamekeeper. If his son became a Protestant, he was withdrawn from paternal custody and intrusted to Protestant rela-
tives, with a suitable provision by the father for his maintenance.
A Catholic was not permitted to own a horse of greater value
than five pounds. If he used a more reputable animal, he was
bound to sell it for that sum to any Protestant who was disposed to buy. If a younger brother turned Protestant, he
supplanted the elder in his birthright. A Catholic could not
inherit from an intestate relative, however near. A Protestant
solicitor who married a Catholic was disqualified from following his profession. Marriages of Protestants and Catholics, if
performed by a priest, were annulled, and the priest was liable
to be hanged. Rewards, varying according to the rank of the
victim, were offered for the discovery of Catholic clergymen.

In the early part of the century, a Catholic who was so daring as to enter the gallery of the House of Commons was liable to arrest.*

The greater part of this profligate legislation had been cancelled during the century which gave it birth. But when the union with England was accomplished in 1801, there still survived laws which forbade the Catholic to be a member of the House of Commons, to hold any important crown office or a commission in the army, to be guardian to a Protestant, to hold any civic office without the written consent of the Lord Lieutenant, to be a gamekeeper, or to have arms in his possession for sale or otherwise, unless he should first renounce the doctrine of transubstantiation and the worship of the Virgin Mary, and receive the sacrament from the Church of England.

Ireland lay for many years utterly prostrate under this cruel Orange domination, unable to express her discontent more articulately than by frequent assassinations or occasional insurrection. Many of the Catholic gentry and traders quitted the country in disgust. At one time five-sixths of the English infantry were employed in maintaining the uncertain tranquility of this unhappy and vilely-governed country.

William Pitt had given to the Catholics a pledge that he would relieve them from their disabilities. But the old king was hopelessly obstinate in his anti-Popish feeling. He thought they were urging him to violate his coronation oath, and he intimated that he would regard every man who did so as his personal enemy. Long afterwards his son, the Duke of York, stated in the House of Lords that the illness which clouded the last years of the king's life was the result of his mental struggles over this question. It is sad to think of the poor old man thus agonized, but infinitely sadder that injustice done to six million Catholics should have been prolonged for twenty years by his incurable dulness and prejudice.

*William III. was applied to by the English woollen manufacturers to prevent that branch of industry from being prosecuted in Ireland. He promised to discourage it to the utmost, and he was as good as his word.

Despite the king, the claims of the Catholics came every year before Parliament with steadily growing support. In Ireland the agitation was governed by Daniel O'Connell. No man was ever more perfectly fitted for the work he undertook. O'Connell's eloquence was irresistible. He roused to white heat the passions of his ignorant countrymen; but, even in the moment of fiercest excitement, his control over the forces which he evoked was absolute. He held Ireland constantly on the verge of rebellion, but he never permitted the law to be broken. With the whole body of Catholic Irishmen obedient to his will, O'Connell became a power which no government could continue to resist.

The Duke of Wellington and Mr. Peel were in full sympathy with the king in his resistance to the claims of the Catholics. · But the time came when they were overborne by the sheer force of unwearied agitation. Peel was the first to recognize defeat. He was able to satisfy the duke that concession was inevitable; and the duke executed the still more difficult task of pursuading the king that the welfare of the empire commanded surrender. A bill to remove Catholic disabilities was introduced, and pressed with all the authority of a strong government. The bigotry of the kingdom rose 1829 A. D. in violent resistance to the proposal that civil penalty should no longer be attached to erring religious belief. But the necessity was too urgent. The bill quickly became law, and its earliest fruit was the return of O'Connell himself to the House of Commons.

The reformed Parliment entered promptly and with vigor upon the undoing of wrongs which the ignorance and selfishness of ages had heaped upon the suffering land. Its very first session is rich with the story of abolished evils.*

* There were still, however, subjects regarding which this meritorious Parliment stood gravely in need of education. In 1833 Mr. Hume's annual motion for the abolition of flogging in the army was negatived by a small majority. A motion pointing towards the abolition of impressment for the navy was also refused.

For a quarter of a century no slave had been imported into our West Indian possessions, but there was in the various islands a slave population numbering six hundred thousand. By the efforts of Clarkson and others, a public sentiment was created which compelled the abolition of the trade in slaves. Later on, Wilberforce and Buxton aroused the national conscience on the subject of slavery. Emancipation was one of the prominent questions of the election, and no candidate dared avow to the people whose votes he sought that he was hostile or even indifferent to the removal of the national disgrace. The harvest of many years of patient toil was now to be reaped. The abolition of slavery was decreed, with the almost unanimous concurrence of all but the slave-owners. That even they should have no reason to complain of the forcible relinquishment of their unjustly held possessions, Parliment voted them the enormous compensation of twenty millions sterling. Economy had become almost a passion of late years; but, to the honor of the people be it told, the great price with which the freedom of the slaves was purchased was paid without a murmer

1833
A. D.

The evils resulting from the unduly prolonged labour of children in factories had attracted the attention which its importance demanded, and had been carefully examined by a Committee of the House of Commons. The subject of legistive inteference between master and servant was new, and the propriety of such inteference was doubted by many. The manufacturers were for the most part strenuous in their opposition.* But the evil was too gigantic; the suffering which it caused was too cruel. It was settled then—and the settlement was ere long cordially acquiesced in even by those who had

* The first Sir Robert Peel, father of the statesman, was a noble exception. He himself had then a thousand children in his employment, and he claimed to know, from his own experience and observation, the urgency of legislative interferance. But the unreformed House of Commons was deaf to his entreaties.

opposed it—that, while grown men could fight their own battle with their employers, and were to receive no help in doing so, the interests of women and children called for protection at the hands of the legislature. An act was passed which prohibited the employment of children **1833 A. D.** under nine; which limited to forty-eight hours weekly the working time of children under thirteen, and to sixty-nine hours weekly that of young persons under eighteen. Ten years later a further . limitation was imposed. Females and those males who were under eighteen might be employed for eleven hours daily during the three years which followed the passing of the act. Thereafter came a reduc- **1843 A. D.** tion to ten hours. It was doubted by many whether our manufacturers, thus fettered, could endure the competition of foreigners, whose hours of labour were not restricted by law. " Manchester," said Daniel O'Connell, " will become a tomb." But the vast enlargment of commerce which followed the adoption of a free trade policy disappointed these fears; and the Factory Act proved an unmingled good.

The uneducated condition of the English people had been ascertained many years ago. The rapid increase of population constantly enhanced the magnitude of the evil. There existed an honest desire to promote education by government support for years before a way could be found. The jealousies which divided churchmen and dissenters interposed difficulties which no government had been able to sumount. But, although government gave no help, private effort, combined with the growing thirst of the people for education, already mitigated the evil. In 1818 there were only one person in seventeen of the population attending school. In 1833 the proportion was one in eleven. Years after, in 1851, when goverement help had long been given*

* In 1850 the government grant was £180,000. Ten years later it had risen to three quarters of a milllion. In 1870 it was close upon one million.

the attendance improved to one in eight. During all these years the Christian churches had been busily engaged in the establishment of Sunday schools. The rapid growth of that beneficient movement is evidenced by the increased attendance from one in twenty-four in 1818 to one in nine in 1833, and one in eight in 1851.

Public feeling now urgently demanded that the reformed Parliament should care for the education of the people. It was yet the day of very small things. A grant of £20,000 was voted, the money to be expended by the National and the British and Foreign School Societies. Such was the lowly origin of the present system of national education. For a few years the same amount was annually voted,—surely a modest contribution to the education of a million of utterly untaught children. In 1839 it was increased to £30,000. It was not without difficulty that this enlarged amount was obtained. The vote by which it was carried was 275 to 273. The educated portions of the community were themselves sadly in want of education. Many of the upper and middle classes cherished and avowed a deeply rooted dislike to the education of the poor, as tending to discontent and an overthrow of that orderly subordination without which society cannot exist.*

The Reform Bill did not bestow upon the people the privilege of self-government in their local affairs. The government of many English burghs was virtually private property. In others, the local authorities were chosen by a small number of the old freemen,—poor, demoralized, and greedy of bribes. The administration of affairs was worthy of its origin. The funds of the community were expended to secure control of Parlimentary elections. Even charitable endowments, the heritage of the poor, were habitually employed in the purchase of votes. In

---

* "The principle was reverenced as indisputable, that the ignorance of the people was necessary to their obedience of law."—LORD COCKBURN.

Scotland the municipal government appointed its successors, and the people endured the humiliation of witnessing their resources applied to purposes of which they disapproved, at the irresponsible will of men whom they despised. This anomaly was quickly marked for destruction. It was unreasonable that the men who voted in the election of a member of Parliament should be without voice in the appointment of a town councillor. The old abuses were indefensible, and they were with little difficulty abolished. In the English burghs, the whole body of ratepayers were in future to appoint their civic rulers; in Scotland, the privilege was limited to those who had the right of voting in Parliamentary elections. The reign of fraud and injustice was closed, and the citizens gained fitness for the duties of citizenship by the habitual exercise of its rights.

1835
A. D.

The evils of pauperism in England had become unendurable, and it was felt that some attempt to remedy them could no longer be delayed. According to the wise practice which about that time came into frequent use, a commission of inquiry was appointed, that legislation might be based on competent knowledge. The investigation of the commissioners revealed a system "destructive to the industry, forethought, and honesty of the labourers; to the wealth and morality of the employers of labor, and of the owners of property; and to the mutual good-will and happiness of all." The enormous cost of the system—nearly eight millions sterling—was not by any means its most serious aspect. It was achieving with appalling rapidity the utter demoralization of the English peasantry. Already the wholesome repugnance to accept the pauper's dole had become almost extinct. In some counties men refused to work, as they preferred the easier and ampler maintenance of the parish. Wages were supplemented from the rates, and in consequence fell so low that they ceased to yield support to the laborer. There were whole parishes in which the labourers were paid partly by their employers and partly from the rates. There were other parishes where cultivation actually ceased, because the revenue yielded by the land was not equal to the sum exacted for support of the poor. Relief was demanded as a right, and in some counties was avowedly given to all who applied. Pauperism had become hereditary. Once conceded to the applicant, the privilege was continued during life, and transmitted to his idle and debased progeny. Money thus acquired was spent freely in vicious indulgence. Tradesmen bribed the parish officers to obtain for them contracts at unjust prices. The parochial administration with fatal rapidity was corrupting the poor, and consuming the substance of the rich.

So deeply were these evils felt that some voices were raised for the total abolition of poor-laws as the only cure. Parliament enacted that out-door relief of the able-bodied, except in cases of emergency, should cease. Henceforth the pauper would not ordinarily receive money to be expended at his discretion; he would receive food and lodging, in order to obtain which he must accept the restraints of a strictly governed workhouse. The supplementing of wages from the rates was forbidden. A central board, with large powers, was appointed to direct the administration of the law. A vast and most beneficent change in the condition of the English peasantry takes its date from that day. Two years after, wages had risen; the able-bodied paupers had found employment, and were self-supporting. The rates had diminished forty per cent. There was, gradually, a marked change for the better in the habits of the working people, and a marked decrease of illegitimate births. But this amelioration has not been progressive; indeed, it has not been permanent. In course of years the practice of giving out-door relief became once more so habitual that now only about one-ninth of the paupers enter

1834
A. D.

the workhouse. One person in every twenty is a pauper.* The annual cost of pauperism in England and Wales exceeds seven million sterling. Nor is the expense of the system its greatest evil. It is a yet greater calamity that so large a proportion of the people have fallen so low as to compete for a disgraceful maintenance out of the earnings of others rather than undergo the labour by which they might honorably support themselves.

It was fitting, in a country whose citizens were assuming the direction of their own affairs, that easy access should be enjoyed to such political information as an unfettered newspaper press may be expected to convey. The heavy tax of fourpence on each copy rendered the newspaper a very occasional luxury to a working-man. The news- papers of the kingdom had only three hundred thousand readers, and their entire circulation was no more than thirty-six million copies annually. The growing thirst for intelligence rendered the tax peculiarly offensive. The revenue which it yielded fell off year by year, notwithstanding the increase in the circulation of newspapers. The excessive tax resulted in an open defiance of the law. The government owned that every effort had been made to suppress unstamped newspapers, but made in vain. It was urgently necessary to modify a tax against which public opinion pronounced thus emphatically. The Whig government proposed to reduce it to one penny. They were resisted with predictions of " a cheap and profligate press." It was urged that the people were not asking for cheap newspapers, but that they were solicitous of cheap soap. They could read the high-priced newspaper in a coffee-house as easily as if it were cheapened; while the high price of soap inflicted filth and disease on the very persons whose minds government professed a desire to illuminate.

1836.
A. D.

* In Scotland the proportion is one in twenty-three. In Ireland—a poorer country, where the workhouse test is more strictly enforced—the proportion is one in seventy-four.

But the House, unmoved by these appeals, struck the fetters from the newspapers, and sent them forth on a career of boundless expansion and inestimable usefulness. A considerable reduction of the duty on paper still further satisfied the lovers of cheap literature.

The postal system of the country presented some features which proved that it was not adequately meeting the wants of the people. During the twenty years which followed the termination of the war population and commerce had largely increased, but the revenue of the post-office had remained stationary. This could result only from restriction imposed by the excessive price charged. The rates were indeed so high as almost to forbid the use of the post-office by the poor, and injuriously to limit its use even for commercial correspondence. The conveyance of a single letter from London to such distances as Aberdeen or Belfast cost one shilling and fourpence; from London to Brighton eightpence. In defiance of law, vast numbers of letters were sent by carrier or other forbidden channels. Peers and members of Parliament had the privilege, practically unlimited, of franking letters. Every one who had access to such a dignitary solicited from him a store of franks, to be used as occasion required, for the free transmission of correspondence.

In 1837 Mr. Rowland Hill offered to the country a daring suggestion. He proposed that all the existing rates of postage should be abolished, and their place taken by a uniform rate of one penny, irrespective of distance, with prepayment by means of stamps. The post-office officials pronounced with emphasis against this revolutionary scheme. Sir Robert Peel —not yet liberalized—condemned it without reserve. But

1839
A. D.
the country at once and warmly approved it; a committee of the House of Commons recommended it; and Parliament adopted it. Our example was gradually followed by every civilized state.

The results of this great measure have largely exceeded the hopes of its most sanguine supporters. Under the old system the correspondence of the British people averaged four letters annually for each of them. In 1875 the average had risen to thirty-three. The incredible aggregate of over a thousand million of letters and post-cards was reached. Of newspapers and book-packets two hundred and fifty-nine million were carried. The gross revenue of the post-office was five million and a half sterling. The net profit realized was one million eight hundred thousand pounds.

The horrors inflicted upon women and children of tender years by their employment in mines and collieries had been fully exposed to public view by the report of a Parliamentary commission. There was such a concord of opinion on that terrible subject as made legislation easy. A measure introduced by Lord Ashley passed through both houses with little opposition and without important change. Henceforth women were forbidden to work in mines. 1843 A.D. Children were not suffered to be employed until they were ten years of age, and then with limitation of the hours of work. Government officers were appointed to exercise supervision over mines, and secure the observance of this salutary enactment.

Very early in the century public feeling began to disapprove of the excessive severities of the penal code. But in those days public feeling did not translate itself quickly into legislative action. The law had to be endured, but its harshness was largely mitigated by the merciful obliquity of jurymen. It was a capital offence to steal from the person or from a shop an article of the value of five shillings, or from a dwelling or vessel on a navigable river an article of the value of forty shillings; but it became impossible to persuade a jury that any

stolen article was so valuable.* Thus theft was growing to be
a privileged occupation, the following of which could not be
effectively reached by law. The penalty was tremendous, but
the machinery which alone could inflict that penalty refused to
be put in operation.†

In 1808, Sir Samuel Romilly, a good man and an eminent
lawyer, began to seek the mitigation of this pitiless code. He
laboured strenuously for ten years, but it was his only to sow;‡
other men were to reap. He was able to do no more than
exempt from death the crimes of picking pockets and stealing
from bleach-fields. He persuaded the House of Commons to
strike various other offences from the roll of those for which
the punishment was death; but the Peers were less merciful,
and maintained without further abatement the terrors of the law.

Sir James Mackintosh took up with success the cause of the
over-punished criminal. In 1820 the mind of the Upper House
ripened a little towards mercy. It ceased then to be a capital
offence to poach by night; unless, truly, the offender blackened
his face, for which enormity no pity could be shown. The protection of the gallows was now withdrawn from Westminster

---

* Sir Samuel Romilly gives some curious instances of the verdicts which humane
jurors returned during the prevalence of those terrible laws. A woman confessed
that she had stolen £5 from a dwelling. It was money she stole, and there was
therefore no ambiguity on the question of value. But, in spite of her confession, the
jury found that the amount was only thirty-nine shillings.—Two men were engaged
jointly in a theft from a shop. One of the two gained the good graces of the jury,
who found that the value of his theft was four shillings and tenpence, and he escaped.
The other had the misfortune to be less acceptable to the jury. His valuation was
fixed at five shillings, and he was hanged.

† The harshness of the law was still further mitigated by the increasing frequency
with which the prerogative of the crown was exercised. Down to 1756 about two-
thirds of the condemned were actually brought to the scaffold; from 1756 to 1772 the
proportion sinks to about one-half; between 1802 and 1808 it is no more than one-
eighth. Dr. Paley argues in favour of a liberal condemnation of criminals, tempered
by a liberal exercise of royal mercy. It is impossible, he asserts, for the law to dis-
criminate with sufficient accuracy between the shades of crime. It is therefore better
to "sweep into the net every crime which under any possible circumstances can
merit death," and leave it with the crown to pardon those offenders for whose crime
death would be an excessive punishment.

‡ Romilly died by his own hand in 1818, during a temporary derangement of mind
resulting from domestic affliction.

Bridge. A gipsy might at length remain for a year in the same locality without danger of expiating his wickedness by death. Even a known thief found in one of the northern counties might hope to live unharmed if he did not anew provoke the resentment of the law.

Very slowly the relaxation proceeded until 1832, when the progress became less timid. During the next few years many crimes ceased to be punished by death. It was long before the mitigation reached the stealing of cattle and sheep, that being an offence against the majesty of the agricultural interest. The legislature manifested an impartial reluctance to spare the forger. At first, Parliament consented to exempt only certain classes of forgeries; and it cost several years, and three several acts of Parliament, before forgery of every degree ceased to be visited with death. After 1834 it was no longer permitted to behead the body of the slain criminal, or dissect it, or hang it in chains. Hitherto the counsel of a prisoner under trial for felony was not permitted (except in Scotland) to address the jury on behalf of his client. In 1836 that privilege was conceded, not without considerable opposition. Until this year a criminal condemned to death had but one clear day between sentence and execution. For that day his sustenance was bread and water, and no friend was allowed access to him. All these needless cruelties were now done away. In 1837 the list of capital offences was further abridged, till it contained no more than seven. The record of sentences passed in these years shows how rapidly the relaxation now progressed. In 1834 there were pronounced four hundred and eighty sentences of death, but only one hundred and sixteen in 1838. In the former year eight hundred and ninety-four persons were sentenced to banishment for life, but in the latter only two hundred and sixty-six. A few changes had still to be made; but the triumph of mercy, after thirty years of effort, was now substantially complete.

9

The unjust acquisition by the powerful and the cunning of advantages which were the rightful property of the weak, occupies a large space in human history. In the darker ages, the persons of the victims were seized and compelled to labour for the profit of the spoiler. When this grosser form of outrage was discredited by advancing civilization, the aggressors followed their designs by process of law, and were contented to possess themselves of the fruits of the labourer's toil. They passed laws compelling him to pay high prices for the articles which he required to purchase, and the poor man's scanty comforts were abridged that the affluence of the rich landowner or manufacturer might increase. And many long years passed before men seemed to suspect that such laws were unjust or hurtful.

In 1776, Adam Smith, a Glasgow professor, and the son of an officer of customs in the small Scotch town of Kirkcaldy, published a book on the Wealth of Nations. In this book he argued with irresistible force that it was an exceedingly foolish thing for a nation to make the commodities which it consumed artificially dear, in order to benefit the home producers of these articles. William Pitt read the "Wealth of Nations" with care. The reasonings of the wise Scotchman were an economical revelation to the great minister. It is certain that he intended to embody them in his own commercial policy, and the era of free trade seemed about to dawn. The Man had come, but not the Hour. Pitt was drawn, reluctantly at first, into the war with France, and the opportunity of commercial reform was never given to him again. Henceforth, during all his life and for years after, enormous war expenditure compelled the indiscriminate levy of taxes, without regard to any result but the immediate possession of money. Pitt's mantle did not fall on his successors in office, nor even upon his great rival. Fox owned frankly that he could not understand Adam Smith.*

* Edmund Burke, whose mastery in every department of thought and knowledge was so marvellous, was a free-trader before the "Wealth of Nations" was published.

Another generation of Englishmen had to bear as they best might the disabling restrictions with which the incapacity and selfishness of the governing class had loaded them.

The protected interests—the landlords, the farmers, and the shipowners—were naturally blind to the mischief wrought by protection. But the classes whose business it was to manufacture and to distribute commodities were quick to discover the evils of a system which limited consumption by making commodities artificially dear. The mercantile class was now becoming powful by wealth and intelligence, and although yet scarcely represented in the legislature, was able to command respectful attention to its wants. The merchants of Great Britain were first to perceive that restriction was injurious to the nation; and the merchants of London, in a petition to the House of Commons, were the first to give forth an authoritative 1820 A. D. condemnation of the system. Their petition is a most full and clear statement of that great doctrine of freedom of trade, the excellence of which was not yet to gain legislative sanction for a quarter of a century.

Under the influence of Mr. Huskisson, various steps in the direction of a free trade policy were taken. A preference for unrestricted commercial intercourse continued 1823-4 A. D. steadily to gain ground in all parts of the country. In 1836, and for two or three succeeding years, the harvest was defective, and much suffering prevailed. Enough had been said about freedom of trade to guide the hungry people to monopoly as the origin of their sorrows. Supported by a growing concord of opinion in all the cities, an Anti- 1838 A. D. Corn Law League was formed in Manchester, and an organized agitation was begun such as no government could long resist.

The soul of the free trade agitation was Richard Cobden, a

Adam Smith spoke of him as the only man he had met who had just views regarding commercial freedom.

man unmatched in the sagacity with which he discerned the true interests of nations, and unmatched, too, in the calm, irresistible clearness and power with which he presented to the minds of the people the truths which he himself perceived. Those who give themselves to the cure of the moral evils which afflict man are apt to look upon Cobden as' if he occupied a lower platform of usefulness than they; as if he strove merely to bring larger gains to the trader, and the means of a more extravagant expenditure to the labourer. It is an impression founded on most imperfect acquaintance with the circumstances. Among moral reformers, no man can challenge a higher place than Richard Cobden. No mission loftier than his, or fulfilled more purely and nobly, was ever undertaken by man. When Cobden, at the opening of his career, surveyed the abuses of his time, that he might determine where his service could be most usefully bestowed, he had almost chosen to devote himself to the cause of education. But he saw that the masses of the people were kept poor by unjust laws, and he knew that poverty brings moral degradation. Material welfare, he believed, was the indispensable foundation of moral progress; or as Sir Robert Peel expressed it after his conversion to free trade—"I am perfectly convinced that the real way to improve the condition of the labourer, and to elevate the character of the working-classes of this country, is to give them a command over the necessaries of life." He devoted himself to the removal of laws which, by estranging nations, lead to war, and by creating poverty create vice. He chose freedom of trade as his life-work; he chose John Bright as his fellow-workman. For his choice of a mission and a colleague all future generations may well be grateful.

The Anti-Corn Law League applied itself to its task with energy unsurpassed in the annals of political agitation. The wealthy mercantile class supplied lavishly the funds required. Tracts were circulated by the million. Skilled lecturers overran the country. The speeches of Cobden and Bright in Parliament and elsewhere were universally read, and lodged in all impartial minds the conviction that restriction of commerce was at once impolitic and unjust. The enlightenment which resulted to the people from the efforts of the League was, apart from all material gain, a magnificent educational triumph.

In 1845, Sir Robert Peel was at the head of a Conservative government, the supporters of which understood that it was pledged to defend the monopoly of the landed interests. Sir Robert had been forced to make concessions to the free trade party. He had modified somewhat the duties on corn, and he reduced or abolished duties on seven hundred and fifty other articles which were taxed by the intolerable tariff of the time. But these concessions, so far from being accepted by the free-traders, merely stimulated them to greater efforts. **1842 A. D.**

The summer had been ungenial, and during the autumn months rain fell unceasingly. In August an alarm was whispered as to the condition of the Irish potato crop. There was a daily interchange of notes between Sir Robert and his Home Secretary, Sir James Graham, who was then at Netherby. Peel's tone was one of deep and ever-deepening alarm. His reports from Ireland, which had been from the first gloomy, soon became tragical from the intensity of the peril which they disclosed. The entire potato crop was rapidly perishing, and still the pitiless rain fell incessantly. The people of Ireland were vissibly to suffer loss of their whole supply of food for the approaching winter. The grain crops of England and Scotland were seriously injured too. Winter was at hand. The supply of food was miserably insufficient, and laws were in force which must have the effect of kepping it so. **1845 A. D.**

Sir Robert Peel summoned his cabinet to the consideration of these appalling circumstances. He would not incur the guilt of maintaining laws which within a few weeks must

inflict the horrors of famine upon the people.*   The corn law
must be, at the very least, suspended.   But if suspended, there
was no prospect, in the present temper of the public mind, that
it could ever be reimposed.   He preferred, therefore, that it
should be at once repealed.

He failed to convince some of his colleagues, and therefore
he resigned.   But there was no other man in England strong
enough to guide the nation in this hour of danger.   Peel was
recalled, and surrounded himself with men who were
in full sympathy with his views.   He proposed the
total repeal of the corn law.   A fierce contest in the
House of Commons ensued, in which Mr. D'Israeli
earned fame and the leadership of the Tory party by his en-
venomed resistance to a measure without which it is difficult to
imagine how the national existence could have been preserved.
But Peel triumphed by a majority of 327 to 229.   The House
of Lords received ungraciously a measure which was deemed
adverse to the interests of the landed class.   But the Duke of
Wellington was still the autocrat of that House, and his grace,
with a wisdom beyond that of his party, recognized and yielded
to the inevitable.   When peers who received their law from
his venerable lips asked permission to vote against the bill, the
duke said to them, "You cannot dislike it more than I do;
but we must all vote for it."   They did vote for it in sufficient
numbers to secure its enactment.

Immediately after, the Tories were able to avenge themselves on Peel by so outvoting him that he at once resigned.
His closing words, on leaving office for the last time, were very
pathetic.   After speaking of the hostility which he had aroused
among defeated monopolists—"It may be," he said "that I

Jan. 19,
1846
A. D.

* Sir Robert's conversion to a free trade policy, although only now disclosed, had
been for some time in progress. Lord Aberdeen told the Queen ("Life of Prince Consort," p. 317). "If it had not been for the famine in Ireland, which rendered immediate measures necessary, Sir Robert would have prepared the party gradually for
the change." So early as 1842 he avowed himself a supporter of free trade in all articles excepting corn and sugar

shall be sometimes remembered with expressions of good-will in the abodes of those whose lot it is to labour and earn their daily bread by the sweat of their brow. I trust my name will be remembered by those men with expressions of good-will, when they shall recruit their exhausted strength with abundant and untaxed food—the sweeter because no longer leavened with a sense of injustice."

The party which placed Sir Robert Peel in power, expecting that he would preserve for them the monopoly which they enjoyed, never forgave him for destroying it. His defence against their vehement accusations of treason is very simple. He was not the servant of the Tory party; he was the servant of the nation. When he became satisfied that the welfare of the nation called for the overthrow of the corn law, there was but one course open to him. The British people, having no sympathy with the rage of defeated monopolists, will long hold in honour the man who, in obedience to his convictions and at the cost of great personal sacrifice, delivered the country from laws which were undermining its greatness and leading it to ruin.*

The corn law was the key-stone of the protective system. When free trade in corn was gained, the other protected industries knew well that their hour was at hand. It was a vast work which the legislature had undertaken, and it was done boldly and swiftly. In 1842 there were twelve hundred articles on which duty was levied at British ports. A few years later there were only twelve, and these were retained merely for revenue. The idea of affording protection by means of duties imposed on imported articles was now completely and finally abandoned. Henceforth the artificial regulation of prices was to cease, and the great natural law of demand and supply was to exercise its uninterrupted, and in the end universally beneficent, dominion.

* The whole foreign commerce of the United Kingdom—imports and exports together—was in 1846 no more than £134,000,000. Thirty years later it had grown to the enormous aggregate of £655,000,000.

Two of the favoured industries were able to plead special
reasons why the protection which they enjoyed should be
spared in the general overthrow.

In the time of Oliver Cromwell, when the Dutch were our
rivals upon the sea, it was considered necessary to repress
the growing competition of that enterprising people. An
act was passed, which by a variety of ingenious restrictions excluded foreign ships from participating in the larger
part of our carrying trade. Mr. Huskisson introduced
an important modification of this law, by offering to
remove the restrictions imposed by our navigation laws
from the ships of any nation which would extend to our ships
a corresponding liberty. Subject to that qualification, the laws
enacted two centuries before, from antipathy to the Dutch, still
regulated the carrying trade of Great Britain.

1651
A. D.

1823
A. D.

Adam Smith, who reasoned so powerfully against all other
restrictions on commerce, bestowed upon the navigation laws
his unqualified approval. They proceeded, he thought, from
national animosity; but yet, strange to say, they were "as wise
as if they had all been dictated by the most consummate wisdom. They were unquestionably injurious to commerce, but
inasmuch as they kept up a large supply of sailors, they were
necessary to the safety of the country; and as defence is of
more value than opulence, it was held by this great economist
that the benefits conferred by the navigation laws outweighed
their disadvantages.

The plea of the shipowners was, therefore, that their trade
would be destroyed by the withdrawal of protection; that the
supply of sailors would cease; and that Great Britain would in
the end lie helpless before any naval power which had been
wise enough to sustain its shipping. But the British
people were by this time very familiar with unfulfilled
predictions of commercial decay. The navigation laws
shared the common doom of monopolies; and the shipowners

1849
A. D.

learned in course of time that their share in the general prosperity which flowed from an unrestricted commerce was
immeasurably more valuable than the paltry advantage which
they had gained at the cost of evil inflicted upon the community. The shipping of great Britain, which in 1849 was only
four million eight hundred thousand tons, increased in a quarter of a century to six million, navigated by crews numbering
two hundred and fifty thousand.

The sugar produced in our West India colonies was admitted
at rates of duty very much lower than those levied upon the
sugar which foreign countries offered to us. The reasons
urged for continuing this protection were, that labour in the colonies had been made scarce and dear by the abolition of slavery,
and that the reduction of duties on foreign sugar would tend to
the encouragement of the slave-trade with those countries
which still maintained that loathsome traffic. But these plans
were not accepted. It was believed that labour was neither
scarce nor dear in the colonies, and that the growing of colonial sugar suffered from no other disadvantage than the rude
and wasteful methods on which it was conducted. And further,
it no longer appeared to the British people that their custom
house should be made a vehicle for conveying to the
foreign slave-owner a knowledge of moral truth. The 1846 A. D.
duties on sugar were equalized, without reference to
the place of production or the kind of labour employed ; but
the process was spread over five years, to give the colonial
growers time to adapt themselves to the change.

It had been confidently foretold that the abolition of slavery
must accomplish the ruin of the West India islands. Predictions of universal ruin are the habitual defence of endangered
monopolies, and the growers of sugar continued to fight their
battle on the old lines. Although the islands had survived the
emancipation of their negroes, it was vehemently asserted that

they must now be utterly overthrown by the law which withdrew the special advantages they had hitherto enjoyed.

Jamaica, the most important of our West India islands, was scarcely in a condition to undergo grave changes. Her soil was largely owned by gentlemen who lived pleasant lives in England, leaving their incomes to be earned for them by overseers. Their estates were heavily mortgaged,* and their management careless and wasteful. They could exist in comfort only while the people of England continued willing to support them by special taxation.. When this could no longer be enjoyed, most of them sank into ruin. The fears which had been entertained were found to be just. The supply of labour was now beyond question inadequate. The negroes were able without trouble to acquire each his little patch of ground, the almost spontaneous production of which maintained him in such comfort as he desired. They were without motive to labour, end they chose to be idle. The exports of Jamaica, which had once amounted to three million sterling, fell to one million. The production of sugar fell to one-fifth of what it had been under slavery. The only crop which increased was pimento; for the pimento tree grows wild in Jamaica, and it quickly overspread the lands which it was now found impossible to cultivate. Jamaica, with every advantage which soil and climate could bestow, proved herself unequal to an open competition with rival producers. Her defeat was regretted by the people of Great Britain, but no shade of doubt was ever cast upon the justice and necessity of the reforms by which her fall had been hastened.

With the other islands it fared very differently. They were more happily circumstanced than Jamaica, in respect that their management had been more careful, and their soil was less heavily burdened by debt; and they passed through the trial

* In 1854 it was stated that nine-tenths of the estates in Jamaica were mortgaged for sums in excess of their value.

which now fell upon them without serious or lasting injury. A few years after the slaves were set free, it was seen that the production of the islands was increasing; that the negroes were purchasing land and prospering; that education was making some progress; that crime was diminishing. This beneficent course of affairs was not impeded by the discontinuance of a protective policy. The welfare of the population continued to increase, and no pecuniary disadvantages revealed themselves to qualify the satisfaction which this consideration was fitted to impart.

The producing and trading classes gained largely by the changes which had now been accomplished. But no gain was comparable with that of the working-classes, who have passed during the last forty years from oppression to power, and from being the victims of undue taxation into a position where the payment of taxation is in large measure optional.

It was estimated, about the close of the war, that a workman paid nearly elven pounds annually to sustain the government and to protect native industry. In the case of a workman paid as the handloom weaver was, this absorbed nearly one-half of his income.

Thirty years later, when their condition had begun to improve, Mr. Cobden reckoned that the working-classes paid to the government from 4s. up to 16s. of every pound which they expended on certain great staple articles of their consumption. "For every 20s. which the working-classes expend on tea, they pay 10s. of duty; for every 20s. they expend on sugar, they pay 6s. of duty; for every 20s. they expend on coffee, they pay 8s. of duty; on soap, 5s.; on beer, 4s.; on tobacco, 16s.; on spirits, 14s." They were now relieved from the tax—impossible to be estimated—which they paid on bread and beef in order to support British agriculture; but still their contribution to the national revenue was unduly large.

Another thirty years have passed, and our method of taxation no longer presents any feature of injustice. The net expenditure of the nation is about seventy-five million. Of this huge sum forty million is levied on intoxicating drinks and on tobacco; five million is levied on tea; the balance is contributed by the wealthier class in the form of income-tax, stamp-duties, and otherwise. The working-man can at pleasure exempt himself from bearing any share of the taxation which is laid upon drinks and tobacco. There remains his tea, the only article indispensable to his welfare on which taxation can be demanded of him. The tax levied on this article averages about three shillings annually for each of the population. For this surely moderate exaction of less than one penny per week, any working-man who chooses can enjoy the advantages of British citizenship. The injustice of ages has been cancelled. The Hampdens of the future must be contented to occupy themselves mainly with the correction of small and uninteresting evils.

NOTE.—There are a few problems which we have, thus far, failed to solve. Of these the following are perhaps the most notable:—

1. THE LAND QUESTION.—In this country the people are wholly dissociated from a proprietary interest in the soil. So completely is this the case that one-half of our land is owned by about a thousand persons, and four-fifths by five or six thousand persons. In all other countries land is, to a very large extent, owned by the people. In France, for example, there are nearly eight million landed proprietors. Had the enormous concentration of British land been brought about by natural causes, it must have been accepted as just and reasonable, or, at all events, inevitable. But it is, in very large measure, artificial. The law of entail withdraws from the market the greater portion of our land; at the same time reducing its nominal owner to the position of holding a mere life-rent interest, and thus weakening his motive for developing its resources. The influence of the powerful legal guild has attached to the transfer of land enormous charges, which go far to prevent small purchases. It results from thus binding up the land into a small number of huge properties that the mass of the people are deprived of one of the most powerful

motives for economy, and that one of the most desirable methods of obtaining subsistence is closed against them. It is said, in defence of the system, that under it the soil is made to produce more largely than in the hands of peasant proprietors. Scotland, where the system is seen at its worst, is the most highly productive country in the world. In Scotland the average production of wheat is thirty-four bushels per acre; in England it is twenty-nine bushels; in France it is only sixteen bushels. But this superiority is traceable to other causes than the land laws; for in Wurtemberg, where land is excessively subdivided, the production is larger than it is in England. Our artificial restrictions on the sale of land are, beyond question, prejudicial to the interests of the British people, and probably cannot be much longer endured. The circumstances of the time put the stamp of urgency upon the land question. In Canada and the United States are enormous tracts of fertile land which will compete year by year more keenly with our own soil in supplying the food of the British people. Our natural disadvantage is sufficiently great; if artificial disadvantage is not removed, the future of British land is gloomy indeed.

2. THE LIQUOR QUESTION.—It is estimated that the people of Great Britain and Ireland expend annually one hundred to one hundred and twenty million on intoxicating liquors. Two-thirds of this sum are received by government in the form of duties, and by manufacturers and distributors in the form of profit. Of the balance a considerable proportion may be fairly set down as yielding legitimate enjoyment to the consumer, and is not therefore to be regarded as a wasteful expenditure. But, after all these deductions, there remains a large sum which is not merely unproductive of good, but which procures by its expenditure the degradation and ruin of multitudes. For upwards of a generation nobly persistent and self-denying efforts have been put forth by associations of men, impressed with the magnitude of those evils, to direct adequate attention to the subject. After many years of discouraging toil they are now being rewarded with a measure of success. But the work is still very far from completion. The public mind has still to be educated to a just appreciation of the enormous evils which flow from the undue use of intoxicants; and the distribution of the agencies by which results so deplorable are produced has to be more effectively regulated and restrained.

3. THE LABOR QUESTION.—Since the emancipation of the workman, his relations with his employer have been troubled, and very often openly hostile. Amicable adjustment of differences has not yet been found

practicable. When working-men desire increase of wages, and cannot
obtain it by asking, they cease to labour in order to force from their employers the concessions which they seek. The employer on his part en-
forces his views by closing his works, hoping that starvation will subdue
his obdurate servants. Some departments of industry have suffered
severely, perhaps irreparably, by the adoption of those barbaric expedients. There is probably little which legislation can do to cure this
serious evil. Industrial war, like the wars of nations, can be averted no
otherwise than by progress of civlization and increase of good sense
among the combatants.

4. EXTRAVAGANT COST OF GOVERNMENT.—The British people spend
annually upwards of seventy million sterling of their earnings in conducting the national business. So imperfectly has the science of government yet been mastered even by the most highly civilized nations, that
we have thus far found it impossible to protect ourselves against each
other and against our unfriends abroad for a smaller sum than this. A
portion of this expense is the penalty we pay for the errors of our ancestors; but the larger portion is incurred by errors which are our own.
The whole subject is in an eminently unsatisfactory position. Expenditure continues to increase; to-day our govenment costs us annually ten
millions sterling more than it did eight years ago. So little instructed
is the public mind that this most unwholesome growth awakens no
interest, attracts almost no attention. The tax-payer carries in silence
and with apparent unconcern the burden laid upon him. No strong or
growing sentiment demands the correction of a monstrous waste which
is constantly, although imperceptibly, sapping our strength and preparing
our decay.

5. The political rights enjoyed by men who live in cities are still
withheld from their neighbors who live in small towns or villages. This
inequality is absolutely indefensible, and it is virtually undefended. The
people know that it must cease so soon as they resolve that it shall.
Their knowledge of this power has made them apathetic, and so allows
the prolongation of the evil.

CHAPTER IV.

THE REDRESS OF WRONGS.—II.

RONGS of the first magnitude yield quickly to the efforts of an earnestly reforming legislature. A progressive diminution in the bulk and pressure of the evils calling for remedy becomes visible in England after the middle of the century. It is pleasing evidence that the political regeneration of a people has well advanced, when they have leisure to engage in removing the less important disadvantages which still impede their welfare.

The sanitary condition of the English people, and the duration of human life, had largely improved. In the year 1710 the annual death-rate was one in thirty-six. In 1800 it was one in forty-eight. In 1810 it had improved to one in fifty-one. During the following twenty years it fell to one in fifty-four. The drainage of farm-lands had greatly diminished the power of those intermittent fevers which used to be so destructive. Vaccination had almost abolished small-pox, under which nine per cent. of the population had formerly perished. Improved houses and more generous diet had done their part in lessening the waste of life. But a new class of evils had arisen from the rapid and unregulated growth of cities. It was vaguely known that the sanitary condition of the city poor was deplorable, and was constantly becoming worse.

A commission was appointed to investigate the subject, and

a copious and valuable report was published. The conclusions
of this report made a profound impression. The supply
1842
A. D. .
of water in cities was exceedingly defective, and so
habitually impregnated with impure matter as to become
poisonous. Houses were crowded without regard to decency
or safety, and ventilation was unknown. There were no drainage. In Liverpool and Manchester one-eighth of the population lived in cellars almost without light, and seldom dry. The
dead were buried in crowded city grave-yards, poisoning the
air of the neighbourhood, and fatally tainting the wells from
which the people had to drink.   There were forty-three thous-
and pauper widows in England, and the commissioners were
satisfied that in a great majority of instances the husbands of
these poor women had been destroyed by causes which were
easily removable. Filth and bad ventilation cost England more
lives annually than she had lost by death in battle or by wounds
during the bloodiest year of her history. It was possible to
reduce by more than one-half the amount of sickness constantly
existing in the country.   The average length of life among the
gentry and professional men of London was then forty-four
years; in the labouring class it was twenty-two years.   Of the
threescore and ten years of life to which the working-man
might reasonably aspire, two-thirds were sacrificed to the unhappy conditions under which his life was passed.   The annual
waste of adult life, from causes which ought to be removed,
was estimated at from thirty to forty thousand.

The anti-corn law strife was raging then, and people had no
thought to spare for the remedy of sanitary evils. But in
course of time, when the agitations of the great contest were
calmed, there were passed, almost without observation, several
acts, by whose operation much disease had been averted and
innumerable lives have been saved. The last resting-places of
the dead were removed to a safe distance from the dwellings of
the living; cities were drained; copious supplies of pure water

were introduced; houses unfit for the abode of man were thrown down, and a more worthy class of dwellings erected in their room; the prevalence of epidemics was gradually abated by the use of sanitary precautions; and a General Board of Health was appointed, with large powers, to enforce such regulations as were fitted to promote the bodily welfare of the population. A Parliamentary election, a change of ministry, a remarkable murder, or a little war with some savage king, would have interested the British people more than those prosaic laws which only removed poisonous filth from their streets, or introduced pure air and water into their homes. But the influence of sanitary legislation traces its benign and enduring record in the high physical condition of city populations, in our comparative freedom from epidemic disease, and in the increased duration of human life, as that is reported to us by the gradual fall in our death-rate.* A large gain has been effected, but the waste of human life is still discreditably great. Of children born in cities nearly one-half die under five years of age. So imperfectly, even in Britain, have we yet been able to turn to account those possibilities of life with which nature has endowed us, that this lamentable proportion of our number fail to gain any footing in the world of living men, and perish when they have only begun to live.

The English dissenters had become powerful by their numbers, intelligence, and high character, but their influence had not yet sufficed to relieve them from ancient disabilities of an irritating and insulting description. They were compelled to contribute to the support of the Established Church, which they regarded as an unscriptural institution. Their own ministers were not empowered to perform the marriage ceremony, and

* This rate, which in 1837 was 24.7 per 1000 persons, was in 1876 only 21. Excepting Sweden and Denmark, England is the healthiest of European states. The death-rate of Italy is 28.7; of Austria, 29.4; of Hungary, 37.2; of Prussia, 25.4. France approaches England in the sanitary scale; her death-rate is 22.7 per 1000.

10

dissenting lovers were constrained to accept union from the clergymen of a church which they abhorred. It happened occasionally that a bridegroom of spirit protested, even at the alter, against the tyranny to which he was submitting, and that the clergyman indemnified himself by reading with special emphasis portions of the service which he knew would be specially offensive. Dissenters might not be buried in the parish graveyard according to forms which they themselves approved; the service of the Church of England must be read over them ere they were suffered to be laid in ground which was the common inheritance of all the parishoners. Their sons were absolutely excluded from Oxford. In more liberal Cambridge they were permitted to study, but denied the privilege of graduation.*

The Jews, in addition to the grievances which they shared with other nonconformists, laboured under the disability peculiar to themselves, that they could not have a seat in the House of Commons. They were, indeed, indulged by being allowed to take an oath on the Old Testament, but were, somewhat inconsistently, required to add the words, "on the true faith of a Christian," and this was necessarily a sentence of exclusion.

Ecclesiastical grievances are exceptionally difficult of redress. Protection, with all the enormous pecuniary interests which it involved, was much more easily uprooted than the wrongs of the dissenters. The tithe—a tax levied for support of the clergymen—was the first to fall. The church rate —a tax imposed for the maintenance of ecclesiastical buildings—was wrangled over for many years. Once in the House of Commons the votes for and against the abolition of the tax were equal, and the Speaker had to decide. Next year, in a very full House, the numbers

1836
A. D.

1861
A. D.

* The statutes by which the nonconformist youth of the nineteenth century were excluded from the universities were framed at the bidding of James I, in 1616, and adopted reluctantly. An immortality of mischief seemed to have been conferred on that follish king. Two centuries and a half after he was in his grave he had not yet ceased from troubling. His senseless and intolerant edicts still provoked strife among the English people.

differed by only a single vote. It was not till 1868 that the compulsory levy of church rates was abolished.

Many attempts were made to compromise the claims of the dissenters in regard to the celebration of their marriages. But no proposal was so fortunate as to satisfy at once the churchmen, resolute to preserve their monopoly, and the dissenters, resolute to destroy it. At length, when the present system of registration was being established, a re-adjustment of old arrangements became indispensable. With little opposition the long-withheld freedom was now conceded, and the marriages of dissenters were suffered to be performed by dissenting clergymen. In regard to their funerals the nonconformists have been less fortunate. The House of Commons still spends a portion of each session in heated debate over this question. It has not yet* been deemed safe to allow to dissenters the privilege of interment according to their own forms in the graveyard of the parish. Many churchmen indicate a belief that dissenters would use objectionable rites which would be a scandal to the sober-minded. On this ground, and others no wiser, the privilege is still refused.

1836
A. D.

The Commons opened their ranks willingly to admit the Jews, and year by year passed a bill bidding them welcome. But the orthodox Peers maintained stubbornly the exclusion of the unbelievers. It was not till the year 1858 that this difficulty was overcome, and Baron Rothschild at length took his seat in the House.†

One of the most tenacious of all the wrongs endured by dissenters was the exclusion of their sons from the universities. Redress of this grievance was claimed from the first reformed

---

* Eighteen hundred and seventy-nine.

† The Peers would not run the risk of having a Jew in the Upper House, but they consented that each House should have the power of modifying, according to its own pleasure, the oath required from a new member. This compromise enabled the Commons to admit Jews.

Parliament. It was not obtained till forty years had passed.

Although the exclusion of any class from the great national schools was conspicuously unjust, it was about the very latest of the great harvest of wrongs which fell to the sickle of a reforming legislature.

The Whigs who carried the Reform Bill of 1832 undoubtedly considered that they had effected a settlement which there would be no occasion to disturb for many years. Lord John Russell has been unjustly charged with the rash assertion that this adjustment was final—not to be modified in any coming time. What he did assert was that "in so far as ministers are concerned this is a final measure." His government would propose no further change; he himself probably did not expect to live into a time when further change would be asked for. But within a period which in the multitude of his years could not seem very considerable, Lord John found himself promoting to the utmost of his power an expansion of electoral privilege large enough to have filled with dismay the sober-minded Whigs who fought with him in the old Reform controversy.

The Reform Bill was a compromise satisfactory to the middle class, on whom it bestowed a reasonable measure of political authority. It was not satisfactory to the working-classes, whom it left wholly unrepresented. Even in the first reformed Parliament there was a party who claimed the suffrage as the right of every householder, who desired the protection of the ballot in voting, and a shortening of the duration of Parliaments. Among the most intelligent working-men, who now took a deep and salutary interest in politics, these views had a large support. The unreasoning violence, however, with which they were urged, as embodied in what was termed the People's Charter, alarmed the timid, and brought general discredit upon views most of which were ultimately adopted when the antipathies aroused by injudicious advocacy had passed away.

Many unsuccessful motions expressed the still unsatisfied craving for reform, and continued to fan the growing flame. At length the Whigs once more took up the question, and Lord John Russell introduced a bill which gained the disapproval of all shades of political belief. Two years later he tabled a proposal of a greatly more acceptable character. But the country was then yielding to its long dormant passion for war, and was visibly drifting into a lamentable contest with Russia. No thought could be given to the tame concerns of mere domestic reform.

1852 A. D.

The agitations of the Crimean War and the Indian Mutiny required to subside before the friends of reform could again gain a hearing. It fell this time to the Conservatives to propose an extension of those popular rights the conceding of which they had opposed so vehemently a quarter of a century before. Mr. D'Israeli proposed a bill which contained so few grains of reform that the House rejected it contemptuously, and the government replied by a dissolution of Parliament. The first division in the newly-elected House inflicted upon ministers a defeat which involved their resignation. They were succeeded by an administration of which Lord Palmerston, Lord John Russell, and Mr. Gladstone were the most influential members.

1859 A. D.

Again Lord John Russell introduced a Reform Bill. This time the popular gain would have been large, for the county franchise was to be based on a £10 rental, while the burgh qualification was reduced to £6. But Lord Palmerston was hostile; the country seemed almost unconcerned; and the members of the House of Commons, from whose memory the trials and expenses of a recent election had scarcely begun to fade, looked coldly upon a measure which invited the immediate return of those evils. Lord John, in sadness of heart, withdrew his bill. The happiness was not to be his of further enlarging the electoral privileges of his countrymen.

1860 A. D.

For some years, so long as Lord Palmerston lived, the question was not stirred otherwise than by the occasional motion of some independent member, always sure to be defeated by a large majority. It was, however, the growing desire of the country that the representation should undergo reform, although, as there were no intolerable grievances to endure, there was no feeling of impatience in the public mind. At length the old Parliament reached the verge of Parliamentary existence, and was dissolved. Soon after, in 1865 A. D. extreme old age, Lord Palmerston passed away. At the elections reform claimed rank as the foremost question, and Mr. Gladstone was its recognized champion.

A new bill was promptly introduced, lowering the franchise to £14 in the counties and £7 in the burghs. This very 1866 A. D. restricted measure of reform did not awaken the enthusiasm of the country. It had again the disadvantage of being proposed to a newly-elected Parliament, and it encountered the hostility of Mr. D'Israeli and his followers—the hereditary enemies of reform—and of Mr. Lowe, with a band of discontented Liberals. Mr. Gladstone was defeated, and his ministry resigned.

A Tory ministry, headed by Lord Derby and Mr. D'Israeli, took its place, and put its hand at once to the work in 1867 A. D. which the Liberals had failed,—the extension of the electoral franchise. Mr. D'Israeli had considered the £14 county franchise and the £7 burgh franchise revolutionary. He himself now offered household suffrage in the burghs* and a £12 franchise in the counties. Lord Derby considered it all a leap in the dark; but he trusted in the sound sense of his countrymen, and he supported the measure because he saw that, with all its uncertainties, it had become urgently necessary.

* Limited to some extent by the provision that the householders must have paid poor rates before being registered, and must have occupied for twelve months the premises on which they qualified. The number of electors in Great Britain and Ireland is now close upon three million.

The bill was passed, and reform was withdrawn for ever from the list of our great questions. What further modifications of our electoral system may be required in the years to come must be of subordinate importance, and cannot now be withheld when the people desire them. A few years later the system of secret voting was adopted, and the poor voter was effectively protected against the petty tyrant who sought to rob him of his political rights.

1872
A.D.

The vast revolution which had been in progress for half a century was at length fully accomplished. The transfer of power was complete. Fifty years ago a few great families guided the destinies of the nation. The people had no shadow of control over the actings of their government, and little knowledge regarding them, excepting such as they gained from the tax-gatherer, the policeman, or the press-gang. Their attitude was that of spectators, their feeling one of dumb acquiescence. They had ceased to petition; they had not yet learned to express their wants by the voice of public meeting. They looked on in silence while men—sometimes able and good, more frequently weak or unscrupulous—expended their scanty substance in enterprises which had no reference at all to their welfare. Wars which were to be fed by their earnings and their lives were entered upon without any one caring to know their opinion. Laws whose injustice was flagrant and shameless were submitted to as unresistingly as the judgments of Heaven. The masses of the British people plodded on their dull life-journey, leaving all its conditions to be adjusted for them by a few men who, by good fortune or dexterity, had contrived to gain the direction of the national resources.

When the Reform bill of 1867 passed into law, the reversal of all these conditions was complete. The people were now in possession of full and instant knowledge of everything their rulers did or intended to do. The platform and the press provided them with the most ample means for the communication of their sentiments on all public questions. Members of the House of Commons enjoyed high consideration on account of the place which they filled, and had thus singular advantages in influencing the formation of opinion. They were powerful to guide public opinion, but powerless to resist it. The voice which could speak decisively at the polling-booth was a voice whose authority no man dared question. It became the care of the politician to discover the wishes of the people, and he was the most successful who was earliest to detect and cherish the yet hidden tendencies of opinion.* The people might conduct the government of their affairs wisely, or they might conduct it unwisely. Experience had to prove that. This only was certain, that henceforth they would conduct it themselves.

But precisely here there arose to view a consideration which gravely qualified the satisfaction of many good citizens at the downfall of class government. There were solid grounds for fearing that the people would not govern their affairs wisely. A fearfully large proportion of them were wholly without education. It was certain, from the school statistics of twenty or thirty years ago, that one-half did not know their letters, and that many of the others knew little more. So great a power was the ignorant voter, that the law had to recognize his existence, and make provision to assist him in recording his vote. Was it not a fatal rashness to intrust political authority to men without even that degree of mental cultivation which an acquaintance with the alphabet is fitted to confer? Undeniably, if the men were to remain thus benighted. But the act which made them formidable created a necessity which all men recognized,—that the danger should be immediately diminished and ultimately removed by means of education.

The new Parliament was chosen in the close of 1868. The

* In the words of Lord Palmerston, the actors continued the same, but they played now to the galleries and not to the boxes.

electors had pronounced so decisively against the Conservative government that Mr. D'Israeli did not wait to have their verdict reaffirmed by the House of Commons. He resigned at once, and Mr. Gladstone came into power. The country had never known a stronger government. Mr. Gladstone and Mr. Bright enjoyed public confidence in a very unusual degree. They were aided by colleagues of recognized capacity, and supported by a Parliamentary majority of about one hundred and twenty.

A bill for the education of the people was introduced by Mr. Forster. In each district it was to be ascertained, by local authorities, what was the existing provision for educating the children of that district. Where there was a deficiency of school accommodation, it was to be supplied up to the full measure of the public need. Funds would be provided by local taxation, supplemented by a government grant. Religious teaching was to be given, but with ample security that it should not be thrust upon any child to whose parents it was distasteful. The management was to be local, subject to the control of a central authority. In England power was given to school boards to make attendance compulsory. In Scotland the law itself compelled attendance under sharp penalties of fine or imprisonment. The children of parents unable to pay the ordinary fees were to receive education without charge.

Feb., 1870 A.D.

The nation thus entered, in good earnest, upon the work of abolishing ignorance by educating—compulsorily, if need be—every child living under its dominion. It is a labour vast and toilsome, but needful to the welfare both of the individual and the state, and it leads to results precious beyond all estimate. The perfect ideal of a state is a people governing themselves, and fitted by intelligence and principle to do so. How mean and vile, in comparison with it, is the absolute rule of one man or of a few men over ignorant and unregarded millions! We

have yet a far journey before we fully realize this high ideal;
but it is much to know that we are in full progress towards it.*

Ireland had shared in the ameliorations of the last twenty
years, and had made very considerable progress in the development of her resources.   She was still, however, unsatisfied;
and reasonably so, for she was still suffering under wrongs of
which the sister countries had no experience.

The Irish Parliament of Henry the Eighth's time had
yielded to the converting influences of that monarch—owning
his supremacy and renouncing that of the pope.   Like the
turning of England to Presbyterianism in the seventeenth century, however, this official conversion of Ireland was not real
or enduring.   It soon became evident that the Irish remained
loyal to their old faith.   But the revenues which had once
maintained the Romish Church continued to be enjoyed by
her Protestant supplanter.   Four-fifths of the people were
Catholics, one-tenth were Episcopalians, and the remainder
were mainly Presbyterians.   While the Catholics, under a
cruel Protestant ascendency, had to endure every imaginable
indignity, they had also to witness a handful of Episcopalians
in possession of those endowments which they regarded as
rightfully their own.   But the Episcopalian Church of Ireland was united with the Church of England, and the great
strength of her powerful sister was pledged for her defence.
While the monstrous injustice under which Ireland suffered was
acknowledged by all excepting those who shared its gains, its

* Since the act of 1870 came into operation there is an increase of one million and
a quarter in the attendance on primary schools in Great Britain.   In other words, a
million and a quarter of persons who would have grown up wholly uninstructed will
now enter upon life with the inestimable advantage of a sound education.   In due
course of years uneducated men and women will become almost unknown in these
islands   The registrar-general gives in a recent report this gratifying proof of educational progress: "In 1837 there were only 58 persons in every 100 who were able to
sign their names to the marriage register; in 1876 the number had risen from 58 to 81,
and is steadily growing."   The amount expended in England upon primary schools
during the year 1878 was close upon four million sterling

continuance was too beneficial to persons of influence to admit the hope of easy or speedy redress.

Towards the close of Lord Palmerston's life Mr. Gladstone took opportunity to express exphatically his opinion that the condition of the Irish Church was unsatisfac- tory, and could not much longer be endured. This declaration was regarded with unusual interest. Lord Palmer- ston was a very old man, and it was certain that no great measure would now be undertaken while he ruled. But the remarkable ability evinced by Mr. Gladstone put it beyond doubt that he would occupy the highest place in the next Liberal administration. When that time came, he was virtu- ally pledged to deliver Ireland from the wrong which she had suffered for ages.

1865 A. D.

It came with little delay. In 1869 Mr. Gladstone was Prime Minister, with an amount of support in public confidence and Parliamentary votes which made it possible for him to uproot abuses even of the greatest age and the highest respectability. He entered without an hour's delay upon the arduous task. Parliament met on the 16th February, and on 1st March Mr. Gladstone introduced a bill for the disendowment and dis- establishment of the Irish Church.

The Irish church was to be severed from her English sister, and was no longer to be recognized by the state. Her bishops were no longer to enjoy seats in the House of Lords, and would not in future be appointed by the crown. She would retain her ecclesiastical buildings without payment, and her glebe lands for half their value. Her clergy would no longer be maintained from public funds, but the life-interest of existing clergymen would be paid for liberally. That portion of the church endowments remaining, after all claims were satisfied, was to be expended for the good of Ireland on objects which were not ecclesiastical or educational. Mr. Gladstone expected that seven million sterling would become available for such uses as Parliament might determine. The bill fought its way against fierce opposition in both Houses,* and on 26th July received the royal assent.

The disestablishment of the Irish Church freed Christianity from a scandal; and if the disendowment had given full effect to the intentions of Parliament, it would have freed Ireland from a perennial source of irritation. But the church was wiser in her generation than the world. However imperfectly furnished with the harmlessness of the dove, she proved herself on this occasion to be amply endowed with the wisdom of the serpent. Mr. Gladstone provided that no new interests should be created after the bill was passed. But five months elapsed from the introduction of the bill before it became law. During that precious interval the church lengthened her cords and strengthened her stakes. Her bishops " laid hands suddenly " on every youth who could be persuaded to accept holy orders. When the bill was passed the curates of the church had increased from five hundred to fully nine hundred; and the incomes of very many of her clergy had undergone a sudden and unprecedented augmentation. It resulted from these very questionable manipulations that the sum which the church had to receive was a little short of thirteen million. After Maynooth and the Presbyterian Church were satisfied, the sum gained for the general good of Ireland was little over three million. The church stooped to the inevitable disestablishment; but in accepting disendowment she contrived to discharge from it nearly all that was offensive to her. She carried off, to solace her widowhood, nearly the whole of the endowments which had made her union with the states attractive.

The tenure of land was of extreme importance in Ireland.

* Lord Derby delivered his last speech against this bill. He was then old and feeble, and within a few weeks of the grave. His very latest words in public were a protest against a measure "the political impolicy of which is equalled only by its moral iniquity."

where more than one-half of the people gained their subsistence, such as it was by agriculture. Irish crime was in a large measure agrarian. The landowners were few in number, mainly poor and non-resident. The cultivators of the soil were tenants at will. There was no law to protect them from being ejected and the improvements they had made from being appropriated by the landlord. The unduly harsh exercise of the proprietor's rights was tempered chiefly by the tenant's power to assassinate.

In course of ages there had grown up certain customs which had gained, in the opinion of the tenant-class, a sanction equal to that of law. In Ulster, for example, where there was no lease, the tenant claimed a right to occupy his holding on payment of rent, just as the owner claimed a right to receive rent. This shadowy right, although unknown to law, was so effectively supported by public opinion, that it had a recognized money value, and was always saleable at a price equal to several years' rental of the property. But there and elsewhere the landowner occasionally declined to recognize this right, especially when it was vested in a tenant who failed to pay his rent. He further declined to compensate the man whom he expelled for the improvements which had been made upon the land or buildings, or he utterly destroyed the value of his tenant's right by laying upon him an unreasonable increase of rent. The aggrieved cultivator thereupon drew public attention to his wrongs by the slaughter of the landlord, or of the new tenant, as circumstances counselled.

Mr. Gladstone undertook to reduce to order the chaos of centuries. The customs which had grown up to shield the tenant were now converted into law. The landlord might exempt himself from their dominion by giving a lease of thirty-one years. If he did not choose that course and wished to be rid of his tenant, he must pay him a sum which ranged from two up to seven years' rental. He must also pay for improvements

effected by the tenant.   Loans of public money were offered to
the occupier who desired to purchase his farm, and to the
owner who desired to reclaim waste lands, or to make roads
and erect buildings.

Ireland was now a country without a grievance, and England expected that she should become immediately a country
without a complaint.   England looked only at the ample justice which she had done, at the lavish kindness which she had
hastened to offer in the hour of her sister's extremity.   But
Ireland thought of the past.   Centuries of cruelty, which even
the rhetoric of her patriots could not exaggerate, branded deep
into her heart a hatred of England.   The cruelty has long
ceased, and in its place there has come an earnest desire to deal
justly and tenderly with Ireland.   The hatred bequeathed by
many generations of sufferers cannot pass so quickly.   Ireland
may still for many years cherish feelings which have long been
without warrant in existing circumstances.   And England
must be patient, remembering that these feelings have their
root in the evils perpetrated by Englishmen of a former day.*

* How broad and deep the foundations of a prosperous future for Ireland have now
been laid, may be read in the fact that in 1875 there were 1,012,000 Irish children attending the national schools. The population is five and a half million, and the
attendance represents thus an educational condition unsurpassed in Europe.

CHAPTER V.

THE Reform Bill of 1832 was not universally accepted as satisfying the demand of the working-classes. It was regarded by some as an installment of justice, valuable chiefly as affording the means of securing the whole. Household suffrage and vote by ballott had many secret adherents in days when men dared not avow such preferences; and they increased largely, both in numbers and in boldness, when the advocacy of political change was no longer attended with personal risk. All the various shades of reforming sentiment were for the moment fused by the enthusiasm of the people into one absorbing desire for the Reform Bill. But when that object was gained, the extreme members of the Liberal party resumed their former position. In a few years they had grown into a party—formidable by their numbers and enthusiasm and by the reasonableness of many of their demands, but enfeebled by injudicious leadership, and by the employment of physical force for the attainment of their purposes.

The leaders of this agitation embodied their demands in a document which they termed the People's Charter. It embraced these six points:—Universal suffrage; annual Parliaments; vote by ballot; abolition of property qualification for a seat in the House of Commons; payment of members; equal electoral districts. In judging to-day the Chartists of thirty years ago, it is necessary to admit, that while we reprobate buildings were strongly fortified and garrisoned. Troops, supported by artillery, were stationed near the bridges. When all necessary dispositions were made, the Chartist leaders were informed that their meeting would not be interfered with, but their procession would not be allowed. The demonstration was, after all, sufficiently harmless. It amounted only to a meeting, at which thirty thousand persons were addressed in the terms customary at such gatherings. A procession was not attempted, and the monster petition, when presented to the House of Commons, was found to contain, not six million signatures as alleged, but two million, many of them fictitious. Ridicule fell upon the cause whose purposes were so poorly supported by performance. Dissension crept into its counsels. Its adherents withdrew in disappointment, and allied themselves with reformers of greater moderation. Under the influence of free trade, the demand for our manufactures began to expand, and employment became abundant. Returning prosperity sapped the foundations of a movement which originated in calamity and suffering; and the agitation for the People's Charter soon passed into forgetfulness.

ployment, the agitation maintained, upon the whole, a formidable vitality. These were mainly years of suffering among the labouring population. They included two violent commercial revulsions, each followed, as usual, by a lengthened depression. Employment was irregular; wages were low; the price of food was kept artificially dear; crime was increasing. Emigration had not yet diminished to any material extent the excessive competition for the means of existence. Chartism had its roots in the widespread suffering of the people, and it expressed, by very rude methods of utterance, the belief that all this suffering was the product of selfish and unjust legislation.

The establishment of a republic in France inspired the Chartist leaders for a supreme effort. The habitual suffering of the period had been intensified by a recent commercial panic, and consequent difficulty in finding employment. Meetings were held everywhere. Incitements to insurrection were addressed to multitudes rendered fierce by hunger, and were received with enthusiasm. A demonstration which it was hoped would intimidate all opponents was resolved upon. A petition of unparalleled dimensions was to be made ready. A meeting on a similar scale was to be held, and a procession of half a million persons would attend the monster petition on its way to the House of Commons. If the overthrow of the monarchy and the setting up of a republic were to be effected by this vast accumulation of popular force, that would be a speedy and therefore a desirable method of gaining long delayed justice. {1848 A.D.}

Government provided London with defence beside which the forces of insurrection were ludicrous. Two hundred thousand men—special constables and soldiers—were enrolled to meet the expected danger. The Duke of Wellington did not deem it unworthy of his fame to assume the direction of the arrangements. The bank, the post-office, and other public

11

tered many hundreds of unarmed and peaceful men and women in the streets of Paris, that he might crush out all thought of resistance to himself by the sheer weight of terror. It was not well for him that the people of France should be suffered to brood over these atrocities. What has been called a spirited foreign policy, to divert the minds of Frenchmen from domestic questions, was indispensable to the existence of the man whom Frenchmen now permitted to call himself their emperor.

He did not possess, nor could he decently create—most likely he did not then desire—a ground of misunderstanding with any of the great powers of Europe. In every way it suited his purpose better to exhibit the vigour of the new reign by urging unreasonable demands upon the feeble government of Constantinople.

The demands by which he broke up the peace of Europe can scarcely be listened to with gravity, but the illimitable evils to which they gave rise invest them with an interest terrible and sad. They related to the privileges of the Latin worshippers at the sacred shrines in Palestine.* Practically they amounted to no more than this, that the Latin monks should have a key to the great door of the church of Bethlehem, and not be asked to content themselves with a key to the inferior door; that they should have a key to each of the doors giving entrance to the cave in which the nativity was supposed to have taken place; that they should have the high privilege of setting up in the same hallowed locality a silver star bearing the arms of France.

Unhappily any addition to the privileges of Latin Christians was a deduction from those of their Greek rivals. And as the Emperor Nicholas was the head of the Greek Church, the amenities of that institution enjoyed a guarantee which it was

---

* That the subject was not a pressing one is apparent from the circumstances that the negotiation which Louis Napoleon now took up had originated with Francis I. and the sultan of his day, but had not been completed by these parties; that it had been resumed in 1819, and again left incomplete, till its present resumption.

somewhat perilous to infringe. But France pressed her demands with such vehemence that the Turkish government was fain to yield. After a year of arduous negotiation, there were delivered to the Latin monks the keys which symbolized their victory over the Greeks. The silver star was borne in triumphal procession to Jerusalem, and victoriously established in its place in the sanctuary of Bethlehem. And the Emperor Nicholas, in wrath at his defeat, straightway directed the march of one hundred and fifty thousand men towards the Turkish frontier.

Feb.
1853
A. D.

He could not with decency go to war about these trivialities, but he lost no time in supplying himself with a ground of quarrel which, at all events was not laughable. He claimed that the rights conceded to the Christian population of Turkey should be secured by treaty with himself.* Such an arrangement was virtually a Russian protectorate extending over three-fourths of the Turkish people. It would terminate the independence of Turkey, and make transfer of her sovereignty from Constantinople to St. Petersburg.

The sultan, acting under the advice of the English ambassador, steadfastly, although with infinite politeness, refused the Russian demands. France, Austria, and Prussia bestowed upon the action of the Turkish government the support of their approval. The passionate czar, unable to effect his purposes by diplomacy, moved an army across the Pruth and possessed himself of the Danubian principalities. He had not even now, as he informed his faithful subjects, "the intention to commence war." He merely

July 2,
1853
A. D.

* Nicholas did not put this forward as a new demand. He asserted that a protectorate of the sultan's Greek subjects was conceded to him by the treaty of 1744, and he merely wished now a more explicit acknowledgment of his right. The sultan of that day had given to the czar a promise that he would "protect the Christian religion and its churches," and this, it was now claimed, made Russia the supreme guardian of Christian interests in Turkey. Turkey and her allies utterly denied this construction of the treaty. Queen Victoria, writing to the Emperor Nicholas, stated that, after careful study of the treaty, she was convinced that it was not susceptible of the meaning which he sought to attach to it.

desired " such security as will insure to us the restoration of our rights "—in the matter of the keys and the silver star, and also of the protectorate.

This invasion imparted to the question a graver aspect than it had heretofore presented, and diplomacy hastened to interpose its good offices, lest results still more untoward should ensue. The representatives of the four mediating powers met at Vienna, and framed a note embodying proposals which, as it was deemed, the estranged governments might honourably accept. This note conveyed to the czar assurances that the ancient privileges of the Greek Church in the Ottoman Empire would be held sacred, but it conferred upon him no new right to enforce fulfilment of the pledge. The czar was willing to accept this compromise, and the mediators recommended it as one which, in their judgment, ought to be satisfactory to Turkey. It was deemed that the difficulty was at length overcome. Members of the English cabinet expressed their confident belief that it would never be heard of more. To the amazement of Europe, Turkey refused to be guided by the advice of her Friends. She would not accept the Vienna note unless certain verbal alterations were adopted. These were insignificant; but Russia, having consented to the note in its original form, would not stoop to have it changed at the caprice of a power which she despised. The mediators stood aside. The Turks, after vainly summoning the czar to withdraw his armies from their territory, declared war against him, Oct. 28, with all the gravity and dignity of a power able to give 1853 effect to the hostile purposes which it announced. The A. D. final differences between Russia and Turkey are scarcely appreciable by the most searching criticism. Europe was led into a bloody war because Turkey demanded, and Russia was too proud and too angry to concede, certain immaterial variations in the phraseology of a settlement which was substantially agreeable to both.

By what malign combination of circumstances was Turkey endowed with power to work this immeasureable evil? How did it come to pass that this despicable government was able to make enlightened and powerful Christian states the ministers of its fanatical and barbarous hatred?

Lord Aberdeen was the Prime Minister of England during the whole of the diplomatic process which terminated thus disastrously. He knew something of war, for in his youth he had witnessed the carnage of Leipsic, and a hatred of bloodshed was perhaps the deepest sentiment in the old man's mind. The premier's horror of war helped influentially to involve his country in the very evil which he dreaded.* In his earnest desire for the peace of Europe, he allowed England to become the adviser of Turkey. The Turkish ministers listened deferentially to the counsels of a friend who had a powerful fleet lying at call in the Mediterranean. No step was taken without the approval of Lord Stratford de Redcliffe. After a time, no step was taken excepting on his suggestion; every note addressed to Russia conveyed the opinions which he had persuaded the Turkish ministers to adopt. His voice was ever raised for resistance to the demands of Russia. Unintentionally and imperceptibly England became committed by the meek acceptance with which the Turks received her warlike counsels. Long before the date of the Vienna note, Lord Clarendon stated that England could not now, with honour, withhold help from Turkey should the czar resent against her the course which she had followed under Lord Stratford's advice. And even so early as May, the sultan was emboldened by a private assurance that the Mediterranean squadron would be summoned to his defence in the event of danger from Russia.

But in truth, although England became bound, unintention-

* "Aberdeen has unfortunately made concessions which bring us nearer war."— PRINCE ALBERT, 15th October.

ally, to maintain the cause of the Turk, she did not become bound reluctantly. The English people had grown willing to have a war. They chafed under the freely expressed Continental opinion that they were no longer terrible in the field, because their energies were now wholly devoted to shop-keeping. For the first time in their history, they had spent nearly forty years in peace. The unwonted calm had become almost irksome. They were ready to be persuaded that any quarrel in which they had been led to take some part was a good quarrel, and that almost any good quarrel was sufficient cause of war.

For France—or, rather, for the Emperor Napoleon—war was highly desirable. There were recent passages in the Emperor's career from which it was most convenient that public attention should be quickly withdrawn, and nothing could accomplish that end so effectively as successful war. Here was a war which promised well to be successful; for the British, who seldom went out of war excepting by the gate of victory, were prepared to engage in it. The enemy was Russia, on whose soil the glories of the First Empire had found a grave,—whose victorious standards had waved in the air of humiliated Paris. Above all, the new Emperor, with his dubious title, certified in part by the blood of slaughtered subjects, would have the inestimable advantage of exhibiting himself to France as on terms of confidential alliance with the ancient and high-toned monarchy of England.* Louis Napoleon lent his willing help to the Turks, because in helping them he was establishing his own throne.

The sultan had thus two powerful allies secured to him. The Turks were of course, eager for war. A rare opportunity had presented itself. The two great Christian powers of the west stood ready to fight, on their behalf, their powerful and dangerous neighbour. Never again could they hope to

* "Louis Napoleon," wrote Prince Albert, in October 1853, "gives way to us even when his plan is better than ours, and revels in the enjoyment of the advantages he derives from his alliance with us."

express so inexpensively and so effectively their fanatical hatred of Russia. By the time the Vienna conference met, it had become all but impossible to restrain Turkey from war.

These various influences were steadily drawing Turkey and her allies towards war, and constantly adding to the difficulties which stood in the way of peaceful solution. This solution was not possible otherwise than by the Emperor Nicholas desisting from claims which had no foundation in reason, and against which Europe had decisively pronounced. His willingness to accept the Vienna note proves that there was a time when Nicholas was well disposed to yield to the opinion of his neighbours. But when Turkey, in her eagerness to drag the western powers into conflict with Russia, refused the note, Nicholas took counsel only of his own pride and passion. The negotiating powers drifted rapidly Nov. 30, 1853 into war. The Russians destroyed with merciless A. D. slaughter, a Turkish squadron lying at Sinope. France and England thereupon intimated that no Russian ship-of-war would be allowed to sail the Black Sea, and moved up Mar. 28, their fleets to enforce the warning. A little later the 1854 final step was taken; and in March, England and A. D. France, as well as Turkey, were at war with Russia.

Austria and Prussia were resolute not to suffer the Russian occupation of the principalities to continue. As their territories were nearer to the invaded provinces than those of England and France, the obligation lay primarily on them to correct the wrong which had been done. At first, they took part in negotiations with a heartiness which pointed towards stronger measures, should these become necessary. But finding that England and France were willing to undertake the heavy burden, they offered abundant counsel to all concerned, and prudently withheld themselves from war.

The allies put their hand promptly to the task which they

had undertaken. Even before the formal declaration of war, French and English steamers were hurrying eastward, bearing the armed men whose business it was to interpose between Russia and Turkey, and preserve for further evil the worst government which Europe has ever known. Throughout all the summer months men and stores were pushed forward, till a powerful army, completely equipped, lay at Varna, on the Black Sea. Lord Raglan, a companion-in-arms of Wellington, a man of large military experience and respectable military skill, commanded the English. The leader of the French was Marshal St. Arnaud, a soldier trained in the Algerian wars, who had made himself serviceable to Louis Napoleon in the revolution by which he had raised himself to the throne.

The seat of Russian power in this region was Sebastopol. An arm of the sea, one thousand to fifteen hundred yards in breadth, stretched for three miles and a half into the land. The city lay mainly on the south side of the bay. It was strongly defended by forts, which the fire of the allied fleets could not seriously affect. A powerful squadron rode secure within the shelter of the forts. There was a population of some forty thousand, chiefly in the employment of the government, for Sebastopol was little else than a fortress.

After delays which to the impatient people of England seemed interminable, an army of fifty thousand men landed on the Crimea, at a point twenty-five miles to the northward of the city which they had come to destroy. They knew imperfectly what forces could be brought to resist them, but they faced the uncertainty with unconcern, confident in their own prowess. A few hours' march southward brought them in presence of the Russian army, strongly posted on a line of hill rising steeply from the little river Alma. The allies waded the stream under a deadly fire of Russian artillery, and forced their way up the heights. The Russians fought stubbornly, and inflicted severe loss on their assailants. So

Sept. 14,
1854
A. D.

steep was the ascent that the wounded as they fell were seen to roll helplessly down the hill. But no effort which the Russians made availed to stay the resolute advance of their enemies. As the infantry pressed them in front, Lord Raglan brought two guns to bear upon their flank. The well-directed fire cut lanes through the masses against which it was aimed. The dismayed Russians broke, and fled. We had fought our first battle, and gained our first victory. Our soldiers had behaved nobly; but three thousand of them lay dead or wounded upon the field.

Lord Raglan was desirous that the army should push forward and make a dash at Sebastopol. But Marshal St. Arnaud rejected this enterprise, on the ground that his troops were fatigued. The truth was that the marshal himself, enfeebled by mortal illness, was within a few days of his grave. Had the general been as fit for effort as his soldiers were, Sebastopol would have fallen an easy prey. But the opportunity passed unimproved. By strenuous exertion, the defences of the city were strengthed, and the allies had no choice but to approach it in the way of regular siege. Nor is the mischance by which this occurred to be regretted. The strife could end now only by exhaustion on one side or the other. Sebastopol was easily reached by the ships of the allies, while, for the Russians, the land journey was long and painful. Nowhere else could this unhappy game be played out more advantageously for the western powers.

Within a month, the allies had been able to bring up their siege-guns to the heights on the south side of the city. Their fleets stood in near to the forts, and the newly- _{Oct. 17, 1854 A. D.} erected batteries opened their deadly career. Twelve or fourteen hundred pieces of heavy artillery maintained for many hours a fire such as no city ever endured before. But Sebastopol emerged from it without any sensible weakening of its defensive power, and it became clear enough that speedy success was no longer to be hoped for.

Meanwhile a Russian army was preparing to attack the besiegers in the position they had taken up. A week after the
ineffective bombardment, the Russians, numbering
thirty thousand, approached the allied position. Their
attack was directed at first towards some redoubts held
by Turks, who hastened to find safety in flight. A large
body of Russian horsemen, moving on in the direction of
Balaklava, came in view of the 93rd Highlanders standing
in line, two men deep. Their commander, Sir Colin Campbell, knowing the quality of his soldiers, did not think it
"worth while" to form them into square. The Highlanders
justified well his confidence. They stood till the rushing
horses came within a hundred and fifty yards, and then gave
forth a fire which emptied many saddles and caused the Russians to retreat in haste. The Heavy Brigade of British cavalry
stood at some distance, waiting their opportunity. A strong
body of Russian cavalry advanced, but as they came near
reined up and paused to observe. The trumpets rang out; the
British horsemen rode at their enemies, rode through them,
trampled them down, chased them away in hopeless rout. Five
minutes sufficed for that magnificent cavalry to defeat the
vastly more numerous force of the Russians.

After these reverses the Russian army drew back, and took
up position at a distance of a mile and a half from the allies.
There whole strength was gathered there, covered from attack
by thirty guns. Up to this time our Light Cavalry Brigade
had not been engaged. Lord Lucan now received, by the hand
of Captain Nolan, a written order to advance nearer to the
enemy. On reading this order, Lord Lucan asked its bearer
how far they were to advance. He received a reply which he
construed, with fatal inaccuracy, to signify that it was his duty
to charge the enemy. The Light Brigade made itself ready to
attack the Russian army. Every man knew that some terrible
mistake was sending the brigade to destruction, but no man
shrunk from his duty of obedience. They rode straight down the

Oct. 25.
1854
A. D.

valley towards the wondering Russians, and in full view of the
chiefs of their own army, powerless now to restrain them. As
the excitement of battle gained power over men and horses,
the pace increased. The shot of the Russian guns tore through
their ranks, but did not abate the speed of their advance, the
fierceness of their attack. They galloped their horses between
the Russian guns, cutting down the gunners as they passed.
They rode down and scattered several squadrons of cavalry.
And then they paused, and turned back, and galloped towards
the shelter of the British lines. The Russian guns reopened
upon them with grape and canister. Their return was beset
by an overwhelming force of Russian cavalry; but they cut
their way through, and reaced the position they had left
scarcely half an hour ago. Six hundred and seventy men
went forth to that memorable ride, but only one hundred
and ninety-eight came back.

But these brave lives were not spent in vain. The splendid
exhibition which they furnished of the high warlike qualities
of the British races, is of greater value than many of the
victories which are supposed to ornament our history. No
guns were brought off, no prisoners were taken; there were
none of the ordinary gains of victorious battle. But deeds of
rare heroism which lay upon an enemy the disabling consciousness of inferiority, may do more to terminate a war than the
capture of many cities.

The Russians utterly failed to shake the hold of the allies
on the position which they had taken up. But some guns
captured from the Turks were carried off the field, and one
of the redoubts abandoned by those timid warriors was held.
These trivial gains being the first which had cheered the
Russians, were hailed as victories of high importance.

A few days after, the Russians made a still more formidable attack upon the allies. They planned and
effected a surprise, which must have proved fatal but for
the invincibly stubborn resistance offered by the British, on

Nov. 5,
1854
A. D.

whom the attack fell. About daybreak of a winter morning fifty thousand Russians advanced, their courage braced for lofty deeds by the presence of a grand duke, the blessing of the church, and a copious supply of stimulating drinks. Covered by the thick fogs which wrapped valley and hill, they were well within striking distance before their approach was discovered. In overwhelming numbers they climbed the heights, and assailed the scanty British force which held the plateau of Inkermann. By all the rules of war they should have had an easy success; for the men they came to attack were fearfully outnumbered, and sufferd the still graver disadvantage of being insufficiently supplied with ammunition. Any general plan of defence was impossible, as the mist shrouded the combatants from the view of their leaders. All along the hill-side were small bodies of British soldiers withstanding, sometimes by shot and sometimes by bayonet, the attack of dense masses of Russians, who strove to gain the plateau. For some hours they successfully resisted attacks which, it may safely be said, no other troops in the world could have sustained. Then the French came to their relief, and the Russians were beaten off with heavy loss. The result of this battle must have brought home to the Emperor Nicholas some unwelcome truths. Eight or nine thousand Englishmen, taken unawares and short of cartridges, baffled for hours fifty thousand Russians, supported by a powerful astillery, and then, with the help of nine thousand Frenchmen, drove them all away.

England was very proud of her brave soldiers; and now, when it had become certain they must winter on those bleak heights before Sebastopol, large provision for their comfort was made. Thousands of tons of wood for huts were sent out; shiploads of warm clothing; food beyond their utmost powers of consumption. The vessels which bore these treasures arrived in safety at Balaklava. Their tall masts could be seen from the heights where our soldiers maintained, amid the severities of winter, the grasp which had been laid upon the doomed city. But yet the men were suffered to perish for want of the comforts which had been brought so near them. The early weeks of the winter had been unusually rainy; the miserable road from Balaklava had become nearly impassable. The idea of constructing a sufficient road to connect the camp and the ships had not presented itself to the minds of the authorities. The extreme difficulty of keeping up supplies under these circumstances was enhanced by faulty administration. A rigorous adherence to form defeated the attempts of officers and surgeons to obtain the food or medicines which were so urgently required. The men were often half-fed; they were clothed in rags utterly inadequate for their protection; they might almost as well have walked barefooted for any benefit which their boots afforded; they slept on the wet ground, under the imperfect shelter of tents; they toiled for many hours every day in the trenches, ankle-deep in mud. Fuel was not to be had, and it was often impossible for them to cook their food. They sickened and died by hundreds, and the British army, always victorious over its enemies, was mouldering swiftly away under the neglect or mismanagement of its own leaders. Several regiments became literally extinct. One had but seven men left fit for duty; another had thirty. When the sick were put on board transports to be conveyed to hospital, the mortality was shocking. In some ships one man in every four died in a voyage of seven days. In some of the hospitals recovery was the rare exception. At one time four-fifths of the poor fellows who underwent amputation died of hospital gangrene. During the first seven months of the siege the men perished by disease at a rate which would have extinguished the entire force in little more than a year and a half. Our total loss in this miserable war was 20,656. Of these, only 2,598 were slain in battle; 18,058 died in hospital.

When the miseries of our soldiers were reported in England,

the indignation of the people was vehement. The care of the army was no longer left altogether to government. All over the country vast contributions were offered of articles fitted to promote a soldier's comfort, and agents were sent out to dispense them. Miss Nightingale, armed with absolute authority, went to bring order out of the infinite confusion which prevailed in the hospitals. M. Soyer, a cook of distinguished merit, was sent to teach the soldiers how to extract from the food supplied to them all the nourishment and enjoyment which it was fitted to yield. A railway was hastily laid between Balaklava and the camp. Henceforth abundance reigned, and the health of the army rapidly improved.

During all these dreary months, while the army was being destroyed by official incapacity, the siege went on. The allies never for a moment loosened their hold on the besieged city. Often their fire was intermitted because of the difficulty of conveying from Balaklava the huge masses of iron which it was their business to throw into Sebastopol. Occasionally it was discontinued for a time that preparations might be made for greater efforts. Very soon it could be seen that Sebastopol was a mass of ruins. But that had no tendency to weaken the defence. The Russians fortified a position outside the town by means of earthworks and rifle-pits. The war lost its character of siege, and changed into a battle of many month's duration between two armies, each holding a strongly entrenched position. It was an artillery duel on a gigantic scale. The allies had five or six hundred guns in operation, and sometimes they launched twelve thousand shells and round shots against the enemy in the course of twenty-four hours. Gradually their trenches drew closer to the Russian works, until at one point the men were within speaking distance. One very strong earthwork, the Malakoff, faced the French position; another, the Redan, was in front of the English. It was determined to carry these works by assault. The French, whose trenches were now within fifteen yards of the enemy, were able, after a brief but violent struggle, to take secure possession of the Malakhoff. The English had a considerable space to traverse under a murderous fire. But they forced their way into the Redan, and looked eagerly for reinforcements which would enable them to hold their conquest. Incapable generalship left them without support, and they were driven out with terrible loss.

Sept. 8,
1855
A. D.

Next day the attack was to have been renewed. But the Russian position had become untenable. Their whole army was conveyed across the bay, and the southern side of the city was abandoned. The war was virtually ended. The Emperor Nicholas had died—broken-hearted by the disasters of this calamitous struggle—and his son, the more enlightened Alexander, was now willing to negotiate. He had maintained the contest in this remote corner of his dominion at enormous cost in men and treasure, and he could maintain it no longer. His ships had been sunk to save them from the enemy. Sebastopol —in ruins—was wrenched away from him; his impregnable forts, his splendid docks, were at leisure mined and blown into the air by triumphant foes. His power in the Black Sea was for the time utterly overthrown. The allies had two hundred thousand men in the Crimea—a force which he was now powerless to resist. Peace had become a necessity for Russia.

As the allies were not unreasonable and their enemy was prostrate, the terms of peace were not hard to arrange. Turkey was made gracefully to promise redress of Christian wrongs, but it was carefully declared that no power was entitled to exact fulfillment of the worthless pledge. No armed vessels beyond a fixed number for purposes maritime police were henceforth to sail the Black Sea. The czar thus endured the humiliation of being shut out from waters on which he had hitherto been supreme. He further became bound not to

12

maintain on the Black Sea any such stronghold as the allies had just abolished.

Europe rejoiced over the close of the struggle. Fifty million sterling had been added to our National Debt. Twenty thousand British youth had perished; many more had come home broken in health or mutilated by wounds. What had we gained by these costly sacrifices? Undeniably we inflicted enormous evil upon Russia; but that happily has long ceased to be a solace to us. We saved for a time the Ottoman government.* We preserved for one or two million Turks the privilege of oppressing and plundering eight million Christians. But we did not secure permanence even for the lamentable success which we achieved. Fifteen years after, Russia declined to submit longer to the irritating restraints we had imposed in her hour of weakness. She required that the neutrality of the Black Sea should cease. She would no longer endure exclusion from waters which were naturally her own. The allies wisely conceded what they could scarcely have withheld, for Russia chose to make her demand while the Germans were lying siege to Paris. A fleet in the Black Sea involved a naval arsenal, and the reconstruction of Sebastopol became only a question of choice and of time. The Eastern Question resumed its habitually threatening aspect. We had not settled it; at enormous cost to ourselves and Europe we had merely postponed the settlement.

1871 A. D.

During more than fifty years of the eighteenth century Great Britain was at war with some of her neighbours. The Continental powers fought with each other so habitually that Europe scarcely ever knew the joy of unbroken peace. These wars were ordinarialy waged in quarrels which were of no real con-

---

* The defence offered for this war by the Duke of Argyll and other members of the government which was responsible for it, is to this effect:—They did not wish to save Turkey, whose decay and fall were plainly inevitable; but, recognizing this fact, and knowing that the place of the Turks had to be occupied by some power, they wished to prevent Russia from prematurely deciding the question in her own favour. They sought to establish the principle that the fate of Turkey was a matter of European and not merely of Russian concern.

cern to the European people. They sprang out of questions
personal to their rulers. What family or what member of a
family was to occupy a certain throne? What advantage
could a prince take of his neighbour's weakness to add to his
own possessions? What increase of power could monarchs
allow any one of their number to gain? Such were the occasions of strife in which the men of Europe uncomplainingly
shed their blood and wasted their substance. Nor was it
customary that these selfish and ignoble contentions should be
confined to the disputants with whom they originated. The
monarch who was about to inflict invasion, or to endure it,
sought to strengthen himself by alliances. And so it happened
that when two kings led their subjects out to mutual destruction, the flame quickly spread, and other kings with their
victim people fell, as an expected thing, into their places on
this side or on that.

A survey of the wars which Great Britain fought during the
eighteenth century, in the attempt to settle questions which
were to her nearly always insignificant, is mournfully suggestive of wasted resources and needless suffering.

In 1702 we allied ourselves with Austria, Holland, and many
smaller states, and we declared war against Spain and France.
It was our high purpose to prevent the grandson of the King
of France from becoming King of Spain. We fought for
twelve years to do that. All western Europe, from the borders
of Russia to the Atlantic, toiled with us or against us in the
vain and bloody enterprise. And after all, the French prince
was King of Spain, and Europe was not perceptibly a greater
sufferer than she would otherwise have been.

In 1715 and 1745 we were obliged to fight in civil war
against ill-advised persons who desired to bring back to the
throne the rejected house of Stuart.

In 1741, England and Austria went to war against France
and Prussia, in order to decide a question about the succession

to the Austrian throne. We fought for five years before we
obtained the decision which we desired.

After a short breathing-time, we resumed our accustomed
toil. In 1756, leagued with Prussia, we entered upon a seven
years' war against France, Russia, Sweden, and Austria. We
had. no apparent interest in the quarrel, but Prussia was in
danger, and had persuaded us to come to her rescue. The
population of the country was then twelve or thirteen million,
and their commerce was small. This war cost us eighty-two
million sterling.

A short war with Spain might almost be deemed a favourite
pastime of the statesmen of the eighteenth century. In 1718,
1727, 1739, and 1762 we waged such wars. We fought altogether seven times with Spain during the century.

In 1775 we took up arms to suppress the rebellion of the
American colonies. It was not till the war had continued for
eight years that we desisted from that enterprise. In addition
to the revolted colonists, we arrayed against us France, Holland, and Spain. The cost of this war was close on one hundred million sterling. It was mainly borrowed, and we have
paid ever since, and will long continue to pay, three million
annually for our stubborn refusal to permit American
independence.

Early in 1793 we began to wage against France a war which
paused twice for a few months, but did not cease till 1815.

Must we deem this bloody century to be representative of the
future, as it too surely is of the past? Are men to stumble on
for ever in this path of mutual destruction? Or dare we hope
that even now the dawn of a better time has come, and that we
ourselves have witnessed the opening of a new and milder era?

The least hopeful must recognize the vast change which has
passed upon the character of European wars since the battle of
Waterloo. England has ceased to take any part in dynastic

strifes. Nay, such strifes have ceased to occur in Europe. The growing power of the people has beneficently diminished the intolerable pretensions of princes. The right of a nation to enthrone or depose its rulers is now undisputed, and the rise or fall of a dynasty has sunk to a just insignificance. The questions which have agitated Europe during the last sixty years have been national, and in no sense personal. The wars of that period have been waged mainly to correct the forcible and unreasonable adjustments of the Holy Alliance. That heavy task now approaches completion. With nations satisfied, and the personal ambition of sovereigns eliminated from European politics, we may anticipate a constantly growing reluctance to seek the solution of international differences by the brutal methods heretofore employed.

England has been engaged in numerous wars during the last sixty years. But these have been nearly all brief and unimportant; and, in their contrast to our earlier wars, furnish evidence that the spirit which drove us so constantly into strife has undergone vast amelioration. The only war which recalls the fighting history of our period was that which we unhappily waged with Russia for the protection of Turkey. Otherwise, we have contented ourselves with little wars and easy conquests over weak and barbarous states. We destroyed the Turkish fleet to secure the independence of Greece. We bombarded Acre to restore the dominion of Turkey over Syria. We sharply chastised the Algerines for their practice of piracy. In India we subdued the Goorkhas, the Pindarees, the Afghans, the Scindians, the Burmese, the Sikhs. We were also constrained to destroy our own native army, in punishment of its aggravated mutiny. Three times we fought with China. Once we bombarded a considerable Japanese town. We had four wars with the Kaffirs. We had a toy war with Persia. We subdued the natives of New Zealand. We waged with the Abyssinians in a doubtful quarrel a war composed of one bat-

tle, and memorable chiefly for its enormous cost. We fought
victoriously against the Ashantees. Finally, we were dragged
by the unwarrantable measures of one of our own public servants into a war with the Zulus, of the origin and early conduct
of which we have the deepest reason to feel ashamed. In these
petty and inglorious strifes it can scarcely be said that England
was at war. She was merely inflicting chastisement, more or
less justifiable, upon barbarians who troubled her. That she
deemed it necessary to do this is not inconsistent with the
increasing prevalence of a genuinely pacific temper among
her people.

England and America have given to the world the first great
example of the peaceful settlement of differences by reference to
the judgment of impartial persons. Influenced by an unhappy
sympathy with the rebel slave-owners, England permitted ships
to sail from her ports to prey upon American commerce. The
time came for America to sum up her losses, and call upon
England to indemnify her. England proposed arbitration, but
America, too angry as yet, rejected the proposal. A few years
passed; more temperate counsels prevailed; the offer was
renewed, and accepted. Commissioners were chosen, to whom
America submitted her claims. The judges found that reason
was upon her side, and ordained that England should pay three
million sterling, as fitting redress for the evil which she had
wrongfully permitted. The transaction is for ever memorable
as the earliest evidence that the differences of states can be
settled on the basis of justice, and not of mere brute strength.

There are quarrels too deep for arbitration. There are
national antagonisms which refuse to be controlled, and drive
men irresistibly to mutual slaughter. Russia and Turkey
could not have referred their differences to arbitration. The
unquenchable hatred of centuries seeks its satisfaction in wasted
fields, and burning villages, and slain men. But such hatred
exists only among the imperfectly civilized. It is scarcely

possible that a difference could arise between England and America, England and Germany, England and France, in regard to which a peaceful solution is not attainable.

But although the English people have made large progress in discovering the brutality and needlessness of war, they are slow to perceive the folly of wasting their subsistance on a continual preparation for it. The traditions of many bloody centuries still exercise a powerful influence over their minds. Their greatest statesmen have been most keenly alive to the value of economy. William Pitt reduced the army to eighteen thousand men, and its cost to £1,800,000. Sir Robert Peel urged that nations ought to run some risk of being imperfectly prepared when war came, rather than weaken themselves by huge idle armaments. Mr. Gladstone has frequently endeavoured to awaken a sentiment favourable to economy. But the people continue to manifest a remarkable apathy to the ill-judged expenditure of their earnings. From a net revenue of seventy-one million sterling,* England expends twenty-eight million in interest on debt incurred by the wars of the past, and twenty-seven million on her preparation for the wars of the future. Her civil charges are sixteen million. War has, in all the ages of her history, consumed the substance of her people, and continues to do so. If Englishmen of former generations had been contented to live peaceably; if Englishmen of this generation were able to put confidence in the good intentions of their neighbours, the cost of their government would be a sum wholly insignificant.

During peace the governments of Europe withdrew three million of young men entirely, and a large additional number partially, from peaceful and productive occupations, and consign them to the demoralizing idleness of the barrack. On these monstrous armaments they expend annually one hundred and twenty million sterling. The loss resulting from the enforced idleness of the soldiers amounts probably to a still larger sum.

*For the year 1876-77. During the two following years it has been greatly, although it may be hoped exceptionally, larger.

The discontinuance of this senseless and lamentable waste is yet far in the future. But nothing in the future is more certain. History is, upon the whole, a record of human progress. It is incredible that men are not to rise above the passion for mutual destruction. War is the fitting employment of the savage. As men become civilized they will no longer attempt to settle their differences by the slaughter of one another. And gradually, as they desist from war, they will cease to maintain the costly appliances which this repulsive occupation demands.

CHAPTER VII.

THE commercial supremacy of England is so over-whelming that we scarcely admit any foreign nation to the honours of comparison. Of the goods exported from all the foreign countries of the world nearly one-half comes to England. Our exports—produced by the labour of a population of only thirty-four million—are equal to one-third of those of all the rest of the world. Of the seventy million spindles employed in the production of cotton fabrics, forty million belong to the people of the British islands. With all woven fabrics—cotton, woollen, linen—with coal, iron, machinery, and many other articles in-dispensable to human well-being, we have spplied mankind, to their advantage and to ours.

This pre-eminence is of comparatively recent origin. It is, indeed, of no higher antiquity than the wars of the French revolution, of which it is in some measure a product. Even now it does not require an exceptionally prolonged life to go back almost to the dawn of the cotton trade. 1785 our ex-port of cotton goods was no more than £800,000. In that year our entire exports were under £14,000,000, and our imports only a trifle more. For many years scarcely any tendency to increase had been apparent.

England was not the birth-place of the industries which have attained upon her soil a maturity so splendid. Calicoes were

185

imported from India long before they could be made in England.*
Silk-weaving was taught us by the Italians and French. The
Flemings brought us our fine woollen trade.   The Venetians
showed us how to make glass. France and Holland were before
us in paper-making, and a German erected our first paper-mill.
Cotton-printing came to us from France.   Although we had
long made coarse linens, were indebted for the finer varieties
to Germany and Belgium.   Our cloth was sent to Holland
to be bleached or dyed. The Dutch caught our fish for us down
to the end of the eighteenth century.   A Dutchman began our
potteries.   The Danes and Genoese built ships for us.   The
Dutch were our masters in engineering, and showed us how to
erect the wind and water mills which presided over the lowly
dawn of our manufacturing system.   Tuscany made our straw
hats.   Much of our salt and most of our earthenware came
from the Continent.   Till nearly the middle of last century we
imported two-thirds of the iron which we used.   The use of
coal for smelting was then only beginning, and the infancy of
our gigantic iron trade was watched with hostile eyes by a
people who saw that it devoured the wood which they needed
for fuel.   The industrial genius of England awoke late, but at
one stride it distanced all competitors.

Until long after the middle of the eighteenth century commerce was strangled by the impossibility of conveying goods
from one part of the country to another. While the English,
with ill-directed heroism, expended life and treasure in the
worthless strifes, of the Continent, they were almost without
roads at home.   In all Europe there were no roads worse than
theirs.   It cost forty shillings to transport a ton of coals from
Liverpool to Machester.   Men could not travel in Lancashire

---

* During the seventeenth century there arose an outcry that the use of Indian
calicoes was ruining our own woollen and silk manufactures.   In 1700 and afterwards
acts were passed forbidding the importation of calicoes, under heavy penalties.
Daniel de Foe, writing in 1708, was of opinion that this prohibition had averted the
ruin of our manufactures!

without considerable personal danger, owing to the condition of the roads. During the winter months traveling was generally impossible. The food of London was for the most part carried on pack-horses. Often the large towns endured famine, while the farmers at no great distance could find no market for their meat and grain. Communication between London and Glasgow was maintained by a stage coach, which undertook this great enterprise only once in a month, and accomplished it in twelve or fourteen days. The seclusion resulting from the absence of roads rendered it necessary that every little community, in some measure every family, should produce all that it required to consume. The peasant raised his own food. He grew his own flax or wool; his wife or daughters spun it, and a neighbour wove it into cloth. He learned to extract dyes from plants which grew near his cottage. He required to be independent of the external world, from which he was effectively shut out. Commerce was impossible until men could find the means of transferring commodities from the place where they were produced to the place where there were people willing to make use of them.

The woollen trade maintained a precarious existence, disabled by a law passed in the reign of Edward VI., which bound the manufacturers to use in their trade no better appliances than the men of the fourteenth century had used. Thus fettered, it is matter of surprise that the export of woollens reached so large a sum as two or three million sterling. Legislation sought in its blundering way to aid the struggling traders. The export of wool was forbidden, and all foreign woollens were strictly excluded.

The splendours of the cotton trade were yet far in the future. For many centuries India had grown cotton and woven it into clothing. But the industry seemed to possess no element of progress, and it remained insignificant.* Down to 1790 America

* The cotton manufacture was introduced to Europe by the Mohammedan invaders of Spain, probably in the tenth century. Four hundred years later it had crept into Italy; but it had no vitality anywhere in Europe till the mechanical inventions of England raised it to sudden greatness.

had not even begun to export cotton;* the trifling supply which we required came wholly from the East. So coldly did our governing powers look upon the infancy of the cotton trade, that till 1721 the weaving or selling of calicoes was penal, and till 1774 it was an offence to weave a fabric composed entirely of cotton. Only one-half of the threads were suffered to be of this suspected material; the remainder must be linen.

The feeble silk trade was struggling in wrath and despondency against French competition. Urgent appeals were addressed to the government, praying for the exclusion of the abhorred rival productions. The prayer, after being supported by destructive riots, was at length granted.

1765
A. D.

The linen trade crept humbly on its obscure way, aided only by the very simplest mechanism, and upheld by government bounties. To the close of the century spinning was done by females in their own houses, and the diminutive home production of linens was supplemented by an importation from Germany and Belgium.

In 1770 the quantity of coal raised in the country was six million tons. Paper was produced to the value of only three-quarters of a million sterling annually. Everywhere we remark a commerce still in its infancy, and exhibiting scarcely any tendency towards increase.

Shortly after the middle of the century there arose in England a passion for the formation and improvement of canals and highways. Ultimately it passed into a species of mania—a miniature of that more violent frenzy under the influence of which the men of a later generation created for themselves more perfect methods of communication. The first great enterprise of this description which was successfully accomplished was the Duke of Bridgewater's canal, connecting Liverpool

* In 1784 an American ship landed eight bags of cotton at Liverpool, and the custom house officers seized them, on the ground that cotton was not a product of the United States! Fifty years later (in 1832) England received two hundred and twenty million pounds of cotton from America.

with Manchester. Many similar works followed. In the four-teen years from 1760 to 1773 four hundred and fifty-two acts were passed for the formation or improvement of high-ways. Before the century closed, England had provided her-self with such length of canal, and had so amended her roads, that commerce was no longer repressed by difficulty of trans-port. A vast expansion of traffic was the immediate result.

But various obstacles still barred the progress of England to manufacturing greatness. In especial, she had no better motive power for her machinery than water. During many centuries little thought had been given to mechanical invention. Of what avail was it to possess machines which there was no power to put in motion? But that disability was now to be removed, and the first condition of greatness in the industrial arts—an adequate moving power—was to be bestowed. On the 5th January 1769 James Watt announced his patent " for a method of lessening the consumption of steam and fuel in fire-engines." That may be regarded as the birth-day of our manufacturing supremacy. Without Watt's improvements, the steam-engine was scarcely of practical value. Now, it became the source and sustaining power of mechanical energy, whose action quickly changed the face of the world.

The value of Watt's great invention was soon illustrated by improvements in cotton machinery, which without it would have been comparatively worthless. In 1767 Hargreaves had invented the spinning-jenny. Two years later Arkwright's frame superseded the earlier invention, and was itself in six years more superseded by the mule of Crompton. In 1787 Mr. Cartwright, a clergyman of Kent, invented the power-loom.* These machines increased the efficacy of each workman two or three hundred-fold.

But the mercantile legislation of European countries was

* Mr. Cartwright's success as an inventor is very remarkable, in view of his own statement that he had not previously turned his thoughts to anything mechanical, and had never seen a loom at work.

fitted to intercept and destroy the good which those beneficent inventions offered to the world.   The system in use was one of regulation and restraint.   Nothing was left to the free action of natural laws.   Every industry was subjected to the operation of artificial encouragements or hindrances which enfeebled its energies and impeded its progress.   Right across the path to which Watt and Crompton and Cartwright pointed mankind there lay obstacles which the ignorance and selfishness of ages had piled up.   These had to be removed, and an appropriate provision for their removal was disclosed at the fitting moment.   In 1776 Adam Smith published his " Wealth of Nations," a book from which Great Britain learned in time to understand the true foundation of economical greatness.   Adam Smith was an indispensable supplement to the work of the inventors.

There was now an insufficient production of cotton to supply the demand which grew apace so soon as men discovered the usefulness and cheapness of cotton fabrics.   America was able to produce ulimited quantities of cotton, but she was not yet able to free the precious fibre from the seeds which clung to it. Until so freed, it was not possible that cotton should be spun and woven.   So utterly were the planters frustrated by the tenacious resistance of those seeds, that for several years after Crompton's spinning-mule had made it indispensable for England to obtain abundant cotton America did not supply a single pound.   But in 1793 Eli Whitney, a New England mechanic, came to the rescue of the strangled industry.   He perfected a machine which easily and cheaply separated the fibre from the seed.   The deliverance which he brought was immediate and complete.   During the next year America sent to England one million six hundred thousand pounds of cotton. The quantity rapidly increased.   In 1801 it had grown to twenty-one million pounds; in 1815 to eighty-three million; in 1730 to over two hundred million. In 1875 the total import of cotton from all countries was sixteen hundred million pounds.

Before the century closed England was thus in possession of the most perfect appliances for spinning and weaving cotton—of ample power to put these in movement—and of raw material cheap and inexhaustably abundant. She alone of all the world enjoyed these priceless advantages. England proved herself worthy of the great opportunity afforded to her. Her cotton manufacture—the youngest, but soon to become the greatest, of her industries—grew with a rapidity to which the world has no parallel. Its progress reads like Oriental romance embodied in solid Western fact. In 1751 the English export of cotton goods to other countries was no more than £45,000. In 1764 it had increased, but only to the trivial amount of £200,000. In 1785 it had crept up to £860,000. In 1810 the amount had swelled out to £18,000,000, and in 1833 to £46,000,000. In 1874 it was £75,000,000.* The home consumption of cotton goods had at the same time increased enormously.†

The woolen trade felt the quickening impulse which had inspired the sister industry. The old restraints by which this manufacture had been disabled for centuries were now thrown aside. Manufacturers were at length permitted to use those mechanical appliances which were best adapted for their purposes. The devices whose use had so signally advanced the cotton trade were found to be substantially applicable to woolens. At once a development began second only in importance to that which the cotton trade enjoyed. In 1874 we imported 344,000,000 pounds of wool, and exported woolen manufactures to the value of £28,000,000.

About the close of the century machinery began to supersede those rude appliances by which the linen manufacture had

* In 1874 we imported raw cotton to the value of £30,696,000, and exported cotton manufactures to the value of £74,247,000, besides supplying our own home requirements. The margin left to cover wages of the labourer and profit of the manufacturer is thus very large.

† The progress from 1833 to 1874 is really much larger than these figures indicate—its true dimensions being concealed by a change in the custom house method of recording values.

hitherto been conducted. .Flax was spun in mills which were
driven by water or steam, and the quaint spinning-wheel sank
into disuse. The hand-loom held its place much longer. The
linen trade was slow to adopt the power loom. This invalu-
able machine had been invented for forty years before the
timid makers of linen began seriously to contemplate its employment.

In every branch of textile industry growth has been rapid
and continuous, until, when the nineteenth century entered its
last quarter there were seven thousand two hundred and ninety-
four factories in Great Britain. Besides supplying the enormous requirements of the home market, these works furnished
the world with cotton, woollen, linen, and silk fabrics to the
value of £120,000,000.

Hitherto there had been obtained from South American and
Russian mines a supply of gold and silver adequate to the
requirements of existing commerce. But that supply would
have been wholly insufficient for the vastly enlarged transactions of the free-trade period; and grave inconveniences
must have resulted if the commerce of the world had been suffered to outgrow the precious metals, on which the security
of all monetary systems depends. These evils were averted
by an opportune discovery. The provision for the want anticipated even our knowledge of its existence. It was
found that gold abounded in California, then recently
acquired by the United States. A little later gold was
discovered in our Australian colonies. Still later, as the
requirements of the world grew, it was found that the Rocky
Mountains, throughout the larger portion of their vast area,
were richly charged with the precious metals. The annual
production of gold and silver rose from ten million sterling to
thirty-five million. In thirty years the store of precious metals
available for the business of the world had received the huge
addition of one thousand million sterling.

1848
A. D.

Vast-quantities of coal became necessary to supply the innumerable steam engines which now gave movement to the productive machinery of the country. Mining took rank as one of the largest and most lucrative of our industries. So great was the consumption of coal that in time a fear seized the public mind that the supply would soon be exhausted; and this fear was not allayed till the report of a royal commission conveyed the soothing assurance that centuries of mining on the present scale would be required to exhaust our enormous coal-fields. The quantity of coal annually raised is over one hundred and thirty million tons,—a production almost as great as that of all the world besides.

It was inevitable that a vast expansion of the demand for iron should attend the growth of our manufacturing system. When the French revolution broke out England was an importer of iron, and her own production did not exceed seventy thousand tons.* Now it is close on seven million tons. So vast were the natural advantages enjoyed by England, so great the energy applied to their development, that we were quickly enabled to supply foreign countries with iron instead of receiving it from them. England has many competitors in the production of iron, but the quantity which they unitedly produce still falls short of hers.

Fifty years after James Watt gave his steam engine to the world, the wind was still the only motive power at sea, and men still depended upon the horse to convey themselves and their productions on land. The large dimensions which the manufactures of the country had now attained called for greater

* In the earlier years of this century our home production of iron was 150,000 tons; our import was 40,000 tons. In 1872 the production had risen to 6,750,000 tons. The iron trade received an immense stimulus after 1824, by a very simple improvement then made in the process of smelting. Hitherto a blast of cold air had been directed into the furnace, while the ore was being smelted. Now the blast was heated to a very high temperature—600 or 800 degrees—before being admitted to the furnace. An economy to the extent of two-thirds of the coal previously consumed was at once effected.

13

facility of transport. The canal boat or the carrier's cart, moving at its leisurely two or three miles an hour, was inadequate to the requirements of a traffic which was growing with unexpected rapidity. The mail coach, which at its best could traverse no more than two hundred miles in twenty-four hours, laid a debilitating restraint upon that free personal intercourse which is so essential in the conduct of business enterprises. More easy and speedy transport of men and commodities was again demanded, and the steam engine was the agency by which it was to be supplied.

The idea of the steamship is older than the idea of the steam carriage. In the sixteenth century, some forgotten genius made a feeble and fruitless attempt to apply steam to navigation. The imperfect mechanical skill of that early time was unable to give embodiment to so high a conception. A century later, 1736, a patent was actually taken for a boat which was to be driven by steam. Towards the close of the century a small steamer was sailing on a loch in Dumfriesshire at the speed of seven miles an hour. In 1807 a steamer, devised by Fulton, sailed up the Hudson from New York to Albany. After the crowning success of that voyage, steam navigation grew apace. A little later there were steamboats on the Clyde, and steamboats plying from Glasgow to London and from Holyhead to Dublin. In 1838 the Atlantic was crossed by steamers. Then the final triumph of steam was assured, and the distant places of the earth were bound together by a new and closer tie than they had known before.

But still, while steam had become a moving power by river and sea, the land communications of all countries were maintained by the agency of the horse. From the earlier years of the century a steam carriage was the dream of mechanicians. Men of inventive genius, withdrawing themselves from the vain and bloody enterprise which then absorbed the national care, sought to find an adequate mechanical embodiment for the splendid conception of steam locomotion. Many efforts, partially successful, were made, culminating at length in the final triumph of George Stephenson. The engine constructed by Stephenson for the Liverpool and Manchester Railway solved all doubts, silenced all objections, and inaugurated victoriously one of the grandest of industrial revolutions.

1830
A.D.

For several years the railway system extended itself with a timidity which the proved value of the invention did not warrant. Fifteen years after the opening of the Liverpool and Manchester line, there were only two thousand four hundred miles of railway in the United Kingdom; and the amount of capital invested in these undertakings was only eighty-eight million sterling. So slowly had the people been educated to a love of travelling that passengers numbered only thirty-three million annually. But in 1845 the British people were smitten with a wild and irrational passion for speculation in railways. The frenzy possessed every rank from peer to peasant. The most extravagant proposals were eagerly supported by a people too greedy of gain to examine the character of the enterprises on which they hastened to stake all they claimed as their own and often very much more. For a time advancing prices filled all speculative hearts with joy, and every one could tell a pleasant tale of profits gained by a few strokes of his pen. But the inevitable revulsion came in due time; and the receding wave swept remorselessly away the easy gains of the deluded crowd.

Under the impulse given by this mania the construction of new railroads was so rapid that in two years the capital embarked in these undertakings was doubled. In four years it had swelled out from eighty-eight million to two hundred and thirty million. A more judicious rate of progress was then established, and has been steadily continued, till now there are seventeen thousand miles of railway in the United Kingdom, for which the enormous outlay of six hundred and thirty

million has been incurred.   The operations of these railways
yield a gross annual income of sixty million.

Commercial intercourse was now fully emancipated from
the restraints which were laid upon it by insufficient means of
transport.   How largely this welcome liberty was made use of
may be estimated from the circumstance that in 1875 the railways conveyed goods to the extent of two hundred million
tons from the localities where they were produced to those
where they were to be consumed.

Still more remarkable was the growth among the people of a
disposition to travel.   During the early portion of the century
men had scarcely the means to go from home beyond such
trivial distance as they were able to accomplish on foot.   Human
society was composed of a multitude of little communities,
dwelling apart, mutually ignorant, and therefore cherishing
mutual antipathies.   At once the causes of separation were
withdrawn.   Men of different towns, of different countries,
were permitted freely to meet; to learn how little there was
on either side to hate, how much to love; to establish ties of
commercial relationship; to correct errors of opinion by
friendly conflict of mind.   The dormant love of travelling, by
which nature protects men from the evils of isolation, wakened
into life so vehement that in 1875 the railways conveyed six
hundred million passengers.   Ancient prejudice melts away
under the fuller knowledge gained by this extensive acquaintance.   Peculiarities of dialect, of manners, of belief, grow
indistinct, and the unity of the people becomes every year
more perfect.

But a still more wonderful mastery over the secrets of nature
was now to crown the patient researches of science, and yet
more closely to unite the scattered families of men.   It was
found that the same mysterious and terrible power which
flashes out of the heavens in storm was ready to traverse con-

tinent and sea with the speed of thought, bearing the messages which men desired to convey to each other. After many experiments, with constantly growing success, a line of telegraph was constructed on the Blackwall Railway **1837 A.D.** and used for the transmission of railway signals. A little later the telegraph was taught to print the messages which it bore. The railway companies hastened to construct telegraphs beside their lines, at first for their own purposes only, but soon for those of the public also. The uses of this marvellous invention spread with rapidity, and soon extended across the sea. Dublin was connected with **1850 A.D.** London; Dover with Calais. In a short time there followed the bold conception of stretching an electric pathway in the depths of the Atlantic, and uniting Europe with America. Ere long all civilized countries were thus **1866 A.D.** connected. Across all lands and seas, the mysterious agency which man had subjugated obediently carried his commands.

In England the state acquired, by purchase, all telegraphs, and so extended the system that soon every village in the kingdom enjoyed the inestimable privilege of **1868 A.D.** instantaneous communication with every part of the inhabited globe.

This use of electricity possesses for us an interest especial and unique. It is the first human invention which is obviously final. In the race of improvement, steam may give place to some yet mightier power; gas may be superseded by some better method of lighting. No agency for conveying intelligence can ever excel that which is instantaneous. Here, for the first time, the human mind has reached the utmost limit of its progress.

The union of distant localities by railway and telegraph quickened the interest which men felt in the concerns of each

other, and awakened an incessant thirst for news. The weekly
journals which had hitherto satisfied the desires of the limited
number who cared to read them, were now utterly insufficient.
It became necessary that the daily history of the world should
be compiled, in such hasty manner as might be possible, and
printed every morning in newspapers. It was further indispensable that these newspapers should be cheap, and
yet of high intelligence and literary excellence. The
abolition of the tax which had hitherto fettered newspapers, and, in a few years more, the abolition of the tax on
paper, made both of these things possible. The price
of nearly all newspapers was reduced to one penny,—a
charge so low that even poor men could afford the
indulgence of a daily paper. From these circumstances there
resulted an increase of newspaper circulation which there are
no means to compute, but which we know to be enormous.*
With increased revenues came a higher excellence of literary
workmanship, and a consequent increase of influence over the
minds of men. Every morning the same topics are presented
to all minds, generally with moderation and intelligence,
often with consummate skill. These topics furnish themes of
thought and conversation for the day. Public opinion, which
is now the governing power of the empire, is thus formed,
expressed, intensified, and guided to the discharge of the great
function which it has assumed.

    The enormous increase of the demand for newspapers
rendered it indispensable that swifter methods of printing
should be found. From the date of the invention down to the
close of 1814 there had been almost no improvement on the
printing-press. A rude machine, yielding at its best no more

1855
A.D.

1861
A.D.

---

   * We can tell the increase in the number of journals, although not the increase of
circulation. In 1857 there were 711 newspapers published in the United Kingdom.
In 1876 there were 1754. The annual circulation has been estimated, or it may more
correctly be said guessed, at one thousand million. Forty years ago the post-office
carried 36,000,000 newspapers; now it carries 250,000,000.

than 150 copies per hour, was still unversally employed. In 1814 the *Times* set up a press of German construction, worked by steam, and giving 1,100 copies per hour. Many years passed without further notable improvement. The urgent necessity arose for more rapid printing. By various steps we have at length attained to machines which satisfy every requirement. A machine, driven by steam, is fed with huge rolls of paper, and gives out newspapers, cut and folded, at the rate of 25,000 copies per hour. A simple process of stereotyping makes it easy to supply from one set of types an indefinite number of such machines.*

The shipping which conveyed the emancipated commerce of Great Britian with foreign countries grew with the traffic to which it ministered. At the beginning of the century our shipping amounted to two million tons. Under the stimulus of the war it rose to two million and three-quarters. Many gloomy years followed the return of peace. At first the number of our ships remained stationary, and then the painful process of decay began. For years there was a steady decline, until English shipping was smaller by three hundred thousand tons than it had been thirteen years before. 1829 A. D. With the coming in of better times, maritime industry was prompt to assert its ancient vitality, and a steady growth was again experienced. When free trade gave us extended commercial relations with the world, the increase became more rapid, until in 1875 our tonnage had swelled out to six million, and the annual arrivals and sailings of our own and foreign ships ran up to the huge aggregate of forty-five million tons.

Much thought was now bestowed upon mechanical improvement, and the power of invention received unexampled stimulus.

* Perhaps the most striking contrast in the Philadelphia Exhibition of 1876 was the press at which Benjamin Franklin once laboured; and near it the Walter machine, throwing off its hourly seventeen thousand copies of a newspaper.

For one hundred and fifty years prior to the middle of the eighteenth century the patents granted for mechanical inventions were at the average rate of eight per annum. From 1763 to 1852 the annual rate was two hundred and fifty. During the next eighteen years it was over two thousand. In 1877 it was three thousand two hundred.*

While the arts which cherish and sustain human life achieved greatness thus rapidly, the agencies by which men seek to destroy each other advanced with equal step. The Crimean war directed the attention of inventive minds to the improvement of warlike implements, and an astonishing success rewarded their efforts in this department. The musket of the Napoleonic wars was loaded tediously at its muzzle, and fired by the uncertain spark struck by a flint out of steel. It was smooth-barrelled, and no one therefore could predict or control the course which its missile would pursue. Its utmost range was under two hundred yards. That primative weapon has given place to a musket whose breech opens to receive the charge, whose rifled barrel enables the possessor to shoot to a hairsbreadth, whose range is sevenfold that of the old musket, whose action is so swift that, skilfully wielded, it will slaughter twenty human beings per minute.† The wooden ships with which Nelson gained his victories, and whose undefended sides were riven by the shot of the enemy, are superseded by vessels clad in armour so massive that almost no weight of shot can pierce it. We have artillery which will throw, with unerring precision, a mass of iron weighing two thousand pounds to a

---

* It is not, however, to be supposed that we are more inventive than any of our neighbours. France issues annually nine thousand patents, and the United States twelve thousand. An unwise patent law still discourages invention in Britain, and gives our industrial rivals an important advantage.

† The slaughter actually effected fully bears out the pretensions of the new weapon. In the Duke of Wellington's campaigns only one bullet in 600 took effect. At Speichern the Germans disabled one Frenchman by the expenditure of 279 catridges. At Woith the practice was better, and one shot in every 147 told. According to Russian statistics, one Turk was struck down in the late war for every 66 shots fired; but these figures are probably to some extent conjectural.

distance of five miles. By the help of electricity we can send against hostile ships an explosive force whose discharge will scatter their timbers to the waves, and utterly destroy the hundreds of brave men who form their crews. Mechanically these inventions are very admirable. It is not, however, beyond hope that civilized man approaches the close of his fighting era, and that the perfecting of the implements of slaughter may be coincident, or nearly so, with their disuse.

Increased command over the necessaries of life by the masses of the people is justly held to mean, not only increased comfort, but an improved moral condition. Judged by this unerring test, the recent history of Great Britain is profoundly gratifying. Her people have it in their power now to consume much more largely than their fathers did of those commodities on which their well-being depends. The true value of our commercial legislation, of our amazing mechanical progress, can be ascertained not otherwise than by its power to raise the condition of the people. No preceding generation of men has witnessed changes so vast and so beneficent.

During the thirty years which followed the repeal of the corn laws the purchasing power of the people experienced an enormous increase. Where in the year 1845 the average consumption of foreign wheat and flour was only seventeen pounds for each of the population, in 1875 it was one hundred and twenty-four pounds. The use of sugar had more than trebled —having risen from fifteen to fifty-one pounds. Tea had undegone a similar increase,—from one and a quarter to four pounds.* The use of foreign bacon had multiplied ninefold,—from less than one pound to fully nine pounds. In butter and cheese the increase was threefold. Thirty years ago we imported eggs at the rate of four to each of the population; now the average is

* Nations differ strangely in regard to their use of tea The annual consumption of America is one and a half pound per head. In France tea is almost unknown. The provincial Frenchman never sees it.

over twenty. Side by side with this increased importation from abroad, our consumption of home-grown articles of food has largely increased. So much larger a number of persons can now afford the use of wine, that the consumption of this beverage has risen from one quarter to rather more than one half gallon. It is an additional evidence of well-being that the use of spirits has increased much less rapidly than that of other articles. In 1840 the average was eighty-three hundredths of a gallon for each person; in 1873 it was not quite one and a quarter gallon.*

These prosaic details write for us a history beside which the annals of our greatest wars sink into insignificance. They reveal to us the toiling millions of our population rising out of wretchedness and debasement, and becoming able to possess themselves of the comforts of life. They give us warrant to believe that the foundations of a corresponding improvement in moral condition are being laid. Nothing in the history of a nation can compare in value with this.

---

* In 1742 the consumption of spirits in England and Wales averaged 8½ gallons for each of the population.

CHAPTER VIII.

THE VICTORIES OF PEACE.—II

THE great outbreak of inventiveness by which our century is distinguished has left no province of human affairs unvisited. Heretofore men accepted as finally perfected every method and appliance which they inherited from their fathers. All at once the imperfections of their heritage seemed to become apparent. All at once an unlimited possibility of improvement seemed to reveal itself. Man's daily life was still burdened with rude and ineffective expedients which for centuries had undergone little or no amelioration. Each of these was now assailed by some thoughtful investigator, whose mind was quickened by the universal passion for improvement, and who, instead of seeing finality anywhere around him, saw only the point from which a new and gracious era of progress could take its opening. In its results this beneficent activity has incalculably enriched and beautified human life.

Nowhere has man more notably widened his empire than in his increased knowledge of his own body, and in his enlarged power to soothe its pains and cure its manifold disorders. Until lately, the healer of diseases groped in darkness—knowing imperfectly the purposes of the great organs, and utterly ignorant of their existing conditions. A series of wonderfully ingenious instruments now open to him the mysteries of the living body. The stethoscope, the speculum, the laryngoscope,

the ophthalmoscope enable him to read with unfailing accuracy
the progress of disease in the internal and hitherto inaccessible
organs.   The microscope, as it is now used, gives him to comprehend the exquisitely delicate organization with which he
deals.   The rejection of remedies applied in ignorance and the
adoption of effective methods of treatment have naturally accompanied this large increase of knowledge.   The use of
chloroform and other anæsthetics has relieved humanity from
the unutterable anguish which, until thirty years ago, attended
all important surgical operations.   The adoption of lithotrity
has nearly abolished the nameless horrors of lithotomy.   An-
eurism is arrested in its deadly course by a device so simple as
the continued pressure of the finger upon the seat of disease.
The contorted limbs of children are made straight and permanent lameness averted by a touch of the surgeon's knife relieving the undue tension of a tendon.   But in nothing are the
results of increased knowledge more acceptable than in the
altered methods of treatment which surgeons now adopt.
Middle-aged and elderly people remark a striking diminution
in the number of mutilated persons who are to be seen in our
streets. From of old the surgeon applied the knife with a readi-
ness which we now recognize to have been as mistaken as it was
lamentable.   The reign of conservative surgery is of recent
origin, but it is firmly established.   Amputation, it has long
been said, is the opprobrium of surgery.   The careful surgeon
has delivered his art from the opprobium of needless amputation.   He extirpates the offending shoulder, or elbow, or knee
joint, leaving to its possessor the stiffened but otherwise
serviceable limb.

Formerly the treatment of the insane was conducted under
a lingering belief that these unhappy persons were possessd by
devils.   They were chained, often in darkness; they were
beaten;* they were starved; they were exhibited for money to

* In 1788 George III., although without any tendency to violence, was subjected to
the restraint of the strait-waistcoat, and was struck by at least one brutal attendant.

a cruel, jeering rabble. Everything was done to make the home of the intrusive demon undesirable. These severities aggravated the evils they ignorantly sought to remedy. A Parliamentary inquiry in 1815 produced a deep impression on the public mind, and fostered the belief that mental disease called for tender and indulgent treatment. In twenty-five years more that belief so strengthened that mechanical restraints were abolished. The professional keepers of the insane defended the methods of government in which they had been trained, and scorned, as the dream of inexperience, the suggestion that madmen could be ruled by kindness. But the persistence of one brave English doctor* triumphed 1839 over their harsh traditions. The barbarous appliances A. D. of chains, and strait-waistcoats, and chairs of restraint were cast out of our asylums, and the reign of gentle and reasonable treatment was inaugurated. The effect was immediate and striking. Insanity, as it hitherto existed, underwent important modifications. The very types of the disease gradually changed. Its unhappy victims, no longer exasperated by continual severity, ceased to be afflicted by the demoniac frenzies which had rendered them so terrible, and gained a gentleness and submissiveness to which they had hitherto been strangers.

It has always been of prime interest to men—savage or civilized—to evoke the heat which lies hid everywhere in nature, and kindle it into flame. Possibly the care which was taken to keep lights continually burning in certain heathen temples, and around which religious sanctions ultimately gathered, had its remote origin in the experienced difficulty of kindling light. But never was any widespread and urgent human want so imperfectly supplied. The earliest method of obtaining fire was by the friction of two pieces of dried wood.

*Dr. Conolly.

The next was the striking together of steel and flint. These two rude methods of obtaining the indispensable assistance of fire have served man during almost the whole of his career. Only so recently as about the time of the first Reform Bill has he been able to command the services of a more convenient agency.

The elements which compose this agency come from afar. Pine trees are brought from Canada or Norway, and cut by powerful and delicate machinery into innumerable little pieces. Sulphur, cast up by volcanic action from the depths of the earth, is brought from Sicily. The bones of innumerable generations of wild cattle are collected on the vast plains of South America, and the chemistry of Europe extracts phosphorus from them. The little pieces of pine wood, dipped in phosphorus and sulphur, form matches, which burst into flame on the slightest friction. So perfect is the machinery employed, that a few workmen produce matches by millions in a day. So cheap, consequently, is the price, that the wholesale dealer buys eight hundred for one penny.

Long after the power-loom had entered upon its career, and cloth was woven by machinery, nothing better than hand-labour had been found for sewing the cloth so produced into the forms required for human use. The poor needle-women of London still slaved during as many hours as they were able to keep awake, and received a daily sixpence or eightpence in requital of their toil. But at length an American mechanic 1846 invented a machine which could sow as much as six A. D. needle-women. The capabilities of this invention were promptly appreciated, and much attention was given to its improvement. In course of years there were twenty different machines, with an annual sale of millions. So highly were the powers of the sewing-machine developed, that it could be driven at the rate of three thousand stitches per minute, The demand for sewing increased with a rapidity altogether unexpected. The starving needle-woman ceased to be one of the scandals of civilization. In her place came the machine-girl, with her moderate hours for labour and her comfortable wages.

Some forty years ago, the surprising discovery was made that the light of the sun reflected from any object could be made to imprint on a smooth, sensitized surface a picture of that object in its minutest details. This beautiful discovery soon proved of the deepest interest to mankind. It was applied at once to portrait-taking. Hitherto the brush of the painter alone had preserved an imperfect resemblance of a few persons in each generation. The cost of the process permited only a very few to avail themselves of it; of the others, no pictorial record was possible. The aspect of the men and women of an age was veiled impenetrably from those who came after them. Photography supplied a new link to connect the ages. It secured for all future generations of men a copious and vivid representation of their ancestors,—their appearance, their dress, their dwellings, their modes of life.* Innumerable are the uses to which this beautiful art has been applied. One of the most interesting of these was suggested during the siege of Paris by the Prussians. The city was so completely encompassed that communication with the outside world 1871 A. D. was altogether cut off. The messages of anxious friends in England were printed in the London *Times*. By a process of microscopic photography the page was copied on a morsal of paper scarcely larger than a postage-stamp, the letters being invisible to the unassisted eye. A number of these morsels were sent by carrier-pigeon into Paris. There, having been

* Recently the power has been gained of preserving a still more wonderful memorial of departed generations. The phonograph stores up for an indefinite period the sounds of the human voice, and gives them off at the pleasure of the operator. Future generations will not merely possess ample pictorial representations of their ancestors; they will be able to listen to the sound of words which were spoken, it may be, hundreds of years before.

health both of man and beast. So well was the value of this improved drainage appreciated, that in 1846 Parliament offered a loan of £4,000,000, to be expended on drains. Science was now enlisted in the service of the farmer. The nature of the plants which it was his business to rear was carefully studied, and the food which conduced best to their growth was ascertained. Agricultural societies collected and compared the experience of observant farmers, and published it for the general good. Machinery was applied to sowing and threshing. In 1852 a machine for reaping was offered to farmers, and accepted with prompt appreciation. Three years later a plough drawn by steam was in use. Steam tillage turned up the soil to greater depth than had been possible before, and was therefore more effective in the production of bountiful crops. It was not only better; it was, to an important, extent, less expensive. British manufacturers have earned for themselves a good degree by the marvellous improvement effected upon all their processes. The British farmer has evinced enterprise and enlightenment not less creditable.

NOTE.—During the last two or three years some doubt begun to be entertained in regard to the permanence of the industrial supremacy which Britain gained so rapidly. The country has been enduring a commercial depression exceptionally severe and prolonged. At such a time anticipations for the future more gloomy than circumstances actually warrant may be expected to prevail. But, after every reasonable deduction has been made for this habit of the human mind under distress, it is impossible to deny that there are aspects of our industial position well fitted to awaken anxiety in regard to the future. Our industrial eminence is in great measure the result of certain British inventions, of which we were able to make large use while our neighbours were engrossed by the work of invading other people's territories or resisting the invasion of their own. We held for many years a virtual monoply of the mechaical appliances essential to industrial greatness. We made a vigorous use of our advantages; our commodities were cheap and good, and the world was satisfied to accept its supplies from us. We assumed it would always be so, and upon this theory we have accumulated on these islands vast aggregates of machinery and of labourers, for whom there could not possibly be found employment if foreign countries should undertake to manufacture for the supply of their own wants. But that is precisely what foreign countries have for many years been endeavouring, with much energy and success to do. A strong and growing desire to establish manufactures exists in all civilized countries. No doubt, if they suffered British goods to enter freely, we could still hold our own against all competition. But we compete under the absolutely fatal disadvantage of heavy protective duties. For many years America has protected her youthful industries, at incalculable cost, but so effectively that the American manufacturer can now produce many articles—notably the lower grades of cotton cloths—more cheaply than his English rival. Moved, to sum extent, by the success of America, the tendency to protect is becoming stronger on the continent of Europe; and the field which formerly was open to the manufactures of Britain becomes, year by year, more circumscribed. Our old outlets are failing us; our hopes must rest on the opening of new outlets. Not the least alarming feature in our position is the circumstance that in America and France much greater thought is given to mechanical improvement than is now the case in England. The English manufacturer has a disabling confidence in the methods which heretofore have led him to success. He rejects novelties, and is unwilling to be bored with experiments. In a world glowing with the love of progress and mechanical improvement, the mechanical conservatism of the English manufacturer is undoubtedly the most perilous form of dry-rot by which our industrial system can be invaded.

The situation and prospects of British agriculture are not more satisfactory than those of our manufacturers. Our farmers have passed through several very unfavorable seasons. Under the protective system, when the quantity of grain produced was small, the price rose so as fully to compensate the farmer. The producer was kept safe; the consumer alone suffered. Now, with all the world growing wheat for us, the miseries of a bad harvest come upon the farmer, whose price does not rise, however low his production may fall. It does not now admit of doubt that America can profitably deliver in this country grain and meat at lower prices than we at present inflated rentals are able to produce them ourselves. During the prosperous year since the opening of the free trade period values of land and rents have been unduly appreciated. A readjustment of such values, to an extent which cannot fail to be painful to many, has now become plainly inevitable.

CHAPTER IX.

IN the foremost rank of powers destined to change the face of the world stand Christian Missions. These may almost be regarded as products of this century, and the imposing magnitude which they have gained is altogether recent. Their beginnings were so small as generally to avert hostility by securing the contemptuous indifference of those who might have been unfriendly. There are few things in human history that wear an aspect of higher moral grandeur than the opening of what are now our great missions. One or two men, sent by this church and by that, are seen going forth, in obedience to a command spoken eighteen hundred years ago, to begin the enormous work of undermining heathenism and reclaiming the world to God. Among the glories of the century is none greater than this. All other enterprises of beneficence must yield to this magnificent attempt to expel debasing superstitions, and convey into every heart the ennobling influences of the Christian religion. The success already attained gives sure promise of results the greatness of which we as yet but dimly perceive.

The early suggestion of missions was received with disfavour. When some good men invited the Church of Scotland to give encouragement to such enterprises, the representatives of that body declined the invitation. They could not well argue against imparting to heathens that

1795
A. D.

212

gospel which it was the business of their own lives to teach. Nevertheless the proposal was unaccepted. One clergyman deemed it visionary; another wished the result to be attained by prayer and waiting; a third saw revolutionary tendencies in every form of united action, and trembled for the constitution. On grounds such as these the Church of Scotland, by an overwhelming majority, refused to sanction missionary effort.

A year or two later, a young Scottish gentleman—Robert Haldane—resolved to sell his patrimonial estate, and along with two friends, to spend the remainder of his days in teaching the gospel to the people of Bengal. 1796 A. D. He applied to the directors of the East India Company for permission to reside in the country and follow this occupation. The directors declined, "for weighty and substantial reasons," to admit within their domain any man who came on such an errand.

Towards the close of last century, a small Baptist congregation in the town of Leicester was ministered to by a young man named Carey. He was the son of very poor parents, who could give him no help during his preparation for the ministry. At first, he maintained himself by the craft of shoemaking. Then, as he rose, he became a teacher. At length he reached what he had striven for during many toilsome years—the office of the ministry. While he laboured among the handful of poor people who formed his congregation, the conviction smote him that something ought to be done for the conversion of heathens. For ten years he brooded incessantly over the undischarged duty which the church owed to the heathen world. At first his brethren listened to him coldly. They regarded him as a dreamer of dreams,—as a man who had allowed a wild and hopeless project to absorb his mind. Carey was not daunted. He preached sermons, published tracts, put forth all the influence of which he was possessed. At length a measure of success was given to him. In the autumn of 1792, while the

French monarchy was tottering to its fall, and Europe was about to plunge into twenty years of incessant war, a few very poor men, yielding to the enthusiasm of Carey, met in Kettering to found a society for the conversion of the world to Christianity. They subscribed on the spot thirteen pounds, two shillings, and sixpence. Thus arose the Baptist Missionary Society,—first-born of all our great associations for sending the Christian religion to heathens,—the annual revenues of which now amount to nearly £50,000.

Next year Mr. Carey went to India to enter upon the work which he had chosen, for he himself was to be the society's first missionary. The territories of the East India Company were closed against the gospel; but the Danes, whose views were more enlightened, held Serampore, and Carey established himself there. He was gifted in the acquisition of languages, and in his early days, while still working as a shoemaker, had made large progress in this department of study. He began at once to translate the Scriptures into Bengalee. So steadily did he continue to apply himself to this essential part of missionary work that, within twenty years, he and his companions had translated the Scriptures into twenty-one Indian languages.

During the first quarter of the century all the great missionary societies of Europe and America were formed, and missionary work was organized into a system. The churches fairly committed themselves to an undertaking from which they cannot desist till heathenism is extirpated. Colleges were established for the training of missionaries. A vast network of auxiliaries for the collection of funds overspread Protestant Christendom. The Bible was translated into many languages hitherto unwritten. Grammers and dictionaries presented to the learner the simple structure of these rude tongues. Teachers of the gospel were to be found here and there in heathen lands, facing with heroic courage the dangers of the Christian pioneer, bearing with heroic fortitude his inevitable and often fatal hardships. Among the snows of Labrador, under the fierce heat of the tropics, in our Indian dominions, among the Hottentots at the Cape, in the islands of the Pacific, among our own negroes in the West Indies, men had begun in simple faith, with means conspicuously inadequate, the gigantic work of driving out heathenism and replacing it by Christianity. A little later, China was entered by the door which the English opened in their determination to force the use of opium on that empire. A few missionaries found their way into Japan. Dotted along the western shores of Africa, and seeking their way into the interior, are numerous mission stations, each the centre of a benign influence which is steadily extending its power, and preparing the restoration of that lost continent to civilization and progress. The sum of these efforts, viewed in relation to the vast proportions of the undertaking, is still inconsiderable. Great Britain sends out 1000 missionaries, and expends annually £600,000. The Continental churches employ 400 missionaries at a cost of £120,000. America contributes 550 men, and £300,000. In all there are now at work in heathen countries 2000 Protestant missionaries, and the churches sustain the work by an annual contribution of about one million sterling.

These attempts to Christianize the world have been in progress for upwards of half a century. There is yet no more than time to open an enterprise so vast. But already there are materials from which it is possible to estimate the prospects of the missionary enterprise, and the grandeur of the results which its success must yield. The gains which have been in some instances already secured may be trusted to guide us in forming our expectations for the future.

In the Southern Pacific, not far from the equator, lie the Sandwich Islands—members of a vast insular family which stretches five thousand miles from north to south. The exist-

ence of these islands was made known to Europe by Captain
Cook, who himself perished here, murdered by the natives. Every advantage of soil and climate has been
bestowed upon them. The grove of bread-fruit trees
around the villages is itself a sufficient maintenance for the
population. The cocoa-nut tree yields food and drink; its bark
can be converted into clothing; from its leaves the natives
manufacture baskets and fishing-lines, and obtain thatch for
their houses. The sugar-cane, the cotton and coffee plants
grow almost without human care. Many trees yield valuable
dyes and gums. Fish swarm on the coasts. Nature in her
most bounteous mood has profusely endowed these lovely
islands with the elements of material welfare.

1778 A.D.

But the inhabitants had sunk to the lowest depth of degradation. They fed on raw fish and the flesh of dogs. They had
found among the products of their soil a narcotic root which
readily produced intoxication, and they used it to excess.
Human sacrifices were frequent. The family relation was
unknown. Licentiousness was without limit or restraint of
shame. Two-thirds of the children born were strangled or
buried alive by their parents. So given to stealing were the
natives that expert divers endangered Captain Cook's ships by
carrying off the nails which fastened the sheathing to the timbers. Population was rapidly diminishing under the wasting
influence of the vices which prevailed.

After some years of intercourse with foreigners the islanders
became dissatisfied with their religion. At the suggestion of
one of their kings they suddenly rebelled against the gods.
The images were cast into the sea; the temples were demol-
ished; human sacrifices ceased; the priests who adhered to the
discarded system were slain. The old faith was overthrown;
but nothing came in its room. The nation left itself wholly
without a religion.

While this revolution was in progress, there sailed from

Boston a small missionary party, intent upon Christianizing the Sandwich Islands. The king, an amiable but drunken young man, received them with kindness. The missionaries quickly acquired the language and began to preach. **1819 A.D.** The king and his court were persuaded to take lessons in reading and writing. The chief people favoured the new religion, and followed the royal example in seeking to possess a little education. The influence of the missionaries steadily increased. In a few years the observance of the Sabbath was enjoined by law; applications for baptism were received; and one of the great chiefs, an old man who had spent his days in war, died professing Christianity. Gradually, as the missionaries were reinforced from home, churches and schools were built, and the whole population were under the influence of Christian teaching. In course of years Christian marriage was adopted; a temperance society was formed; and one-third of the people were attending school.

Christianity made its way steadily, until in twenty years it had become the accepted faith of the nation. The deeply ingrained vices of the old days were hard to conquer, and many disappointing falls grieved the missionaries. But upon the whole the progress in virtue kept pace with the progress in faith. The people became quiet, orderly, industrious. From among themselves an adequate number of young men were trained for the ministry. It was deemed that the Sandwich Islands had ceased to be a field for missionary operations. The nation was Christianized. The native church afforded men enough for her service, and means enough for their support. Fifty years from its opening the mission was closed. Its entire cost—the cost of turning this little nation to God—had been £250,000, greatly less than the cost of one iron-clad ship-of-war.

Hitherto, as in politer despotisms, the only law was "the thought of the chief." With Christianity came constitutional government, The chiefs formed a parliament, which met

annually for despatch of business, and was opened by a speech
from the throne. A code of laws was prepared, and, after
discussion, adopted by the parliament. A charter was granted
in which the king recognized and guaranteed the rights of his
subjects. A government system of education was established.
Even a patent law was provided for the protection of inventive
islanders.

The missionaries taught how to cultivate the cotton-plant,
and how to spin and weave its fibre. They taught how to
extract sugar from the cane. They instructed a docile people
in the decencies and comforts of civilized life. Roads were
made; bridges were built; a newspaper was established; industry prospered even among the seductions to idleness which a
tropical climate presents. The islands took a respectable place
in the records of commerce. In 1867 the imports were
£400,000 or the exports—consisting of sugar, coffee, arrowroot,
timber, beef, and hides—amounted to £500,000, and were
steadily increasing. The government expenditure was £100,-
000. Even that crowning evidence of civilization, a national
debt, was not awanting. The country had borrowed £25,000
to promote the development of its resources.

A complete success had been achieved. Heathenism had
utterly disappeared from the islands; Christianity had come
instead, bringing in its train security to life and property,
peace, industry, and progress; raising the wasteful and treacherous savage to the dignity of a God-fearing, law-abiding citizen, who bears fairly his part in contributing to the common
welfare of the human family.

Southern Africa was the home of the Bechuanas—a fierce,
warlike race, cruel, treacherous, delighting in blood. No
traveller could go among them with safety; they refused even
to trade with strangers. They had no trace of a religion, no
belief in any being greater than themselves, no idea of a future
life.

In the early days of missionary effort, Dr. Moffat, with some companions, went among these discouraging savages. For years he toiled under manifold difficulty. No man regarded his words. The people would not even come to church until they were bribed by a gift of tobacco; and their deportment when they came was unbecoming in a high degree. They stole the missionary's vegetables, his tools, the very water which irrigated his fields. They destroyed his sheep, or chased them in utter mischief into dangerous places.

But Moffat, a heroic Christian man, laboured patiently on, and in time a vast success crowned his noble toils. Almost suddenly (1828) the people began to attend church in large numbers, and to evidence deep interest in the instruction of the missionaries. Dr. Moffat translated the Bible into the native tongue, and there arose an eager desire to be able to read. Many persons professed Christianity, and applied for baptism. Soon they manifested a disposition to clothe themselves and to keep clean their persons, which heretofore were filthy. They began to improve their dwellings, and in a simple way to furnish them. They wanted ploughs, wagons, and other agricultural implements. They entered readily into commercial relations with foreigners; and in a few years their imports of foreign manufactures amounted to £250,000, paid for in the produce of the soil. Christianity is now almost universal among the Bechuanas. Education is rapidly extending; natives are being trained in adequate numbers for teachers and preachers; Christianity is spreading out among the neighbouring tribes. The Bechuanas have been changed by Christian missions into an orderly, industrious people, who cultivate their fields in peace, and maintain with foreigners a mutually beneficial traffic.

The greatest of all fields of missionary labour is India. Thirty-five societies carry on their operations among the swarming millions who own British rule. Upwards of six hundred foreign missionaries, besides a larger number of Christianized natives, are employed in communicating a knowledge of religious truth. From the printing-presses of the missionaries there have issued during the last twenty years three million copies of the Scriptures, and twenty million school-books and other works.

Early in the history of Indian missions, it was perceived that preaching alone would not yield the results which the missionaries sought. The Hindu clung tenaciously to the religion which his fathers had held for twenty-five centuries, and which was wrapped closely around every detail of his daily life. He preferred it to any new faith which the foreigners offered for his acceptance. The first indispensable step in the process of his conversion was to show him that his religion was a mere aggregate of fables. The missionaries established schools and applied themselves to the work of teaching. At first their instruction was given wholly in the native tongues. But the question arose, and was keenly debated, whether it was not better to teach the youth of India in the English language. In 1829, a missionary from Scotland—Alexander Duff—virtually solved the momentous question. He satisfied himself that English should be substituted for the vernacular; not otherwise could European enlightenment and the Christian religion possess India. In that belief he founded an institution for the training of young men of the better class, and his signal success led to the general adoption of his system. In a few years the governor-general was able to state that Duff's labours had produced " unparalleled results."

For fifty years Hindu youth in increasing numbers have received an English education. A revolution of extraordinary magnitude has been silently in progress during those years, and even now points decisively to the ultimate, although still remote, overthrow of Hindu beliefs and usages. A vast body of educated and influential natives acknowledge that their ancient faith is a mass of increditibilities. A public opinion has been created by whose help such practices as infanticide and the burning of widows have been easily suppressed. From time immemorial the Hindu people have been broken by the superstition of caste into innumerable fragments, each of which is taught as a religious duty to despise and shun the others. The missionaries from the beginning declared war against a system which prohibited the free intermingling of men and filled their minds with unreasonable prejudices and antipathies. Their policy was based on the principle that the followers of Christ are brethren, and they taught the converted Brahman to receive the cup of communion from the hand of a man whose touch he was accustomed to regard as hopeless defilement. The mischievous delusion of caste is gradually losing its power over the Hindu mind. The debasement of Indian mothers enfeebles the Indian character. Irreversible physical as well as moral laws secure the degradation of races who deny to women their rightful position. A desire for female education has sprung up in India. Educated natives seek the companionship of educated wives. The missionaries have entered with eagerness upon the indispensable work of elevating the women of India. Multitudes of women are being taught in their own houses. Native female teachers are being trained to carry on this vitally important work.

Through the open gateway of the English language, English knowledge and ideas and principles are being poured into India. The educational progress already made is large, and the desire for education steadily increases. The Hindu mind is awakening from its sleep of ages. A knowledge of the English language is widely coveted; English usages are regarded with admiration and studiously imitated. A higher moral tone is becoming familiar to the people. In the words of the Indian government, "the blameless example and self-denying labours of the missionaries are infusing new vigour

into the stereotyped life of the great population placed under
English rule, and are preparing them to be in every way better men and better citizens of the great empire in which they
dwell."

The direct results of missionary labour in India are not inconsiderable. In 1852 the number of native Christians was 128,-
000; in 1862 it had increased to 213,000; in 1872, to 320,000.
But the value of missionary labour is not to be estimated by
the returns of avowed conversions. Christianity has not, thus
far, been accepted by India. It is found that the vanity of the
old faith has to be shown before a new faith can gain a footing,
and this indispensable work is being successfully accomplished.
Hinduism is evidently yielding before the resistless force of
Christian education. Large numbers of the people who have
enjoyed the advantages of an English education find it impossible longer to believe in their hereditary faith. They have been
raised by education to a point at which Hinduism is to them no
more credible than nursery tales. This is the first stage in the
conversion of a heathen people. The adoption of a purer faith
will in due time follow.

These illustrations of missionary success could be multiplied
almost indefinitely. They show that already vast progress
has been made, although the work is still scarcely more than
in its infancy. Every year increases the power of the agencies
which are employed and widens the sphere of their influence.
In the priceless results already gained, we discover warrant to
expect that in some not very remote future the missionary will
fulfil his daring and glorious programme—the educating and
Christianizing of the whole heathen world.

CHAPTER X.

THE CHARITIES OF THE NINETEENTH CENTURY.

NE of the noblest traits of the century is the growth of organized voluntary effort to relieve the suffering and to raise the fallen. The humane spirit in which such efforts originate has never been absent from the Christian world, but its energies were grievously repressed by the brutalizing influence of incessant war. Towards the close of the eighteenth century it is seen struggling towards a wider dominion than it had hitherto been able to assert. Howard had already devoted his life the amelioration of prisons, and his revelation of their horrors had fallen upon a people not indisposed to listen or reluctant to correct. A Society for Bettering the Condition of the Poor* was in active operation in London. A little later Sir Samuel Romilly was striving to mitigate the severities of our criminal code. The iniquities of the slave-trade and of slavery itself became more apparent in the growing light, and awakened a constantly increasing abhorrence. But still men's minds were hardened to human suffering by the years of bloodshed through which they lived. A spirit of universal hatred pervaded society. Personal bitterness was intense. Difference of political or religious belief was a recognized warrant

---

* Founded in 1796 by Wilberforce and some others, with the king as patron. It operated chiefly in the way of collecting and diffusing information on topics of interest to the poor,—as the improvement of dwellings; the improvement of cottage fire-places and chimneys; the establishment of parish mills, of village shops and soup-kitchens; the improvement of county jails; the means of procuring an adequate supply of fuel, &c.

for the extremest hate. When the body of Lord Castlereagh, pierced by self-inflicted wounds, was borne to the grave, the mob expressed their indecent gratification by a cheer. At the

1803 A. D. funeral of Lord Chancellor Clare, the mob bombarded with dead cats the coffin of the unpopular judge. A quarrel, however trivial in its origin, was held to lay the disputants under constraint of honour to seek the destruction of each other.*

But with the return of peace the bland spirit of forbearance and toleration which Christianity and cultivation inspire gained a large increase of energy. A gradual amelioration of temper crept over society, and in course of years it became possible for men to hold different opinions without diminution of mutual regard. As the softening influence grew in strength, men turned with ardour unkown before to the work of helping the helpless and lightening the burden of suffering which lay heavy on so large a portion of the people. An enumeration of the leading charities of any of our great cities enables us to estimate the vast amount of kindly energy which men now put forth to ameliorate the condition of their less fortunate neighbours. The charities of the Scottish capital will suffice for this purpose.†

Edinburgh has a vast hospital in which a poor man who has fallen under disease or accidental hurt receives the benefit of careful nursing and the highest medical skill. Lest his recovery should be impeded by the impure air and defective nourishment of his own home, a residence some miles out of town is provided for him during the glad days of convalescence. Those who are never to know the sweetness of returning health are received into institutions provided for sufferers against whom the sad

---

* "The frightful thing," says Lord Cockburn, writing of Edinburgh at the close of the last century, "was the personal bitterness. The decent appearance of mutual toleration was dispised, and extermination seemed a duty."

† London has upwards of five hundred charitable societies, which expend annually about one million sterling, voluntarily contributed by benevolent individuals.

doom of incurable has been spoken. There every possible alleviation of their sorrow is afforded while they wait for the final shelter of the grave. Little children who are sick have an hospital provided for themselves, where the tenderest care is lavished upon them. A separate home is maintained for children who are the victims of disease in spine or hip-joint. There are several institutions in which medical advice is given gratuitously to the poor regarding the manifold ills to which they are heirs. Poor women about to become mothers find the doors of an appropriate institution hospitably open to them in their hour of trial, or they may receive from either of two societies the help of physicians in their own homes. Skilled nursing does much to promote the comfort and the recovery of the sick. The humane and thoughtful people of Edinburgh have provided two establishments where women who desire to become nurses of the sick may accomplish themselves in their merciful vocation.

One association establishes lodging-houses, where the very poor can live in comfort free from the allurements of vicious companionship. Another employs its resources in improving the condition of the poor by every device which Christian thoughtfulness suggests. Another watches over the destitute sick; and to the kindly words of its agents, adds an open-handed dispensation of comforts which are so needful in sickness, and yet so often unattainable. Indigent old men, indigent old women, decayed gentlewomen, enjoy the care of three societies. A philanthropist, whose bounty was under guidance of her orthodoxy, makes a provision for decayed old men and women "being Protestants." The blind and the deaf and dumb are received into home where suitable occupations are found for them. Children, on whose youth there has fallen the calamity of loss of parents, are maintained and educated and equipped for the work of life. There are houses of refuge where homeless wanderers may turn aside to obtain shelter for

15

the night. The deserving foreigner who finds himself in the
Scotch metropolis penniless and friendless is straightway taken
in hand and relived by a society founded for his especial
benefit. Nor is philanthropy altogether without its humours.
One lover of his kind makes provision that when oatmeal is
selling at more than a shilling per peck, poor householders of
Edinburgh shall be supplied at tenpence.

The moral interests of the poor are cared for with an enlightened zeal which is beyond praise. Children who are without
guardianship are snatched by merciful hands from the perils
which surround them, and safely bestowed in institutions where
they are taught simple industries and receive a wholesome education. In the early stage of a boy's industrial development
one society sends him forth to polish the soiled boots of pedes-
trians. Boys who love, or think they love, the sea, are sent
to a training-ship. For agricultural aspirants a farm-school is
provided. The government of these institutions is intrusted to
some of the wisest and best of the citizens of Edinburgh, by
whom unwearied personal care is given to the interests of their
unfortunate clients. Women who have fallen from virtue are
sought out and gathered into an institution whose influences are
directed towards their restoration. Criminals whose term of
punishment has expired are taken charge of by a society, whose
agents find for them honest employment and consequent deliverance from the temptation to commit fresh offences. Self-denying persons, impressed by the enormous evils which our drinking
usages produce, have banded themselves into societies, and
strive with unwearied and heroic effort to lead drunkards back
to sobriety.

A vast machinery, worked with noble devotedness, seeks to
carry the light of religious truth into the dark places of Edinburgh. One society distributes copies of the Holy Scriptures
gratuitously or by sale at low prices. Another circulates religi
ous tracts by the million. A third maintains a large body of

city missionaries, whose work it is to bear the gospel into the squalid homes of the poor. A fourth, combining the cure of physical with that of moral disease, employs a staff of medical missionaries. Nearly every Christian congregation has selected a district, where its members visit the lapsed poor, and strive to awaken, in hearts dulled by suffering, some interest in the magnificence of eternity. Hundreds of Christian men and women labour in Sunday schools to give to the children of the poor that religious knowledge which otherwise would not be given at all.

Nearly the whole of these organizations have had their beginning since the close of the great war. This disposition to raise the fallen, to befriend the friendless, is now one of the governing powers of the world. Every year its dominion widens. and even now a strong and growing public opinion is enlisted in its support. Many men still spend lives which are merely selfish. But such lives are already regarded with general disapproval. The man on whom public opinion anticipating the award of the highest tribunal, bestows its approbation, is the man who labours that he may leave other men better and happier than he found them. With the noblest spirits of our race this disposition to be useful grows into a passion. With an increasing number it is becoming at least an agreeable and interesting employment.* A future of high promise awaits that community whose instructed and virtuous members occupy themselves in carrying to their less happily circumstanced neighbours the good which they themselves enjoy.

* It is said on the monument to John Howard in St. Paul's, that the man who devotes himself to the good of mankind treads "an open but unfrequented path to immortality." The remark, so true of Howard's time, is happily not, true of ours

CHAPTER XI.

OUR INDIAN EMPIRE.

IN the year 1593 and adventurous Englishman named Stevens landed on the western shore of the great Indian peninsula. He found a country richer than he had ever dreamed of, inhabited largely by a simple and submissive people. The field for commercial adventure seemed tempting in an eminent degree. Stevens came home, and described in a book the splendours which he had witnessed. He spoke of ivory, of perfumes, of silk, of pearls, of gold. Some merchants of London hastened, as men do still, to found a company, and thus turn to account the dazzling possibilities which Stevens had revealed. But the confidence of the city was less easily gained then than it has been of recent years, and in 1599 only one hundred and one shares, representing a capital of thirty thousand pounds, had been subscribed for. Even that moderate sum was not fully paid. Many subscribers, repenting their untimely boldness, withdrew from the enterprise, leaving the more daring partners to assume the entire responsibility.

In 1600 the company obtained a charter from Queen Elizabeth, and began its modest trading. It earned large profits, but these were frequently neutralized by losses of similar magnitude; and thus it came to pass that the dividends enjoyed by the shareholders were not always of a very satisfying character. But the prospects of the company were full of promise. Its

228

capital was largely increased. Its transactions became year by year more considerable. In a few years the company was permitted to set up four establishments of a permanent description for the more convenient conduct of its business. Thus was gained its earliest foothold on the peninsula.

Other European traders had perceived the rich commercial promise of India, and the English were soon involved in irritating competition with Dutch, Portuguese, and French rivals. Unlicensed Englishmen, too, vexed their souls, by a course of trading which was visably more profitable than their own. Such irregular persons were seized and ruthlessly shipped home to England. On every side there were springing up questions which it was obvious could be solved more conveniently by force than reason. In 1640 the company set up a fort at Madras, and garrisoned it with a few native warriors, whose arms were bow and arrow, spear and shield.

England and France did not find, during the eighteenth century, that the battle-fields of Europe sufficed for the expression of their mutual hatred. They must needs carry the noise of their contention also into Asia and America. In the valley of the Ohio, on the Heights of Abraham as well as on the eastern coasts of the Indian peninsula, the deadly rivalries of these great European powers strove for supremacy. In India it seemed that France was to find compensation for her reverses on other fields. Dupleix, a capable Frenchman, drove the English out of Madras, and so guided affairs that common expectation pointed to the final expulsion of the English and the triumph of the French.

But all this was quickly changed. A young man named Clive was then serving as a clerk in the employment of the company. When the need arose, it was found that, although wholly without military training, he possessed military genius of the highest order. He organized a little force of English and native troops, led mainly by civil-

1750
A. D.

ians and soldiers who had never seen war. He attacked Arcot, the capital of the Carnatic, and took it. He was in turn besieged by an overwhelming force of French and natives, but he held Arcot against them all. In numerous other engagements he vanquished his enemies. The influence of France was destroyed, her discomfited general went home in disgrace, and England was supreme in southern India.

The company had established itself in India for purely commercial purposes, and had no higher ambition than profitable trading and liberal dividends. A career of military conquest was of all things the most repugnant to its peaceful and prosaic instincts. But now such a career was thrust upon it. The factory at Calcutta was attacked by Surajah Dowlah, the wicked sovereign of Bengal. The English governor fled from his post. One hundred and forty-six Englishmen were made captive and mercilessly thrust into a dungeon. Next morning all but twenty-three had perished. In December, Clive was before Calcutta with a force adequate to avenge his murdered countrymen. He repossessed the English settlement. The native forces and the handful of audacious strangers met at Plassey. Of the former there were sixty thousand; of the latter, three thousand two hundred. Even Clive hesitated in presence of a disparity so excessive, and his officers counselled immediate retreat. But his heroic spirit could not brook to turn away from the presence of an enemy. He fought, and obtained an easy victory. With no greater loss than that of seventy men, he gained for England unquestioned dominion over Bengal, with a population of thirty million. He laid the foundation of our Indian Empire.

June 1757 A. D.

The cares of extended sovereignty had now devolved upon an association which sought nothing more than a profitable sale of broadcloths and cutlery—a favourable purchase of silks, muslins, and pearls. Nor was it found possible to prevent the growth of these unwelcome responsibilities. Orissa and Bahar were added to Bengal. The territory of Benares followed, and certain large tracts lying along the Bay of Bengal. The still more formidable addition of the Carnatic could not be resisted, although for a time the company upheld there a native prince, whose rule was, however, merely nominal. When the century closed, the company was one of the governing powers of the world, keeping great armies on foot, fighting great battles, controlling vast revenues, holding in its hands the destinies of of many races and nations.

As a traiding association, the company had not achieved remarkable success. Its dividends, begining with six per cent., had crept up to ten, and for a brief space even to twelve and a half per cent., but quickly sunk once more to six. As a sovereign, it was a manifest failure.* 1769 A. D. The anomaly of permitting a company of merchants to exercise dospotic rule over a population many times larger than that of Great Britain was now to be corrected. A bill was introduced by Mr. Pitt, and passed into law, leaving to the company wide powers of management, but 1784 A. D. giving to the crown the appointment of a board by which control should be exercised over every detail of the civil and military government of India.

In 1798 the Marquis of Wellesley was sent out as governor-general. It seemed to the new governor that some decay of assendency had been incurred by the timid policy of his predecessor. He wished to make Britain feared for her strength as well as trusted for her integrity and wisdom, and his earliest care was to augment his army. He found ample employment for the military resources which he provided. During the seven years of his administration, he subdued four powerful states, whose chiefs had opposed themselves to British supre-

* "Different plans," says Adam Smith, writing in 1784, "have been proposed for the better management of [the company's] affairs. All those plans seem to agree in supposing, what was indeed always abundantly evident, that it is altogether unfit to govern its territorial possessions."

macy. He subjected to our rule provinces larger than France. He estabished a predominating influence over many princes, whose thrones, as yet, he spared. He increased the revenue from seven to fifteen million sterling. At the close, he bore rule over a population of seventy-five million. All this had been accomplished by forces which never exceeded twenty thousand British troops, supplemented by three or four times that number of Indian auxiliaries.

The british had gained a position which made their presence indispensable to the welfare of India. Incessant strifes had from time immemorial devasted the country, and were only now restrained by British power. The aggressive Mohammedans waited to overrun the gentler followers of the Hindu faith. The fiercer races were ever ready to spring upon the less fierce. The native governments were little better than organizations for the plunder of their unhappy subjects, save where they were laid under beneficent restraint by the strangers. All around us were bandit princes, whose barbaric splendours had been maintained till now by the hereditary policy of rapine. The nabob of the Carnatic lived magnificently on that portion of his revenues which was allowed to him, and left his wasted lands to be governed as the English deemed best. To the west was Mysore, which had been delivered from Tippoo and restored to its ancient sovereigns, now submissive to the will of their deliverers. Still farther west lay Malabar, whose prince was now swayed by hatred of the British, and now by fear of his robber neighbours, from whom the British protected him. To the north was Hyderabad, a huge territory, where a British resident guided the sovereign, and watched the miserable intrigues of a court which was justly described as a experiment to prove with how little morality it was possible for human beings to associate. All these and many others depended on the British to avert anarchy, For the first time in its his-

tory, the peninsula had rest from war, and men were suffered
to enjoy in quietness the fruits of their industry.

The directors, with pathetic earnestness, bewailed the conquests which were forced upon them. The company hung on
the perilous verge of bankruptcy, and could not regain its
position otherwise than by a course of peaceful trading. Each
new governor-general was commanded to abstain from war, to
avoid with his utmost diligence the acqusition of new territory.
But no effort of the directors sufficed to stay the career of conquest. With distressing frequency came reports of great battles, of brilliant victories, of new empires cast upon the burdened authorities. Ever it seemed that on our borders there
lay some treacherous ally who plotted mischief against us, or
some neighbour whose flagrant misrule disturbed our tranquility. When forbearance had reached its limits, we were constrained to reduce to subjection those disorderly powers, in the
hope that beyond the territory which we now absorbed we
might gain the blessing of a settled frontier. Thus, about the
time of Waterloo, we subdued the Goorkhas, a fierce people
who had been deemed almost unconquerable, and whose conquest now gave us a resting-place on the Himalayas. The
Pindarees came next—a banditti rather than a nation—who
swept over the land, plundering, slaying, torturing. These
savages were now effectively quelled, to their own advantage
and that of all who were near them. Across the Bay of
Bengal, a long series of differences with the Burmese
government seemed at length to leave no alternative   1824
but war. We conquered the Burmese, and annexed   A. D.
part of their territory in that still unsuccessful search after a
quiet frontier. Influenced by a prevailing jealousy of Russia,
it seemed to us needful to depose the rule of Afghanistan, and set up in his room a claimant better affected to   1839
ourselves. We reached Cabul; we established the prince   A. A.
whom we favoured; we placed besides him a political resident

to direct his policy.   But we did not provide a force adequate
to hold the position we had taken, and the ill-judged expedition
was closed by a catastrophe unparalleled in British his-
Jan.   tory.   A retreat was ordered, and four thousand soldiers,
1842   ill-supplied with food . and ammunition, and bur-
A. D. dened with the presence of a multitude of camp-follow-
ers, sought to regain friendly territory.   Only one man accomplished the terrible march.   The rest perished of cold and hunger, or by the sword, excepting a few who fell into the hands
of the enemy.   A new expedition retrieved in some measure
this disaster, and retook Cabul—only, however, to evacuate it
and leave Afghanistan to its habitual anarchy.

As one of the results of our reverse in the north-west, it was
found that the princes of Scinde proposed, by murder or otherwise, to remove all Englismen from that province.   Sir Charles
Napier was sent with a small army to reduce those reprobate
potentates to a wholesome subjection.   At Meeanee he encountered, with two thousand four hundred men, an
1843   enemy of thirty-five thousand, and defeated them with
A. D. heavy slaughter.   A few months later another victory
at Hyderabad completed the conquest, and Scinde was formally absorbed into British territory.   The government of the
native princes had been exceptionally wicked.   Villages by
the score were burned down to leave room for hunting-
grounds.   Every form of property which could be tracked out
was wrested from its unhappy owner.   Men rendered desperate by wrong wandered in robber bands over the land, perfecting the ruin which the government had begun.   The province
was constantly scoured by famine.   After a few years of
Napier's rule, Scinde had a surplus of grain over the supply of
its own wants, and actually became an exporter.   The robbers
returned to honest pursuits, population increased, and the
rescued people entered gladly upon a career of secure and
prosperous industry.

Yet further: disturbances arose among the Sikhs of the

Punjab, and an army was sent to the frontier to restore order. The Sikhs, nothing daunted, advanced to meet us on our own territory. We had never met before, on Indian soil, foemen so worthy. The battle of Moodkee closed indecisively. That of Ferozeshah lasted for two days. When evening fell of the first day, the British scarcely held their ground, and the victory of the second did not prevent the Sikhs from making an orderly retreat. At Aliwal and Sobraon we were decisively victorious, and the enemy submitted. It had been hoped that the annexation of the Punjab might be unnecessary, and the experiment of a protectorate had been tried. This experiment was now held to have failed, and the Punjab was added to the British possessions.

1848
A.D.

1849
A.D.

Last of all came the absorption of the kingdom of Oude. For fifty years we had upheld the throne of Oude. But the government became so intolerably vicious that the population fled from the extortion which made their lives bitter, and this rich province was lapsing into wilderness. The revenue was habitually collected by armed men, infantry and artillery. In two years eleven thousand persons had been murdered. By proclamation of the governor-general, the pernicious rule of the native princes was terminated, and the government of the province assumed by the British.

1856
A.D.

Our Indian Empire was now completed. We had reached the great natural boundary of the Himalayan mountains. Britain ruled a territory equal in area to that of all Europe, excepting Russia, and yielding a revenue of thirty-one million sterling. Her own subiects numbered one hundred and ninety million, and tnere were besides these four hundred and fifty tributary states, containing a population of fifty million, under her guidance. The prosaic enterprise of a few London merchants was now a great empire—magnificent beyond the wildest dream of romance. Upon no people before had there devolved a heritage so glorious, responsibilities so vast. But we were to pass out of the era of conquest into that of peaceful progress by the gateway of a sharp and lamentable trial.

British rule, notwithstanding its manifold errors, had been eminently beneficent, and the natives were wise enough to perceive that life was more desirable now than it had been in the days of their fathers. There is no reason to believe that there existed among them any widespread dissatisfaction with the government which had brought them the novel enjoyment of security to life and property. But the Mohammedans hated us, of necessity, with the fierce hatred which their religion inspires. The Hindus feared our interference with the faith to which they were devoted. It was believed that the British meditated the forcible conversion of all their subjects to Christianity. Already we had forbidden some observances to which they attached religious significance. Human sacrifices might no longer be offered to the gods. Infanticide was no longer a religious service; it had become a crime. Women could not be consumed on the funeral pile of their departed husbands. Nay, an act was now passed which removed all legal obstacles to the marriage of Hindu widows. Still more extended desecration of sacred things was generally apprehended. Our usages differed from those of the people whom we ruled. Our domestic life incurred their contempt. They could not satisfy themselves as to the religious tendency of our railways and telegraphs, and they viewed with inarticulate mistrust the vast mechanical revolution which began to develop itself on every side. Dethroned princes and Brahmans, conscious of decaying authority, did not cease to intrigue against us. And there sprang up and spread itself widely among the people the persuasion that the term of our dominion was reached, and our fall imminent. A slow aggregation of dislikes and suspicions contrary to all reason built up the catastrophe which was now at hand.

1856
A.D.

The army by which Britain maintained her authority over India was composed mainly of natives.* The early annals of the sepoy army were not without stains of mutiny and massacre and the fierce retribution of the enraged Englishmen. But for many years all had been tranquil, and the sepoy had become a proverb for fidelity to those who employed and fed him. But here also a lamentable change was in preparation. Special care had been successfully used to foster disaffection among the native soldiers. Their superstition was cunningly appealed to; their loyalty was sapped by prophecy and insinuation, by fear of our profane innovations, by promise of advantage from our fall. Sir Charles Napier had given warning of the changed temper of the troops, and since his time other officers had perceived and reported the same ominous indications. The soldiers had ceased to manifest the accustomed deference to their officers. Occasionally they objected to some descriptions of service; occasionally they refused; frequently they made stipulations with their officers. The officers, widely separated from the soldiers by diverse customs, faith, and language, knew little of the character and power of those mysterious influences by which the men were becoming visibly deteriorated. But enough was known to awaken grave apprehensions of impending calamity.

At the opening of 1857 it was well understood that discontent and alarm existed in the army, and that everywhere fallen native dignitaries intrigued busily to compass the expulsion of the invaders. But the British, confident in their strength and their honesty of purpose, went calmly on their course, trusting that untoward symptoms would disappear as they had done before. The expectation was not unreasonable, and might well have been fulfilled but for the occurrence of circumstances which maddened the sepoys with fear, and carried them hopelessly beyond restraint or control.

* The sepoys in the company's service when the mutiny occurred numbered two hundred and thirty thousand; the Europeans forty-five thousand.

Hitherto the Indian troops had been armed with no better
weapon than the smooth-bore musket. It was now determined
to substitute for that antiquated contrivance the Enfield rifle.
The sepoys hailed with a soldier's joy the increased efficacy of
their arms. But in order to secure accuracy of aim it was
needful that the cartridge should fit tightly to the grooved barrel, and without lubrication the tightly-fitting cartridge could
not be easily rammed home. In the government factories animal
fat was the lubricant employed. This seemingly trivial detail
became known, and the knowledge spread among the troops
with extraordinary rapidity. It thrilled the dusky legions with
horror such as they had never known before. The Mohammedan perceived that he must in future defile his lips with the
fat of the abhorred swine. The Hindue perceived that he   .
must offer indignity to the venerated cow. The worst fears of
all were confirmed; the English government had planned the
destruction of caste, the overthrow of the native religions, the
fraudulent conversion of the people to the faith of the white
man. The sepoy was in presence of a revolution which was, to   .
him, of terrible significance. He and his children were in danger of losing religion and social position—their place both in this
'world and that which is to come. When he returned to his
native village his friends would disown him as a recreant. A
great fear had fallen upon him, under the influence of which
deeds of abject foolishness and of savage cruelty became possible.
The governor-general sought to allay the growing agitation by
assurances that no evil had been intended. The offensive cartridges were not served out, and the men were suffered to apply
with their own hands a lubricant of whose integrity they were
able to satisfy themselves. But reason had no longer power
over the excited soldiery. The wildest rumors were eagerly
received. It was believed that animal fat was used in the
manufacture of paper for the cartridges. It was believed that
flour was served out mixed with the bones of the cow ground

to powder. Confidence in the government was gone. Every feeling of loyalty and fidelity, every memory of ancient kindness, every sentiment of soldierly honor had perished. Nothing remained but hatred and fear of the white men and their unholy devices.

The men who sought advantage by the overthrow of British power hastened to avail themselves of the great opportunity. The dethroned king of Oude pressed upon the discontented sepoys offers of a lucrative service under the standard which he hoped soon to raise. Nana Sahib, the heir of a dispossessed prince who had long been a pensioner of the government, had failed to obtain a renewal of the lapsed inheritance, and sought to avenge himself by organizing a hostile combination of aggrieved chiefs. At first he met with little encouragement, but now he redoubled his diligence, and his overtures were widely accepted. Everywhere it was believed that the British rule would, as the old prediction ran, pass away at the close of a hundred years from its establishment.

The greatness of the danger was first disclosed at Meerut, where the native regiments slaughtered their officers and many European ladies and children. At Delhi the same horrors were perpetrated, and the deposed king raised his standard over the ancient palace of the Mogul. Before May closed the soldiers had mutinied at twenty-two stations in the Bengal presidency, everywhere murdering, without discrimination, all Europeans who fell into their hands. At Cawnpore there was committed a crime of appalling magnitude and baseness which will hold for ever a foremost place in the annals of human guilt. A force of revolted sepoys directed by the Nana Sahib besieged Cawnpore, which was held against them by General Wheeler and the Europeans * who were with him. When a bombardment of twenty days had been endured, and one hundred brave men had fallen, a

May 10, 1857 A. D.

* About three hundred fighting men.

capitulation was agreed to, by the terms of which the besieged were allowed to leave Cawnpore. They reached the boats; some were in the act of embarking, others were settling quietly to their oars, when suddenly from every side there opened upon them a fire of musketry and artillery. In a few minutes half of the little party were killed or wounded. The others were seized and carried back to Cawnpore, where the men were at once shot. The ladies and children, in number two hundred and six, were held captive in a large apartment which had been used as an assembly room. Eighteen days later five men armed with sabres were seen in the twilight to approach the building. They entered the room and quietly closed the door. Shrieks were heard and low groans, and the sound of blows as the savages hewed to death the unresisting women and little children who filled the room. Thrice a hacked and blunted sabre was passed out, and a sharper weapon received in exchange. Next morning the mutilated bodies were dragged forth and cast into a huge well. When, two days, after, the avenging English, under General Havelock, reached Cawnpore, the blood of the victims still lay on the stone pavement of the hall; fragments of ladies' and children's dresses, soaked in blood, were scattered all around. The traces of this foul crime filled the men with horror, and steeled their hearts for the work of relentless vengeance to which England was now committed.

British dominion in India was shaken to its foundations. The governor-general, Lord Canning, recognized the greatness of the peril, and braced himself to maintain the empire which Clive had gained a hundred years ago. All British troops were gathered up from the other presidencies and hurried to the revolted north. A few regiments on their way eastward to inflict chastisement on the offending Chinese, were turned aside to the more urgent work of saving India. A petty war with Persia had been opportunely closed by the submission of he enemy, and the returning troops were available for immediate service. A little later on the sufficient help which had been called for from England was sure to come. On the final result no doubt rested, but many weeks of difficulty and lamentable suffering must first be endured.

The dark period during which the mutineers were free to work their evil pleasure came quickly to a close. The British, weak in respect of numbers, but mighty in their personal supremacy and the just wrath which burned in every heart, went forth to the reconquest of India. Within two months from the first outburst of mutiny a little army July 7, 1857 A. D. set out from Allahabad. It numbered two thousand men, and it was under the command of General Havelock, one of the noblest example of the Christian soldier of which even the Indian army can boast. General Havelock was a veteran of forty years' service, and till now it had not fallen to him to enjoy an independent command. His career approached its close, and the high soldierly qualities with which he was endowed were still unrevealed. But now, even at the close, there came the opportunity for which his soul thirsted. Only a few months of life were left, but these sufficed to gain for him a foremost place among soldiers, and to earn the enduring gratitude of his countrymen.

Cawnpore had fallen before Havelock's march began. For several weeks the affairs of the province had been administered in name of the Nana Sahib, but there was no semblance of effective government. The emancipated ruffianism of the district, associating itself with bands of mutinied sepoys, roamed at large over the country, plundering, burning, murdering. The army passed many villages which had been destroyed, and some towns wholly deserted by their inhabitants. The quietness and security which the strong government of the foreigners bestowed had wholly disappeared, and in their place had come back, at one stride, the old reign of violence and disorder. Everywhere the English perceived evidence

16

of the hatred with which they were regarded. Their churches were laboriously desecrated; their telegraphs were destroyed; their locomotives were battered with cannon-shot; their very milestones were dug out or defaced. It was the dream of the rebels that English authority was subverted. Their concern now was to obliterate every memorial which recalled the detested supremacy of the strangers.

The Nana had large forces at his disposal, amply supplied with the artillery of which he had been able to possess himself.

July 17, 1857 A. D. Thrice he met the avenging British, and thrice he sustained bloody defeat. Havelock entered Cawnpore, chasing away the disheartened rebels. The Nana himself disappeared, and no diligence of search was ever able to bring him to the punishment which his unparalleled crime had earned.

Havelock had no leisure to bestow upon the triumph which he had gained. At a distance of forty miles, in the city of Lucknow, a small and diminishing band of Englishmen held, with the courage of despair, a position which competent military authority would have declared to be utterly untenable. Lucknow was the capital of Oude, and contained a population of nearly three quarters of a million. Oude, the latest of our acquisitions had wholly risen against us. We had not gained the favour of our new subjects, notwithstanding the benefit we brought them. Certain taxes which we imposed were highly distasteful. That influential class who profited by the vices of the old government were earnestly hostile to the new. The great land-owners, whose crimes had been flagrant and whose reputation was exceedingly bad, had been ruthlessly overthrown, and now thirsted for restoration and revenge. The king's disbanded army was a formidable weapon ready to the hand of the evil-disposed.

Sir Henry Lawrence, one of the many Christian heroes and strong wise men whose names adorn the annals of our Indian administration, was then chief commissioner of Oude. He was not attacked at once, and he had time to make some preparation for resistance. By the end of June the little garrison of Lucknow, with a large dependency of English ladies and children, were gathered into the Residency. Around them on every side swarmed a savage enemy eager for their blood. From every available point artillery, served by the men we ourselves had trained, played without ceasing upon our crumbling defences. One or two days after the siege began a shell burst close to Sir Henry Lawrence, and wounded him so that he died. The fire of the enemy searched every corner of the building, and the losses sustained by the garrison told fearfully upon their strength. The heat was excessive, and the mortality of children and of wounded men were very great. Every privation was patiently endured; every danger was bravely faced. But the time was too plainly at hand when failing supplies and loss of life in battle must bring the heroic defence to a terrible close.

During the three months of agony through which the imprisoned British passed they looked continually for help from without, and they were sustained by occasional intima- Sept. 25. tions that Havelock was fighting his way to their deliv- 1857 erance. At length there came a day when in the streets A. D. of the city people were seen thronging about in visible excitement—some with bundles in their hand, as if in contemplation of immediate flight. And then, too, it was seen with joy beyond expression, that the fire of the besiegers was in part turned against an enemy approaching from without. Finally, British soldiers were seen fighting their way toward the Residency, and Havelock's relieving army was hailed with tears and shouts of welcome by the men and women whom it came to save. Havelock secured the safety of his besieged countrymen, but he could not yet secure their escape. The rebels, through whose swarms he had cleft a path, closed again around the Residency, and the siege continued. Two months later Sir Colin Campbell reached Lucknow with a force of five thou-

sand men. Many of his soldiers had seen the well of Cawnpore, and the just wrath which its horrors kindled nerved every
arm and steeled every heart. Sir Colin forced his way to the
Residency with fearful slaughter of rebels, and removed in
safety all the females and children who had been so long shut
up there. He had scarcely left when Havelock was seized with
dysentery, and died—worn out by the labours of those five
terrible months during which he had served his country so
well.

After the massacre at Meerut the mutinous sepoys fled at
once to Delhi, as if fearing instant retribution for their crime.
Delhi was the capital of the Mogul empire, and the feeble old
man who was nominally the successor of Timour had his residence there. The native troops of Delhi sympathized with
May 11, those who came from Meerut. All the English resi-
1857 dent in the city, civilians and soldiers alike, were murd-
A. D. ered, or fled for their lives out into the jungle. The
king was prevailed upon to raise the standard of his
house, and the outbreak which at Meerut was only a mutiny
assumed at Delhi the immeasurably graver aspect of a rebellion headed by the king.

The flight of the mutineers from Meerut left available for
service elsewhere a small force of British infantry and dragoons. After some delay this brigade was marched on
May 27. Delhi. A week later it was joined by a force sent from
Umballah. The sepoys came out from the city to meet the
advancing enemy, and twice sustained bloody defeat. And then
the British took firm hold of a ridge which commanded Delhi,
where they made for themselves a position impregnable to any
force the king could send against it. They were yet too weak
to attack the city. Indeed, they were themselves subjected to
the continual attack of greatly superior forces during the three
months which passed while they waited for additional strength.
It was not till August closed that they had guns to breach the
walls and men to storm the city. The artillery quickly opened

access to British troops burning to meet the despised and abhorred enemy. All the lamentable occurences of a storm— in the indiscriminate slaughter of the guilty and the innocent together—darkened, inevitably, the great triumph. The defence ceased, and the enemy fled. The old king was taken prisoner. Three princes of his house after being captured were shot dead by a bold captain of English cavlary. The British flag waved once more over the city of the Mogul. The rebellion was beaten down in the very centre of its power, and a great fear of the terrible British now filled the minds of those who but a little while ago had been rejoicing in the expectation of our final overthrow. *Sept. 20, 1857 A. D.*

Lucknow was still in rebel hands, although a strong English force held securely the Residency. Once more Sir Colin Campbell advanced with a force sufficient to quell resistance and complete his conquest of the revolted capital. This time the work was done thoroughly and with enormous bloodshed. Oude was forced back to her subjection. *Mar. 22, 1858 A. D.*

In central India the rebels still held their ground. But the force of the insurrection was now well-nigh expended, and the troops which England eagerly supplied found employment in trampling out the disheartened and hopeless resistance which was still on foot. Sir Hugh Rose besieged Jhansi, and took it by a storm which cost many rebels lives. Some weeks later Gwalior fell, and the war was over. There was no longer an enemy in the field. Here and there small bands of mutineers wandered over the country, but these were quickly exterminated or chased over the frontier into Nepaul, and order was finally restored. *April 1,* *June 19,*

From the first outburst of the mutiny the English determined upon a policy of merciless retribution towards the offenders. The governor-general telegraphed to his commander-in-chief to make a terrible example of Delhi. 'No amount of severity can be too great," were his words. " I will support you in any degree of it." *May 23, 1857 A. D.*

These stern instructions expressed the universal feeling.   The
slaughter by mutinous soldiers of so many unoffending persons
filled every heart with wrath unutterable.   The English,
rejoicing in their conscious superiority, had been habitually
arrogant, overbearing, contemptuous.   Now, when the despised
natives turned upon them, their rage knew no bounds.   As
the relieving forces passed northwards, the soldiers made strict
search for guilty persons, on whom they might express the
wrath which burned within them.   A native suspected of cruelty to a British fugitive was hanged without formality of
trial.   The soldiers did not scruple to prick with the bayonet
the wretches whom they were about to execute.   It was
gravely proposed by officers high in command that torture
should be inflicted on natives guilty of murder; and there is no
reason to doubt that to some extent, although not largely, this
was actually done.   Power was given to civil officers to inflict
death without judicial procedure.   Mutinied sepoys, when
captured, were hung in groups upon any convenient tree, or
were fastened to the muzzle of cannon whose discharge shat-
Mar. 3, tered their bodies into fragments.   A proclamation of
1858   the governor-general confiscated all lands in Oude
A. D.   whose proprietors had not aided the British.

While India was still in process of being reconquered, Lord
Palmerston introduced into the House of Commons a
Feb. 9.   bill vesting in the crown the government of our great
dependency.   Hitherto the East India Company had shared
in the exercise of political functions for which, by its origin
and character, it was wholly unqualified.   This inconvenient
partition was now to cease, and the government of India was
in future to be conducted by a minister responsible to public
opinion and to Parliament.

When the restoration of order was complete, and punishment,
which did not err on the side of leniency, had been inflicted on
its violators, England resumed her efforts for the elevation of

the Indian people and the development of the boundless resources amidst which they lived. Much as there had been to
regret and to blame in her administration, England had always
sought the good of the subject races. Her zeal grew warmer
now after she was so fearfully reminded of the errors of her
government. She applied herself with a noble earnestness to
the vast and fruitful labour of raising the condition of the
Indian people. Her efforts have been sustained and their scope
widened as the years have passed. She has striven to educate,
to afford adequate protection to life and property, to save from
the ravages of disease, a people helpless for their own defence;
to draw out the vast wealth of the soil, to open up the country
by the construction of railways and roads, to lay the foundations of a system of self-government under which the India of
the future may become capable of guiding her own destinies.
And although the work accomplished bears an insignificant
proportion to that which remains, yet has a progress been
made most beneficent in itself and rich in its encouragement of
future effort.

Government fosters "every kind of education, from the
highest to the lowest." In especial it aims to bring the whole
of the poorest classes under instruction. The gigantic enterprise is yet only at its beginning. In Bengal, for example,
the government expenditure on schools is only £400,000, and
the attendance, composed wholly of boys, is no more than
twelve in every thousand of the population. But year after
year marks a steady if not a very rapid increase. The education
of females is at length receiving some attention. The great
majority of the people still see more harm than good in the
education of women, but among the higher classes the education of girls is eagerly desired. In this new and delicate task
the missionaries and their wives achieve greater success than
it is possible for the government to reach. The desire for an
English education is universally prevalent among the better

class. The universities are attended by increasing numbers.
Schools of art, medical and engineering colleges are largely
resorted to. The supply of teachers in the primary schools is
of course utterly inadequate, and the quality of the teaching
is often very inferior. The establishment of normal schools
will gradually alleviate this evil. In literature the native mind
shows some activity. The press of Bombay sends forth
annually four hundred to five hundred original works and sixty
to seventy newspapers.

A commencement has been made in preparing the people
of India, by municipal self-government, for those larger
political functions which ultimately they will be called to exercise. As yet the experiment is new, and it extends to a very
inconsiderable number of persons. In the capitals of the three
presidencies, and in a few hundred towns and cities besides, the
people elect their own rulers. In the capitals a moderate
degree of interest is evinced; elsewhere the privilege is little
understood or regarded. In Lucknow, at a recent election,
only seven votes were recorded. The initiation of an Oriental
people in the exercise of governing functions is exceedingly
slow. But the desire will grow with the fitness which increasing intelligence confers.

A large and reasonably efficient police force gives increasing
security to life and property. The police-officers are wofully
ignorant. In Bengal more than one-half of the men are
wholly without any pretext of education, and they blunder
vexatiously in the discharge of their duties. But year by year
this evil diminishes under the encouragement which government affords to the educated policeman. Local gentlemen are
admitted to participate in the administration of justice—a dis-
tinction which is eagerly desired. The care of youthful
criminals is being provided for by the establishment of reform-
atories and industrial schools. In the Punjab a steady increase
of civil actions is observed—an appeal to law coming now in

place of the violence by which sufferers formerly righted their own wrong, or of the despairing silence in which they submitted to it. Crime is gradually decreasing over the larger portion of India. The traditional crime of the Hindu races, the slaughter of female infants, lingers tenaciously in some districts, notwithstanding the watchfulness of the magistrates. But the extent to which it is now practised is very limited and constantly lessening.

Government is owner of the greater portion of Indian soil, and one-third of its revenue is rent of land. Many embarrassing questions have arisen out of this relationship. It is needful to provide for the cultivator a tenure which he shall seem secure, along with a rent which he shall not deem oppressive or inequitable. This has not been found an easy work, and a perpetually recurring controversy rages between landlord and tenants as to the proportion which the former ought to receive of the gross produce of the land. But the desire of the government is sincere,—to foster the prosperity of the people and secure their good-will, and their efforts in that direction have met with a reasonable amount of success. Rents are collected promptly and with little pressure. It is obvious that a large increase of prosperity has been experienced by the classes who are engaged in agriculture. Very much has been done by the government to stimulate the intelligent cultivation of the soil. Model farms, schools of agriculture, and agricultural shows have been established, and are fairly successful. Selected seeds have been liberally distributed to all who applied for them. Experiments are constantly in progress with the purpose of ascertaining by what methods of sowing and manuring the amplest yield may be extracted from the soil. The agricultural implements of India are still strangely rude, and the efforts of government to introduce more effective appliances have not yet produced very marked results. The gigantic work of a first survey of all India has been in progress for many years, and now approaches com-

pletion. Year by year the area under cultivation increases,
and live stock continues to multiply and to improve in quality.

In central India something is being done in the mining of
coal. But here the labour difficulty has proved to be very
serious. The work is too severe for the liking of the natives,
who, moreover, have not yet overcome their timid reluctance
to descend into the bowels of the earth.

The foreign trade of India, including both imports and
exports, exceeds one hundred million annually. The amount
is steadily, although for some years not rapidly, increasing.
The chief increase in exports is in grain, tea, and tobacco, all
of which articles are rising to importance. The prosaic trade
returns which the government furnishes tell, in regard to many
of the provinces, a tale of most impressive and romantic interest.
Twenty years ago Oude was wasted by evil government, till
the miserable inhabitants fled away into other states, and the
country was lapsing into wilderness. To-day Oude supplies
liberally her own wants, and conducts a foreign trade of three
million sterling. Scinde, equally oppressed and impoverished,
has a foreign trade of two million. The warlike Sikhs have
laid down their arms and betaken them to more profitable employment. The annual dealings of the Punjab with the outside world amount to twenty million; those of British Burmah
to nine million. The vast and beneficent revolutions which
these figures express stand alone in the rapidity of the steps
by which great populations have been raised from the extremity of wretchedness to the enjoyment of solid although
humble well-being.

The Indian government has expended large sums on works
fitted to quicken the development of the country. In seasons
of drought only copious irrigation can save the thirsty soil from
barrenness and the population from famine. Large canals and
reservoirs are being constantly constructed, in which the super-
fluous water of the rainy season is stored against the day of

need. India is being opened up by means of communication hitherto unknown. Stately bridges span her great rivers. New roads cut though pathless jungles connect districts whose separation had been absolute. Above all, seven thousand miles of railway have been opened for traffic, and India is aided in rising out of her barbarism by an agency which other nations gained only as the result of years of civilization. The people avail themselves of the railways in sufficient numbers to yield a net revenue of three or four per cent., although the fares go down as low as to one farthing per mile.

Persevering efforts are made to protect from disease a population wholly ignorant of sanitary laws, and living in a climate peculiarly favourable to the prevalence of epidemics. Cholera, small-pox, and malarial fevers waste Indian life to a lamentable extent. The death-rate of Calcutta is thirty-five per thousand, while that of London is only twenty per thousand. Small-pox admits of more direct control than the other leading types of Indian disease. The government employs a great army of vaccinators, who are constantly in the field. Native prejudice is always at the outset very intense and often almost invincible. There is a goddess of small-pox, whose rights it is profane to invade, and in whose territory the death-rate is very high. Elsewhere vaccination gradually makes way, and the mortality from small-pox is being stayed. Considerable progress is being made in the drainage of cities. Lunatics are being gathered into asylums. Medical schools for the training of native doctors are very successful. An attempt to make female doctors signally failed. The pupils did very well, and were extremely promising. But in the East women do not enjoy the consideration which is necessary to the successful prosecution of a learned calling. No one would employ a female doctor.

The revenue of India is sixty million sterling. Fully one-third of this sum is furnished by rent of lands. A sum of eight to nine million is gained by a tax on the opium which we force the Chinese government to admit. Six million is received from a salt monopoly—a source of revenue as indefensible on economical as the opium-tax is on moral grounds.

The progress of India is evidenced by the increased demand for postal communication. During the ten years which followed 1866 the number of letters and newspapers which passed through the post-office was doubled. India, however, is not yet a land of newspapers. The number which passes annually through the post office is no more than ten million copies.

England maintains her possession of the great Indian peninsula by an army of one hundred and ninety thousand men, of whom sixty-six thousand are British and the others native. The British-born civilians who represent the authority of England amidst this vast population number sixty-two thousand. About one hundred and twenty thousand British soldiers and civilians govern a population which, if we include the tributary states, amounts to two hundred and forty million. England has undertaken to rescue from the debasement of ages that enormous multitude of human beings. No enterprise of equal greatness was ever engaged in by any people. Generations will pass away while it is still in progress, but its final success cannot be frustrated. We who watch it in its early stage see mainly imperfections. Posterity will look only upon the majestic picture of a vast and utterly barbaric population, numbering well-nigh one-fourth of the human family, subdued, governed, educated, Christianized, and led up to the dignity of a free and self-governing nation by a handful of strangers who came from an inconsiderable island fifteen thousand miles away.

CHAPTER XII.

OUR COLONIES.

NTIL the vast commercial expansion of recent years, the population of Great Britain was obviously in excess of the means of subsistence. Employment was often difficult to be obtained; wages were scanty; food was scarce. To aggravate the evil, the country refused to receive food from abroad, and men were suffered to go fasting in time of peace, lest they should become dependent on foreign supplies, and so be obliged to starve in time of war. An isolated, self-sufficing national life was the prevailing idea, and a relationship with foreign countries hostile when it was not neutral. In Britain were multitudes of half-employed, half-famished men and women. Beyond the sea were continents of rich land lying unused by man. The idle people and the waste lands had merely to be brought together, and the giant evil of the time would be redressed. But this expedient was too simple and natural to be readily adopted.

During the earlier years of the century there was so little emigration that in 1815 only two thousand persons quit.ed the kingdom. From that time, when peace had been restored with America, and increase of misery came as the result of the long European war, the tendency to emigrate grew in strength year by year. In 1852 it had reached its great maximum of three hundred and sixty-eight thousand. During the sixty years beginning with 1815, seven and a quarter million of persons have left the British Islands to find homes beyond the sea. Of these, the larger proportion, probably three-fourths, have passed away from British citizenship and settled in the great republic. The remainder have gone to our own colonies.

While the thirteen American states were still dependencies, England was in the practice of sending a few of her convicts there. Occasionally political offenders were disposed of thus, but more frequently they were mere vulgar criminals who were sent. The war of independence stopped this convenient outlet, at the same time that the wretchedness which that war caused stimulated the increase of criminals. The efforts of John Howard had disclosed the insufficiency of prison accommodation. Some new method of disposing of criminals had to be found.

1788
A. D.
England had just taken possession of a huge territory, to which the name of New South Wales was given, and she determined to send her criminals there. For half a century this unwholesome practice was continued, and the foundations of new empires in the Southern Seas were laid by the very refuse of the population. Colonization became in consequence discredited. Reputable people would not take up their abode in a land whose inhabitants had for the most part committed grave crimes.

In course of years, as the colonies increased in strength, the honest inhabitants refused to allow their territory to be longer defiled by the convicted ruffianism of the parent state.

1846
A. D.
The idea of convict settlements abroad was finally abandoned. Colonization recovered its respectability, and the stream of immigration assumed at once important dimensions.

The largest of our colonial possessions are on the North American continent, where we rival in area the great republic itself. The dominion of Canada is destined in process of years to become a powerful empire;* but thus far her progress is

---

* It is probable that the progress of Canada in the future will be greatly more rapid than it has been in the past. A few years ago the Dominion of Canada acquired from the Hudson Bay Company a territory situated far in the north-west, and covering an

extremely inferior to that of the states which touch her frontier on the south. As yet she bears a population little larger than that of London, scattered over an area greater than that of all Europe. She has never been able to make herself so attractive to men of quest of a new home as the United States, and even as the Australian colonies do. Of late, few persons have left the mother country for Canada,* and even of these a considerable proportion cross the frontier, and settle finally in the United States. For the number of her people, Canada maintains an important foreign commerce. She supplies the world with grain, timber, and other products of her soil; receiving in exchange the iron manufactures and textile fabrics of Europe. Her exports are sixteen million sterling; her imports, nineteen million. So free are the colonies to frame their own commercial arrangements, that not more than one-half of this trade is done with the mother country.

The extension by Great Britain of her dominion over vast subjugated populations is without parallel in the history of the human family. She bears rule over fully one-seventh of the surface of the globe and one-fourth of its population. Her possessions abroad are in area sixty times larger than the parent state. She owns three million and a half of square miles in America, one million each in Africa and Asia, and two and a half million in Australasia. These enormous acquisitions area equal to three-fourths of that of Europe. This enormous region proves to be of marvellous fertility. Cultivated plants are said to attain their maximum of productiveness near the extreme northern limit of growth. The production of wheat in Manitoba illustrates this natural law. In the valley of the Mississippi the average yield of wheat is fourteen bushels per ac e. The soil of Manitoba yields forty bushels under careless tillage, and without the application of manure. During the last two or three years the capabilities of this magnificent region have begun to attract attention to such an extent that last year three million acres were put for the first time under cultivation. The inflow of settlers continues to increase. As yet railway and river communication is inadequate, but it is being rapidly extended. In the not remote future a large population may occupy the vast and fertile plains which lie around Lake Winnipeg; Britain may draw her supplies of grain mainly from her own dependency; and Canada may rise to importance and authority by the development of the boundless resources which have been intrusted to her.

* In 1875, the emigrants from the United Kingdom to the North American colonies numbered only seventeen thousand three hundred and seventy-eight.

have been grained chiefly within the last hundred years.
There are thirty-eight separate colonies or groups of colonies—varying in area from Gibraltar with its two miles,
to Canada with three million and a half.   Their population aggregates eleven million,* and continues steadily to
increase.   At one time they were all governed in London,
and it was held that they existed solely for the advantage of
the parent state.   But all this has been long abandoned.   In
all colonies where self-government is possible, the colonists
elect their own parliament, ordinarily by universal suffrage.
The chief executive officer is a governor appointed by the crown.

Our important colonies have almost ceased to be burdensome to us, as they now bear the charges of their own government and defence.   They have also ceased to be specially
advantageous to us, and they do not scruple to impose protective duties upon our products when it seems good to them.   In
an age when the lust of territorial conquest has died out, they
do not require that our strength should guarantee them against
invasion.   The connection has ceased to be of political value.
But so long as a perfectly good understanding exists between
the mother country and those of her children who are building up new empires abroad, so long the alliance will be a source
of pleasure to both.   When it ceases to be agreeable to either,
its discontinuance will be unattended with difficulty.   The vast
folly of 1776 will not be repeated.

* Our smallest settlement is the island of Ascension, with a population of sixteen
males and eleven females.   The destinies of Ascension are controlled by a governor
appointed by the crown.

Book Third.

CHAPTER I.

FRANCE: THE RESTORED MONARCHY.

THE condition of France after the overthrow of Napoleon was miserable beyond anything which the experience of modern Europe presented. Although the defeat of Waterloo visibly closed the war, and left France without the means of further resistance, the armies of the allies continued their advance. Nearly every European nation was represented in this majestic scene of triumph and of vengeance. British, Russians, Austrians, Prussians, Belgians, Italians, Bavarians, Saxons, Hungarians, Hanoverians, Spaniards—all combined to humiliate the unhappy people from whose merciless hand they had all endured injuries so deep. The tide of armed men did not cease to flow into France till there were eleven hundred thousand foreign soldiers within her territory. All these had to be maintained by France. Indemnities amounting to sixty million sterling were exacted by the allies, and untold sums were rung from the defenceless people by the half-savage hordes of unrestrained soldiery. The remnants of Nopoleon's army were disbanded. A foreign army of one hundred and fifty thousand men, commanded by the Duke of Wellington, was for five years to maintain order, and preserve the stability, if not the dignity, of the restored dy-

17 257

nasty—France bearing the heavy cost of this occupation.
Taxation could not be collected, for the exactions of foreigners
left to the people nothing beyond the barest subsistence. The
miseries of the fallen nation were deep, abject, unutterable.

And yet it cannot justly be said that the allies were unreasonable in the severities which they inflicted. The territory
of France was suffered to remain undiminished from its extent
in 1792. The works of art of which Napoleon had plundered
the galleries of conquered states were reclaimed, but nothing
to which France had any just title was withdrawn. And
huge as were the pecuniary exactions which the allies levied,
they bore a small proportion to the sums which Napoleon
had wrung from his victims during the years of his ruthless
supremacy.

Nothing in France is more wonderful than her power of
recovery. Her miseries had been unexampled. In 1815 she
was utterly defenceless; her army was extinct; her soil was
held by her bitterest enemies; the strength of her population
had perished in war; her trade was destroyed; the enormous
demands of her conquerors drained the remnants of her substance. Her five per cent. funds were selling at fifty-seven; a
forced loan was resorted to in order to meet the most urgent
liabilities. In 1816, as if to bestow upon her sorrows the last enhancement of which they were susceptible, the harvest was exceedingly deficient, and prices ranged up to famine level. Government was obliged to sell grain at reduced rates to avert widespread mortality among the poor. Three years later, and the
sun was again shining on poor wasted France. Her trade had
largely increased; her agriculture had become greatly more productive; the claims of her conquerors had been satisfied, and
their forces withdrawn even before the period fixed by treaty.
She was again a respectable military power, and was beginning
to regain her lost consideration among the nations. France had
thrown off her gloom. The wealth of her soil, and the patient,

cheerful industry of her people, had already in great measure restored her fallen fortunes.

The Bourbons, returning to France in the train of the conquerors, were forcibly restored to the high place from which the nation had flung them a quarter of a century before. It seemed probable that they would become in consequence a symbol of defeat and humiliation to a large portion of the people. But fickleness, as the French historian* feels bound to acknowledge, is the vice of the nation. France suffers from an instability "more sudden and prodigious" than that which characterizes the movements of public opinion among any other modern race. This quality of mind made the restoration easy, and prepared for the Bourbons a reception which was embarrassing only by its extravagant warmth. Every family had suffered bereavement; every interest had sustained intolerable loss; every political party,—republican, royalist, and liberal,—had seen its cherished beliefs ruthlessly trampled down; every town and village had endured the presence of a triumphant invader, and had groaned beneath the weight of his merciless exactions. And now, by a universal impulse, these sorrows were avenged on Napoleon. A "paroxysm of anger burst from every heart" against the fallen chief, the glories of whose career had so lately been the pride of France. The French people accepted with eagerness the refuge offered to them from the destructive and now abhorred rule of Napoleon. They elected a legislative chamber which was more royalist than the king himself. The first care of this body was to enact laws of a severely repressive character for the protection of the restored government against the wiles of the disaffected. A cry seditious or insulting to the king was punished by prolonged imprisonment. It was a capital offence to display the flag under which Napoleon had led his soldiers to victory. Individual liberty was placed, without limitation, in the power of the police. The king viewed

* Lamartine.

these severities with just disfavour; but the flaming loyalty of
the deputies refused to be modified.   In the southern provinces
the reaction assumed a still darker aspect, and numerous mur-
ders of Bonapartists, and of Protestants suspected of sympathies
with the fallen cause, stained the skirts of the restoration.

Louis XVIII. was in his sixtieth year when he ascended the
throne from which Napoleon had been driven.   It was no easy
task which the old man undertook.   He had to appease the
just indignation of Europe, and negotiate peace on terms which
would not inflict undue humiliation upon France.   He had to
lead a people to whom he was unknown, and who had been
long used to the intoxication of military glory, back to the love
of peaceful industry.   He had to hold with firm and impartial
hand the balance between fiercely contending and irreconcilable factions.   He brought to the difficult work no remarkable
capacity; but he brought good sense, firmness, a kind heart,
and a disposition to conciliate.   He could read with tolerable
accuracy the time in which he lived, and adapt himself to its
requirements.   "He possessed the temperate, flexible, and
negotiating genius of restorations."   Where men greatly his
superiors would have ignominiously failed, Louis achieved a
measure of success creditable to his own skill in ruling, and
eminently advantageous to France.

But the reign of the first restored Bourbon could not be
otherwise than bitter.   The nation was humiliated; worse
than that, it was poor.   The early fervours of the restoration
passed away, and a sharp reaction set in among the unstable
people.   Those who had purchased for nominal prices, or
obtained on still easier terms, the estates of emigrants, were
suspicious and apprehensive.   The disbanded soldiers yearned
for the old excitements.   The Bonapartist faction, bereaved of
honour and emolument, missed no opportunity to promote the
general discontent.   Republican feeling, held in abeyance by
the glories of the empire, regained strength under the prosaic

Bourbon rule. The mob of Paris, disapproving highly of certain government measures, waged for days incessant war with the troops. In the provinces there occurred insurrections, which were quenched in bloodshed greatly more copious than their importance seemed to warrant. Secret societies maintained the perilous organization of revolt. The heir to the throne—the Duc de Berri—was stabbed to death by a Bonapartist fanatic, who expressed by the felon blow nothing more intelligent than the rancour and hatred which raged throughout the baffled and suffering nation. Under the influence of that same feeling, M. Decazes, the prime minister, was gravely charged in the Chamber of Deputies as an accomplice in the murder of the prince, and was driven from office by the popular belief in his guilt.

After a reign of eight years Louis XVIII. died. Those years had been unquiet, but they had not been unfruitful. Political strife did not stay the course of French industry. The French peasant ploughed and reaped; he spun and weaved; he hoarded his earnings, and soon began to feel himself passing rich. Agriculture became more intelligent; food was abundant; steamers multiplied on the rivers; the coasting trade doubled in a few years. Silk and cotton manufactures were especially prosperous — a gratifying evidence that the people were gaining an increased command of the comforts of life. The foreign trade increased by one-half. The funds, which had been so low as fifty-seven, were now one hundred and four. The revenues exceeded expenditure, owing, not to the imposition of new taxes, but to the increasing productiveness of the old. And France was again a formidable power, with an army of two hundred and fifty thousand men, and a fleet of ninety ships of the line and frigates.

The king died childless, and was succeeded by his younger brother Charles, then a man of sixty-six. Charles had spent the best years of his life in exile, but even in the school of adversity he had learned little. He was a man of pleasing and affable manners, quick of apprehension, ready and felicitous in his talk, but superficial and frivolous. He was a matchless rider, and retained to the last a boyish delight in the joys of the hunting-field. A piety sincere but unenlightened enabled the priests to gain control over his conscience, and thus to exercise disastrous influence over his policy.

His reign opened hopefully. There had been a succession of bountiful harvests, and the people were prosperous and contented. The king uttered liberal and loving sentiments; he pledged himself to rule by the charter; on the evening before he entered Paris he signed an edict releasing the press from the censorship which his brother had established. The satisfied people hailed the opening of a happier era than had ever dawned upon France.

One bold and wise measure confirmed the general hope. Till now those families which had been despoiled of their estates by the revolution had not ceased to remonstrate against the wrong which they had endured. The new possessors experienced the discomfort of insecurity. The value of all landed property was injuriously depressed by the uncertainty of the titles under which it was held. It was now resolved to silence for ever, by one great act of tardy justice, the murmurs of the disinherited, and to free the land of France from the evil of a doubtful tenure. A sum equal to forty million sterling was distributed among those whom the nation in its fury had wronged. The measure was warmly opposed in the chambers, but the general opinion of the French people approved a liberality whose justice was indisputable.

But very early in his reign it began to be whispered that the priests exercised an undue ascendency over the mind of the king. Ere long the apprehension with which the people regarded the superstitious piety of their monarch received fatal confirmation. The ministry introduced and carried a law which decreed the penalty of death as the punishment of sacrilege. The offender who profaned the sacred vessels suffered death. He who was guilty of the graver offence of profaning the consecrated wafer endured some measure of torture before he was permitted to die. The church blindly availed herself of the royal weakness to make her odious ascendency conspicuous. The streets of Paris now witnessed sacred processions, in which there walked the royal family, the great officers of state, and the members of the two chambers. Among the rest was to be seen Marshal Soult, walking with reverential mien and bearing a penitential candle in his hand. The people looked on with ill-disguised contempt. In time the rumour ran that the king himself was a Jesuit, sworn to gain for that dreaded society supreme power in France. It was certain that he appointed an avowed Jesuit one of the tutors of the heir to the throne. The confidence of the nation in its sovereign perished, and a sinister meaning was attached to every action which he performed.

1826 A. D.

The liberated press criticised freely and denounced with vehemence the hated domination of the priests. The king sought to free himself from this annoyance by the re-establishment of a rigid censorship. But the public indignation forced him so to modify the proposed enactment that little of it remained. The popularity of Charles was now entirely gone. At a review the national guard—the citizen army of Paris—hissed him and insulted him by seditious cries. Next day the king in wrath disbanded the national guard, leaving, however, to the indignant warriors their arms, ready to be used against him when occasion called.

1827 A.D.

Ever the popular mistrust deepened. Growing suspicion and hatred waited upon every step of the unhappy monarch. A ministry, somewhat less bigoted and unwise than himself, wrung from him edicts which limited the number of the Jesuits, and excluded them from taking any part in the education of the people. But soon this ministry fell,

1828 A. D.

and the king chose the Prince de Polignac as the head of the new government.

The prince was an amiable man, but a shallow politician—unreasoning and fanatical in his love of royalty, and animated by a narrow, monk-like piety. His appointment gave hope to the banished Jesuits and all the party of the priests, but it awakened gloomy forebodings everywhere else.

Between the Chamber of Deputies and the new ministry there existed from the first a violent hostility. The chamber addressed the king in polite but unsparing denunciation of a government which it was alleged was not in sympathy with the people. The government avenged itself by dissolving the chamber. The angry people elected new representatives more obdurately hostile than before.

. The newspaper press of Paris was at that time conducted with remarkable ability, and exercised in consequence a commanding influence upon public sentiment. The liberal papers were vehement in their hostility against the government, and never ceased to fan the flame of popular resentment. The Prince Polignac had persuaded himself that the people were contented, and that the dangerous agitation which now prevailed was due wholly to the malign influence of the newspapers. The king, remembering how, as it had seemed to him, concession ruined his brother and led him to the scaffold, determined that no repetition of similar weakness should endanger the restored throne. He would maintain the royal dignity against the evil persons by whom it was impugned. To do this effectively it was judged needful that the king, ceasing for the moment to govern constitutionally, should for public safety assume a temporary dictatorship. Ordinances were prepared which dissolved the new chamber before it had even met; which modified the electoral law so as to secure the choice of a more courtly representation; and which suspended the liberty of the press. There was profound silence in the royal cabinet as Charles and his ministers put their hands to those awful documents which sealed the ruin of a line of sixty kings. So obvious was the peril, that even the printer to whom the publication of the ordinances was committed hesitated to enter upon the task until he had besought ministers to reconsider their decision.   But the Prince Polignac pledged himself that the tranquility of Paris would be unbroken, and the king consoled himself with the persuasion that the step which he had taken was indispensable.

July 25, 1830 A. D.

Next morning the readers of the *Moniteur* were stuned by the discovery that their liberties were abolished and that they were living under a despotism. The news diffused itself quickly among the more intelligent citizens.   Men, gathered into little groups in all public places, discussed with Parisian warmth and expressiveness of gesticulation the enormities of the government.   As the day wore on, and the gravity of the situation was more fully perceived, the public funds fell, business ceased, the great employers of labour closed their works, and the people gave themselves up to the agitating influences of this supreme hour.   But there was yet no such excitement as threatened immediate disturbance of the peace.   The king spent the day in hunting.   Prince Polignac at its close retired calmly to rest, satisfied with the events of to-day and serenely confident of the morrow.

Next day the office-doors of an offending newspaper were forced by orders of the government, and the printing machinery was seized.   By this time work had utterly ceased in Paris, and the streets were crowded by dense masses of angry men.   The excitement had now reached down to the lowest of the population. The men of the faubourgs appeared once more, ragged and fierce as they looked on that day, now thirty-five years ago, when the cannon of Napoleon quelled their last uprising.   During the afternoon stones were thrown at the soldiers, who replied in haste by a discharge of musketry.

July 27.

Slain men now lay on the streets, and the long surpressed fury of the people burst forth. Gunsmiths' shops and powder factories were plundered. The students of the École Polytechnique seized the foils which were used for fencing, and ground the points to effective sharpness on the stones of the corridor. The pavement of streets was torn up, houses were stripped of their furniture, omnibuses were thrown down, and soon the leading streets were furnished with barricades, with the support of which the people could successfully resist the attack of the troops. Paris was in arms against the tyrant government.

During the next two days their was stubborn and bloody fighting between the people and the slender body of soldiers who formed the garrison of Paris. At its close the people were victorious, and the defence of the crown ceased.

The unhappy king realized, when his troops were driven out of Paris, the calamitous significance of the error he had made. He withdrew the fatal ordinances, but concession was unavailing. He lingered in the soft shades of St. Cloud, loath to resume in his old age the sad life of the exile, till his personl safety began to be threatened; and then, with his family and a strong guard, he took his way to Cherbourg, weeping bitterly, like King David, as he went. Slowly the fallen monarch rode northwards during twelve dreary days. There journeyed with him the Duchess d'Angoulême, the daughter of Louis XVI., stately and beautiful, and used to adversity. She had spent some of her earlier years in prison, and many of them in exile, to which she was now finally returning. The Duchess de Berri, frivolous and irritable, fared northwards too—she whose husband had been snatched from her by the assassin's knife, and who now carried with her away from France the boy who would have been its king. As this mournful family passed, the people looked on them in silence, with the pity which misfortune so great was fitted to awaken. At Cherbourg two ships waited for the exiles. On the beach the king parted from his guard. England had offered an assylum in the remote palace of Holyrood. There the dejected old man lived, with his mimic court, till, at the ungenerous wish of Louis Philippe, the English government requested him to go. He wandered to Bohemia and to Göritz, where he died. 1836 A. D.

The Duke of Orleans, the son of him who was beheaded in 1793, returned to France at the period of the restoration. King Louis considered that the duke, as the head of the younger branch of the Bourbon family, was already sufficiently near the throne, and took good care that he should come no nearer. Charles, more confiding, heaped honours upon him, and restored to him the enormous possessions which had been confiscated forty years before. The duke was one of the wealthiest men in Europe. He was ambitious, astute, patient; his long experience in the school of adversity had given him the power to wait. He laboured to become acceptable to all political parties, veiling his designs under a subtle and impenetrable reserve. He had been successful, and was now the hope of the revolted nation. During the agonies of the revolution the duke withdrew from Paris, and concealed his place of residence to escape the necessity of premature revelation of his purpose. When the crown was offered to him by the chambers, he affected reluctance, and yielded only to the urgent entreaty which the universal voice addressed to him. He ascended the throne amidst the raptures of a delighted people who had placed him there, and he chose to reign as Louis Philippe, king of the French. He owed his elevation to the citizens of Paris—the bankers, manufacturers, and shop-keepers; but the workmen gave their cordial support, and the provinces quietly acquiesced in the choice which Paris had made.

It was natural that the agitations which had resulted in a victory so brilliant should not immediately subside. The people could not at once bring themselves down to the level of the prosaic toils by which it was needful they should live. The government addressed to them a soothing proclamation. " Brave workmen," it besought them, " return to your workshops." But the revolution had given to the industries of Paris a shock from which they were slow to recover. Capital withdrew in terror from a city whose streets had been changed suddenly into a battle-field. Industrial enterprise languished; the imports and exports experienced an alarming decline; the revenue fell to a point far under the expenditure; employment was scarcely to be found, and its wages had fallen so miserably low that the workman could no longer live by his labour. The first care of the new government was to devise expedients by which thousands of workmen, who had just gloriously overthrown a tyrant monarchy, could be saved from death by hunger, till returning confidence permitted commerce to resume its beneficent course.

The task which the citizen-king had undertaken was one of extraordinary difficulty. Arrayed against him were the adherents of the fallen dynasty, those who cherished the brilliant memory of Napoleon, and the republicans, who were now rapidly increasing in numbers. Each party was actively engaged in conspiring its own future triumph, and none of them shrank from the idea of employing force to compass its ends. The agitations of the revolution were slow to subside, and the public tranquillity was disturbed by a yearning for fresh excitements. Universal mistrust prevailed. A complex organization of police found ample employment in watching the movements of men who were suspected of dangerous projects.

A few weeks after he gained the crown, there occurred circumstances which cast a shadow on the reputation of the king. The Duc de Bourbon—last of the great house of Condé, and father of that Duc d'Enghien whom Napoleon so basely murdered—was an old and feeble man, living under the influence of an evil woman, who exercised over the decaying mind of the aged prince a relentless tyranny. Driven unwillingly by this woman, he made a will by which the bulk of his vast fortune was left to a son of Louis Philippe. About a year after this was done, the duke was found strangled to death, apparently by his own hand, but in reality, as men believed, by the hand of a murderer. The king's son was the chief gainer by his death, and the king was therefore suspected of the crime. His majesty, calmly disregarding these injurious surmises, assumed control of the dead man's wealth, and bestowed honours upon the woman by whose help it had been gained. He endured a lawsuit, in which he was successful; but he was less fortunate before the tribunal of public opinion.

From another quarter odium burst in upon the new monarch. He was enormously rich, but instead of uniting his private property with that of the state, as law required, he transferred it to his children. And then he claimed from the country a sum of about one million sterling for his civil list. The details of his expenditure drew upon him showers of damaging ridicule. This robust monarch, it was pointed out, cost the nation a larger sum for medical attendance than the frail and gouty Louis XVIII. had done. The royal chapel, now little used, was upheld at an expense tenfold greater than in the days of the superstitious Charles. Each of the king's horses, of which there were three hundred, cost as much as a counsellor of the Cour Royale. The subterranean furnaces of the royal kitchen were heated at an annual charge of fifty thousand pounds. An obsequious chamber voted all that was asked for, but the people could never make out why a citizen-king adopted a scale of expenditure so inconsistent with the circumstances of his subjects. For at that very time it was found that in the manufacturing departments of France nine-tenths of the young men drawn for military service were infirm or deformed; and even in the agricultural departments four-tenths were similarly disabled. So heavily had excessive toil and imperfect nutriment pressed upon the physical condition of the people.

The first four or five years of the new reign were years of
unquietness and fear.   There were constant strifes with the
press, in which government was generally worsted.   The
public mind was distinguished by an unwonted activity, directing itself with inconvenient persistency to the discussion of
political questions.   This state of mind demanded, as one of
the conditions of its maintenance, a copious issue of cheap political literature.   Uustamped papers, abhorred of the police,
were openly vended on the streets in defiance of law, but with
popular sanction so emphatically expressed that the authorities
scarcely ventured to interfere.   There was a powerful and
widely-ramified society for promoting the rights of man,
whose methods were universal suffrage, an executive elected
and temporary, public education, a more equitable distribution
of property, freedom of trade, and the federalization of Europe.
Twenty-seven members of this society were prosecuted by
government, but acquitted by the jury.   So sensitive was the
liberalism of the deputies, that when one of their number
erringly spoke of the people as the king's "subjects," the
chamber absolutely "quivered with indignation," and ad-
journed in irrecoverable confusion.   "The men who make
kings," it was logically said, "are not subjects."

The government attempted to suppress associations for political discussion.   The indignant republicans prepared to defend
their inalienable rights.   They meditated a new revolution.
Old M. Lafayette, now very near the close of life, who had
spent fifty years in conspiring to overturn thrones, held meetings of the discontented in his own house.   An organization
ready for revolt overspread France.   When the normal excitement which burned in the hearts of the Parisians suffered and
accidental enhancement, it expressed itself in formidable riots.
Twice the distressed weavers of Lyons rose in open rebellion,
and drove out the troops after a severe and bloody conflict.

While the elements of disturbance were thus abundant, a

wretched fanatic, named Fieschi, set up at a window, before
which the king and his sons were to pass, a machine
composed of twenty-five gun-barrels, which he dis- **1835**
charged simultaneously against the royal family. Forty **A. D.**
persons fell, slain or wounded, but the king passed on unharmed,
although a bullet grazed his forehead. This outrage profoundly
impressed the public mind, and silenced for the time the enemies
of the monarchy. Instant advantage of the auspicious opportunity was taken to enact despotic laws in the interest of public
safety. One series of measures made it easy for the government to secure the conviction of a political offender; another
fettered the press. No man now might publish a newspaper
without giving such security as only the rich could find. Nothing might be published offensive to the person of the king.
No man might express a wish for the overthrow of the new
government or the restoration of the old, or subscribe money
to defray penalties inflicted on newspapers. No picture could
be offered for sale until approved by the censor. No man might
venture, under a heavy penalty, to call himself a republican.
M. Thiers and M. Guizot were members of the administration
which originated these measures.

Gradually confidence returned to the terrified commerce of
France. With confidence there came prosperity. The hungry
and irreconcilable agitator found employment and an income,
and ceased from troubling. The government was hated, but
its cold, remorseless strength was undeniable. Every social
disorder found itself in presence of force adequate to silence
an l restrain. Sedition was dealt with by stern laws sternly
administered; insurrection was promptly confronted by bayonet and cannon in overwhelming strength. The election of
1834 gave the king a triumphant majority. The revolution
was closed; personal government was established; and France,
if not contented, was tranquil.

France had not till now made provision for the education

of her people.   In the early days of the first revolution noble
plans had been devised and utterly forgotten in the wild strifes
which swept over the country.   Napoleon desired soldiers; he
had no need of educated men.   Under the restoration it was
deemed easier to govern an ignorant than an educated
people, and education was not encouraged.   Now the
very foundations of an educational system had to be laid.
A scheme was prepared by M. Guizot, and readily adopted,
which provided and adequately endowed thirty-five thousand
primary schools.

1833
A. D.

In the year 1829, when the troubles which were soon to
bring its overthrow were gathering around the restored monarchy, Charles X. sought to regain the favour of his people by
the conquest of Algiers.   It was a work which the European
powers ought to have performed long before.   For centuries
the Algerines had been the scourge of the Mediterranean.
Charles V. attacked them, and almost perished in the attempt.
During the seventeenth century the English, the French, and
the Venetians sent fruitless expeditions against them.   Louis
XIV. bombarded Algiers twice, and the daring freebooters
ravaged his coasts in return.   In 1816 England battered down
the defences of Algiers, and exacted worthless promises from
the government, without, however, taking trouble to close their
evil career.   The Algerines continued to follow the occupation
of piracy; still sold into slavery or held for ransom those Christians whom they captured; still received tribute from Christian
states.   M. Arago—eminent in politics as in science—had once
been a slave on board an Algerine pirate-ship.

It was now resolved that France should deliver Europe from
this shame.   A powerful expedition took, without serious difficulty, the town of Algiers, and preparations were made for a
permanent occupation by French troops on the African shores
of the Mediterranean.   France was pleased with the achieve-

ment, which, however, was unavailing to turn the tide of disfavour now flowing so strongly against the government.

Down to the very close of Louis Philippe's reign, France
toiled to establish her supremacy over that portion of northern
Africa which she had marked as her own. It was a fair and
ample region—the Libya of tl e Romans, and one of the chief
sources of their supply of wheat. In extent it is nearly twice
as large as Great Britain. Once it had maintained a population of twenty million, but these were now dwindled to one-
tenth of their former strength. The natives refused to yield to
their new masters. Incessant and pitiless war was waged.
One tribe, which had especially displeased the French commander, was annihilated. Another tribe had found refuge in a
vast cave, and refused to come fourth and submit. The soldiers
piled fagots at the entrance to the cave, and kept up the fire till
five hundred persons were suffocated. This atrocity was
loudly condemned in France, and even Marshal Soult, who
was then minister of war, offered no defence.

The most formidable antagonist encountered by the French
was the emir Abd-el-Kader. This chief ruled the Arabs in
the province of Oran with the double authority of prince and
prophet. His reputation for piety, his military genius, and his
frequent success gained for him an extraordinary ascendency
over the wandering tribes by whom he was obeyed and who
listened to his words as to those of Deity. For thirteen years
Abd-el-Kader withstood the invaders. Often he was defeated
and his forces scattered to the winds—only to recombine, formidable as ever, in some unexpected quarter. Occasionally he
was able to inflict a sharp repulse upon the invaders. France
continued to accumulate forces until she had over one hundred
thousand men in Algeria. Her people seemed pleased to have
the excitement of a perpetual war which did not cost many
lives and did not add appreciably to their burdens. In Algeria
glory was gained cheaply. The generals were skilful, the

18

soldiers were brave, and the delights of victory were enjoyed at a cost which, to those who remembered the awful triumphs of Napoleon, seemed utterly insignificant. At the battle of Isly the French gained a really brilliant and decisive victory over the Moors with no greater loss than twenty-seven men killed and ninety-six wounded. And all the while their soldiers and officers were acquiring the experience of veterans, and qualifying themselves to play their part on bloodier fields should the occasion arise.

1845 A. D.

At length the fortune of war pronounced so conclusively against the emir that he offered his submission to General Lamoricière, on condition of being allowed to retire to Egypt. The general accepted this surrender, and the Duc d'Aumale, the king's son, confirmed it. But the compact was basely violated by the French government. Abd-el-Kader was sent to France and kept in close confine-ment for five years. He was set at liberty at length by Louis Napoleon, and received from the government an allowance suitable to his former rank.

1847 A. D.

1852 A. D.

France was now in undisputed possession of her African territory. Twenty years ago, when she put her hand to the chastisement of the Algerines, England exacted from her a pledge that she would attempt no permanent occupation in Africa. The benefits which France has conferred show how idle and pernicious are frequently the jealousies which divide the European powers. Under French rule the imports of Algiers have risen from two hundred and eighty thousand pounds to five million. Her exports are seven million. Where the wandering Arab camped are now roads and bridges and four hundred miles of railway. Where the pirate lurked are lighthouses and harbours. The civilian population has grown to three million, of which two hundred thousand are European. The discounts of the Bank of Algeria amounted in one year to eight million sterling. The inhabitants peacefully cultivate the fertile soil, and add to the comfort of mankind by raising abundant crops of wheat, cotton, grapes, olives, oranges, tobacco, flax, and silk.

For several years, after the early agitations of Louis Philippe's reign were quelled, France was tranquil and apparently satisfied. No voice of complaint reached the royal ear. The press used with moderation the liberty allowed to it. The tone of the chamber was loyal and dutiful. The questions presented to that body were ordinarily of an unexciting character, and, after being subjected to a temperate and decorous examination, were decided in accordance with the wish of the government. The country enjoyed unwonted prosperity. The king's chief care in his foreign policy was to preserve his country from the calamity of war. Never before had France enjoyed for so lengthened a period the blessings of peace; never, therefore, had her wealth grown so rapidly. Her population, her commerce, her revenue were all steadily increasing. The citizen class, to which the king owed his elevation, and which alone was influential in the national affairs, approved with its whole heart the unexampled reign of peace and commercial expansion.

France had surpassed England in the excellence of her roads —insomuch that the Englishmen who traveled in France during the eighteenth century never failed to remark the surprising contrast. But, in her construction of railways, France was content to borrow the inventions and wait for the experience of her neighbour. Several years after the Liverpool and Manchester railway was opened, M. Arago 1838 was directed by the French government to prepare a A. D. report on the subject of railways. A system of great trunk lines was sketched out, radiating almost wholly from Paris out to the extremities of the kingdom. But it was not proposed to construct these at once. M. Arago prudently recommended

to proceed slowly, so that advantage might be taken of the
improvements which were to be expected. A strong party
desired that these great works should be wholly executed and
controlled by the state. But those who preferred private enterprise with the larger opportunity afforded for private gain
were in the ascendant, and it was determined to leave the construction of railways to the voluntary combination of capitalists.

1840 A. D. But the French were slow to put confidence in this new
form of investment. In two years only one of the proposed lines had been constructed. The government
was at length obliged to undertake the work, but not until
France had fallen very far behind her neighbouring states.

The course of peaceful years brought forgetfulness of the
miseries which the empire had inflicted and a reviving pride
in its glories. The heart of the nation was turning once more
to the hero who had raised France so high and brought her
so low. A pension was granted to his sister, the dethroned
and widowed Queen of Naples. Numerous monuments to the
emperor were erected, and the strength of the party which
favoured the restoration of his dynasty constantly increased.

1840 A. D. M. Thiers, on the part of the government, gave expression
to the changed national feeling when he asked England
to restore to France the bones of Napoleon. Lord
Palmerston acceded courteously to the request. He
hoped that all remaining animosity between the nations would
be buried in the tomb of the emperor. A French ship-of-war
was sent to bear the remains home to France. The lonely
grave under the willow tree at St. Helena was opened. The
body has been so skillfully embalmed that nineteen years of
death had not effaced the expression of the well-remembered
features. Men looked once more with reverence and pity upon
the almost unchanged countenance of him who had been the
glory and the scourge of his age.

The funeral procession passed slowly through the streets of Paris to the Church of the Invalides, attended by countless multitudes of the population. The king and all the royal family took part in the ceremonial. The enthusiasm of the people was boundless, and the cries which proceeded from the crowd showed that Paris thought no more of her agony and shame, but remembered only the unmatched splendours of the emperor's reign.*

While these honours were bestowed upon the remains of Napoleon, his nephew and heir had just entered upon a captivity which was to continue for six years. Louis Napoleon—silent and inscrutable then as afterwards—reading with a too hopeful eye the indications of returning popular favour, deemed that the time had come for the assertion of his claims. With a small band of comrades he embarked at London and landed at Boulogne. He proclaimed to his countrymen that " the ashes of the emperor should not come but into regenerated France," and that he had arrived to effect that needful renovation. It was not impossible he should succeed, but his fate must depend upon the attitude assumed to his enterprise by the troops whom he first encountered. The officer in command at Boulogne refused to be corrupted, and was able to hold his soldiers to their duty. Prince Louis and his friends fled to their boats, but were all captured, and he was condemned to imprisonment for life.

From an early period in the reign of Louis Philippe the fortification of Paris had engaged the attention of the government. Recent history revealed a twofold danger from which protection had to be sought. Twice the capital had been taken with ease by foreign invaders. Many times had it been in lawless possession of its own rabble. To the government of the barricades it probably seemed that, of the two, the internal

* Down to 1858 the will of Napoleon remained in Doctors' Commons. The interesting document was presented to France under the influence of the cordiality which prevailed during the early years of the second empire.

danger was the more real and urgent. The king favoured
defence by means of a series of detached forts, each independent and capable from its own resources of enduring a siege.
Each of these forts must be silenced before an assailant could
approach the city, and they were to be so placed that their fire
could be made to converge, destructively, upon any point where
insurrection revealed itself. The opposition supported defence
by a wall surrounding the city, and strengthened by bastions
and a ditch—a scheme which, it is supposed, would not prevent
the citizens from taking up arms when they saw grounds for
doing so. Ultimately a combination of the two methods was
adopted, and carried out at a cost of six million sterling. The
government consented, by way of concession, that the forts
should not be armed without a vote of the chamber. Two
thousand pieces of artillery were stored at some distance, to
be ready when the emergency arose.

Underneath the peaceful surface of French politics there were
elements of disturbance which were steadily consolidating towards revolution. The middle class was rapidly accumulating
wealth and was satisfied. But wages were low, and the working
population did not appear to participate in the prosperity of their
employers. The small owners of land—forming with their families almost one-half of the population—were so heavily burdened with taxation and debt, that they obtained with
1840   difficulty the means of a scanty and precarious subsist-
A. D.   ence. In Paris trade combinations were formed, and resulted in extensive strikes. Numerous arrests took place; for
by French law it was an offence for a number of men simultaneously to desist from work. Alarming riots followed, and
to secure tranquility it was necessary to fill Paris with troops.
The distressed labourers attempted to protect themselves
against the abhorred despotism of capital by schemes of co-
operation. But the time was not ripe for such undertakings,
and no relief was gained.

Peaceful as his reign had been, the government of Louis Philippe had been enormously expensive. The army by which he supported his throne and maintained the national dignity numbered six hundred and forty thou- **1841 A. D.** sand men. Over twenty million sterling was expended on public works. The total expenditure of the country had swelled from the moderate forty million of 1829 to the enormous aggregate of sixty million. The revenue was not sufficient for these outlays, and there was for years a deficit, larger than that which hastened the first revolution. A heavier rate of taxation was deemed impracticable, but it was resolved to order a new valuation, whereby the area on which taxation was levied might be enlarged. This resolution encountered grave opposition, and produced results permanently injurious. A multitude of local authorities openly counselled resistance, and the valuation was not completed without rioting and copious bloodshed.

The population of France was then thirty-four million, and the privilege of the political franchise was vested exclusively in those who paid in direct taxes a sum not less than eight pounds. This class numbered little more than two hundred thousand. It was a class with interests which were held to be antagonistic to those of the great mass of the people, and was not, therefore, in any sense representative of those who were excluded from political influence. The chamber elected by this inconsiderable body did not enjoy the confidence of the people. Nor, in truth, was it deserving of this confidence by its character more than by its origin. A large proportion of its members were needy adventurers, who made their way into the chamber with no higher aim than that of selling their support to the government in return for lucrative places to themselves and their friends. Nor were such hopes often diappointed. The government had one hundred and thirty thousand places at its disposal, and the use which was made of these during the eighteen years of Louis Philippe's reign was productive of corruption more wide-spread and shameless than France had known since the first revolution.   In the scarcely exaggerated language used by M. de Lamartine, the government had " succeeded in making of a nation of citizens a vile band of beggars."

It was obvious to all who desired the regeneration of France that reform must begin with the representation of the people. To this end the liberals directed much effort.   They did not as yet propose universal suffrage, and their leaders were divided between an extension of the franchise to all who paid two pounds of direct taxes and an extension which went no lower than four pounds.   The demand for reform was resisted by the government.   The king himself was opposed to it.   It was " a malady of the age," he considered, and it would pass away. His majesty was growing old, and looked coldly upon all political novelties.   And at best his views were narrow, his perceptions were not acute, and his sympathies with the age in which he lived and the people over whom he ruled were extremely imperfect.

Among the leaders of the liberal party were men of high character and commanding influence.   Arago, Odillon Barrot, Louis Blanc, Thiers, Lamartine, were formidable assailants for the strongest government to encounter.   Under their guidance the agitation for reform assumed dimensions exceedingly embarrassing and even alarming.   For once France borrowed from England her method of political agitation. Reform banquets, attended by thousands of persons, were held in all the chief towns, and the pressure of a peaceful public opinion was employed to obtain the remedy of a great wrong.   The police made feeble attempts to prevent such gatherings, but were ordinarily unsuccessful. But the king and M. Guizot, strong in the support of the army and a purchased majority of the deputies, and apparently little aware of the vehemence of the popular desire, made no effort to satisfy or propitiate.

Louis Philippe had wisely set a high value on the maintenance of cordial relations with England. During many years
he clung so tenaciously to the English alliance as to bring upon
him at home the charge of undignified subserviency.
The Queen of England gratified him by a visit, which   1843
he returned a few months after. He did not conceal that   A. D.
he was pleased to have the world made aware that personal
regard was added to political alliance.* During these visits
there was much coversation regarding a Spanish matter which
was then of some interest. The Spanish government was
looking around to find suitable husbands for their young queen
and her sister. The hands of the princesses were offered to
two sons of Louis Philippe. But however anxious the king
may have been to make provision for his children, he was
aware that the traditional policy of England looked with disfavour upon a close alliance between the crowns of France
and Spain. The king would not offend England. He declined the hand of the Spanish queen, but accepted that of her
sister for his fourth son, the Duc de Montpensier. Queen
Victoria and her minister approved of that marriage on the
condition voluntarily offered by King Louis, that it should not
take place till the Spanish queen was married and had children. But in a few years the king violated his pledge,   1846
and pressed upon Spain an arrangement under which   A. D.
the two marriages were celebrated together. Looking
back upon this transaction we readily perceive that the views
entertained regarding its political significance were altogether
mistaken, and that the order in which the Spanish ladies were
married, and the choice which was made of husbands for them,
were questions of importance only to the persons immediately
concerned. But thirty years ago the decay of despotism had

* "The family of Louis Philippe have a strong feeling that, for the last thirteen
years, they have been placed under a ban, as though they were lepers, by all Europe
and by every court, and expelled from the society of reigning houses; and, therefore,
they rate very highly the visit of the most powerful sovereign in Europe. The king
said this to me over and over again."--PRINCE ALBERT TO BARON STOCKMAR, 10th
September, 1843.

little more than begun, and the ideas of men were still moulded
upon the traditions of personal government. A marriage union
between the royal families of France and Spain still seemed to
involve a junction of fleets for an attack upon England.

To Louis Philippe himself the transaction was calamitous.
He had broken his kingly word, and he stood before Europe
and before his own people a dishonoured man. The support
which he had hitherto drawn from his cordiality with England was lost to him forever. The English newspapers condemned in unmeasured terms the royal duplicity, and their
denunciations were eagerly reproduced by the liberal journals
of Paris. Queen Victoria, it was believed, had even written
with her own hand a letter of courtly but firm rebuke.* To
the causes which ma le Louis Philippe unpopular at home,
there was now added the humiliating circumstance that he
had incurred the contempt of Europe.

The king was not unaware of the hatred with which his
government was now regarded. He would gladly have been
more acceptable to his people, but he would not seek their
favour by changing the policy which incurred their displeasure.
His sole dependence was on the chamber and on the army, and
he could bind them more closely to his cause only by favours
which were degrading to him who gave and to them who received.

Circumstances made it easy for the opposition to enhance the
general discontent. Many evidences of shameless corruption were at this time brought to light. A cabinet min-
1847
A. D.
ister was found guilty of accepting bribes; the ministry
was accused by a newspaper editor of having sold peerages,

* Two years after, when the mob sacked the Tuileries, there were found the draft of
a letter of vindication, written by Louis Philippe to his daughter, the Queen of the
Belgians. So much in earnest was the king, and so difficult does the task seem to
have proved, that he sat writing on three occasions till four in the morning, notwithstanding that his family "maintained he was killing himself" by the unwonted toil.
The king mentions the lett r of Queen Victoria, and states that it greatly grieved him.
It was addressed to the Queen of the French. A long and very able letter of remonstrance and rebuke was also addressed by Queen Victoria to the Belgian queen. The
entire correspondence was afterwards published in the "Life of the Prince Consort."

and of having been bribed to grant license for a theatre; an arsenal was burned down to conceal, it was believed, the delinquencies of certain officials; the provisions supplied to the navy were found to be adulterated to an enormous extent. "Public morals," said M. de Tocqueville, " are degraded, and private morals have come too closely to resemble them."

The crops failed in 1845 and 1846, and prices rose to a famine point. So gravely did public tranquility seem to be endangered that the municipality of Paris borrowed a million sterling, and expended it in artificially cheapening the price of bread. The revenue fell off so seriously, that the last budget of Louis Philippe's reign showed a deficit of 1848 twelve million sterling. A. D.

The enemies of the government mustered their forces for a supreme effort. When the chambers met a debate took place which stretched over twenty days, and in which the fiery rhetoric of the opposition charged home upon the king Dec. 28, and his ministers all the manifold evils afflicting the 1847 state. The demand for parliamentary reform became A. D. constantly more urgent; but M. Guizot heeded it not. The reformers took up again their work of agitation. They announced a great procession and reform banquet. The police, somewhat hesitatingly, interdicted the demonstration, and its promoters resolved to submit; but the people, insufficiently informed of these movements, gathered for the pro- Feb 22, cession in the early morning. All that day the streets 1848 were thronged, and the excitement of the people in- A. D. creased from hour to hour; but few soldiers were seen, and consequently no conflict occured. Next morning the strategic points of the city were garrisoned by a strong force of soldiers and national guards, and the people saw that the government feared them. Business was suspended, and the constantly rising agitation foretold irrepressible tumults. The men of the faubourgs appeared once more. Towards evening a few barricades were thrown up, and a few gunsmiths' shops were plundered. Worst of all, the national guard appeared to sympathize with the people.

Terror-stricken by these fearful indications, the king and his ministers met for counsel at the Tuileries. To appease the angry mob, no measure seemed so hopeful as the sacrifice of the ministry. Guizot resigned. Theirs and Odillon Barrot, cheifs of the liberal party, were received into the cabinet. Marshal Bugeaud was appointed to command the troops. But before the day closed a disaster had occurred which made all concession vain. Before one of the public offices there was stationed a battalion of infantry, around which there surged an excited crowd. A shot came from the crowd, and was promptly responded to by a volly which killed or wounded fifty persons. The bodies of the victims were placed on waggons and drawn along the streets, that the fury of the people might be excited to the highest pitch.

During that sleepless night, Marshal Bugeaud, skilfully directing the forces which he commanded, had taken the barricades and effectively checked the rioters. But in early morning the new ministers ordered him to desist and withdraw his troops. They deemed it useless to resist.

Feb. 23, 1848 A. D.

Concession was, in their view, the only avenue to tranquility. The soldiers retired; the crowds pressed on to the Tuileries.

The king had breakfasted, and was now in his cabinet surrounded by his family and great officers, waiting the course of events which he had no longer any power to direct. From afar the shouts of the approaching multitude were borne to the royal ears. The king took up his pen to write the names of a ministry still more radical than that which he had appointed a few hours before. Suddenly there entered the royal chamber Iile de Girardin, editor of a Paris newspaper, who, in abrupt and uncourtly terms, informed the helpless monarch that his immediate abdication was necessary. The king hesitated, but the urgency of his advisers and the sounds of strife, which waxed ever louder, overcame his reluctance, and he put his name to an abdication in favour of his grandson.   The insurgents were now at the palace gates, and the personal safety of the dethroned monarch required to be secured without further delay.   Along with the ladies of his family the king left the Tuileries and reached a cab-stand, where happily two vehicles stood waiting to be hired.   Availing themselves of the only means of safety left them, the royal family drove away from Paris.   A week later they reached the coast and embarked for England, the home of so many expelled French sovereigns, their majesties travelling under the lowly but well-chosen incognito of Mr. and Mrs. Smith.

Mar. 2,
1848
A. D.

Another of the numerous experiments which France made in her preserving search for liberty had thus closed in disappointment.   The French people intended that Louis Philippe should represent their grand ideal of the sovereignty of the people; but he represented only the sovereignty of a small caste, and even that was transferred by the employment of corrupting agencies into his own hands.   He was a despot not less than his predecessors had been.   The French somewhat abruptly discharged him from their service, and resumed the weary search which for sixty years they had vainly prosecuted.

Immediately on the departure of the king a provisional government was organized, with M. Lamartine at its head.   Never surely did any body of men enter upon a more arduous task. The mob of Paris was excited beyond any capability of being guided by reason; the streets were cumbered with dead and wounded men; supplies of food had ceased to come from the provinces; already multitudes were famishing, and soon the entire population would suffer the pangs of hunger; a band of insurgents seized the Tuileries, and were holding high festival over the contents of the royal larder and cellar; a vast crowd surrounded the Hôtel de Ville, and thronged the lobbies and stairs and even the rooms where the members of the government sat at work.* But M. Lamartine and his colleagues were equal to the occasion. A stream of decrees flowed, incessant, from that busy workshop of legislation. Within a day or two they had abolished all titles of nobility; engaged to find employment for the whole population; arranged for supplies of food; rewarded the patriots who had overturned the monarchy; changed the position of the colours on the national flag; planted trees of liberty; ordered the words *Liberte, Egalite, Fraternite*, to be inscribed on the walls; organized a new military force; abolished the punishment of death for political offences,† and set up national workshops in which one hundred and twenty thousand citizens found, if not employment, what suited them as well, a daily wage of two francs.

An election of deputies was ordered, and the right of voting was at once extended to the adult male population. The work of framing a constitution was intrusted to a committee of the wisest members, and in due time a scheme was produced

Nov. 4.
1848 so acceptable to the assembly, that it was adopted by
A. D. an almost unaniomous vote. The form of government was declared to be republican. The legislature was one chamber, elected by universal suffrage. The executive was a president, elected for four years, appointing his own ministers, having control of the army, empowered to declare war and conclude treaties with foreign powers, and re-eligible indefinitely. He also was chosen by universal suffrage, and all votes were to be given by ballot. The vote by which this constitution was adopted (737 to 30) is sufficient evidence that grovernment by the people was the deliberate choice of France; but years of

* "We proceeded to the Hotel de Ville at the head of a column of people, and were borne amidst a wall of pikes, sabres, and bayonets to a small table, on which we or. ganized the government" (LAMARTINE). Twenty times during the first seventy-two hours M. Lamartine was "led, carried, or dragged" to the door or window, to harangue "those men of a former age" who were clamorous for a new reign of terror.

† "Never shall I forget the moment when this proposition, emanating from our hearts, was carried unanimously; and throwing ourselves into each other's arms, we exchanged a long embrace."—LAMARTINE.

cruel frustration were yet to elapse before she could reach what she had long desired.

While these peaceful labours were in progress, the rabble of Paris, dissatisfied with the insufficient provision made by government for their comfort, burst into an insur- June 23, 1848 rection of gigantic dimensions. General Cavaignac was A. D. appointed to command the national troops, and immediately after was named dictator. The mob was powerful in numbers and courage, was well armed and led with skill. Barricades arose in every street, until there were nearly four thousand of these fortifications, chiefly in the faubourgs. During three days there was severe and bloody fighting. Cavaignac employed mortars and heavy siege-guns against the insurgents, and quelled them at last with enormous slaughter on both sides.

CHAPTER II.

ERY speedily after the fall of the monarchy it became evident that their old love of the Emperor Napoleon was still cherished by large numbers of the French people. Prince Louis Napoleon, the heir to the empire, hastened from London and lost no time in offering his help to the government—to whom, however, his overtures were not acceptable. But soon he was elected by four constituencies, and his name was heard with ominous frequencey among the street-cries of Paris. He duly took his place in the assembly, and occasionally ascended the tribune. His purposes were impenetrable, but his manners were bland and his sentiments unexceptionable. The dearest object of his desire was peace. He was wholly without personal aims. "Those who accuse me of ambition, little know my heart." He sought only to gain the esteem of good men by labouring to serve France, and uphold the institutions which she had established. He became a candidate for the presidency; and in the provinces his name, recalling as it did the glories of the empire, was received with enthusiasm. The people enjoyed perfect liberty of choice, and they elected Price Louis by an overwhelming majority. The prince received five and a half million of votes, while his five competitors did not together receive two million. The new president swore to maintain the constitution, and

Dec. 10, 1848 A. D.

288

in his address to the assembly gave detailed and impressive assurances of his loyalty to that order of things which " entire France had established."

The president and the assembly were enemies from the beginning. The assembly seemed to devote its energies chiefly to the task of watching and thwarting the president. Many of its measures were unacceptable to the people. It limited the suffrage by disfranchising three million of voters; it handed over the primary instruction of the people to the priests; it fettered the press more heavily than Louis Philippe had done. Always it was before the public eye as a body given over to unprofitable wrangling,—its action constantly suggestive of danger to the national repose.

The president wielded with a firm hand the powers intrusted to him. When the customary insurrections arose, they were suppressed with the ease of overwhelming strength. The enemies of order were silent in presence of a power which they felt it vain to resist. In his controversies with the assembly, the president kept himself scrupulously within his constitutional rights. He was prudent, silent, always effective. His measures were framed with a conspicuous regard to the welfare of the masses. He cared for the sanitary condition of the poor man's dwelling, and for the purity of the food which was sold to him; he transferred taxation from the necessaries of life to its luxuries; he retained at the public expense priests whose duty it was to furnish gratuitously the rites of the church to those who were without the pecuniary means of obtaining this advantage; he increased the pay of the common soldier; he stimulated the construction of railways, canals, telegraphs; he largely increased the powers of local authorities, and freed them from an injurious dependence upon the central government. The beneficent results of his enactments were immediately apparent. The trade of the country revived; prices rose; employment was becoming abundant; deposits increased in the

19

savings-banks; the number of poor supported by the city of Paris diminished rapidly. France craved for rest under a strong government; she had found it, and was satisfied.

The assembly was actuated by a conviction that the president was moving steadily towards a restoration of the empire. To frustrate that design, it attempted to gain some measure of control over the army. But it was foiled by the superior strategic skill of the president, who had gained not only the army, but the magistracy, the police, and indeed the whole executive force of the country.

The president was satisfied that the time had come to rid himself of his enemies. With the shameless selfishness of his race, he was now to grasp the scepter which was visibly within his reach. No regard to the constitution which he had sworn to maintain was suffered to lay restraint upon his action, for he knew that the army was prepared to obey and the people to absolve. The forces at his disposal rendered success sure and easy.

With the help of the Count de Morny, General St. Arnaud, and M. de Maupas, the president framed the details of his plot. On the night of its execution he entertained a large assemblage at the Palace Elysée. No man in all that glittering company wore a more smiling and gracious aspect, or seemed more entirely unencumbered by care, than the man who was about to overthrow the liberties of his country. So soon as his guests had taken their leave, the president turned to the execution of his enterprise. In the middle of the night the prominent members of the assembly were wakened from sleep and carried off to prison. The leaders of secret societies and other organizations of the disaffected, whose names had been searched out by the police, were now carefully gathered up. Before daybreak every man who was likely to raise his voice too loudly against the contemplated outrage was in confinemet. When the Parisians rose in the

Dec. 1, 1851 A. D.

morning, they learned from official placards on their walls that
their assembly was abolished; that their most influential representatives were in prison; that a state of siege had been proclaimed; and that Louis Napoleon, supported by an army of
half a million of men, had France at his disposal.

But it was not necessary for the president to place his dependence for the future on force. Popular sanction of what
he had done was confidently reckoned upon, and he at once
made his appeal to a people whose feelings had been carefully
ascertained, and whose support he knew was safe. He summoned them to judge between him and the assembly. He
told them he had not power sufficient to fulfil the mission with
which he had been charged; that the assembly had become
the centre of factious designs; that if they desired to perpetuate the existing condition of affairs, they must choose another
in his place, as he would no longer consent to remain " chained
to the wheel when he could not prevent the ship from drifting
to destruction." * He proposed a new basis of government,
which included a responsible chief elected for ten years, a cabinet appointed by him alone, and a legislature composed of
two chambers. A fortnight later, the French people, by an
almost unanimous vote, gave to the president the powers he
asked. Of eight and a half million of voters, seven and a half
million voted affirmatively, while only six hundred and forty
thousand gave a response unfavourable to the new proposal.

But in the meantime the faubourgs had claimed to express
themselves in regard to the *coup d'etat*. On the next day after
the dissolution of the assembly armed crowds began to appear,
and barricades were thrown up. The insurrection was of no
considerable extent, and the blood shed in its suppression was
unjustifiably great. Anticipating disturbances, the president
had massed a strong military force in Paris, and held securely

* This figure may have been suggested by a saying of Sir Robert Peel when he was
preparing to abolish the corn laws: "I will not stand at the helm during the tempes-
tuous night, if that helm is not allowed freely to traverse."

every point where the insurgents sought to gain a footing. It
was said to have been the intention of the president to give a
bloody warning to all persons who were ill-affected to his government, and the troops were copiously supplied with liquors
to render them more fitting agents in the execution of his
cruel purpose. When the drunken soldiery began to massacre, the streets were thronged by citizens intending no evil
and expecting none. Suddenly, and without warning, the
troops lowered their muskets and fired among the people who
were moving about beside them. A large number of unsuspecting persons fell wounded or killed. Women, little children, helpless gray-haired men were found among the slain.
At one point a mother and child lay dead together. A house-
wife, returning from market with her simple provision for
the family dinner, was gathered out from a heap of dead. A
printer's boy, lying dead in a pool of blood, still grasped the
proof-sheets which he had been sent to deliver. After this
execrable massacre was accomplished, multitudes of the suspected were taken into custody. The prisons were crowded.
The president gave no account of the thousands of unhappy
persons who had fallen under his displeasure. Many were
sent to die in the pestilential climate of Cayenne. It was asserted that citizens who lived near the Champ de Mars had
their rest broken by musketry firing in the stillness of night,
and shrieks as of men in pain, and it was believed that the
president was thus secretly, and without form of trial, ridding
himself of men who were or might become enemies.*

In a few days the president was able to announce: " The
disturbances are appeased; society is saved." A year
later, the senate issued a decree restoring the empire,
and declaring the imperial dignity hereditary in the male
descendants of Prince Louis Napoleon. The nation con-

Dec. 8,
1852
A. D.

* The prefect of police denounced this report as "nothing but a hateful lie." According to this authority, there were only 175 insurgents killed in the street fighting,
and 115 wounded; but the prefect's statements have not been accepted as reliable
evidence.

firmed this restoration by an affirmative vote of eight million against only a quarter million of dissentients.

No beneficial results following from the *coup d'etat* can vindicate its author from reprobation. He destroyed the constitution which he was bound to uphold, and he ruthlessly slaughtered, in so far as he could, those who condemned his action. It is difficult to concieve any combination of circumstances which could have justified his conduct, and assuredly no such combination existed. But he is entitled to whatever benefit can be drawn from the virtually unanimous approval of the French people. He had rightly interpreted the wishes of the nation. France, yearning for quietnees, bestowed her approval upon a monstrous violation of law and of honour, and condoned a crime of almost unparalleled baseness, because it promised to result in the creation of a strong and permanent government. The fact may be humiliating, but it is undeniable. *

The emperor proceeded, as his first great work, to select for himself a partner in the splendours of his new position. It was said, although on insufficient evidence, that he sought in vain the hand of more than one European princess. But his throne—set up only a few weeks ago—was as yet insecure, and he was not deemed an eligible connection for the daughter of a well-established monarch. Whereupon he discarded "dy-nastic prejudices" and the "calculations of ambition," and announced that, inspired by Providence, he had made a choice in which he regarded only "the qualities of the heart," and sought only domestic happiness. The lady who thus became the Empress Eugenia and the leader of fashion throughout Christendom, although not without high qualities, failed to become an elevating power in French society. She was the slave of the priests; the patroness of bull-fights and other debasing amusements. The French peo-

Jan.
1853
A. D.

* The addresses of congratulation received by the emperor form a collection of six quarto volumes, each containing eight or nine hundred pages.

ple never learned to sympathize with her amusements or her religion, and she never gained their love.*

It was a maxim of the emperor that liberty never helped to make a durable political edifice; it could only crown a political edifice which time had consolidated. The constitution which he now bestowed upon submissive France was based upon this valuation of liberty. His government was a despotism founded on universal suffrage. The lower chamber was appointed by the people, but it could originate nothing; it could only discuss the measures submitted to it by the emperor, and the amendments which it suggested could be adopted or rejected by the council of state, a body nominated by the emperor. The senators were mainly chosen by the emperor, and although their services were gratuitous, his majesty was empowered to grant liberal salaries to those whose conduct merited such recognition. This structure was an exquisite embodiment of the Napoleonic idea. It claimed to harmonize democracy and despotism. It surrounded personal government with the sanction of popular choice. It amused France with a conviction of liberty, while she was given over to the operation of an unrestrained despotism.

It was fortunate for the empire that from the beginning there were exciting foreign questions to occupy the public mind. The difficulty with Russia in regard to the holy places was ripening into a quarrel, and under the fostering care of the new government it was guided into war. The alliance with England pleased the French people. The emperor and empress came to visit Queen Victoria, and all London was moved with delight

* Fifteen years later the emperor wrote a little memoir of his wife for one of the Paris journals. It seems that Mademoiselle Montijo was powerfully attracted by the early career of Prince Louis. After the *coup d'etat* she commended herself to the favourable regard of the president by offering to place her whole fortune at his disposal. When his married life was nearing its close, the emperor wrote of her virtues with enthusiasm. She was pious without being bigoted; well-informed without being pedantic; she discussed, in a charming manner, with men of authority the most difficult economical and financial questions; she engaged with efficacious activity in manifold works of beneficence; she had on two occasions exercised the regency with moderation, political tact, and justice. It is a very pleasing picture, such as a youthful lover might have been expected to produce.

at the presence of the august strangers. The war was costly and prolonged, but it yielded glory; and Sebastopol was accepted as in some measure an expiation for Moscow. When peace was restored, the empire presented the aspect of a stable government, resting solidly upon the approval of a contented and thriving people. The horrors of its origin were fully atoned for by its splendid success.

During the next three years France was at peace. But this was the period when the activities of the imperial mind were in their fullest development. Some new and dazzling enterprise was not merely politically beneficial, it was a necessary outlet for the energies of a mind rejoicing to wield the vast powers of which it had at length been permitted to assume the direction. The deliverance of Italy was the work which now lay most convenient to the emperor's hand. It had been begun by his uncle, in whose steps he desired to tread. It was pledged to Count Cavour as the reward of help given against Russia. On New Year's day, the emperor spoke to the Austrian ambassador words which were justly held to convey intimation of a hostile purpose. War quickly followed. After a campaign of a few weeks the emperor returned to Paris in triumph, victor in two hard-fought battles and saviour of Italy.*

1859
A. D.

But about this time the universal activity of the emperor began to awaken alarms in Great Britain. The British people have been liable to occasional panics on the subject of invasion.†

---

* See chapter v.

† This was the third panic on the subject of French invasion within a few years. In 1847 Louis Philippe's son, the Prince de Joinville, wrote a foolish pamphlet. The Duke of Wellington, in the decay of his great powers, wrote a letter which ought never to have been published. The English people straightway became alarmed lest the king of the French should invade them, and were not comforted till they learned that that monarch, dethroned and fugitive, had sought refuge on their shores. Again, after the *coup d'etate*, the alarm burst out afresh. It was promoted by Lord Palmerston, who was bold enough to assert that a French army might land on our coasts without our knowing before that such a measure was in contemplation. Soon after, we were allied with the French to defend the Turks. The emperor was our guest—welcomed with enthusiasm; and the senseless and humiliating fear passed as quickly as it had risen.

There was not now any shadow of warrant for alarm which prevailed. But none the less firmly, in utter defiance of reason and evidence, did the British people cherish the fear that the Emperor Napoleon designed their overthrow, and was probably able to effect it. The fear was childish, but the action following upon it was manly. The people offered themselves to the government for military training and service in such numbers that within a few weeks two hundred thousand men were under drill, of whom forty thousand were reported able to take their place in line of battle. The confidence of England was of political value to the emperor, and it, vexed him to be so mistrusted. But he bore the annoyance, as Mr. Cobden, who was then in Paris, informs us, with calmness, and watched in surprise the strange mania which was running its course among his neighbours. He appealed to Lord Palmerston with abundant protestations of the excellence of his

intentions. "Let us," he said, "understand one another in good faith, like honest men, as we are, and not like thieves, who desire to cheat each other." But it was

July 1860 A. D.

vain to reason with a nation in panic. In course of time the alarm subsided, but men never admitted that it had been baseless. The opinion continued to prevail that the intentions of the emperor had been bad, and that the volunteer movement alone restrained him from attempting the subjugation of the British people.

A few months after the restoration of peace with Austria, disorders of an aggravated character broke out in Syria.

1860 A. D.

Many hundreds of Christians were massacred; the French consulate of Damascus was destroyed, and its inmates owed their preservation of the timely friendship of Abd-el-Kader. The Turkish troops who should have repressed these excesses themselves aided the murderers. Here was an attractive field for the beneficent activities of the emperor. An English government would have addressed vain remonstrances to the Sublime Porte. The emperor perferred to seek redress by more direct methods· With admirable promptitude* an expedition was despatched to Syria, and order was at once restored. The troops were not recalled when their work was done. It seemed that the emperor meditated a continued occupation. In that case, the French would, at their own cost, have made roads and railways and harbours, greatly to the advantage of Syria and the world. But Lord Palmerston would not suffer this to be. He was still the protector of the Turks. Most likely he trembled for our communications with India. The French troops were withdrawn, and Syria returned to her habitual lawlessness.

But Europe and Asia did not afford adequate scope for the scheming and restless emperor. The western shores of the American continent were the home of a people given over to perpetual revolution and wasteful civil strife. Mexico, always a wild chaos of misrule and disorder, had become lately so intolerable that France, England, and Spain were provoked into sending out a military force, in the futile hope of applying a remedy to evils which were a scandal to. Christendom. Napoleon, as it may be supposed, originated the design.† England. joining the league with some hesitation, was contented to play a subordinate part. She contributed one line-of-battle ship and two frigates, with seven hundred marines; France and Spain sent six thousand soldiers. The United States government wisely declined to share in the enterprise. England and Spain after a time withdrew their forces, having made the discovery that their efforts could not result in good. The more tenacious emperor adhered to his purpose, and his troops passed on to the Mexican capital. The Mexican president fled, and Napoleon had upon his hands a country without a government. He procured from a Mexican assembly a resolution

1861
A. D.

---

* The massacre at Damascus began on 9th July; the French troops sailed 4th August.

† His object was "to assure the preponderance of France over the Latin races, and to augment the influence of these races in America."

to found a hereditary monarchy, and to offer the crown to the
Archduke Maximilian, brother to the Emperor of Aus-
1863 tria. The unhappy young man accepted with joy the
A. D. fatal gift. So long as the French soldiers upheld him,
he maintained with success an incessant conflict with the republican authority which he had displaced. But France became wearied of this expensive and useless strife. Her
1866 army was withdrawn. The Emperor Maximilian sent
A. D. his young wife to Europe to beg for help. In an inter-
view with the pope, the poor empress revealed the first symptoms of the insanity by which the whole of her remaining
life was darkened. But help, even if European powers had
been disposed to afford it, would have come too late. Maximilian was betrayed into the hands of enemies who
1867 knew no pity, and by whom he was promptly put to
A. D. death. So great had been his misery that death, he
said was for him a happy deliverance, and not an agony.
Thus disastrously closed the intervention of the Emperor
Napoleon in the affairs of Mexico

The emperor could not keep his hand from the concerns of
his neighbours. (He ardently desired to recognize the independence of the revolted American states, and repeat-
1863 edly urged the British government to join him in doing
A. D. so. His overtures were received with judicious cold-
ness; and one of his despatches, as he complained, was communicated to America. Happily for his credit he was "determined to act with England" on the American question, and
the better judgement of the English ministers saved him the
folly which he was eager to commit.

But the empire was not exclusively intervention in the affairs
of foreign countries. The emperor did some more useful work
than this profitless "making war for an idea." England had
now enjoyed for thirteen years the vast benefits which a policy
of free trade bestowed upon her. It had been expected that
all civilized nations, instructed by the experience of England,

would, like her, have emancipated themselves from the evils
of restriction. But this had not come to pass. Disappointed
by the prevailing blindness, Richard Cobden informed
his government that it was his intention to visit Paris,   1859
and there if possible to convince the emperor of the   A. D.
evils of a protective policy. The emperor received him, and
discussed the subject at great length. The influence which
the reasoning of Mr. Cobden exercised on the minds of the
emperor and his ministers was such that a commercial treaty
between the two countries was agreed upon, and Cobden himself was appointed on the part of England to arrange the
details. It was a difficult task he had undertaken. The French
protectionists were powerful and resolute. The emperor,
whose conversion was imperfect,* vascillated painfully during
the early period of the adjustment. No reinforcement
of his infirm purposes was to be gained from public opinion,
which was wholly unenlightened. Then, at the very crisis of
the negotiation, Lord Palmerston proposed a scheme for the
fortification of arsenals, and spoke openly of the danger of
French invasion. Even then the emperor, inspired by his trust
in Cobden, did not suffer the work to be interrupted. After
twelve months of toil the treaty was perfected. Its purpose
was to remove, in so far as was possible, all obstacles to commercial intercourse between the countries. England swept
out of her tariff some fragments of protection which still
lingered there, and reduced her duties on wines and brandy.
France, on her part, substituted moderate duties on the chief
articles of British export, many of which her tariff had till now
altogether prohibited. Since these changes were effected the
exports of France to England have increased from seventeen
to forty-six million sterling, and the exports of England to
France from five to fifteen million.

* His leaning to a more liberal commercial policy was not, however, entirely new.
Six years before, he had reduced the import duties on corn and cattle, on iron and
coal, despite the clamour of protectionists.

For centuries France had been to Germany a most undesirable neighbour. It had been her hereditary policy to repress
and weaken to the utmost the multitudinous states which lay
beyond the Rhine—to maintain their paralyzing divisions, to
foster every antipathy, to exercise a destructive predominance
in the internal affairs of a race which might become a formidable rival. France, united, aggressive, and swift in movement,
found an easy prey in Germany—divided, discordant, unwieldy.
Louis XI. frustrated Burgundy in her natural desire to unite
with Germany, and held her as his own. Francis I. intrigued
to gain the dignity of emperor, as Louis XIV. did after him.
Louis XIV. took Alsace and Lorraine, and would have taken
much more unless he had been prevented. Louis XV. devised
the erection of four German kingdoms, whose policy France
would direct.   Napoleon stole German territory, and gave it
away or kept it in his own family as inclination dictated.   He
assumed the subserviency of Prussia as his right, and chastised
her hesitating assertion of independence by blows which were
almost annihilating.   For fifty years after his fall Prussia had
rest from French aggression, and grew in power by the wisdom
of her government and the peaceful industry of her people.
Her rise was regarded with unfriendly eye, and with a jealousy
which became, year by year, more intense. In process of time
there occurred the war in which Prussia was signally
1866 victorious over Austria. She was now at the head of a
A. D. united northern Germany, and all men foresaw the early
adhesion of the southern states also. France resented as an
affront to her own majesty this unparalleled increase of power.
A cry rose for immediate war. But the army had been lately
reduced, and it was not yet furnished with the new musket
which in Prussian hands had proved so deadly. The emperor
perceived that he was not ready, and he "resisted with all his
strength," as he himself tells, "the bellicose ideas which had
taken possession of a portion of the public. " He restrained

the untimely zeal of his followers, but he addressed himself with diligence to the work of preparing to abate the audacious strength of Germany. The law of 1868 increased largely the number of his recruits; breech-loading muskets were served out as rapidly as they could be produced; vast stores were accumulated, or appeared to be so; the emperor himself gave much thought to the organization of the army, and wrote voluminous memoranda regarding its minutest details.

In a short while it seemed to her chiefs that France was now ready to set about reducing the intolerable strength of her neighbour. The minister of war asserted his possession of an army which, after all needful deductions, would enable him to place four hundred thousand men on the frontier. Organization was faultless. The stores of clothing were inexhaustible; not even " a gaiter-button " was awanting. There were cartridges enough to maintain for years the slaughter of offending Germans. Elaborated in secret, and known to the world only by dark whispers, was the terrible mitrailleuse, whose prowess was now to be revealed in destruction hitherto unexampled. The emperor satisfied himself that northern Germany could place on the Rhine no more than three hundred and thirty thousand men. Even should the southern states cast in their lot with their northern brethren—a contingency which he scarcely apprehended—this number would be raised only to four hundred and twenty thousand. He might thus outnumber his enemies; he could not be appreciably outnumbered by them. With a natural confidence in the fortune of his house, in his own military skill and the high fighting qualities of his people, the expectation that his march would lead him to Berlin did not appear wholly unwarranted.

There was only required now some pretext of quarrel—not necessarily credible, but at least susceptible of being expressed in the decorous language of diplomacy. This was opportunely found. The distracted Spaniards, searching among the royal families of Europe for a king, chanced upon a certain Prince Leopold of Hohenzollern, to whom they addressed the prayer that he would rule over them. This potentate was kinsman to the King of Prussia. He stood in a closer degree of relationship to the emperor himself, but the king might be regarded as head of the family of which he was a member, and might therefore plausibly be held responsible for his actions. It was intimated that France would not approve the occupancy of the throne of Spain by any member of the house of Hohenzollern. The king, caring little about the affairs of the Peninsula, disclaimed all knowledge or responsibility in regard to the proceedings of his relative. What was still more to the purpose, that relative himself, who at first inclined a favourable ear to the petition of Spain, announced decisively his refusal of the vacant throne. It seemed that France had lost her pretext for declaring that war upon which she was resolved. But the emperor was equal even to this emergency. He demanded, with premeditated rudeness, a pledge that the king would never, in any future time, permit his kinsman to accept the overtures of Spain. The desired refusal was promptly given. Prussia, said the king, was in no way concerned in the transactions of Prince Leopold and the Spanish government, and would not mix herself up with them. Eight days later, the formal declaration of war was delivered at Berlin.

July 4, 1870 A. D.

July 11.

July 19.

There is no room to doubt that in the visible decline of the second empire a successful war had become, for personal and dynastic reasons, necessary to the emperor. The country had prospered under the empire—as France must always do when she is suffered to be at peace. But in the process of years the unreasonable restrictions laid upon their liberty had become irksome to the French people. In 1866 the emperor stated that "persons of uneasy minds desired to force the liberal progress of the government. He advised them to cease from discussing constitutional theories, and apply to moral and social ameliorations." But the "persons of uneasy minds" rejected his counsel; and their influence was sufficient to force him, after fifteen years of despotism, into the path of reform. He partially removed the fetters which the newspaper press had long worn. He permitted meetings of an economical and industrial character. Next year he announced that in future he would choose his ministers from the majority in the chambers, thus granting the large concession of ministerial responsibility. His prefects were instructed to please the people by promises of new roads, bridges, and railways, and hint to voters that they would be leniently dealt with in regard to payment of taxes. Finally, liberty of the press was granted, and "every class of public sentiment was allowed free expression." Hoping that these concessions would revive his waning popularity, the emperor submitted to a plebiscite the constitutional changes which he had introduced. He begged the people for a favorable vote, which, he said, "would seat order and liberty on a solid basis, and render easier the transmission of the crown to my son." Seven million and a quarter of the voters granted and a million and a half refused the support which he desired. The minority was larger than it had been before, and the ominous fact was known that many of the soldiers voted in opposition to the wish of the emperor.

1868 A. D.

1870 A. D.

In truth, the country was becoming tired of his government. It was said he had grown old and ineffective. His rule was very expensive—more so than any republic, or monarchy, or empire which France had ever known. His foreign policy had brought mainly disgrace; his plots had all been found out, his intrigues had all been baffled. Even the good which he had done became a fault. Thiers and the liberals reproached him that he had helped to make Italy great. France now demanded that he should mar the threatening greatness of Germany, and perpetuate her enfeebling divisions. Probably he would not have undertaken the task if he dared shun it. But the voice of France was for war. The chambers were unanimous; Paris was enthusiastic; the provinces blindly acquiesced. France, with shameful unanimity, sanctioned the great crime which the emperor, not without reluctance, consented to commit. Six weeks later, when his career had closed, and he was a prisoner in the hands of the Germans, he assured Count Bismarck that he himself had not wished for war, but had been compelled to wage it by the pressure of public opinion.

The emperor joined the army at Metz, prepared to lead his eager troops across the Rhine and on to Berlin. Expres-
July 28, sions, loud if not deep, of devotion to his person and
1870 enthusiastic approbation of the war were showered upon
A. D. him at every stage of his journey. But there met him at the very outset discoveries fitted not merely to disappoint but also to alarm. He should have found himself at the head of four hundred thousand men, perfectly disciplined and equipped. To his dismay there were no more than two hundred and twenty thousand. The men of the reserve, not breathing the general enthusiasm, " took an infinite time," as the emperor mourns, " to rejoin their corps." Moreover, it quickly appeared, when they came, that many of them had not been drilled in the use of the breech-loading musket, and their education had now to be commenced in this perilous hour when the highest accomplishment in the use of weapons was so indispensable. The officers who were familiar with the mitrailleuse had been carelessly drafted off to other duties, and this formidable weapon was of necessity intrusted to men who were strangers to its qualities. Supplies of every description, even of money and food, were awanting. Vast accumulations were piled up in two or three great depots, whence they could not be rapidly delivered. The transport-wagons were stored at one point,

their wheels lay elsewhere at a distance, and weeks elapsed before the inopportunely scattered members of those waggons could be recombined. The artillery were without horses until they borrowed from the cavalry. The only maps which were provided were maps of Germany.

It was the intention of the emperor to cross the Rhine before the Germans could gather strength to prevent him. But he quickly perceived that the incompleteness of his own preparations rendered this impossible. He concentrated his troops for an advance into the valley of the Saar. At Saarbrück * there lay a small force of Germans who, adventurously, disputed with him the passage of the river. They were Aug. 2, 1870 A. D. driven away and the river secured. But no use could be made of the success. The emperor was not to enter German territory till four or five weeks had passed; and then he was to enter it as a prisoner. His army lay inactive for two days, and then fell back towards Metz. Already the idea of invasion was seen to be hopeless. For, almost from the day that war was declared the armed manhood of Germany had been hurrying to the frontier—admirable in discipline, marvellously complete in organization, guided by the highest military genius of the age. Internal divisions yielded to the first pressure of a common danger, and the states of the south marched with their countrymen of the north. By day and night railway trains followed each other at brief intervals, laden with soldiers, horses, and artillery. Fourteen days sufficed to place four hundred and fifty thousand perfectly equipped Germans face to face with the rash and ill-prepared armament of France.

The Germans lost no time in beginning the invasion of French territory. The crown prince crossed the Lauter—at

* It was at Saarbruck the Prince Imperial received his "baptism of fire." The emperor writing, in exile, regarding this incident. expresses himself thus:—"In this affair the Prince Imperial displayed a coolness beyond his age, but indiscreet friends having exaggerated the merit of his behaviour, the malevolent turned into ridicule that which in reality was worthy of praise."

20

that point the boundary which divides the two countries—and
at Weissenburg, with an ovetwhelming force, fell upon
Aug. 4, the French and defeated them. The victorious Germans
1870
A. D. passed immediately southwards towards Wörth, where
Marshal Macmahon was striving to draw his scattered
forces together. The French kept careless watch, and it was a
painful surprise to the marshal to be attacked in early morning
by a force which here, as elsewhere, largely outnumbered his
own. Macmahon had every advantage of position, and his
troops fought with desperate courage. But they failed to hold
their ground against their assailants. Both sides endured heavy
Aug. 6. loss, and the French, beaten and disordered, fled from
the field. Nor was this the only calamity which befell
France on that unhappy day. At Speichern the French, under
General Frossard, occupied heights which were deemed almost
impregnable. But the Germans, after hours of heavy fighting,
scaled the heights and drove the French away, with lamentable slaughter on both sides.

This accumulation of disaster filled the emperor with dismay.
He was at Metz, vainly endeavouring to hasten the concentration of his whole force, but frustrated at every point by this terrible flood of armed Germans who overran his country and
dashed all his combinations into hopeless ruin. He already
thought of returning to Paris to resume the reins of government. But the empress counselled him to delay his return until
he should have gained an important success, and he remained.
His military reputation, as he himself states, was not sufficiently
established to resist evil fortune, and the confidence of his
troops diminished. He made over the command of the army
Aug. 13. at Metz to Marshal Bazaine. Henceforth he was
borne helplessly along, scarcely regarded either by his
government or his soldiers—" condemned to impotence while
he saw his armies and his government on the road to
destruction." To the evils of this sad position it has to be

added that he was suffering physical pain, constant and often intense, from the disease which ultimately proved fatal.

It was yet only eleven days since the first blow had been struck, and already the war was lost beyond hope of recovery. During the first week of August the cry of Paris was still, " On to Berlin." So sudden was the collapse of these vain hopes, that during the second week the concern of Paris was for her own defence.   The Parisians, who so lately urged their government into war, now assailed those in its direction, overthrew a ministry, and assumed an attitude threateningly hostile to the throne.   It was determined that Macmahon, who had withdrawn to Chalons, where the emperor had joined him, should retreat in the direction of Paris, for the protection of the capital.   But the next day brought a new policy.   Bazaine had been left at Metz surrounded by the enemy, and government " feared the worst " in Paris if he should be aban- Aug. 21, doned to his fate.   Macmahon must therefore hasten to 1870 A. D. his relief.   The marshal hesitated, for he knew the enterprise to be impossible.   His troops—one hundred and forty thousand in number—were not all of the best quality; they were exhausted by toilsome marches, discouraged by defeat, and insufficiently provided with the most indispensable supplies.   Their flank must be exposed during their long march of one hundred and ten miles to the attack of an enemy of unknown strength, of whose energy they had already had terrible experience.   Confidence in their leaders was gone; and the gloom which forebodes and invites disaster was in every heart and on every face. But the fear of revolution in Paris overruled all other considerations, and the marshal set out on a march Aug. 23. which he scarcely hoped could end elsewhere than in ruin.

Meanwhile Bazaine had suffered fierce attack from the Germans. He vainly attempted to escape from Metz. He fought two bloody and indecisive battles at Rezon- Aug. 16, 18. ville and Gravelotte.   He found it impossible to break through the German lines, and he drew back his disheartened troops to the shelter of the forts.

Tidings of Macmahon's movement were immediately carried to the Prussian camp. His purpose could at first only be guessed; but it was rightly guessed, and prompt measures were taken for its frustration. Two German armies, numbering one hundred and sixty thousand men, were sufficiently strong to shut in Bazaine till hunger forced his surrender. The other two armies—the third and fourth—with a strength of two hundred and thirty thousand, were available for service elsewhere. It was possible for this great force to fall upon Macmahon while still on his march and before he could receive help from Bazaine. The two armies were immediately turned northwards.

As the French drew near the little town of Stenay, where they proposed to cross the river Meuse, the Germans Aug. 26, had approached them closely, and in overwhelming 1870 numbers were concentrating on their flank. The country A. D. was densely wooded; the watch of the French was, as usual, careless. At Beaumont a German force, issuing from forest roads, burst upon the unexpectant French occupied in cooking. In the engagement which followed, the French were forced aside from the advance which would have led them to Metz and were driven northwards towards Sedan. About midnight the wearied men set out on this dismal journey. The night was dark; heavy rains had made the roads difficult; the confusion which prevailed was extreme. All night the men toiled forward, and reached Sedan at nine next morning. The emperor had gone to the little town of Carignan to rest for the night. A message from Macmahon told him of the enforced change of route, and required him to repair to Sedan. He arrived there late at night, without baggage or escort, and walked almost alone from the railway-station into the little town where the crowning agony of his career was to be endured. His advisers urged him to go further and save himself, but he refused.

Life was little worth saving then. He would stay with his army and share the fate which no power could now avert.

Next day the French busied themselves in restoring some measure of order in their ranks, and in making such preparation as they found possible for the approaching conflict. All that day the German advance continued. When night fell their two armies had gathered themselves around the French so closely and in such strength that resistance was hopeless, and escape, in the event of defeat, impossible.

The French occupied a range of heights which overlook Sedan and the valley of the Meuse. Before daybreak the indefatigable Germans advanced to the attack. Their coming was not expected at so early an hour, but the French stood their ground. The marshal, hastening to Sept. 1, 1870 A. D. the front, was struck down and disabled by a fragment of a bursting shell. As they bore him from the field he was met by the emperor, who spoke some kind words and road onward to the battle.* It was their final parting—tragical and mournful as few partings have been.

No one understood the position of the two armies, or knew anything of the marshal's plans—if indeed he had any plan beyond a resolution to fight stubbornly to the last. He made over the command to General Ducrot, who began to order certain new dispositions. But an hour or two later the command was claimed by General Wimpffen, who had just arrived from Africa, and who bore a commission from the minister of war. This new leader at once reversed the arrangements of Ducrot. The manifest vacillation in command destroyed confidence among the troops and accelerated the now inevitable ruin. For many hours, however, they maintained with heroic courage the hopeless struggle—enduring and inflicting lamentable

* In his own words, "with the conviction that either his life or his death was, on this fatal day, equally useless for the public safety, he rode on to the field of battle with that frigid resignation which faces danger without weakness, but also without enthusiasm."

slaughter of brave men.   The fortune of war was so decisively adverse, that the utmost hope of the general was to
hold his ground till nightfall, and then to break through and
escape.

The Germans attacked the French positions and carried them
one by one, along the whole line four or five miles in length.
They established artillery on the heights, until at the close there
were five hundred pieces whose fire commanded every foot of
ground on which a Frenchman stood. By four o'clock resistance
ceased.   The French had been driven into Sedan, or scattered
or captured.   Sedan was a prey to the wildest confusion. The
streets were crowded with soldiers, many of whom had cast
away their arms, and now, regardless of authority, sought only
for food and for shelter from the withering fire of the German
guns.   Through these crowds mounted men and panic-stricken
waggoners forced their desperate way heedless of the wretches
whom they trampled down.   Loud imprecations rose on every
side against the leaders who were responsible for these disastrous results.   And over all rose the thunder of the German
guns, which, converging their fire upon Sedan, sent an incessant
storm of shells among the Discomfited troops. The miserable
emperor, worn by fatigue and sorrow and physical pain, had
vainly exposed himself, seeking death in the midst of his
soldiers.   Now he ordered a flag of truce to be hung out; he
surrendered himself to the king, and sent General Wimpffen to
make what terms he could for the army   •

The German chiefs were all before Sedan. The king, his son
the crown prince, Count Bismarck, Count Moltke, Von Roon
the minister-at-war, were present to drink the delight of this
marvellous triumph. Late at night the general of the defeated
French met at Donchery with the officers empowed by the
king to negotiate. He pled earnestly that his beaten soldiers
should be allowed to pass the Belgian frontier—only seven
miles away—and there be disarmed. Generous terms, he said,

would awaken the gratitude of France; rather than submit to disgrace he would renew the fight, and Germany would be guilty of the blood which would be vainly shed. Count Moltke showed him that eighty thousand Frenchmen, with food for only twenty-four hours, were surrounded by two hundred and forty thousand Germans, and under fire of five hundred guns, which would utterly destroy them in a few hours; that the suggestion of renewing the fight need not, therefore, be discussed. Bismarck treated contemptuously the idea of national gratitude, and intimated with perfect frankness that, having France now in their power, they intended to provide for their future security. With much reluctance General Wimpffen consented to an unconditional surrender, and eighty-three thousand Frenchmen laid down their arms. No such shame had ever before fallen upon the arms of France.

The King of Prussia, accompanied by his son, came to visit the fallen and captive emperor. The two monarchs met last in Paris, three years before. The king came then as the emperor's guest during the Paris Exhibition, when Napoleon, at the pinnacle of human greatness, received all the crowned and otherwise illustrious persons of Europe. The altered circumstances of the present meeting were referred to in sympathizing terms by the conqueror, and good-naturedly attributed to imprudent advice. A castle in Germany was assigned as a place of residence for the emperor, who now finally disappears from history.

And now the way to Paris was cleared of every obstacle, and the Germans without loss of time began their march on the capital. So soon as the disaster of Sedan was known there, the Parisians deposed their emperor and erected a republic. The new government determined upon a strenuous defence. The Germans completely surrounded the city, and effectively cut off communication with the world

Sept. 4, 1870 A. D.

outside. They did not inflict the horrors of bombardment, and
Sept. 19, were contented to wait till famine compelled surrender.
1870– During four months the Parisians endured the miseries
Jan. 30, of partial starvation—consuming animals whose flesh
1871 they loathed; maintaining postal communication with
A. D. the world by the aid of balloons. At length endurance
reached its limit; Paris was given over to the enemies of France;
the humbled Parisians looked on while the countless hosts of
Germany, entering by the Arc de Triomphe, marched in triumph down the magnificent avenue which leads to the Tuileries, and possessed themselves of the city. Their occupation
was soon terminated by a treaty; but so miserable had the
condition of Paris become, that she had reason to lament the
departure even of her great enemy. For the communists,
exasperated by privation, and emboldened by the humiliation
of the authorities, undertook to found a government of their
own. They seized Paris, manned its defences, and announced
April 2 defiance of the republican government. For many weeks
to a French army besieged and shelled the capital. At last
May 21, an entrance was forced. The wretched insurgents, fight-
1871 ing with a savage disregard of life, were in large measure
A. D. slaughtered or taken prisoners, but not till some of the
finest buildings of Paris had perished by their incendiary hands.

During the German siege the king had occupied the palace
of Versailles. The divisions of Germany were now healed;
the last obstacle to the long-desired unity of the race was now
overcome. For ages it had been the wicked policy of France
to maintain the divisions which kept her neighbours weak. So
Dec., complete was her discomfiture that the union of all the
1870 German states was now consummated in a French palace
A. D. by the coronation of King William as the first emperor
of united Germany.

The terms exacted by the conquerors expressed with terrible
although not unreasonable severity the woe which waits upon
the vanquished. Germany took back Alsace and Lorraine,

once her own, and still, after two centuries of separation, retaining their use of her language. She demanded an indemnity of two hundred million sterling, in reimbursement of the charges to which France had unjustifiably put her. A German army would remain on French territory, upheld at French expense, till this huge claim was fully met. The entire cost of the war to France, apart from destruction of property and injury to commerce, was three hundred and seventy million. It seemed to many observers that France was hopelessly ruined, and it is probable the victors themselves intended that the enormous burden which they imposed should break the power of France to become again dangerous to her neighbours. But once more the ability of France to recover from pecuniary disaster was an astonishment to the world. M. Thiers was now president of the republic. He was able to discharge in full the claims of Germany, and terminate the occupation within the period fixed for that purpose by the treaty.

May 10, 1871 A. D.

The sight of an empty throne naturally quickened the mischievous activities of those who claimed a right to occupy it. The adherents of each of the pretenders deemed that the hour of success was near, and busied themselves with vain intrigues. For a time it might be feared that a reaction in favour of some one of the rejected houses had set in. But the reaction was only apparent. M. Thiers, who resigned the presidency in May, 1873, was succeeded by Marshal Macmahon, who claimed to be "an honest man and a soldier," and who proved no more successful in political than he had been in military life. Guided by the legitimist and priestly factions, he seemed ready to defy the wishes of the people, betray the republic, and force a new revolution. The French people, confident in the strength of the republican cause, exercised a calm forbearance which even their friends scarcely ventured to expect. The elections gave forth a voice so decisive that

the marshal submitted to the popular will and ultimately
1879 resigned, yielding his authority to M. Grévy, whose
A. D. views were fully in accord with those of the people.

The constitution under which France is at present governed
is sufficiently democratic to have satisfied even the patriots of
1789. There are two legislative bodies — the Chamber of
Deputies and the Senate. Every citizen who is twenty-one
years of age is entitled to vote in the election. Any citizen
of twenty-five may be a deputy; any citizen of forty may be
a senator. The legislators receive payment for their services.
The head of the government is the president, elected for seven
years by the Senate and Chamber of Deputies met in national
assembly. The president appoints his ministers, who are
responsible to the chambers for their policy.

France is Catholic to the extent of ninety-eight per cent. of
her population, but all religions are equal in law. A system
of concurrent endowment prevails, the beneficiaries under
which are Catholics, Protestants, and Jews. The Catholics
receive about two million sterling; the Protestants sixty thousand pounds; and the Jewish rabbis five thousand pounds,—an
even-handed distribution strictly according to numbers.

The education of the country is necessarily in large measure
controlled by the Roman Catholic clergy. The amount annually expended on public instruction is about two million sterling, about the same amount as the church receives. Thirty
per cent. of the French people above six years of age are still
wholly without education—unable either to read or write. It
is evident, however, that progress is being made; for while
thirty-four per cent of persons above twenty years of age are
unable to read, only twenty-four per cent. of those between six
years and twenty are in that condition. That progress is extremely irregular; for while in the north-eastern departments
the wholly uneducated are only seven or eight per cent. of the

population above six years of age, in the south-west they range as high as sixty per cent.

The first care of France after the fall of the empire was to create a new military system in room of that which had disappointed her so fatally. Copying now the system of her triumphant enemy, it was declared that every Frenchman owes to his country personal military service. Every citizen not physically disqualified must serve five years in the active army, and must then stand enrolled for fifteen years in the various reserve forces. Service by substitute is strictly forbidden; but the severity of this law is tempered by merciful exemptions in cases where family circumstances render the presence of the conscript specially needful at home. Practically these exemptions relieve from service about one-fourth of those who are liable. France maintains an army which, on its peace footing, numbers seven hundred and nineteen thousand men. Altogether she has two and a half million trained men ready to assume arms. She expends upon these enormous forces twenty million sterling.

The war navy of France consists of four hundred vessels, manned by conscription, and costing about seven million annually. Like other European powers, France has cumbered herself with the large number of sixty huge ironclad steamers, in which the maximum of cost is so happily combined with the minimum of usefulness.

It has been the unvarying experience of the French, in all their recent political changes, that each of their new governments has been more costly than that which preceded it. The government of the first Napoleon was inexpensive because it was in large part supported by plunder. The expenditure under the restoration averaged forty million sterling. Louis Philippe raised the average to fifty-one million. The republic brought it up to sixty-three million. The second empire, with its practice of "fighting for an idea," cost France eighty-three million, and bequeathed entanglements which resulted in an annual expenditure of one hundred and seven million—the most enormous waste of the fruits of industry to which human mismanagement has yet attained.

The national debt of France has swelled out to the extraordinary aggregate of nine hundred and forty million sterling, and the annual interest is thirty million. This huge debt is the favourite investment of the careful French peasantry, and it is important to remark how large and how rapidly growing is the number of persons who by this means have become interested in the stability of French institutions. In the last year of the empire the creditors of the state numbered one million two hundred and fifty thousand; five years later they numbered four million three hundred and eighty thousand. Every second householder in France is in the position of having lent money to the government. The era of revolution may be presumed to have closed when a conservative influence so unprecedentedly powerful has been called into existence.

French law divides all landed possessions equally among the children of the owner, This arrangement has resulted in an extraordinary diffusion of ownership. Nearly two-thirds of French householders are land-owners.* Their holdings are of necessity very small. While fifty thousand persons own properties which average six hundred acres, and half a million whose average is sixty acres, there are five million whose possessions are under six acres. The subdivision of land is not without its inconveniences, but it is immeasureably more conducive to the general welfare than the absorption of the entire surface of the country by a very few individuals, as in Great Britain.

The French people increase more slowly than any other of the western nations of Europe. For several years after the fall of Napoleon stopped the waste of life in battle, the average

* Only one British householder in every four is an owner of land.

gratitude of France; rather than submit to
renew the fight, and Germany would be
which would be vainly shed. Count Moltke
eighty thousand Frenchmen, with food for
iours, were surrounded by two hundred and
rmans, and under fire of five hundred guns,
rly destroy them in a few hours; that the
ewing the fight need not, therefore, be dis-
k treated contemptuously the idea of national
imated with perfect frankness that, having
ieir power, they intended to provide for their
With much reluctance General Wimpffen
unconditional surrender, and eighty three
imen laid down their arms. No such shame
fallen upon the arms of France.
Prussia, accompanied by his son, came to visit
aptive emperor. The two monarchs met last
years before. The king came then to a
: during the Paris Exhibition, when Napoleon,
of human greatness, received all the crowned
illustrious persons of Europe. The scenes
if the present meeting were referred to, ...
s by the conqueror, and good nature, ...
ent advice. A castle in Germany was assigned
residence for the emperor, with whom ... /
a history.

... when Paris was denuded of every soldier able
without loss of time regain their ranks ... ...
son in the disaster of ...am was ...
ritans deposed their emperor and ... ...
he new government be carried ... ...
lace. The German ... ...
effectively cut off ... ...
I to put
there be ...

they import are purchased in Great Britain. We send them some coals and iron products, a few cotton and linen goods, and almost exactly the same value of woollen articles which we receive from them. Some silk goods also we succeed in disposing of to them; but the amount they buy from us is only one-third the amount they sell to us, and for some years it has been decreasing.

Notwithstanding the growth of her foreign trade, the mercantile navy of France has not increased since 1866, and is now only one million tons—about one-sixth that of Great Britain.

France is imperfectly supplied with railways. She has only twelve thousand miles, and even of these one-half could not be constructed without a guarantee from the state. The people have not yet learned to travel so freely as the English do; for while in England the annual receipts of the railways are equal to about forty shillings for each of the population, in France they are less than half that amount. The French are still contented with a smaller amount of postal and telegraphic communication than their neighbours across the Channel. The average correspondence of every Englishman gives thirty-three letters per annum, but the Frenchman's average is only ten, and even this has shown a slight tendency to decrease since the German occupation of the country. Thus, too, the English use the telegraph at the rate of one message annually to each person, while the French average is only one message to five persons.

One-half of the French people are directly engaged in agriculture; three-fourths live in the country or in small towns, subject to rural influences. The changes of recent years have given to the provinces their just political authority, and the French peasant is now, therefore, a figure of prime importance in politics. He is extremely ignorant of all that is to be learned from books and newspapers, which indeed he shuns rather than courts, believing that education would unfit his children for the life of monotonous toil which is their destiny.

Although thus uneducated, he is acute, observant, is possessed
of much tact, and is not without a certain native dignity of
character and manner. He is superstitious, but also sceptical,
and goes no further towards reception of religion which the
priest offers than to believe that it may do him some good, and
can do him no harm. His wife maintains the family relations
with the church, and is ordinarily under the dominion of the
priest. He is frugal, industrious, patient, simple, and inexpensive in all tastes and habits. In politics he is inclining more
towards a conservative republicanism; although not wholly
delivered from a lingering suspicion that the republic will one
day sieze and divide his possessions. He hates monarchy because of the traditions of old oppression, and his own bitter
experiences of the miseries of war. He cares for no dynasty;
in truth, he does not care greatly what form of government he
lives under, so long as he is suffered to live quietly and accumulate his small earnings. The ballot protects him in his exercise of the franchise, and he votes independently. Very possibly he will vote under some ludicrous misconception, but
neither the priest nor the local magnate will be suffered to
guide his action. No man in Europe is more regardless of
military glory, or less likely to go voluntarily into war. The
French towns are fiery in their temper, and prone to a solution
of difficulties by a recourse to violence. Rural France is peaceable, apathetic, penurious. Even now the French peasant is
a valuable power on the side of peaceful government, and his
value will grow with the progress of his education.

It has been said by Carlyle that "the thing we call French
Revolution became a thing that was" on the day when
Napoleon quelled the revolt of the sections. Four years
later, when Napoleon obtained supreme power, he, and
France with him, believed that he had then closed the era of
revolution. When Louis XVIII. ascended the throne of his

1795
A. D.

fathers, it was to heal the wounds of the revolution—now at
length terminated. Louis Philippe came on a like errand—to
give stability to the institutions of France, and finally calm the
agitations of the now accomplished revolution. Years passed,
and the same necessity, grim and fierce as of old, confronted
the Frenchmen of a later time. Louis Napoleon announced
that he had arisen to close the era of revolution. But despotism heals no wounds; it solves no great problems; it only delays their solution and enhances their complications. The
gulf which had yawned since 1789 refused to close till it
had swallowed down the last pretender to the throne of
France.

The era of revolution in England stretched across the half-
century which intervened between the breaking out of hostilities in 1642 and the establishment of a constitutional monarchy
in 1688. The era of revolution in France opened in 1789, and
cannot close otherwise than by a establishment of a republic
—the free choice of the French people.

For ninety years—nearly the life-time of three generations
—the French people have yearned for political equality. They
were sufficiently enlightened to desire liberty, but too little
enlightened to use it wisely. Their early success bewildered
them. After giving, as it seemed, high example to the world,
and awakening the hope of oppressed humanity they suffered
their revolution to be covered with shame by crimes of unparalleled atrocity. Then they proved, for a time, disloyal to the
cause of freedom, and dazzled by the glory of a brilliant soldier,
became his willing slaves. They paused in their pursuit of
freedom to conquer the world, and raise their emperor to the
throne of a universal despotism. The restoration found them
penitent, caring only for quietness after the long frenzy. In
time their love of freedom regained its ascendency, and they
chased from the throne two kings whose rule was becoming
unduly absolute. Once more their dream of liberty and equali-

ty embodied in a republic was realized. But disappointment was still in store for them. The nephew of Napoleon robbed them of their liberties by shameful violence. They were not free to return to the government of their preference till the Napoleon despotism perished in a war which its own arrogance had provoked.

There has been charged against the French a blind, aimless love of change; a mere insatiable restlessness, incapable of content. Many observers fail to discover progress in her history, and see only a barren, oft-repeated alternation of despotism and license. These impressions are, however, inconsistent with obvious facts. France has not followed liberty with wisdom or with moderation, but she has followed it tenaciously under unprecedented difficulties. If she has been led aside from the pursuit, she has not failed to return to it when the circustances which tempted her deviation passed away. Nor are the other nations of Europe guiltless regarding the aberrations which darken her record. At the opening of her revolution the time seemed to have come for the emancipation of Europe from the political and ecclesastical systems of the Middle Ages—now grown obsolete and injurious. France pointed the way to the great deliverance. But the nations were unprepared to follow, and their hostility provoked the excesses by which the hopes of mankind were for the time frustrated.

Perhaps the most injurious legacy bequeathed by the earlier years of the revolution was the vehement antipathy with which monarchists and republicans have been taught to regard each other. Despotism had been very cruel to its victims. Republicanism had exacted a terrible revenge. Political antagonism has been in consequence peculiarly tenacious and bitter. For well-nigh a century the adherents of the opposing principles have contended for supremacy in a spirit of mutual abhorrence, beside which the mild rivalries of England sink into

21

insignificance. But even under this disadvantage the cause of liberty has steadily gained. There is yet a strong party which seeks for rest under a government of divine right. But its influence wanes in the growing political light; and the danger that pretenders to the throne will awaken renewed discords constantly diminishes.

Once more France is free and self-governing, with a better prospect than she has ever before enjoyed of retaining her dearly-won privileges. All her royal houses have had their opportunity—closed, in each case, by rejection which thus far appears to be final. The mob of Paris can no longer make a revolution it can make only a riot. In 1848 the provinces complained that they had to receive their revolutions by mail from Paris. Previously they accepted such consignments without even complaint. Now they do not complain; they are able to prevent. Railways and the telegraph have taken away the usurped dominion of the capital, and summoned all France to share in her own government. In a few hours the voice of the country pronounces with authority on political questions. Paris is no longer France. The rural population of France—industrious, peaceable, economical, although still sadly uninformed—is now a controlling power in the state. The military spirit, whose predominance has brought calamity so great, is curbed by the calmer and wiser influences originating among those classes by whom the miseries of war have been most severely felt.

Now indeed it is possible to hope that the era of revolution is at length closed, and that France, satisfied with glory chastened by sorrow, and finally delivered from the curse of personal government, will become a stable, powerful, and peaceable republic.

CHAPTER III.

PRUSSIA did not enhance her military renown by the part which fell to her in the great revolutionary wars. At Jena and Auerstadt her armies were so utterly broken that for seven years she held no higher place than that of a subjugated and tributary country. In the campaign of 1814 she fought stoutly, but without important success. At Ligny her army yielded the honours of the field to an inferior force of Frenchmen; and at Waterloo she performed merely the useful but not glorious task of pursuing an already beaten enemy.

But although she gained few laurels, she was a member of a victorious association of powers, and she reaped the rewards of victory. Napoleon had stripped her of nearly one-half of her territory and population. All this was now restored, and the liberality of the Congress of Vienna added to it Swedish Pomerania, the Rhinelands, and a portion of Saxony, whose king had been so injudicious as to maintain his loyalty to Napoleon after wiser potentates perceived that the time had come to abandon a falling cause. Prussia was again a great power, with a territory of over one hundred thousand square miles, and a population of ten million.

Even amid the humiliations and agonies of the war, the German people solaced their minds with the hope of constitutional government. Their wishes even then were not restricted to deliverance from French tyranny. They already in their hearts rejected a management of their national affairs in which they themselves had no voice. So well was this perceived that their princes stimulated them to efforts against the common foe by promises of reform. During the Hundred Days the King of Prussia explicitly promised "representation of the people." A few days later the same pledge was given by the German diet. Even when there was no actual promise, it was the general expectation of the people, tacitly sanctioned by their princes, that peace was to usher in the era of representative institutions.*

May 25, 1815 A. D.

It was not easy to devise convenient political arrangements for Germany. The old system—the combination of states under an emperor who was held to represent the Cæsars—had been dashed to pieces by Napoleon, and in its place had partially come the Confederacy of the Rhine. But that association had fallen with its author, and Germany was now an incohering multitude of independent and for the most part of petty states. The Congress of Vienna undertook the correction of a disorder so threatening to the general weal. Thirty-seven German states were united in one great confederation, under the presidency of Austria. This alliance embraced thirty million people, and had at its call three hundred thousand armed men. The states which composed it sent representatives to a diet which met at Frankfurt. The leading objects which occupied the diet were the internal peace of Germany and its defence against foreign attack; but an assembly of sovereign powers was necessarily at liberty to widen indefinately the range of interests which it was pleased to regulate.

1815 A. D.

When the war closed, the German people looked that their

* Thirty years after, it was asserted at a sitting of the three estates of Prussia that the country had risen in 1813 for the sole purpose of gaining a constitution. Bismarck denied this statement, and asserted that the uprising had no other motive than to rid the land of foreign tyranny. The house contradicted him by violent and prolonged marks of disapprobation. There is no room to doubt that the combination of the two statements yields the true explanation of the great movement of 1813.

princes should redeem the pledges given in the hour of need. The wish for constitutional government was widely spread, not merely among the artisans, but also among the educated and influential middle class. In some of the smaller states—as Hanover and Würtemberg—the people compelled the fulfilment of their desires. But in Prussia the government was too strong to be concussed, and it manifested from the beginning an indisposition to concede the popular demands. The liberal newspapers were suppressed when any pretext for severity could be found. When certain petitioners once ventured to remind the king of the promises he had made, 1817 they were angrily informed by one of his ministers that A. D, "those who admonish the king are guilty of doubting the inviolability of his word." Moved by the same impulse, the diet adopted certain measures which were intended to make it impossible for the small states to grant constitutions, and which, for a time, most fully served that purpose.

The revolutionary movements which agitated Spain and Naples awakened grave anxieties among the German princes. The Prussian government announced 1818–20 that there existed " a fermentation of ideas fitted A. D. to cause most serious alarm;" that there were numerous secret societies; that there prevailed among the people " a sentiment of hatred for kings and governments, and an enthusiasm for the phantom which they call liberty." To meet these alarming symtoms the diet adopted such measures of repression as were deemed adequate. The press was strictly bound. No word might now be printed in which the sharp eye of the censor discovered any sympathy with the threatening liberalism of the time. The more active reformers were silenced or driven away. Meetings in which the people presumed to criticise the acts of their rulers were prohibited. An enforced and reluctant silence. prevailed. Prince Metternich Dec, 1819 was able to announce from Vienna that the agitation has A. D. sensibly diminished."

To the severe conservatism of the German diet the prox-
imity of France was eminently disquieting. Every throb of
the great revolutionary heart went pulsing through the mass
of German liberalism, threatening the overthrow of the order
which was maintained so laboriously. But the idea of making
the people contented by granting their reasonable demands
was yet many years in the future. When the French
1830 overthrew the throne of the Bourbons, the agitation
A. D. over whose subsidence Prince Metternich had rejoiced
swelled out to alarming dimensions. But there was no hope
for revolution in presence of a union of governments which
commanded three hundred thousand available bayonets. The
diet, with unshaken authority, betook itself to measures more
sternly repressive than before. Political associations were interdicted; political speeches at meetings duly authorized were
visited with heavy penalties; the states bound themselves to
give up political offenders and to maintain a vigorous watchfulness over their subjects; the introduction of newspapers or
pamphlets printed abroad in the German language was forbidden; workmen were no longer allowed to pass from states
in which there were trades-union into states as yet free from
the taint of those objectionable organizations. The people
petitioned for some relaxation of their bonds; but the diet had
now assumed powers more absolute than ever in regard to such
requests, and the people prayed in vain. A few riots which
were intended to emphasize the popular demand were easily
quelled. The German people cherished in silence desires
which were steadily consolidating into a fixed and unalterable
resolution.

A habitual submissiveness, while it did not prevent the
growth of such desires in Prussia, made their progress slow,
and enabled the nation to suffer their frustration patiently.
Every man had been for three years a soldier, and carried with
him into civil life the soldier's habit of obedience. Nearly

every man could read, but the faculty was not generally exercised. The people had no newspapers, and few books. They were without the educational agencies which develop the mental powers of a free people. They had no acquaintance with the proceedings of their government; they had no part in any description of public business. They were held in a condition of pupilage. Everything was compulsory. There was no free exercise of mind. Government undertook everything, and expected from the people the unreasoning obedience of children.*

Government interference and popular submission extended fully even into the province of religion,—a domain in which intrusive rulers have ordinarily encountered the obstinate resistance of their subjects. Protestantism in Prussia was divided into Lutheranism and Calvinism. The Lutherans held a modification—now scarcely intelligible—of the doctrine of the real presence, which the Calvinists rejected. The Calvinists believed in predestination, which the Lutherans abhorred. Divergences vastly less important than these have generally been deemed sufficient to keep Protestant churches apart. But the King of Prussia intimated to his people that the separation was maintained altogether about outward things, and ought to cease. He compelled the union of two specimen congregations, and himself partook of communion in the united church, expressing emphatically the hope that his example would be followed. It was followed. A majority of the churches submitted to union, not because they themselves wished it, but because the king wished it.† A multitude of educated Prussians accepted from the royal hand what was to them virtually a new religion with no greater apparent hesita-

1817
A. D.

* "The power of the government presses upon the partially developed faculties of the youth as with a mountain's weight. When the children come out from the school they have little use either for the faculties that have been developed or for the knowledge that has been acquired."—HORACE MANN, 1843.

† Predestination was left an open question. In the celebration of the Lord's Supper the officiating minister was directed to indicate no opinion on the question of real or symbolical presence, but simply to relate the historical fact that Christ said, "This is my body," &c.

tion than if the matter had been one of mere police or custom-house regulation.

The confederation of 1815 looked only to political interests, and had no regard to the commercial welfare of its members. Each state was left to impose and levy its own duties. The result was a series of barbaric arrangements, according to which goods required to pass through twenty-seven custom-houses upon the Rhine alone. The removal of these vexatious hindrances to commercial intercourse must largely promote the interests of German trade, and crown with public favour the state under whose auspices a reform so valuable was established. The rivalry between Prussia and Austria, which closed forty years later by the defeat of Austria at Sadowa, already power-fully influenced both. Prussia saw her opportunity. She organized a commercial league of all the German powers with the omission of Austria. The internal trade of all the allied states was now freed from restriction. Foreign goods were subjected to a uniform scale of duty; the amount collected was divided among the several states in proportion to their population, as ascertained by a triennial census. Every state, great or small, had an equal voice in the council of the league. The duties imposed were intended to protect domestic manufactures, especially against English goods, and in avowed retaliation for the English corn law of 1815. Under the fostering influences of this league the commerce of Germany made progress so rapid that in ten years the receipts of the custom-house had doubled.

1833 A. D.

Among the liberals of Germany there grew up slowly during many years a desire for a closer union than the loosely-knit confederation supplied.* There were forty million Germans,

---

* This desire, which was all the time acquiring increased strength, burst out with redoubled vigour when circumstances drew special attention to the evils of disunion. This was notably the case when the Franco-Italian war broke out in 1859. Germany, smitten, as England has so often been, with sudden fear of France, became vehement in her demand for union.

occupying fertile territories in the centre of Europe. Effectively united, this population would form one of the most powerful of European states. But their influence was neutralized by their separation into a multitude of petty states, and by the jealousies which resulted from an arrangement so unhappy. Nor was it found that voluntary alliance in a confederation sufficed to cancel the manifold evils of division. The people saw with ever-growing impatience that the power of Germany was frittered away by a foolish political system, and the cry for unity waxed ever louder.

The great factors in recent German history gained increasing prominence as the years passed. Steadily growing among a population of average intelligence and of notable steadfastness of purpose, there was a desire for national unity and also a desire for government according to a constitution, and no longer according to the pleasure of a few individuals. There was further a rivalry between Austria and Prussia for pre-eminence in Germany. These causes, more powerfully than all others, have contributed to mould the political system of Germany into its present form.

In Prussia the antagonism between the opinions of king and of people was so complete as to give assurance of a stubborn conflict. The people had persuaded themselves that, like their neighbours of France and of England, they possessed of right a voice in the management of their own public affairs. The king, on his part, claimed to have received from Heaven an exclusive control over these affairs. Bismarck, afterwards chancellor of the German empire, defines with much clearness, in one of his early speeches, the royal position. "The Prussian sovereigns," he sets forth, "are in possession of 1847 a crown, not by grace of the people, but by God's grace; A. D. an actually unconditional crown, some of the rights of which they have voluntarily conceded to the people—an example rare in history." The adjustment of a divergence of opinion so grave might well be attended with difficulty.

The smaller despotisms of Germany, smitten with fear by the tidings of the revolution in Paris, yielded instantly to 1848 the demands of their people. The kings of Saxony and A. D. Würtemberg hastened to grant constitutions. The King of Bavaria was troubled at this inopportune moment by an insurrection, whose object it was to expel from his palace the fascinating but unworthy Lola Montes. Encouraged by the news from Paris, the insurgents widened the scope of their movement, and exacted from their reluctant king liberty of the press and parliamentary government. A crowd of less considerable princes entered with equal haste and equal reluctance upon the work of erecting liberal institutions. Even the German diet, lately so irresistible and so arrogant, was fain to bend to the storm, and cancel some of its more offensively despotic edicts.

To the King of Prussia* it seemed, after the first days of alarm had passed, that he might hope to gain advantage by assuming the direction of a movement which he perceived to be irresistible. He hastened to announce numerous liberal measures, and to indicate a purpose of shortly increasing the number. But above all he proposed the union of Germany into one federal state, of which federation it was obvious that his majesty desired to become the head.

The king's sudden liberalism did not command the confidence of his people..† On the day after the royal proclama-Mar. 18, tion, a bloody conflict raged for hours in the streets of 1848 Berlin between the populace and the troops; barricades A. D. were erected within sight of the palace; numerous dwellings were sacked and burned. Next day a new and more liberal ministry was appointed, and the king's asseveration of his ardent desire to secure the liberty of his people became more emphatic than before.

* Frederick William IV., crowned 1840.

† " The poor King of Prussia has made a sad mess. Never has he made a move or a concession but it was too late; ·nay, when it would have been better had he done nothing."—BARON STOCKMAR to PRINCE ALBERT, 31st March

Royal and popular liberalism having thus united their forces, the transition from a despotic to a democratic form of government was quickly accomplished. His majesty proposed household suffrage as one of the bases of the new constitution, and his offer was rapturously accepted by the chamber. But not even by a concession so extreme did the king succeed in restoring harmony between the government and the people. . The assembly fell into interminable debate Regard trival details of the constitution. They eliminated from the royal title the words "by the grace of God," leaving it to be understood that his majesty ruled merely by the will of his people. They abolished his nobility. Their profitless discussions paralyzed commerce and roused the passions of the populace. Employment could not be found; multitudes of workmen, idle and hungry, roamed the streets of Berlin; destructive riots were of frequent occurrence,—and still the assembly prolonged its vain debates.

April, 1848 A. D.

The king was deeply chagrined by the untoward results which his new institutions had produced. He had also to endure the mortification of seeing an Austrian prince chosen regent of the German confederacy—a dignity which he ardently desired for himself.* It became evident that he had entered upon a path which did not lead to tranquility, and he resolved to retrace his steps. His cabinet announced that "a limit must be put to the revolution." Berlin was filled with troops, under the command of General Wrangel, a soldier of approved fidelity and vigour. The too loquacious assembly was forcibly dissolved, and its president, seated in his official chair, was borne out by the irreverent soldiery and deposited in the street. A new constitution was announced, with changes of a highly conservative character. It is true that every Prussian who had attained his twenty-fourth

Nov. 1848 A. D.

May 1849 A. D.

* He was proposed for the office by a Prussian deputy, but the proposal was received in the diet with general laughter.

year received the franchise. But the voters were ranked in three classes, according to the amount of taxes paid. By the method adopted the small minority of persons who were rich and highly taxed exercised in an election equal authority with the vast majority of workmen and others who paid inconsiderable amounts. This principle still regulates the electoral system of Prussia.

Among the members who formed the united diet, on which the king had bestowed increased powers, was Otto von Bismarck. He was a younger son of a family whose estates had been seriously encumbered by the extravagance and faulty administration of many years. He was then a man of thirty-two, of vast stature, and physical strength such as few men possess. His youth had been wild, but the energies of a great nature now demanded worthier occupation, and he had chosen a political career. He was the uncompromising enemy of liberalism. The divine right of the Prussian monarchy was a fundamental article of his political creed. He regretted the concessions of the king; he condemned with vehemence the demands of the people. His voice was often raised in defence of absolute authority, and his commanding ability quickly gained for him a foremost place among the defenders of the endangered monarchy. There is no reason to believe that even then Bismarck was in his heart a lover of despotic government. But from an early period in his political life he satisfied himself that order could not be brought out of the prevailing chaos otherwise than by the action of a strong Prussian government. His first care was to establish the affairs of Prussia and Germany on a solid and permanent basis, and he did not believe that result could be gained by such parliamentary government as Prussia was then able to supply.

The king bestowed favourable regard upon this formidable champion of an authority which men were threatening to reject.

Feb. 1847 A. D.

He employed him as his representative in the German diet at
Frankfurt. He sent him as ambassador to St. Petersburg. And when Frederick William died, and his *Jan.*
brother became King William I., the influence of Bis-   **1861**
marck was yet further increased. He was sent on a   **A. D.**
short mission to Paris, where the emperor, "looking well, and
by no means fat and aged, as he is caricatured," and the
empress, " still one of the handsomest women I know,"   **1862**
received him "in a friendly manner," little dreaming of   **A. D.**
that terrible interruption to friendship which the swift years
were soon to bring. And then he was summoned to Berlin to
undertake the government of his country in the capacity of
prime minister. It was a work of unwonted difficulty, for the
policy which he had determined to pursue was in direct opposition to the wishes of a strong parliamentary majority. But he
had gained the full confidence of the king, whose mind, slow to
comprehend the policy of his new minister, was tenacious in his
adherence to that which he once adopted. He had the powerful support of his colleague, Von Roon, the minister of war,
and of Von Moltke, whose military genius would add to the
purposes of the new government the sanctions of irresistible
force, the prestige of unexampled success. Above all, he had
his own clear preception of the country's need, and a resolution,
which never faltered, to make Prussia great and Germany
tranquil in defiance of all opposition.

Bismarck entered immediately upon a strife between the king
and the lower house which was already of some continuance.
The king had pressed a scheme of army reorganization. The
house refused him the means to carry it into effect. Bismarck did
not hesitate to suspend parliamentary government, and
to restrain illegally the liberty of the press. He closed the   **1862**
diet with the despotic intimation that, since the house   **A. D.**
refused its sanction to the budget, he found himself obliged to
carry on the administration of affairs even in the absence of

sanction. During four years this violence continued to be offered to the constitution. The liberals denounced a method of government so offensive. But gradually, as the foreign policy of the great minister was successfully developed, the clamour ceased. Even the liberals forgave the means which had been used, in view of the splendid results which were gained. After the defeat of Austria there was no longer any temptation to govern by irregular methods, for the country elected a house which was prepared to give willing support to the government. Bismarck asked for, and obtained by a majority of two hundred and thirty to seventy-five, a bill of indemnity for his violations of the constitution. Henceforth success gained acceptance for his measures, and he governed according to law. The king still maintained a belief in the divine right of his own authority, and was not easily convinced that there was any power in the state higher than the royal will. The most influential members of the cabinet cherished the same political faith. But Bismarck was wise enough to see that every desirable result could now be gained in the safe path of constitutional government, and he was strong enough to impress his own views upon his master and his colleagues.

1868 A. D.

The relations existing with Austria formed for the Prussian government the grand question of the day. For ages Austria had been supreme in Germany, and she was wont to treat Prussia with scant ceremony as a manifest inferior. But Prussia—compact, wisely guided, and long in the enjoyment of peace—increased in power; while Austria, burdened with distant and dissatisfied provinces, wasted by costly wars, and frustrated in her career by injudicious government, was steadily dwindling. Prussia aspired to supremacy in Germany. A long diplomatic strife was maintained over trivial differences evolved from the growing animosity of the two governments; but it was obvious that the high dispute was, in the hands of diplomacy, merely ripening for its inevitable solution by the sword.

Bismarck had secured the "benevolent neutrality" of Russia and France in the long-foreseen conflict. The active friendship of Italy could be safely assumed.

But while the great controversy was still at some distance from its close, Bismarck succeeded in inducing Austria to join him in wresting from Denmark the duchies of Schleswig and Holstein. After a brave defence againt the overwhelming strength of the invaders, Denmark was forced to yield. The plunder was easily acquired, but grave difficulties arose in regard to its distribution. Bismarck took measures which pointed to the absorption by Prussia of all the newly-gained territory. Austria favoured its erection into an independent state, under a certain Prince Frederick of Augustenburg, who might be trusted to rule according to Austrian maxims. Ultimately it was agreed that the gains should be divided; that Holstein should be made over to Austria, and Schleswig to Prussia. But this settlement gave no satisfaction to either of the disputants. Some months ensued of mutual complaint and recrimination, growing ever more bitter. Early in the year it became plain that war was at hand. The reorganization of the Prussian army was complete, and Bismarck had resolved that·the time had come to expel Austria from the German confederation and unite the remaining states in a close alliance under the Prussian king. The Emperor of Austria summoned a council of his most distinguished soldiers. General von Moltke sat down to prepare the plan of the approaching campaign.

1864
A. D.

1865
A. D.

1866
A. D.

Austria was able to strengthen herself by the support of some of the smaller states. During the spring months all Germany was arming. Mutual demands of explanation and of disarmament were exchanged, and mutually refused. Austria at length annouced herself as the "upholder of the freedom, power, and integrity of the whole German Fatherland" against a power influenced only by "the dictates of

June 17

egotism and an ungovernable craving after aggrandizement."
June 22, Prince Frederick Charles led his army into Bohemia,
1866   in order to defend his country against "Austria, faith-
A. D.   less and regardless of treaties." With the exchange of
such amenities the war opened.

But during the last sixty years—even from the hour of Prussia's deepest humiliation—there had been evolving, with slow
and silent but unswerving progress, a marvellous train of circumstances, which were now to exercise a commanding influence on European history.   In the year 1806 a Prussian boy
finished his apprenticeship, and went fourth upon his travels in
quest of employment.   His name was John Nicholas Dreyse;
his age nineteen; the occupation to which he had been bred
that of locksmith.   The battle of Jena had just been fought,
and Dreyse chanced upon the field, still cumbered with the
Prussian dead and with the arms which they had wielded so
vainly.   From time to time, as he walked among these ghastly
memorials of national ruin, he lifted and examined with care
the musket which had dropped from some dying hand.   He satisfied himself that it was the least effective musket in Europe,
and that his poor countrymen had been sent out, imperfectly
armed, to wage hopeless combat with the genius of Napoleon
and the prowess of his well-equipped veterans.   He resolved
that he would amend that faulty weapon.   In the purpose of
the young locksmith lay wrapped up much of the political
future of Germany and of France.

Dreyse found his way to Paris and obtained employment in
the workshop of a Swiss gunmaker, named Pauli, who enjoyed
the favour of the Emperor Napoleon.   The industrious, intelligent Prussian lad quickly gained the confidence of his master.
One day Pauli told him that he was charged by the emperor to
construct a musket which should be loaded at the breech.   It
was a revelation to Dreyse, whose mind now brooded continu-

ally upon the idea of breech-loading fire-arms. His master was similarly occupied, and even constructed such a gun. Napoleon encouraged him to further effort by a gift of money and the Cross of the Legion of Honour.

It is one of the striking situations of history. The genius of the tyrant had given him possession of an idea whose embodiment would have laid Europe at his feet. The man who was ultimately to create that embodiment was face to face with him, seeking labouriously to do it now. But a safe expanse of years still lay between Europe and the success of this perilous attempt. Long before the invention was perfected the conqueror slept beneath the willow-tree of St. Helena.

The musket constructed by Pauli was complex and unsatisfactory, and never came into use Just as the war closed the percussion-cap was invented, and Dreyse turned his attention to the manufacture and improvement of this important novelty. But the idea of a breech-loading musket was never abandoned. At length, in 1835, nearly thirty years after his first efforts, he succeeded in constructing a breech-loading needle-gun which promised to be of practical service. It was tried by the Prussian government, and approved, and means were given to Dreyse for the erection of a factory of such weapons. The new musket was first brought into action, experimentally, against the Danes, and yielded satisfactory results, **1864 A. D.** to the high delight of King William, who at once ennobled the inventor. Measures were now taken to arm all the Prussian forces with this terrible weapon and train them to its use. From time to time the other powers heard of the Prussian needle-gun, but failed to appreciate its significance. And now Austria was drawn into war against a neighbour whose power to destroy was fearfully in excess of hers. The Austrians advanced to a hopelessly unequal conflict and a vain expenditure of human life.

The Prussian armies entered Bohemia by different routes, with orders to drive back the Austrians and concentrate towards Sadowa. In all the preliminary combats they were successful. The Austrians fought bravely, but the terribly rapid fire of the new Prussian musket inflicted losses which para-

June 27, 1866 A. D. lyzed them. In the first engagement which took place an entire battalion of Austrians was struck down almost to a man. Within a week the Austrians had fallen back upon Sadowa. Here, in a position of considerable strength, they were attacked by the first Prusian army,

Junly 3, under the nephew of the king, Prince Frederick Charles. The Austrians, with a splendid artillery, made good their defence, and inflicted severe losses.* After three or four hours' fighting, it seemed that the attack had failed. But then there burst fourth suddenly on the Austrian right a deadly fire of musketry. The second army, under the crown prince, had arrived at this opportune moment on the field. The dark-blue regiments multipled with appalling rapidity and the wither-· fire of their needle-guns was quickly reinforced by a powerful artillery. They had struck full on the most vulnerable point of the Austrian position. For an hour or more the Austrians stood their ground, enduring bravely the fearful losses which the enemy was now able to inflict. But at every point the Prussians cut their way into the Austrian lines, their murder-·ous fire covering the ground with dead. Resistance ceased, and the shattered Austrian army withdrew, weakened by the loss of thirty-two thousand men in killed, wounded, and missing. The Prussians had lost only nine thousand.

After a defeat so crushing, the continuance of the war was impossible. Two days after, the emperor made over Venetia to France; to be by this mediator delivered to Italy. Nego-

Aug 5, tiations for peace were entered upon, and easily completed. At the opening of his chambers, the Prussian

* The 27th Prussian regiment, for instance, went into battle three thousand strong, and only three hundred or four hundred men came out unwounded.

king was able to give thanks for God's gracious goodness in bestowing upon the army this rapid career of victory, and thus "smoothing the course for the national development of Germany." The campaign had occupied seven days; between the declaration of war and the formal conclusion of peace only seven weeks had elapsed.

Austria was forced to yield all that her conqueror was pleased to demand. She paid a heavy contribution towards the expenses of the war; she surrendered the duchies which she had helped to seize; she sanctioned the union of Venetia to Italy; above all, she consented to a new organization of Germany, from which she herself should be excluded. Prussia absorbed Hanover, Hesse, Nassau, and Frankfurt, and reigned without a rival in Germany.

These momentous changes were looked upon by the Emperor Napoleon with an evil eye. France was accustomed to regard herself as the arbitress of Europe. The emperor could boast with truth that when France was tranquil Europe was satisfied. But now, at no greater distance than the width of the Rhine, there had arisen a power whose sudden greatness threatened to dim the grandeur of France. The emperor reminded Bismarck of his "friendly inactivity" during the war, and suggested, as an acknowledgment of the same, that Prussia should bestow upon him certain frontier towns which he had long coveted. Bismarck, with much frankness, refused to yield a single foot of German soil, and even allowed it to be said to the French ambassador that, if these demands were insisted on, grave complications might be expected. The emperor, deeply chagrined, retired with some loss of dignity, from the position which he had too hastily assumed. Henceforth there was reason to fear that the unity of Germany involved war with France. But it was for the interest of Prussia to delay, if she could not avert, that fiery ordeal. The northern states were already in full accord, but the cause of unity was less advanced in the south. It was the aim of Bismarck to avoid a rupture with France until he could reckon upon a union of the whole German people to resist their ancient enemy. Meanwhile Prussia made herself ready for the expected struggle.*

King William returned from the war with France emperor of a united and satisfied Germany. The long-deferred vengeance due for centuries of French aggression had been exacted with terrible completeness. The divisions which had enfeebled and wasted the nation were cancelled. Germany, which had been little more than a geographical expression, was raised to the position which her strength and intelligence entitled her to claim. She was supreme in central Europe; and discerning men everywhere recognized in the greatness of this peace-loving and industrious people a new guarantee that the tranquility of Europe would not in the future be so lightly disturbed as it had been in the past.

For upwards of fifty years Prussia had been patiently and silently preparing for this supreme effort. The cost had been to her incalculably great, not in money alone, but still more in the wasted years of her sons and in the false direction given to the national mind by the prominence necessarily assigned to that lowest form of power—military force. Now the harvest of her great self-denial was reaped. Had her chiefs been wiser, the error of maintaining her preparation **for** a work which was fully accomplished would have been avoided; a milder and more liberal spirit would have pervaded the administration of the new empire. But the king and Prince Bismarck had grown old—too old to change—in massing the forces of the nation for the purpose of striking down France and vindicating the unity of Germany. The spirit which nerved Prussia to the toilsome and gigantic accumulation of

* See chapter ii., Book III.

forces needful for the success of her enterprise still animates the men who rule the powerful and peaceful German empire. The despotic energy of the German executive still restrains the wholesome freedom which the constitution ought to secure. This undue prolongation of the dominion of force will probably continue during the lives of the emperor and his chancellor. Not till the men who have contributed so largely to the greatness of Germany have passed away will the nation which they have made enjoy the full advantage of the service they have rendered. The German people have submitted to the abridgment of their liberties in order to gain their unity. Under a new and weaker executive it will be easy to regain the rights which they have temporarily relinquished.

The population of Prussia is now twenty-six million; that of the other twenty-four states which make up united Germany is seventeen million. The Prussians are governed by two chambers,—one of which is almost wholly nominated by the king, and the other is elected by the people. For electoral purposes the people are divided into three classes, according to the amount of taxation paid by each. Each class has equal influence in the election, and thus the vote of a rich man who is heavily taxed is greatly more powerful than the vote of a poor man whose taxation is light. Indirect election is practised,—the people choosing electors, who appoint the representatives. The members of the lower chamber are paid about one pound sterling per day, acceptance of which is compulsory.

Prussia is, in her religion, Protestant to the extent of nearly two-thirds of her people, and Roman Catholic to the extent of rather more than one-third. Government endows partially both denominations. It appoints the consistories or provincial boards which rule the Protestant Church, and reserves a right of control over the election of the Catholic clergy.

Education is compulsory, and in practice almost universal.
Four million children, or nearly one in every six of the popu-
tion, attend the elementary schools. A small fee is charged,—
one penny per week in the country, and threepence per week
in towns. The balance is contributed by a local tax. The
minister of public instruction is at the head of the educational
system.

All Prussians are trained to military service. Every young
man enters the army at twenty, and serves for three years
For the next nine years he is in the reserve, liable to serve in
offensive war. Thereafter, for another eighteen years, till he
has attained the age of fifty, he may be called on to serve at
home in oase of invasion. This system dates from 1814, and
has been copied from Prussia by most of the other great powers of Europe. The Prussian army in time of peace numbers
three hundred and thirty thousand, and can be raised in time
of war to almost a million, available for foreign service. So
perfect is the organization that this vast force can be made
ready for the field in fourteen days. In the war of 1870 with
France nearly the whole army was on the Rhine within this
time. The Prussian army has now, strictly speaking, no separate existence, but forms a portion of the forces of the empire,
of which the King of Prussia, as emperor, is the commander-
in-chief. So well has the empire prepared herself for all untoward possibilities that, out of a population of forty-three
million, she can place two million and a half of armed and
disciplined men in the field, and still leave a force at home for
defensive purposes.

In respect of debt, Prussia is the most happily circumstanced
of all civilized countries. Apart from money borrowed for
construction of railways, she owes no more than thirty million
sterling. Her total revenue, upon which she lives, like a prudent nation, without running further into debt, is only thirty-two
million. One-half of this comes from her crown lands, her

forests, her railways, mines, iron-works, and other industrial
enterprises. The national taxation levied from her people is
no more than ten million. In addition to this, the Prussians
have something to pay towards the expenses of the empire.
The imperial revenue is drawn mainly from customs and excise
duties, of which Prussia pays a large share. The revenue is
not always equal to the imperial expenditure, and in such cases
the deficiency is made up by the several states in proportion
to their population. The Prussian contribution is about one
million five hundred thousand pounds.

Prussia is rich in minerals, and prosecutes this description of
industry so diligently that nearly four hundred thousand persons are employed in her mines, smelting-works, and foundries,
which deal with the products of these mines. She raises
annually forty-two millon tons of coal,—about one-third the
production of Great Britain. She yields also iron, zinc, lead,
and copper in considerable quantities. One-half of her people
depend upon agriculture; and about one in every five has a
proprietary interest in the soil. Land is so much subdivided
that there are a million of proprietors whose possessions are
under three acres.

For purposes of foreign commerce Prussia is merged in the
empire, and keeps no separate accounts. Germany sends to
England all manner of agricultural produce, including flax,
wool, and timber; glass-ware; toys, to the value of nearly a
quarter of a million sterling; sugar; and even spirits. She
takes from us coals (although in lessening quantity) and iron;
cotton, woollen, linen, and silk cloths; herrings; leather; chem-
ical products. She is one of the few customers who take from
us more largely than we take from them. Her imports from
Britain are over twenty-three million pounds, and her exports
under twenty-two million pounds.

Prussia has ten thousand miles of railway, nearly one-half
of which are owned or administered by the state. It is proba-

ble that, ere long, all Prussian railways will pass into the hands of the government.*

The German people are indifferent correspondents. They write annually five hundred million letters; while the British, who are only two-thirds of their number, find occasion for over one thousand million. Their diligence in letter-writing scarcely exceeds that of their neighbours, the French, who, with a population one-seventh less, write three hundred and sixty million letters. The Germans are great readers of newspapers, and the imperial post-office carries annually as many papers as the post-office of Great Britain does. They use the telegraph more freely than the French do, but their messages are in number only one-half those of Great Britain.

* In four of the youngest American states,—Iowa, Kansas, Nebraska, and Minnesota,—with a population of three million, there are ten thousand miles of railway,—as much as Prussia owns.

CHAPTER IV.

THE throne of Austria was occupied by the Emperor Francis during the momentous years which intervened from 1793 to 1835. Francis meant well by his subjects: he desired to see them contented and happy; but his views differed extremely from theirs in regard to the methods by which these desirable conditions were to be attained. His theory of government dispensed not only with popular interference but with popular criticism. He allowed no liberty of thought or speech; he kept his people in abject submission, believing that to be for their good. He enforced a strict censorship over the press of Austria, and a vigorous scrutiny of all printed matter which came from abroad, that foreign agitators should not disturb the happy tranquility which the absence of thought might be expected to produce. He upheld a minutely ramified system of secret police, by which he should have timely warning if unhappily the contagion of liberalism reached his people. In all his measures for repressing the intelligence of his subjects* and preserving untarnished that ignorant loyalty without which he believed government impossible, he was ably supported by his wily and unscrupulous minister, Prince Metternich. A more absolute despotism never existed among men than that which was maintained to the close of the emperor's life. Thirty-seven

* "I want obedient subjects," he said to the professors at Laybach, "and not men of learning."

345

million people held their lives and their property and their
right to form and express an opinion at the pleasure of the
government. The emperor, although weak, selfish, and obstinate, was good-natured. His people had passed with him
through the terrible years of Napoleon's supremacy, and the
recollections of their common danger and suffering, gained for
the errors of the aged emperor a tolerance which was little
likely to be extended to those of his successor.

The accession of the new emperor marks the opening of a
new era. In most European states men were awakening to a new political life. Exclusion from participation
in the management of their own national affairs was
becoming insufferable. The demand for self-government grew
year by year louder and more importunate. The precautions
of the government had not been able to shut out from Austria
the subtle and pervading impulse. Deep and wide among the
Austrian people spread the desire for free institutions. The
cities were full of secret societies—the perilous resort to which
despotism compels its victims. The government made no concession. Discussion of political questions was stifled; every
amelioration even of admitted evils was delayed. The finances
of the empire were in a miserable position, and large annual
deficits had to be covered by loans. Universal discontent prevailed; faith in the emperor and his ministers was utterly gone.
Besides the general dissatisfaction with the form of government, there existed special causes of complaint. The Slav
populations alleged that, under the influence of dislike to
Russia, the government postponed their interests to those of
their German fellow-subjects. The Hungarians refused to be
contented without a restoration of government separate from
that of Austria proper. The whole empire seemed ripe for
revolt; and no wiser policy than that of forcible suppression—
no worthier aim than that of indefinite postponement, had been
discovered by the Emperor Ferdinand and his advisers.

1835
A. D.

Upon a people thus prepared the news that France had once more conquered a tyrant king fell like the voice of the trumpet which summoned them to instant battle. Mar. 1, 1848 A. D. The government, and all those whose interests were identified with the government, received with dismay the tidings of that awful event. The citizens of Vienna perceived that the hour of their deliverance had struck. A few days passed, in constantly growing excitement, and then the mob sacked the palace of Prince Metternich, and were driven away by the soldiers not without bloodshed. A new ministry was appointed. Under the influence of fear, the government hastened to offer concessions which reason had failed to obtan. The press was set free from its fetters; an assembly ot the estates of the empire was convened; political prisoners were liberated; such reforms as the people desired were bountifully promised; even universal suffrage was decreed. But so little did these enforced and reluctant gifts conciliate the people that the emperor deemed it wise to withdraw secretly from his capital. He did so, he intimated, rather than employ force against his subjects, and he was ready to welcome the return of his prodigal sons. May 19.

Some weeks after his flight the assembly which he had convened met in Vienna. The hopes which usually cluster around revolutionary parliaments invested this assemblage with an interest deep although ephemeral, and the presence of the emperor alone seemed wanting to the happy inauguration of the new era. The emperor listened to the voice of his repentant prodigals and returned to his capital. But the penitence of the Viennese was not enduring. In a few weeks disturbances of an alarming character broke out. The arsenal was captured; Count Latour, the aged minister-at-war, was brutally murdered; the emperor once more betook himself to flight; and Vienna was entirely in the hands of the insurgents. Aug. 12. Oct. 4. Oct. 7.

The perils which surrounded the empire seemed now to

threaten its dissolution. Lombardy and Venetia were in revolt, aided by the King of Sardinia and encouraged by the universal sympathy of Italy; Hungary had declared herself independent; the Slavs of Bohemia and Silesia had taken up arms; Vienna was held by rebel hands, and the palace of the emperor no longer afforded him personal safety. Still further, the impulse which animated these movements was the impulse by which all the surrounding populations of western Europe were pervaded.

But the empire, experienced in danger and accustomed to defeat, proved to be tenacious of life. Within a few months her difficulties were surmounted, and she was again at peace. Prince Windischgratz suppressed, without extreme difficulty, the Slavonian revolt. General Radetsky enjoyed an easy triumph over the ill-prepared Italian patriots, and restored tranquility by the defeat of the Sardinian king at Novara. Three days after the flight of the emperor, Jellachich, Ban of Croatia, was before Vienna with an army of thirty thousand men, resolute to maintain the monarchy; and this force was speedily raised to seventy thousand. The insurgents stood firm, and the city endured bombardment. It was not surren-
Oct. 31,
1848 dered until the frightful slaughter of its defenders ren-
A. D. dered further resistance impossible. The emperor, hope-
less now of a reign useful to his people or tolerable by himself, abdicated in favour of his nephew, then a lad of eighteen.

The Hungarians were still in arms. They were a people numbering about eleven million, and occupying a territory somewhat larger than Great Britain and Ireland. Under Austrian rule they suffered wrongs which fully justified revolt. Taxation was borne exclusively by the labouring classes. The nobles were exempted from burdens which pressed so heavily on the poor. The peasant supported church, school, and army; tilled the fields of the proprietor without recompense; yielded at nominal prices such supplies as the military service required;

and if a nobleman owed him money and was unwilling to pay it, there was no law by which the claim could be enforced. A yearning for independence had long existed, especially among the Magyars, who composed nearly one-half of the Hungarian nation. The thrilling news of what the French had done quickened the purposes of the Hungarian chiefs, and precipitated the inevitable conflict.

Austria made such preparations as were possible amid the vast difficulties which surrounded her to reclaim her revolted vassal. The Hungarian government, at the head of which was Louis Kossuth, drew out the resources of the country as for a contest the issue of which was national independence or utter ruin. The Hungarians stood on the defensive, and during the first few months of the war it appeared that they were able to maintain the liberties which they had asserted. Their forces grew with success. Poles, French, and Italians whose revolutionary sympathies had been frustrated at home, now hastened to Hungary. Georgey, the skilful commander of the patriot army, found himself at the head of a hundred and twenty thousand veteran troops, well equipped by help of the paper money which Kossuth issued in profusion.

Austria recognized the hopelessness of her attempt to quell the defense of this heroic people. In her distress she appealed to Russia for help, and the Czar Nicholas, to whom successful democracy so near his own border was highly distasteful, intimated his intention to send a hundred and fifty thousand men to the relief of discomfited Austria. *May 8, 1849 A. D.*

The Hungarians prolonged during several weeks a brave defence against enemies now of overwhelming strength. Everywhere they were overmatched and driven back. Dissensions among the leaders hastened the fatal close of their noble efforts. Kossuth resigned his office after investing General Georgey with the powers of dictator. But Georgey had

lately despaired of success. The sole use which he made of
his new authority was to negotiate with the Russian general,
Aug. 12,   Prince Paskiewitch, an unconditional surrender of his
1849   troops. Resistance ceased; Hungary was again the
A. D.   slave of Austria; the scaffold was set up, and the Austrian general, Haynau, barbarously put to death all the
Hungarian generals who fell into his hands.

    The advisers of the new emperor could not fail to perceive
Dec. 5,   the necessity of conciliating the liberalism whose
1848   vitality had been so terribly asserted. A proclamation
A. D.   in the emperor's name boldly avowed the excellence of
free institutions, and announced a restoration of the
empire on the basis of true liberty and the equality of rights.
Mar. 7,   A few months later, while the Hungarians were still
1849   making good their defence, a constitution was promul-
A. D.   gated. Henceforth laws were to be made for Austria
by a parliament elected by household suffrage. The
press was to be unfettered. Complete religious freedom was
guaranteed; universal education was provided. The empire
had offered terms which the most advanced liberals of the
time could not fail to regard as satisfactory. But it did so under
the fierce pressure of necessity; and ease quickly recanted
Dec. 31,   vows made in pain. After a languid existence of three
1851   years the constitution was cancelled and the ancient
A. D.   despotism reimposed.
    There survived, however, the provision which had been
made for the education of the people. Austria has maintained
her loyalty to the cause of education, with results upon her own
career which have been highly beneficial. All children from
six to twelve are obliged to attend school, and three-fourths of
them actually do so. Education is free; and although it was
long under control of the priests to such an extent that one-half
of the teachers were themselves ecclesiastics, Austria has at-

tained an educational position immeasurably higher than she occupied thirty years ago.

It was now too late in the world's history for a purely despotic government to maintain itself in Central Europe. Once more a liberal policy was adopted, and now, it seemed, with an honest purpose. The emperor "entered suddenly," as it was said, "on the path of constitutionalism." Representative institutions were established based on a right of voting which came near to household suffrage. So well satisfied was the emperor of the wisdom of these changes that he foretold as their result "the salutary transformation of the whole monarchy."* A few years later Hungary obtained the satisfaction of her long-cherished desire. She had her own legislature, chosen by the almost universal suffrage of her people; and the emperor and empress were crowned at Pesth king and queen of Hungary.

1860 A. D.

May 1, 1861 A. D.

1867 A. D.

The empire was still saddened by the awful memories of Sadowa, by the loss of her Italian possessions, by her fall from the pre-eminent position which she had long held in Germany.† "Austria," said the emperor to his people, "has been severely visited by misfortune, but she is not humiliated or bowed down." Her sorrows had indeed been great; but from the greatest of them all she had at length obtained deliverance. She was no longer the victim of an oppressive government. She was no longer defrauded of her rights. Her people were contented because they were no longer wronged. They were loyal to their government, because it was their own choice. The secret organizations by which a wronged people maintain their protest againt despotism had wholly disappeared, for the Austrians could now express openly through their freely chosen representatives every political aspiration which they enter-

---

* Notwithstanding the apparent ardour of the emperor, constitutional government was suspended from 1865 to 1867.

† See page 334.

tained. Even the emperor saw and approved the excellence
of the new method. " By the system of direct popular elec-
1874   tions," he stated, "the empire has obtained real inde-
A. D.   pendence."

Austria, as a constitutional state, no longer enfeebled by the
just discontent of the multitudinous races which she governs,
enjoys abundantly the elements out of which a prosperous
career may be fashioned. Her population is thirty-six million,
and increases at the rate of one per cent. per annum. Her industrial progress gives evidence of steady industry, and therefore of growing prosperity. Her imports, which ten years ago
were only twenty-five million sterling, were in 1874 fifty-three
million—figures from which may be inferred a vastly increased
command by the people of the comforts of life. Her exports
show only the very slight increase from thirty-four million
sterling in 1865 to thirty-six million in 1874; and as her production has grown much more rapidly, it is evident that the
consumption of native as well as of foreign products must have
largely increased; Two-thirds of the population are engaged
in agriculture, or labour in the vast forest which overspread a
large portion of the surface. Austria sends to her neighbours
grain, timber, flax, hemp, wool, fruits, wine, olive oil. In the
southern portions of the empire the growing of silk is prosecuted, and the annual production of cocoons accounts to two
and a quarter million pounds. The keeping of bees is quite
an important branch of rural industry. A census of the bee-
hives of the empire gives the number at fifteen million, and the
annual yield of honey at eight million pounds.   Minerals are
annually raised to the value of nine million sterling.
    Austria endeavours, by such encouragement as protective
duties afford, to establish textile manufactures· on her soil.
Her progress is not contemptible, but neither as yet has signal
success crowned her efforts. She employs in the spinning of

wool three quarters of a million spindles, and in the spinning of
cotton not quite two million. Great Britain, it may be stated,
employs nearly fifty million cotton spindles, and the United
States of America ten million. Austria has also a manufacture
of linen, hemp, and silk which has not attained very important
dimensions. She is, however, mighty in the production of beer,
having no fewer than three thousand two hundred breweries,
which supply annually two hundred million gallons of beer for
the assuagement of the public thirst. She has two hundred
sugar works, in which one and a quarter million tons of beet
are consumed. Her manufacture of leather and of paper is
large. In some of the more delicate handicrafts her people
have attained much skill, and her mathematical, surgical, and
musical instruments enjoy high reputation.

The railways of Austria have a total mileage of twelve thousand. The post-office conveys on an average twelve letters
for each of the population—rather less than the average for
Ireland and only one-third that of England. The people
have not yet learned to avail themselves freely of the telegraph,
and the messages delivered average only one to seven of the
population.

Austria has been notable among the impoverished Continental
states for the unvarying insufficiency of her revenue. During
the last ninety years her revenue has on no single occasion been
equal to her expenditure. The result has been an enormous
increase of her national debt. In 1789 her debt was only
thirty-five million sterling; it is now three hundred and fifty
million. Her total expenditure is sixty-four million sterling—
not very much less than that of Great Britain. Among the
sources from which she gains the means of this huge expenditure are two which may be accepted as evidences of very
unenlightened finance. One is a sum of nearly two million
sterling earned by a state lottery, and the other a similar
amount drawn from a tax laid on salt. There is, however,

23

the redeeming feature in the budget of an expenditure upon education of one million and three quarters sterling.*

In conformity with the barbarous usage which still prevails among the European powers, Austria expends a large amount of her insufficient revenue upon military preparations. All her males are trained to arms. Three years of his youth have to be spent by every citizen in active service, and for a further term of seven years he stands enrolled in the reserve, liable to be called out in case of war. The army numbers, on its peace-footing, nearly three hundred thousand men, and may be increased to eight hundred and forty thousand when danger is held to be at hand. Although her relations with the sea are inconsiderable, Austria has indulged in a fleet of war-ships of enormous cost and slender utility. A large proportion of her force is ironclad—a contrivance which promises to be gradually discredited by improvements in the methods of attack.

* This is only a small portion of the amount expended on education. A much larger amount is provided locally.

CHAPTER V.

ITALY.

WHEN the Roman Empire fell, Italy, helpless and demoralized, was at the mercy of the destroyers. The barbarians took her cities and beat down their walls; they possessed her wealth; they overan and desolated her fertile plains. The Goths, the Lombards, the Franks, the Germans by turns exercised their fierce pleasure over her. She was the unresisting prey of the victor. The timid and defenceless communities which survived the shock of constant invasion purchased freedom from fresh assault if they were able, or meekly endured it if they were not. No prostration could be more complete than that of the Italians during four centuries after the overthrow of Rome.

Towards the close of the tenth century the dawn of a better time becomes visible. The Italian cities were moved by a desire to restore the defences which the jealousy of their conquerors had forbidden. They began to surround themselves with massive walls, to dig moats deep and wide, to erect strong forts, to manufacture or purchase arms. When these things were done, the cities rose quickly out of their degradation. They were no longer mere assemblages of unarmed and spirit-less men waiting to be plundered at the convenience of an avaricious noble or gang of roving barbarians. With arms in their hands, and strong walls which they were now able to defend, they breathed the spirit of men free and self-governing, caring for the favour of none. Their wealth and numbers grew apace. The inhabitants of the country, who held life and

property at the pleasure of oppressive nobles, sought the sweet
security of the neighbouring city. These welcome immigrants
added to the wealth and power of the communities which shel-
tered them.   The advantages offered by the cities compelled
the nobles to ameliorate the condition of the peasantry. Thus
encouraged, agriculture made important progress, and the rural
population largely increased its numbers.

During three centuries Italy enjoyed a life beside which that
of other European nations was barbarous and miserable. Her
land-owners strove by copious irrigation to increase the productiveness of the soil. Her peasantry were affluent and contented.   The agriculture of Lombardy and Tuscany was
deemed a model for the world.   In the cities abundant capital
gave life to all industries. The manufacture of silk was pros-
perously established. The citizens learned the art of manufacturing paper from rags. They made glass for mirrors.
They practised the art of engraving. A widely extended foreign commerce yielded them vast wealth. The costly products
of the distant East traversed on camels the dreary wastes which
lie between the Red Sea and the Mediterranean, and were then
shipped for Venice. Italian merchants had possessed themselves of this lucrative traffic, and enjoyed the enormous gains
of the commerce which Europe carried on with Asia. When
the crusading mania prevailed, Venice found profitable
employment for her shipping in transporting the persons and
stores of the devout warriors. Venice, Pisa, and Genoa owned
ships which outnumbered those of all the other states of
Christendom.   The cities of Italy had become the grand
commercial and maritime powers of the world, and wielded
an influence which had then no parallel.

While London and Paris were little more than groups of
mud cabins, the cities of Italy possessed buildings to which
men still make pilgrimages—on which they still gaze with
wonder and admiration. Noble bridges spanned their rivers.

Their streets were admirably paved centuries before the streets of other European cities were anything better than muddy paths. Churches and palaces unequalled in beauty even now, canals which England began to rival only a century ago, quays massive and enduring, attest the supremacy of the Italians in engineering and architecture. In painting, in sculpture, in literature they were no less eminent. Withal the manners of the people were simple, their tastes were inexpensive, their spirit was high and bold. Italy in the ancient time had given law to the world. Once more she filled the highest place, and offered to the barbarous nations of Europe a marvellous example of enlightenment and progress.

So many independent, prosperous, and well-armed republics could not long exist side by side in peace. The larger cities compelled their weaker sisters to enter into alliances, with the natural result that the strong ultimately ruled and absorbed the weak. Venice, Genoa, Milan, Pavia each commanded the allegiance of many smaller cities, and became each the head of a strong republic. Quarrels springing out of obscure jealousies broke out among the rival states. Often they suffered themselves to be drawn into the quarrels of others. In the twelfth century the pope and the emperor fought about the right to create bishops, and the Italians ranged themselves on this side and on that of the idle strife.

In their numerous wars the citizens lay under the fatal disadvantage of being without cavalry. The horse was the soul of medieval battle. The stout men-at-arms of the Italian cities, having no adequate force of horsemen in their ranks, were unable to stand in battle before the knights who came against them. Out of this inferiority there sprang perilous alliances with nobles who could bring cavalry into the field. During the fourteenth century the Italian cities sought and obtained the support of such dignitaries, who helped them in ther wars; who built and strongly fortified residences within their walls; who surrounded themselves with mercenary soldiers; who possessed themselves lawlessly of the resources of the state, and gradually disarmed the people. The foundations of absolute sovereignty were laid. The fall of Italy had begun. In the fifteenth century the easier route to India by the Cape of Good Hope was discovered. The Italian seaports lost their enriching Eastern trade.* The cities began to decay; the unarmed citizens lost their boldness of spirit. The neighbouring powers began to take a deadly interest in the concerns of the peninsula, and Italy became once more the battle-ground of ambitious monarchs. The German, the French, the Spaniards, each fastened their demands upon the fair and defenceless land. The Swiss looked from their hills upon fertile plains and opulent cities which offered a sure reward to the soldier of fortune. The Turks, driven by the wild impulse which made them at that time a terror to Europe, inflicted their abhorred and desolating presence upon Italy. For three centuries Italy was trodden down by foreign spoilers. These were centuries of weakness, of humiliation, of shame. The people had lost their aptitude for war, and were given over to the will of despots. But they never lost their love of liberty. During those ages, the memory of which is a degradation, the desire to take rank as an independent nation, still lingered in the minds of the Italian people.

It was Napoleon Bonaparte who rendered possible the fulfillment of this desire. When Napoleon first crossed the Alps to enter upon his marvellous career, he found the Austrians in possession of Lombardy. He found one of the Spanish Bourbons on the throne of Naples. The pope governed considerable territories. The remainder of Italy was parcelled out into five republics and several duchies. The ancient glories of Italy

---

* During the last few years Italy has begun to regain a portion of the traffic which was alienated from her when the route by the Cape was adopted. The opening of the Suez Canal is drawing the traffic of the East with Europe back into the channel by which it flowed in the Middle Ages. For four centuries English ships, sailing by the Cape, have carried Eastern products home to England, making London the great trading centre of the two continents. Now, once more, these products come by the Red Sea and the Mediterranean; and Italian seaports are beginning to intercept, as they did of old, the gainful traffic which Europe maintains with Asia.

impressed deeply the imagination of the youthful conqueror, and the Italian blood which flowed in his own veins naturally quickened his interest in the concerns of this unhappy land. Even then he thought of her unity and freedom. And long afterwards, at St. Helena, when his feverish dream of universal sovereignty had passed away, he loved to argue that the unity of Italy in manners, in language, and in literature established her claim to unity of government. He himself went far towards gaining for her this coveted unity. He drove the Austrians out of Lombardy. He emptied every Italian throne. He united nearly six million Italians into a republic, raising them at once to the dignity of free and self-governing citizens. He united to France an equal number of Piedmontese, Genoese, Tuscans and Romans. He bestowed on seven million Neapolitans a government greatly more free than they·had ever known before. He established for all a code of laws, enlightened and just. He held out hopes of a union yet wider than that which he had been able to form—of a union which would embrace the whole Italian family.

The restoration of Italy seemed ready to be accomplished. It was indeed now rendered inevitable, but many years had first to pass and much patriot blood to flow. Napoleon fell. The Congress of Vienna cancelled his regeneration of Italy, and reimposed the old separations—the old and hateful despotisms. Italy was again, in the language of Prince Metternich, nothing more than a geographical expression. But Italy had tasted the sweetness of freedom and union. She could never more know rest till these blessings were permanently assured to her.

Borne down by the strength of the tyrant monarchs, the Italians seemed to submit without resistance to their fate. But they took measures which pointed to the coming of a happier time. They enrolled themselves as members of secret societies in which the love of unity and representative government was kept in vigorous life. In the cities, and especially among the educated classes, this movement quickly assumed an aspect of commanding importance. Seven hundred thousand of the most intelligent and patriotic Italians formed the membership of these unseen organizations.*

The revolution in Spain furnished an early occasion to test the vitality of the patriot sentiment. In Naples and Piedmont successful insurrections established for a few days universal suffrage and representative government. But the allied despots could not permit such irregularities. Austria, Russia, and Prussia met in solemn deliberation over the crime of men who sought to govern themselves. England wisely held aloof. France maintained a neutrality which the liberals stigmatized as a real though concealed support of despotism. The Emperor Alexander, more liberal than his royal brothers, considered that the spirit of the age demanded liberal institutions. These, however, must come voluntarily from the gracious hand of the sovereign. As the privileges seized by the Italians enjoyed no such origin, it was indispensable to the security of monarchs that they should be forcibly withdrawn.† An Austrian army entered Italy. The patriots, ill prepared for war, were swept almost unresistingly away, and despotism for a little longer reigned supreme.

1820 A. D.

More than a quarter of a century passed, and order almost unbroken prevailed in Italy.‡ Austria maintained in Lom-

* The most powerful of these societies was that of the Carbonari. The views of this association were set forth (1820) in a remonstrance addressed to the pope, and admirable for the enlightenment and elevation of its tone. "The Society of the Carbonari breathes only the religion of Jesus Christ. It preserves that respect for sovereignty which the apostle requires from Christians; it loves the sovereign; it preserves the state; but it supports democracy, which, instead of attacking monarchy, forms that happy addition which endears it to the nation." The associated despots, regarding these principles as inconsistent with orderly government, spared no effort for their suppression.

† The sovereigns of the Holy Alliance claimed "an incontestable right " to take common measures against any state whose people had risen against their rulers. No matter how vile and insufferable the misgovernment might have been, the great despots would uphold it against the discontent of a suffering nation.

‡ The only considerable exception was the abortive rising in 1831 against the government of the Pope.

bardy and Venetia a dull, changeless, leaden despotism, abhorred more on account of its foreign origin than its active cruelty. King Ferdinand of Naples, obeying his Bourbon instinct, despoiled the goods of his unfortunate subjects, and tortured their persons, according to his own evil pleasure. Pope Gregory, guiding himself by the traditions of the Vatican, was watchful to suppress human thought, and preserve untarnished the loyalty of his people by preserving uninvaded their profound ignorance. Italy was dumb. Her leaders had perished on the scaffold or been chased into exile. Nothing, it seemed, was left to her but submission to the tyrants into whose power her hard fate had cast her. But all the while opinion was steadily ripening towards freedom. Numerous political organizations fanned the rising flame. Severed as they were and oppressed, the Italians knew that they were silently growing into a nation able to vindicate its unity and independence.

France gave the signal which called the Italians to a fresh effort. In 1848, when France once more cast out her king, and the revolutionary flame burst forth also in Vienna and Berlin, the Italians deemed that their hour of deliverance had struck. Driven by an impulse passionate and irrepressible, all Italy rushed to arms. The welcome news called back from exile men who had scarcely hoped to see their country again. From all European cities they came where banished men were allowed a home. Mazzini hastened from London; Garibaldi sailed from Monte Video, to attempt, not yet successfully, the marvellous work of deliverance which was reserved for his later years. Gray-haired soldiers, who had spent their blighted years in poverty and obscure toil, stood once more on Italian ground, side by side with the eager students of Pisa, the resolute burghers of Genoa and Leghorn, the Romans not unworthy to bear a name so renowned. All were full of hope that their efforts would be crowned with the glory of a rescued Italy. All offered their lives gladly in her cause.

The grand aim of this national uprising was to expel the Austrians, and thereafter to assert the national life and unity, under the guidance of any Italian prince who might worthily assume the sacred task. Pius IX., who had recently become pope, had given some unexpected evidences of a sympathy with the popular desire. During some moments of a happy delusion the Italians dreamed of a Papacy inspired by human sympathies assuming the guidance of a restored national life. Had it been possible for Pio Nono to fulfil the fond predictions of an enthusiastic people, he would have become the object of such love and devotion as never before had been kindled in the Italian heart. But the influences which bear rule in the Vatican are necessarily and inexorably hostile to popular claims. His holiness, quickly repenting the short-lived weakness, sought the congenial refuge of despotic alliance. He had permitted a body of Roman volunteers to join the patriot ranks. He now withdrew his permission, and commanded his subjects to detach themselves from an enterprise which no longer enjoyed the favour of Heaven. He was the minister of a God of peace; he was the impartial father of every member of the Christian family; he could give no sanction to the shedding of Christian blood. The rage of the disappointed people knew no bounds. Papal influence over the Italians was henceforth a comparatively feeble thing.

April 29, 1848 A. D.

The sole remaining hope of the patriots was Charles Albert, king of Sardinia, a prince well disposed to the popular cause, but unwise and infirm of purpose, unreliable as a statesman, fatally incompetent as a soldier. The popular impulse, which now surged around his throne, drove him, single handed, into an invasion of Lombardy. Some successes in the opening of the war shed a momentary gleam of hope over the desperate enterprise. But the incapable leadership of the king brought swift ruin upon the patriot forces. After much waste of life in battle and by hardships needlessly im-

Mar. 24, 1849 A. D.

posed on the troops, the defeat of Novaro closed the war, and the humiliated king resigned to his son the crown whose dignity he had failed to uphold.

Meanwhile the subjects of his holiness the pope, as their contribution to the cause of Italian unity, had relieved the pontiff of his temporal sovereignty, and formed themselves into a republic. The pope sought refuge in Gaeta, where his brother in adversity, the expelled King of Naples, extended to him a sympathetic welcome. From this secure retirement his holiness issued unregarded protests against the profane violence which had wrenched the patrimony of St. Peter from the hand of St. Peter's successor. But a powerful arm of flesh was near to give unexpected emphasis to the ineffectual spiritual menaces of the pope. Louis Napoleon had become president of the French republic. Personally, he cared nothing for religion or any of its ministers. But if France delayed her intervention, Austria would hasten to snatch the precious opportunity. The support of the priesthood was of high political importance, and the unbelieving president did not hesitate to become suddenly one of the most devout sons of the church. He sent General Oudinot with a force which, in the end, numbered forty-five thousand French soldiers, to restore the pope.* It was a delicate task for a people who had lately expelled their king, and set up a republic, to announce to the world that they were about forcibly to reimpose upon their neighbours an overthrown despotism. But the new president was equal to the occasion. He informed the Romans that his troops were sent in the interests of " peace, order, conciliation, and true liberty," and he expected that they would receive with eagerness an army which came " to accomplish so kindly and disinterested a mission."

Feb. 8, 1849 A. D.

Dec. 29, 1848 A. D.

---

* The president asserted that this expidetion was urged upon him by a force of opinion which he could not resist. "That door," he said, "has not opened once since I have been here, except to advisers who had said to me 'To Rome.'"

The Romans, led by General Garibaldi, prepared themselves to defend like free men the liberty which they had asserted. During the months of May and June they held the mouldering walls of the ancient city against all the strength of France.

But at length the heroic defence was crushed, and the French army enjoyed a shameful triumph. One of the keys of the city gates was sent off in haste to the pope. His holiness publicly blessed his deliverers, and returned to Rome to resume his intermitted despotism.

July 2,
49
A. D.

Order once more reigned in Italy. A French army held Rome, and maintained the pope's unstable throne. The Austrian troops swept over northern Italy, and trampled out the embers of patriot resistance. The leaders of the rising betook themselves once more to their exile, or expiated their offence on the scaffold or in the yet more terrible dungeon. All seemed lost. Italy had measured her strength with that of her oppressors, and had been beaten to the ground.

But even then, when all hope seemed gone, the man who was to lead Italy to an early and splendid triumph stood ready to begin his work. The Count Camillo di Cavour was then a man of thirty-eight. He had inherited a competent fortune, and was now a member of the Sardinian parliament, of growing political reputation. His figure was not of heroic mould, for he was short and unduly inclined to corpulence; but it was crowned by a massive head, and a face which expressed intellectual power and strength of will, marvellously sweetened by kindly good-humour. He had travelled much, and had studied carefully the institutions of self-governing countries. He returned with a deep conviction that national welfare was impossible without liberty, constitutional government, and freedom of trade. His love of country was an absorbing passion. To gain unity and freedom for Italy was the object of his life. It had been the dream of his youth that he would one day be the

minister of emancipated Italy. In 1850 he was received into
the Sardinian cabinet. Henceforth, to the day of his death,
the historty of Cavour is the history of Italy. Providence had
given to this long-afflicted land a man with wisdom to decern
her needs, and strength to conduct her victoriously through the
unparalleled difficulties by which she was beset.

After the disasters of 1848, Cavour was persuaded that
foreign help was necessary to the deliverance of Italy. Sardinia ruled a population of only four million, while twenty
million owned the sway of Austria, Naples, the pope, and the
dukes. The brave little kingdom which alone upheld liberty
in the peninsula was surrounded by despotic forces of overwhelming strength. It became evident that this was a political
condition which could not endure. Italy could not exist partly
free and partly enslaved. Liberty must drive out the despotisms, or be crushed by them. Cavour believed that it was
possible to liberate and unite the Italian people, and he lived
to justify his confidence by magnificent success.

In a few years the wounds of the war were healed, and Sardinia, with growing resources and unbroken courage, commanded increasing respect among European powers. The time
came when England and France deemed it necessary for them
to declare war against Russia. That might fairly have been
regarded as a war in which Sardinia was not called to interfere.
But Austria, her irreconcilable enemy, had taken such part
in the counsels of the warring powers that it was certain she
must have a voice in the congress which would be held when the
strife was over. Cavour saw his peril. A European congress
in which Austria was represented while Sardinia was excluded
might well be fatal to the hopes of Italy. He offered to join the
allies, and to put an army of twenty-five thousand men at once
in the field. The proposal was very acceptable, especially to the
English government, which had then some difficulty in keeping
the force in the Crimea up to its expected strength. England

offered a subsidy; but Cavour upheld the dignity of his country, and resolved that she should go to war upon her own charges. The men whom he sent did valiantly, and rendered effective service to the allied cause.

Thus was the foundation laid on which Cavour hoped to build the restoration of Italy. It is true the congress did nothing either for him or against him; but his relations with England and France were now of the most friendly and even confidential nature. England, indeed, would contribute only good advice—would give no more valid support than the support of her sympathy and approval.* But the throne of France was occupied by a man who "made war for an idea." Cavour sought and gained the favour of the Emperor Napoleon. A treaty was concluded between France and Sardinia. France was to drive the Austrians out of Italy, and procure the union of Lombardy and Venetia with Sardinia. Nor was she to war purely for "an idea." In the event of success, her help was to be recompensed by the cession of Savoy and Nice.

On New-Year's Day of 1859 the foreign ambassadors went, according to their custom, to make a visit of compliment to the emperor at the Tuileries. When his majesty approached the Austrian ambassador, he said to him, in a tone of well-assumed anger, that although the relations of the two countries were not such as he could desire, his personal feelings towards the Emperor of Austria were unchanged. This proceeding, unprecedented excepting by the still more insulting remarks addressed

* Although England acted on a wise determination to abstain from armed interference in the affairs of the peninsula, her support of the Italian people in their progress to freedom was given heartily, and was of undoubted service. In 1859 the Emperor Napoleon proposed an Italian confederation, under conditions which would have given Austria undue authority. At that time, as Lord Palmerston remarked, the emperor's mind seemed full of schemes as a warren is full of rabbits. Palmerston opposed the confederation scheme, on the ground that it would not satisfy the reasonable wishes of the Italian people. Again it seemed that Austria might use force to replace the fallen Italian dukes. Lord Palmerston protested against such action, and favoured a joint determination with France and Sardinia to prevent forcible interference in the affairs of Italy, even at the risk of a war with Austria. So highly was the friendly help of England appreciated that, after the annexation of Namples, numerous addresses of thanks were sent to Lord Palmerston from all parts of Italy.

by the first Napoleon to the British ambassador in 1803, was justly regarded as the intimation of hostile purposes. And so it proved. The three powers had been arming as for an inevitable conflict, and they were now ready. After some fruitless attempts at meditation by England, the Aus- ^{April 29,} trians entered Sardinian territory, and a French army _{A. D.} hastened to the rescue.

Throughout, that war went ill for Austria. In some engagements of inferior importance her troops were unable to keep the field, and in the battles of Magenta and Solferino ^{June 4} she suffered crushing defeat. At Solferino her losses in ^{and 25,} killed, wounded, and prisoners were nearly thirty thousand.

The troops were much demoralized by continued defeat, and it was not doubted that very decisive success was now within easy grasp of the allies. But during a period of two weeks the French lay inexplicably idle. The resumption of active hostilities and their glorious issue were eagerly looked for. But one day the awful whisper ran through the camps ^{July 6} that a French officer had been seen to drive towards Verona, where the Emperor of Austria had for the time his lodging. At first the report was discredited, till next day the messenger was seen to return and seek at once the presence of the Emperor Napoleon. Soon the tidings went abroad that an armistice had been offered to Austria, and accepted, and that peace would follow

The Italians were roused to vehement indignation by this unexpected desertion of their cause. Forgetful, in their wrath, of the vast service already rendered them, they denounced the emperor as their betrayer. Cavour resigned rather than sign a treaty of peace which he bitterly condemned.

Peace was quickly concluded. Austria acknowledged defeat by yielding Lumbardy, with a population of nearly three million; but she was allowed to retain Venetia, with a ^{July 11,} population of two and a half million. The duchies of Tuscany,

Parma, and Modena had driven out their rulers, and a portion
of the subjects of the pope had rejected the authority of his
holiness. The treaty provided that the people of these states
should return to their allegiance. But it was found that this
restoration could not be accomplished otherwise than by military force, which neither France nor Sardinia would

March
1860
A. D. apply. The wise resolution was adopted to leave the
people themselves to fix their destiny. Almost unani-
mously the people elected to join themselves to Sardinia.

By a war which lasted not quite three months Sardinia had
thus been enabled to add nine million to the population over
which she ruled. She owed this great accession wholly to the
help of France. But the Italians thought less of the advantages which they had gained than of those in regard to which
they suffered disappointment. General Garibaldi told them it
was foolish to have put their trust in the man who had overthrown liberty in France. Especially was the emperor hated
when it was known that his service was not wholly disinterested, and that Savoy and Nice, the earliest possessions of the
royal house of Sardinia, were now to be surrendered to France.
Garibaldi, himself a native of Nice, indignantly denounced an
arrangement which made him a foreigner in his own country.*

The emperor made war for the avowed purpose of libera-
ting Italy from the Alps to the Adriatic, and he had now to
explain why performance had fallen so far short of promise. He
expressed warmly his regret to see " noble illusions and patriotic hopes vanished from honest hearts." He had not abandoned the noble cause which he had desired to serve, but the
interest of France left him without alterative. The area of the

---

* The English government refused to acknowledge the cession. Lord Palmerston
spoke of it as objectionable on many grounds—among others, for the multitude of
false denials, and of promises apparently never intended to be kept, by which the
negotiation had been accompanied. It is not to be overlooked, in judging this transaction, that in respect of language and of sympathy the people of Savoy were French
rather than Italian, and that the same remark applies in some, although not so large a
measure, to Nice. The popular vote in both provinces was nearly unanimous in favour
of annexation to France.

war threatened to widen, and he "found himself in face of Europe in arms." In especial, he had either to close the war or " to accept a conflict on the Rhine as well as on the Adige." As subsequent events showed, he had done enough. What was wanting to the complete deliverance of Italy could be gained without further bloodshed.

At the close of the war Naples, containing a population of nine million, was still ruled by a Bourbon, who maintained over the unhappy people a shameful despotism. The Neapolitans were quick, intelligent and good-natured—a people capable of high civilization, but cruelly debased by centuries of wicked government. They were ignorant, idle, superstitious, and without just ideas of right and wrong. Their towns swarmed with beggars. A traveller passed to his hotel between lines of the halt, the maimed, and the blind, all imploring his excellency's bounty. If he ventured to look from his window, a tumult of supplication assailed him, a forest of withered legs and mutilated arms revealed itself to his horrified gaze. Every one begged; the indolent lazarone sought alms that he might be spared the hard necessity of labour; the friar begged that he might free unhappy souls from purgatory. The country was overrun with priests and monks. The endowment of the church yielded ten million sterling, and were in reality worth a much larger amount. The people lay under the power of priestly influnces, which were constantly exercised to shut out enlightenment and avert the dangers to which intelligent reflection would subject existing institutions.

Ferdinand II. was then king, the last of a line of bigoted tyrants. His government was regarded with abhorrence by his subjects, and with strong disapproval by Europe. Some years before an eminent English statesman, Mr. Gladstone, had visited Naples. He was led to make inquiry into the relations maintained by the government with those of

its subjects who were supposed to be disaffected. He gave to
the world the result of his researches in letters addressed to
Lord Aberdeen. He showed that there were probably twenty
thousand persons held in prison by the Neapolitan government
for political reason; that men were habitually arrested without
any offence being charged, simply because the government
desired to have them out of the way; that unoffending citizens
were imprisoned for years, without trial, among the vilest
criminals, often in heavy irons, which were never for a moment
removed; that the dungeons were dark, airless, crowded, inex-
pressibly filthy, and often so low-roofed that the prisoners could
not stand erect; that the doctors refused to enter these loathsome cells, and caused such prisoners as required medical care
to be brought to them; that the police habitually inflicted torture; that trial was a mockery of justice; that prisoners who
had the rare good fortune to be acquited were liberated only if
the government pleased.

These revelations brought upon Naples the reprobation of
the civilized world, and left her, in an age of revolution, without a friend. Lord Palmerston sent copies of Mr. Gladstone's letters to the British ministers at all European courts.
The Neapolitan government felt so acutely the damage done
to its reputation that it caused a reply to be prepared, which,
as Mr. Gladstone showed, virtually admitted the substantial
accuracy of his statements.

The great events which had come to pass in northern and
central Italy sent their thrilling influences among the people
of the south. An insurrection broke out in Sicily. General
Garibaldi summoned about him two thousand men, old
soldiers of liberty, and sailed from Genoa, to strengthen
and direct the movement. His battle-cry was to be,
"Italy and Victor Emanuel." The king's government
was not a little embarrassed by this invasion in the king's name
of the territory of a friendly power. Cavour, who had just

May 5,
1860
A. D.

returned to office, pronounced it the most difficult conjuncture in which he had ever been placed. He could not, without the sanction of France, give encouragement to the conquest of Naples. But the people of the north felt deeply the wrongs of their brethren in the south, and would not suffer any effort for their deliverance to be thwarted. The government officially disapproved of Garibaldi's expedition, but stood prepared to accept the advantages which its success would offer. After a little the king himself wrote to Garibaldi, July 27, 1860 begging him to desist. The general replied, with many A. D. loyal and dutiful assurances, that he was called for and urged on by the people of Naples; that he endeavoured in vain to restrain them; that the king must, on this occasion, permit him to be disobedient. But when it became evident that marvellous success was to crown the patriot efforts, Cavour's difficulty vanished. It was necessary that Sardinia should assume the leadership of a great national movement. Otherwise the unity of Italy would have been endangered.

Garibaldi quickly possessed himself of Sicily He crossed over to the mainland and began his advance to Naples. His march was a triumphal progress. The troops of the Aug. 19. king retired as he drew near; the rejoicing people hailed him as their deliverer. They gave expression to their rapture by illuminations. They brought gifts of fruit and wine to the soldiers. They embraced, with Italian demonstrativeness, the rugged and travel-stained heroes. Garibaldi pressed forward rapidly, and in three weeks he entered Naples. The king and queen fled on his approach. The people received him with enthusiasm, such as the ancient city had probably never witnessed before.

A portion of the Neapolitan army made a stand on the Volturno, where Garibaldi inflicted upon it final defeat. Garibaldi became for a time dictator, and governed Naples. The people were asked to declare their wishes in regard to their political future. They voted, by vast majorities, in favour of union with Sardinia. The king, in accepting the new trust, summoned the people to concord and self-denial. "All parties," he said, "must bow before the majesty of the Italian nation which God uplifts."

Garibaldi did not remain in the kingdom which he had won. He cherished against Count Cavour a bitter antipathy, and sought to have him dismissed from office. He intimated in the official gazette of Naples his determination never to be reconciled with the man who had sold an Italian province. He felt that he was not in harmony with the political conditions which surrounded him. In three months he had overthrown a despotic government, and added a population of nine million to the free kingdom of Italy. And now his work was done. Unostentatiously he quitted the land which he had saved, and returned in poverty to his little island of Caprera.

The foundations of Italian unity had been laid by the judicious interference of Sardinia in the strifes of the great European powers. A judicious repetition of the same strategy was once more to yield results of the highest value to the national cause. In course of years it became obvious that questions had arisen between Austria and Prussia which could not be solved otherwise than by the sword. Austria's extremity was Italy's opportunity. A treaty was arranged by which Prussia bound herself not to make peace with Austria until Venetia should be gained for Italy. King Victor Emanuel engaged, on his part, to attack Austria on land with eighty thousand men, and at sea with all his naval force. On both elements he was unsuccessful; the Austrians defeated his army and his fleet. But better fortune crowned the arms of Prussia. Two days after the battle of Sadowa, it was announced that Austria had ceded Venetia to France, thus, it may be supposed, lessening in some slight degree the humiliation which her final expulsion from

1866
A. D.

July 5.

Italy involved. The Emperor Napoleon gracefully handed his acquisition to the Italian government. It had always been his purpose, he intimated, to restore Italy to herself, so that she should be free from the Alps to the Adriatic, and this programme, interrupted by the hasty peace of 1859, was now all but completed.

The sole remaining obstacle was the pope. The holy father still bore rule over the city of Rome and a considerable portion of those unfortunate regions which the church claimed to possess as the patrimony of St. Peter. To north and south lay the now united states which made up free Italy. Wedged in between was a population of half a million of Italians longing to be united with their countrymen, enduring impatiently a government which they believed, with reason, to be the worst in Europe. This was a condition whose continuance was impossible. Italy could not tolerate, in the very heart of the kingdom, an alien state with a blindly despotic government and a discontented population. Moreover, Rome was the inevitable capital of united Italy. A few months before his death, Count Cavour "thought it his duty to proclaim this truth to the country with all the solemnity in his power."

But the tottering throne of the pope was still upheld by French bayonets, and the "eldest son" of the church gave ominous warning to the Italians that his filial duty was to be inflexibly discharged. The King of Italy was firmly bound by a convention with France, not only to abstain from making any attack upon the territory of the holy father, but also to resist any such attack if made by others. And when the Italian government manifested some disposition to forget that agreement, the Emperor Napoleon sternly intimated that France was prepared to insist upon its fulfilment. Sept.
1864
A. D. Nov. 1,
1867
A. D.

But events proved stronger than the Emperor Napoleon. The impatience of the Italian people became irrepressible. In-

surrection burst out in Rome. Garibaldi gathered around him
a band of unlicensed liberators, most of whom fell into the
hands of the French and Papal troops. The Italian question
became again a cause of European anxiety. Queen
Nov. 19,
1867
A. D. Victoria expressed to Parliament her hope that the
emperor would, by the early withdrawal of his troops
remove any possible ground of misunderstanding between himself and the King of Italy. A week or two later
the French quitted Rome, but next day the French government intimated angrily that "France would never submit to
such a violence on her honour and on Catholicity" as the occupation of Papal territory by the Italians.

Three unquiet years passed, bringing vast changes. The
Emperor Napoleon was a prisoner in the hands of the Prussians; his armies, shamefully defeated, had found refuge in
surrender; the King of Prussia was setting out on his triumphal march to Paris; the church was bereaved of her "eldest
son." Undutiful Italy did not neglect the opportunity.
Sept. 20,
1870
A. D. Her troops forced an entrance into Rome. The
Popish world shrieked loudly. The Empress of France
exclaimed, "Rather the Prussians in Paris than the
Italians in Rome." The Archbishop of Paris foretold approaching desolation. "Revolution," he said, will overwhelm
the world, and God will know how to create a new order out
of its chaos." The holy father did not cease to lavish in-
nocuous curses upon the disturbers of his tranquility. But
neither prophecy nor malediction shook the steady purpose of
the Italian people. The subjects of the pope joyfully united
themselves with their countrymen, and the liberation of Italy
was at length a completed work.

But long before these crowning successes which raised Italy
from a mere "geographical expression" to a rank among the
great powers of Europe, the statesman whose wisdom prepared
the restoration of her national life had passed away. During

the months which followed the annexation of Naples, the work which fell to Count Cavour was overwhelmingly great. In the following May, worn out by anxiety and toil, he was struck down by congestion of the brain. For a week he hung between life and death. When it became known that he was dying, the people of Turin crowded around he palace, eager to have tidings of the man they loved, dismayed by the sudden calamity about to fall upon the nation. Near the close the king had come to visit him, and when about to leave said that he would return to-morrow. "I will not be here to-morrow," said the dying statesman. And so it proved. $\begin{smallmatrix}\text{June 6,}\\ 1861\end{smallmatrix}$ Next morning, about sunrise, he died. A. D.

Cavour was not permitted to witness the completion of the work to which he had devoted his life; but he knew that what he had done made its completion sure. The rapture of the final triumph was reserved for others, but the higher glory of having rendered unparalleled service was his.

The desire vainly cherished by so many generations of Italians was at length fully satisfied. For centuries Italy had been parcelled out in fragments, each the pleasure-ground of a paltry despot. These enfeebling separations were now cancelled, and she stood before the world a great and united nation, in the full enjoyment of constitutional liberty, with a population equal to that of Great Britain, and an area equal to that of Great Britain and Ireland. Every natural advantage seemed to be hers,—a fertile soil; a genial climate; an ample sea board, and easy communication with all the world; unity of feeling among her people, growing out of the prosecution of a common aim; a history full of enobling memories, fitted to rouse men to worthy deeds. It remains for a later time than the present to show in what measure the Italians are able to avail themselves of their great opportunities; but the history of their few years of national life is full of promise.

Liberty and unity work no miracles. The degradation which
it has taken centuries to inflict may well require the life-time
of two or three generations to cancel. Priestly influences had
been studiously hostile to education, and the expelled despots
bequeathed to free Italy the care of a fearfully ignorant population. In 1864, eighty Italians in every hundred were unable
to read or write; and in 1870, sixty-four in every hundred of
the young men who came up for military service were similarly
uninstructed. The Italian government applied with becoming
energy a remedy to evils which were justly deemed incompatible with the stability of free institutions. A parliamentary
grant, which has now swelled to nearly one million sterling,
was voted for public instruction. No time was lost in adding
to this grant the greater portion of the revenues enjoyed by
the monastic establishments. Of these there were two thousand four hundred, inhabited by nearly thirty thousand idle
and unprofitable men and women. The act of 1866 dissolved
all these institutions; and after providing for life-interests on a
scale* which could not be considered inappropriate to persons
who had undertaken vows of poverty and self-denial, the
property was devoted to the education of the people.

The industrial progress of free Italy has been rapid. Only
two-thirds of her available soil are yet cultivated at all, and her
cultivation is often barbaric and wasteful; but she is making
such progress that her exports, which in 1868 were only
twenty-two million sterling, had risen in 1875 to forty-two
million. She taught England, centuries ago, the weaving of
silk, and she still continues to send abroad large quantities of
this article, both raw and manufactured. She supplies hemp,
oranges, spirits, brimstone, and after satisfying her own liberal
consumption of olives and olive oil, she has still a large surplus of these articles for shipment. The growing prosperity

---

* The pensions given to the various grades of "religious persons" ranged from ten
pounds up to twenty pounds annually.

of her people is expressed in the increase of her power to consume the productions of foreign countries. Her imports, which
in 1868 were thirty-four million sterling, were in 1874 fifty-two
million. She imports grain, her own production being still
insufficient, cotton and woollen manufactures, coal and iron.
A liberal commercial policy gives reason to expect that her
intercourse with other nations will continue to increase.

The modern Italian has inherited none of the aggressive-
ness of the ancient Roman. Her own concerns have been so
absorbing that Italy has not been tempted to occupy herself
with those of her neighbours. Her inclination as well as her
interest is altogether pacific. She has not, however, been able
to deny herself the dignity of a large and costly warlike establishment. She has under arms in time of peace two hundred
thousand men, and she maintains a powerful and expensive
fleet of ironclad and other vessels. Nay, so enterprising is
she in this profitless direction that she anticipated England in
the development of artillery, and possessed a gun of one hundred tons while our most powerful implement was a gun of
only eighty-one tons.

The expenditure of Italy has grown with an unwholesome
rapidity. From thirty-eight million sterling in 1862, it had
risen in 1875 to sixty-three million. Her income has not kept
pace with this increase, and there have been annual deficits
ranging from two million sterling up to twenty-four million.
This unhappy disparity has resulted in portentous additions to
the national debt. The debt, which in 1862 was only one
hundred and thirty-five million sterling, is now four hundred
million, and still increases, although the income seems at
length to approach equality with the expenditure.

Unfortunately the progress of Italy in the formation of railways has been much less rapid than the growth of her public
expenditure. She has only four thousand six hundred miles
of railway; and so little does private enterprise favour this

description of investment, that government has been obliged
to construct or to purchase one-half of the lines.   Of telegraph
she has thirteen thousand miles.   Her requirements in respect
of postal and telegraphic communication are still limited.
While in England the average number of letters received
annually is thirty-three for each individual, in Ireland fourteen,
and in France ten, in Italy it is only four.   Thus, too, while the
people of Great Britain receive telegrams in the proportion of
nearly one to each of the population, in Italy the proportion is
one telegram to six persons.

The modern career of Italy is yet only at its opening, and its
character therefore belongs to prophecy rather than to history ;
but the materials on which prediction may be safely based are
abundant.   The Italian people are in possession of the ennobling
privilege of self-government,* and they have thus far proved
themselves worthy of the trust by an ardent loyalty to their
institutions, and a cheerful obedience to the laws which they
contribute to frame.   They are being delivered by education
from the darkness which has so long rested upon them; they
have perfect liberty of thought, and speech; they are satisfied
with their political circumstances, and are therefore peaceable.
Industry is bringing them comfort.   The great conditions on
which prosperity depends are thus present.   Italy, which until
lately was a constant source of anxiety to Europe, may be
expected to make steady progress in enlightenment and power,
and to exercise a growing influence in the interests of peace on
the policy of the other European powers.

* All citizens twenty-five years of age, and who pay taxes to the amount of £1, 12s.
exercise the franchise. The number of registered voters does not exceed six hundred
thousand,—perhaps a fortunate limitation in the present uneducated condition of the
people.

CHAPTER VI.

RUSSIA.

RUSSIA was scarcely known as a European power till the close of the seventeenth century. No army of hers had been seen in the west till almost the middle of the eighteenth century. Her vast and thinly-peopled territory was the home of many races—European and Asiatic—who were separated by great distances, and ordinarily had no relations which were not hostile. They owned allegiance to the same monarch, and had centuries ago accepted a shadowy Christianity at the bidding of one of their kings. But they remained wholly barbarous. They had no commerce, no manufacture but the very rudest, and no softening intercourse with other nations. They had no roads, no education, no regular army, no shipping. A primitive agriculture furnished their subsistence, and their days were divided between savage indolence and the fierce delights of war.

The European history of Russia may almost be said to open in the year when the people of England finally rejected absolute monarchy, and peacefully settled themselves under a constitutional government. In 1689 a boy of seventeen ascended the Russian throne. His name was Peter, in course of years surnamed, with some reason, the Great. It suited the wicked purposes of an elder step-sister to hold him under the debasement of ignorance and vice. He was wholly without education. He was encouraged to the practice of drunkenness and

379

gluttony, and every degrading form of self-indulgence. But the energy of his nature quickly surmounted the disadvantages thus basely laid upon his youth. Peter hastened to provide himself with what education he could obtain. He shook off the fetters of vicious indulgence. He had no great wealth of years before him, for he died at fifty-three, and the task which he undertook was unparalleled in its magnitude and its difficulty. But he did with his might what his hand found to do, and his short span of life sufficed for a revolution such as the will and the efforts of one man had never accomplished before.*

A little intercourse with the people of the west revealed to Peter the immeasurable inferiority of Russia. Unaided by the wisdom, as he was unrestrained by the caution of others, Peter resolved to force upon his subjects the civilaztion of the west. He created an army—at first so ineffective that ten thousand Swedes under the heroic madman Charles XII. routed eighty thousand Russians. But Peter, undismayed, perfected the discipline of his troops, and raised them to an equality with the soldiers of the older European states. He had no fleet; indeed there was not in the language a word by which that idea could be expressed. He had no ship-builders. At Deptford and Amsterdam Peter worked with his own hand to acquire the art of the carpenter. He carried skilled artificers back with him to Russia, and in a few years a formidable Russian fleet commanded the Baltic. Moscow, the seat of government, was too remote from European interests. Peter determined to establish on the shores of the Baltic the new capital of his empire, from which, as " from a window, he could look out upon western Europe." He chose for its site a marshy island in the Neva. Thither came, at his despotic call, three hundred thousand men

---

* Although animated by an enlightened love of improvement, Peter still retained much of the savage in his nature. On one occasion he not only looked on while a crowd of defeated insurgents were put to death, but even wielded the executioner's sword with his own royal hand. Habitually he applied his cane to the shoulders of his clergy and courtiers, whose actions displeased him.

to clear forests, drain marshes, construct roads, and otherwise prepare for the new city. Inundations destroyed his works; epidemics swept away by thousands his crowded workmen. The undaunted czar held on his way, and in five month his capital was founded and so fortified that his enemies of Sweden could gain no advantage over it.

He introduced into Russia silk and woollen manufactures, the art of printing, and even some slight knowledge of western literature. He made roads and canals. He established police and a postal service. He framed a code of laws drawn from those of more civilized countries. By the help of a Scotch mathematician he caused arithmetic to be adopted in the government offices, where heretofore accounts had been kept by a system of balls threaded on wire. He established a council of mines and began to develop the vast mineral wealth of the country. He founded hospitals and medical schools. He watched over and encouraged all his innumerable enterprises. And among all crafts, from the founding of cannon to rope-making, there was none with which Peter did not possess some acquaintance and to which he could not put his own hand.

He ventured to reform the church, meeting the objections of the clergy by telling them that, as he had reformed everything else, civil and military, he would be wanting in gratitude to the Most High if he did not render the same service to the church. He assumed the control of her revenues. He would have no pope, and therefore he replaced the patriarch by a synod. He forbade the adoption of a monastic life by persons under fifty, deeming that population was more valuable to Russia than monasteries.

Many of the customs of his people bore traces of an eastern origin. Women lived in oriental seclusion, and marriages were arranged by the parents of those chiefly interested. Peter forbade bethrothal until the parties to such contracts had been acquaited for at least six weeks. He introduced assemblies where young persons could meet and vindicate to themselves the western privilege of choosing their own partners for life. The Russian dress was of the loose and flowing eastern type; the Russian beard was long. Peter ordained the substitution of western fashions. He commanded his masculine subject to shave off their beards.* He punished by heavy fine those who ventured abroad with long beard and loose robe. With grim jocularity he hung model garments at the city gates, and his officers mercilessly shortened the apparel of those conservative citizens who perversely maintained the ancient costume.

The Russian year began in September, in which month, as it was believed, God had created the world. Having no respect to this commemoration, Peter caused the year to begin in Russia as it did in other European countries.

This sweeping reconstruction was eminently successful. The manufactures planted by the czar took root and prospered; the arts flourished under his munificent patronage; his laws were obeyed; his fashions were accepted; his new capital assumed, under his eye, metropolitan dimensions and beauty. He had prepared Russia to take rank as a great European power. She was still remote from the centres of European political life. Turkey interposed between her and the Mediterranean. Poland shut her out from the west. An extension of her frontier line was indispensable to the increase of her greatness. She was patient and sagacious; strong, united, unscrupulous. Already more powerful than her neighbours, and urgently in want of their territories, her increase southward and westward was now rendered inevitable.

When Peter asscended the throne, Russia exercised dominion over five million square miles of the earth's surface. To-day the Emperor Alexander gives law to territories which extend

* Orthodox Russians, mourning the bereavement, preserved the beards which they had been compelled to sacrifice, to be placed by their side in the coffin. Not otherwise could the favourable regard of St. Nicholas be secured in their hour of need. With many Russians the beard was an essential portion of religious belief.

over nine million square miles. During the intervening period the history of Russia is a record of incessant expansion on every side. The world has no parallel to this monstrous growth. The vast acquisitions of England in the great Indian peninsula, extending as they do to one million square miles, are almost insignificant beside those of a power which, since the beginning of last century, has added to its possessions a territory equal to the whole of Europe.

Sweden was one of the earliest sufferers by the avarice of this unquiet neighbour. Livonia, Carelia, and Finland were required to supply Russia with access to the sea; and as they were wanted, they were taken. Poland stood inconveniently between her and western Europe, in whose affairs it was now her desire to take part. Russia marked for her own a large portion of Polish territory. By three gigantic acts of spoilation, the guilt and the gains of which were shared with Austria and Prussia, Poland was effaced from the map of Europe.* The southern march of conquest began while Peter was on the throne. Azov was yielded by the Turks in 1711. Kherson followed, and Kertch and the Crimea; Bessarabia, and certain portions of the Black Sea coast. She occupied, as her own by right, Kirghis and the Steppes, a vast region stretching northwards from the Areal Sea. All the while Russia was steadily extending her sway over fertile but thinly-settled regions in the east. Persia yielded Georgia and Tiflis. From time to time, as the century advanced, the Caucasus fell to the victorious arms of Russia.

* Russia has been justly blamed for the severities which she inflicted on Poland. In judging of the relations of the two countries, it should, however, be remembered, *first*, That for six centuries there had been continual war between Poland and Russia; that Poland was habitually the aggressor; that, being then the stronger, she inflicted terrible evils upon Russia, and sought, by diplomacy as well as by war, to strangle the national life of her rival. When Russia, now grown strong, shared in the final assault upon Poland, she was not attacking a harmless neighbour, she was avenging centuries of cruel wrong. *Second*, At the time of the dismemberment the Poles were "in the lowest state of degradation—ignorant, indolent, poor, drunken, and improvident." The recent reports of the English consuls represent the condition of Poland as most satisfactory. There is "a very remarkable progress in commerce, agriculture, and manufactures." "The country is becoming rich and prosperous beyond all expectation."

In 1847 began her great eastward march into central Asia. England had just possessed herself of the Punjab, and Russia feared, or pretended to fear, our growing control over the lucrative commerce of Khiva, Bokhara, and the great valley of the Jaxartes. She launched upon the Aral Sea a little fleet of warships. She advanced steadily, without hasting but without resting, towards the south, overcoming with ease the resistance offered by the scattered population. The exhaustion resulting from the Crimean war induced for a few years a pause; but with returning strength there came resumed progress. In 1864 she had seized Chemkend, and held securely the fairest portions of the rich valley of the Jaxartes. At this time Prince Gortschakoff explained to the world that these conquests had been forced upon Russia by " an imperious necessity," and had now reached their limit. But none the less for this announcement was the career of appropriation continued. Tashkend and Kokan were seized. Khiva, despoiled of much territory, was reduced to vassalage, and Bokhara was threatened with a similar fate.

Since her career of acquisition began, Russia has carried her frontier eight hundred miles westward into Europe. She has advanced four hundred and fifty miles nearer to the Mediterranean, and three hundred miles nearer to the capital of Sweden. In Asia she has moved southward and eastward towards Afghanistan, until her outposts are now a thousand miles nearer India, and within three hundred miles of territory which is under protection of the British flag.

It was held by many persons of political sagacity that the fall of Napoleon transferred the empire of the world to Russia. Her magnificent success had raised her to a place of commanding authority in the direction of European affairs. A century before, Russia was unknown to the politics of Europe; now she was their supreme arbitress. Soon the belief was widely entertained that power so vast, guided by ambition unbounded and unscrupulous, involved peril to all other European nations. Nowhere perhaps was this impression more firmly held than by the Russians themselves, who now indulged in arrogant contempt of the institutions and customs of their neighbours, and claimed for their own arms a supremacy which was wholly irresistible.

For forty years the national vanity suffered no abatement. The influence of Russia continued to increase, and it was centered more exclusively in the person of the emperor. During the latter years of the reign of Nicholas his despotism was absolute almost beyond example. There was no will in the state but his. He could brook no contradiction; towards the close his most trusted counsellors dared not to offer any—so terrible became the wrath of the aged tyrant. Mute submission was the attitude of the people. Education was discouraged because the universities might be nurseries of liberal tendencies. The slightest breath of political criticism in a newspaper was instantly punished by the ruin of the too daring journalist. All the interests, material and intellectual, of a great nation were fashioned according to the unrestrained pleasure of an honest but narrow and obstinate man. Nicholas learned to dislike western ideas. Progress and culture were distasteful to him. He would fain shut out all foreign influences, and to that end he put a stop to the extension of railways. He avowed his contempt for the arts of peace, and deemed it the grand work of his life to enhance the military greatness of Russia.

The Russians entered upon the contest with England and France in the rejoicing conviction that their emperor and his army were invincible. It was impossible to believe that the power which for forty years had wielded unlimited authority was now to stoop to defeat and humiliation. The nation took up arms in the fullest confidence that their emperor would lead them to victory. Nicholas perilled upon the issue of the war not only his military greatness, but the whole enormous fabric of despotism which he had builded so laboriously.

25

The triumph of the western powers produced a vast change on Russian opinion. Not only was the believing devotion of the people to their emperor overthrown, but the policy which he had established was utterly discredited. The ruthlessness of his despotism was lightly regarded in days of success; now that the blight of defeat had fallen upon him, its enormous evils became at once the subject of deep and universal reproba-

1855
A. D.
tion. And when the aged monarch passed away from among the ruins of his political system, a sense of relief was experienced. It was deemed better that Nicholas should die, for he could never have adapted himself to the changes which his own blind obstinacy had rendered inevitable.

Under the rule of his successor the despotic system of Nicholas was to an important extent departed from. The newspaper press experienced sudden enlargement. So urgent was the demand for political discussion, that within a year or two from the close of the war seventy new journals were founded in St. Petersburg and Moscow alone. The government censors discharged their functions with the mildness which the liberal impulses of the time demanded. For a brief space the press enjoyed a virtual freedom from restraint, and availed itself boldly of the unprecedented opportunity. Western Europe had been shut out by the Emperor Nicholas. Its libelal ideas, the history of its recent political revolutions, its marvelous progress in science and the arts—all were un-known to the Russian people. Educated Russians were eager to acquaint themselves with this long-forbidden knowledge, and a crowd of journalists, burning with a love of liberal ideas, hastened to gratify the desire. An enfranchised press began to call loudly for the education of the people, for their partici-pation in political power; for many other needful reforms Chief among these, not merely in its urgency, but also in its popularity, was the emancipation of the serfs.

Forty-eight million Russian peasants were in bondage—

subject to the arbitrary will of an owner—bought and sold with the properties on which they laboured. This unhappy system was of no great antiquity, for it was not till the close of the sixteenth century that the Russian peasant, became a serf.* The evil institution had begun to die out in the west before it was legalized in Russia. Its abolition had long been looked forward to. Catherine II. had contemplated this great reform, and so also had her grandson Alexander I.; but the wars in which they spent their days forbade progress in any useful direction. Nicholas very early in his reign appointed a secret committee to consider the question; but the Polish insurrection of 1830 marred his design. Another fruitless effort was made in 1836. In 1838 a third committee was appointed, but its work was suspended by "a bad harvest," and never resumed. Finally, it was asserted that the dying emperor bequeathed to his son the task which he himself had not been permitted to accomplish.

And thus it came to pass that when Alexander ascended the throne the general expectation of his people pointed to the emancipation of the serfs. The emperor shared in the national desire. At his coronation he prepared the somewhat reluctant nobles for the change which to many of them was so unwelcome. A little later he nominated a committee chosen from the proprietors, whose duty it was to frame, in accordance with certain principles laid down for their guidance, the details of this great rovolution. Three years followed of discussion, adjustment, revision, and then the decree was published which conferred freedom upon nearly fifty million Russian peasants.†

Aug. 1856 A. D.

Feb. 19, 1861 A. D.

The position of the Russian serf, although it had much to

---

* The Russian word which we translate serf carries merely the idea of being fixed to one locality. Their Tartar instinct impelled the peasants to roam about, to the ruinous neglect of agriculture. They were made serfs with no worse purpose than that of restraining this wasteful indulgence, and obliging them to stay at home and till their fields. Even now the emancipated peasant may not go from home without permission of the elder—the chief whom the villagers elect.

† This decree applied only to the twenty-two million common serfs. The twenty-six million crown and appanage serfs were emancipated by a separate act.

degrade, was without the repulsive features of ordinary slavery. The estate of the Russian land-owner was divided into two portions. The smaller of the two—usually not more than one-third—was retained for the use of the proprietor. The larger was made over to the village community, by whom it was cultivated, and to whom its fruits belonged. The members of that community were all serfs, owned by the great lord and subject to his will. He could punish them by stripes when they displease him; when he sold his lands he sold also the population. He could make or enforce such claims upon their labour as seemed good to him. Custom, however, had imposed reasonable limitations on such claims. He selected a portion of his serfs to cultivate his fields and form his retinue. The remainder divided their time equally between his fields and their own: three days in each week belonged to their master, and three days belonged to themselves. Many of them purchased for a moderate payment the privilege of entire exemption from the work of their owner. It was customary for these enterprising bondmen to settle in the nearest city, where occasionally they attained to wealth and consideration. Instances have occurred of wealthy bankers and merchants who still remained the property of a master, to whom a humiliating recognition of their servile estate was periodically offered.

The lands which were in possession of the villagers were divided by lot among the separate families. As the number of claimants fluctuated, a fresh division was made every ninth year. A villager never lost his right to participate in the common inheritance. He might be absent for years, seeking his fortune in the city, but when it pleased him to return and claim his interest in the lands of his native village, the claim could not be resisted.

The law of emancipation bestowed personal freedom on the serfs. For two years those who were household servants must abide in their service; receiving, however, wages for their work.

Those who had purchased exemption from the obligation to labour for their lord were to continue for two years the annual payment. At the end of that time all serfs entered on possession of unqualified freedom.

The villagers continued in occupation of the lands which they had heretofore possessed; but they became bound to pay a purchase-price or a sufficient equivalent in rent or labour. The continued occupation was not voluntary, but compulsory; and no peasant may withdraw without consent of the whole commuity, which, in the northern parts of the empire, is gained only by purchase. The lands thus acquired are not owned by individuals, but by the community. All obligations to the former proprietor or to the state are obligations of the associated villagers. The land-system of the greater portion of Russia is thus a system of communism. The industrious villager is the co-obligant of the idle and vicious. The motive which impels a man to the careful cultivation of his land is weakened by the knowledge that in a short time he will have to change fields with his neighbour. The peasant is assured of a maintenance which no misconduct on his part can alienate, but he is left almost without hope of rising to a better position. The portion of land assigned to him furnishes only partial employment. Recent changes in the excise laws bring stimulants within easy reach of all. Promoted by idleness, ignorance, and abundant opportunity, durnkenness has fearfully increased since the abolition of serfdom.* The indolent peasant works reluctantly for hire to his former lord. Notwithstanding an abundance of labourers, there is a serious insufficiency in the supply of labour. It is believed that over much of the country the productions of agriculture are diminishing.

* Nearly one-half of the national revenue is obtained from duties on liquor, and the government will not suffer this important source of income to be trifled with. The consumption of vodki, the great intoxicant of the peasant. is deliberately promoted by officials, cival and ecclesiastical. Any attempt to propagate temperance opinions is sternly repressed.

In 1862 Russia completed a thousand years of national existence, and the anniversary, occurring as it did while the liberal
tendencies and hopes of the educated classes were in the full
vigour of youth, was joyfully held to mark the opening of a
new era.   Some demanded complete religious liberty; others
persuaded themselves that the emperor was about to bestow
upon his people the boon of a free press.   Others yet more
ambitious expected that the second millennium of Russian life
would be inaugurated by the establishment of constitutional
government in a broadly democratic form.   In lands where
men are free political hopes compel their own fulfilment.   In
Russia it is not so.   The widespread desire of the people was
calmly disregarded by the little group of men whose prerogative it was to give or to withhold

But Alexander's love of reform, although narrow, was sincere,
and he honoured the great anniversary by enacting certain
measures which soothed the disappointed feelings of his subjects.

Hitherto the administration of justice had been incredibly
corrupt.   All judicial proceedings were secret.   Government
officers could at pleasure arrest or modify the course of justice.
A favourable judgment could almost always be obtained by
purchase.   Appeals were so numerous, that a wealthy litigant
could avert almost indefinitely a judgment which was unacceptable to him.   The judges were ignorant; the forms and pre-
cedents by which they ought to be guided were cumbrous and
inaccessible.   The people had, with reason, utterly lost confidence in the courts of justice.

Suddenly the emperor applied a remedy to these disorders.
In future competent judges were to be appointed by the
Sept.   state; all judicial transactions were to be public;
1862   government interposition was excluded; trial by jury in
A. D.   criminal cases was established, and a wholesome limit to
the right of appeal was imposed.   These reforms have proved

to be of the highest value; and the newly appointed tribunals soon began to gain the confidence of the people.

Hitherto there had been no shadow of self-government even in municipal or provincial affairs. All depended on the arbitrary pleasure of the sovereign and his ministers. Outside the circle of individual interests there was no will but that of the executive. The peasant ploughed his field, the merchant directed his commercial affairs; but all beyond, whether local or imperial, was under the irrepressible control of the government.

This unhappy condition of public affairs was now to experience a certain measure of amelioration. A system of district and provincial assemblies was organized. The district assembly was chosen by all classes of the community—proprietors, citizens and peasants. These assemblies elected certain of their own members to form the provincial assemblies. The interests confided to the new organizations were wholly local. They were empowered to maintain highways, to make arrangements for the welfare of local trade and industry, to levy those taxes which government had imposed. With politics they might not intermeddle, and the government watched jealously any disposition to stray into this forbidden field. The ignorant peasant class preponderates in these assemblies, and their action thus far has not been attended with any notable advantage to the community. The Russian peasant manifests little desire for the possession of self-government and no aptitude for its exercise. His performance of public duty does not therefore tend to educate and elevate his character. He seems to be contented with autocratic rule rather than those popular institutions which are the glory of the enlightened western nations.

Nor were these the only reforms which Alexander bestowed upon his people. Flogging in the army was discontinued. Some measure of toleration was extended to the strange and fanatical sects who by their irrepressible dissent had long troubled the orthodox church. Considerable pains have been taken to improve the church herself, and raise the standard of intelligence in the priesthood. An amnesty permitted the return of many of those who had suffered banishment under the savage rule of Nicholas. The construction of railways was promoted. The cost of a passport—heretofore eighty pounds—was reduced to a trifle which no longer restrained persons of moderate income from travelling. A milder and more liberal spirit pervaded all departments of administration.

The progress of Russian reform was, however, seriously interrupted by the Polish revolt of 1863. The liberal party befriended the discontented Poles, but a powerful sentiment sprang up in favour of maintaining unimpaired the national unity and dignity. Under its influence the Poles were ruthlessly suppressed, and liberalism was discredited. Since that time the short-lived ardour of the Russian government and people in the cause of reform has not regained its former power.

The Russian peasantry remain almost without education. In most country districts not more than one in fifty of the population attends school.* Until recently only eleven in every hundred soldiers could read. Even in towns the artisan who can read and write is exceptionally cultivated. Only the children of the rich receive education. In the early part of Alexander's reign it was usual for the newspapers to deplore the uneducated condition of the poor. The liberal tendencies of that time expressed themselves by a spasmodic attempt to establish voluntary schools in the large towns. Some progress had been made in this work, when the schools fell under suspicion of government as diffusing revolutionary influences. They were first discouraged, and then destroyed. The church is the only

* Finland, which has an educational system peculiar to itself, is greatly in advance of the rest of the empire. Nearly the whole population of Finland can read. Recently certain advantages have been offered to those soldiers who learn to read and write. A marked success has attended this scheme, and an increasing proportion of Russian soldiers are now able to read.

channel by which any measure of education can reach the people. Government, recognizing this truth, bestows considerable care upon the education of the priests. But the system followed is miserably unenlightened. That the young priest may not be tempted to interfere in politics, he is not allowed to see any newspaper; he is debarred from all secular literature, and his instruction is confined to the theology which has been handed down by the Greek Church of the Middle Ages.*

It does not appear that agencies are at work which tend in any important measure to the elevation of the Russian peasant. The church does little for him; indeed, it may very well happen that his clergyman is scarcely less ignorant and drunken than he himself is. Of the schoolmaster he knows nothing. The village in which he lives is a collection of miserable wooden huts, ordinarily of a single apartment, in which the whole family sleep on the bare floor. In a large portion of the empire his food and climate impose upon him an imperfect physical and mental development. He can no longer be beaten or sold by a master, but his fellow-villagers may assemble in public meeting and decree that he shall be flogged—a sentence from which there is no appeal. His attitude to the great lord of his district is still utterly slavish. He can be moulded into a soldier of exceptional excellence. He endures without complaint extreme privation and fatigue, and in the ranks he encounters dangers without shrinking; but he is without natural daring, and when alone is a prey to childish terrors.

Russia is imposing by her vast bulk. She is a huge embodiment of brute force. In defensive warfare she will always prove invincible; in aggressive war on barbaric oriental powers she will always be formidable; for purposes of aggression on the civilized and powerful west she must happily remain harmless.

*In the Russian Church the marriage of priests is compulsory. The sacred office may not be filled by an unmarried man or by a widower. Nor is the bereaved priest allowed to marry again; he quits his charge and retires into a convent.

But it is not surprising that an empire so gigantic should inspire with awe the states which are overshadowed by her enormous dimensions. In point of extent Russia is the largest dominion in the world. The waters of the Arctic Sea wash her northern shores; on the south she looks out upon the Mediterranean; the Pacific bounds her on the east ; the Atlantic may almost be said to bound her on the west. The czar gives law to one seventh part of the earth's surface. From his palace in St. Petersburg he governs a people seven thousand miles away on the remotests coasts of Asia. His subjects number eighty-five million. They would be well-nigh irresistible were they less widely separated; but they are scattered thinly over nine million square miles—an area twice that of Europe.

The eighty-five million Russian people have surrendered to a single family all control over the management of their national interests. Russia is, in the fullest sense of the term, an absolute monarchy. All power—legislative, executive, judicial, ecclesiastical—centres in the emperor. His will is the law of Russia. He appoints and dismisses all the officers by whom his will is executed, and answers to no one for his actions. He enjoys an income which, it is believed, amounts to two and a half million sterling. The people suffer in silence, as if sent by the judgment of Heaven, the miseries which his pride or folly may inflict upon them. When he dies all these vast perogatives and emoluments are occupied by his son.

The emperor supports the dignity of his crown by an ample military establishment. Following the example of Prussia, he has decreed universal liability to military service. Every young Russian must spend the six years from twenty-one to twenty-seven in active service, and thereafter stand enrolled for nine years in the reserve. During peace there are three-quarters of a million men under arms; in war the number rises to a million and a quarter. Besides this enormous army, there are one hundred and thirty thousand

1871
A. D.

Cossack horsemen, who give military service instead of rent or taxes, and who equip themselves for the field at their own cost. The emperor spends thirty million sterling annually upon his preparations for war; the education of his people costs him two million; he dispenses justice at a cost of two million; religious instruction is supplied for one million two hundred and fifty thousand pounds. The total expenditure is eighty million. Until recently the financial position of Russia was not upon the whole unfavourable. During the last fifty years she has borrowed largely, but by the operation of sinking funds she has also repaid largely, and her total debt before the war was three hundred and sixty million.

The late war against Turkey has involved Russia in no inconsiderable financial distress. The costs of that war are officially stated at a sum which, under the present depreciation of the currency, is the equivalent of one hundred and thirty million sterling, and will represent a greatly larger amount if Russia shall ever regain the blessing of a healthy currency. Much of it has been met for the time by enormous issues of paper money, the uncertain value of which is highly injurious to the commercial interests of the country. The credit of Russia has been gravely impaired, and her power to borrow has almost ceased. Her people are already taxed beyond their capability; vast irrecoverable arrears defy the well-proved skill of her most experienced collectors. The universal dishonesty of officials inflicts year by year losses which seriously enhance the sufferings of the people and the difficulties of the government.

Russia exports annually products to the value of fifty-two million sterling. Her shipments consists mainly of wheat, flax, hemp, timber. She receives to a somewhat larger value the manufactures of the west. Her foreign commerce does not tend to increase.

The resources of Russia are enormous, but as yet their development has scarcely begun. Her coal-field equal in area those of Great Britain, but she raises only one million five hundred thousand tons of coal—scarcely over one-hundredth of the British production. She has abundant gold, but her processes are so rude that the real capabilities of her mines have not been ascertained. She has a prodigious area of fertile land under cultivation, but her agriculture is barbarous, and her land laws preclude the hope of improvement. There is a magnificent future in store for Russia, but it is still remote.

With vast effort the emperor has provided twelve thousand miles of ill-constructed and ill-conducted railways by an outlay of two hundred million sterling. But the country is still miserably supplied with means of communication. Where Britain has one mile of railway to seven square miles of area, and the United States one to forty, the proportion in European Russia is one to one hundred and fifty-seven. There are many parts of the country where the price of wheat is nominal, and where access to a seaport or the market of a large city is wholly impossible. New lines have been projected, the construction of which would hasten the development of the empire. Several lines are to pierce the great coal-fields of the Don. One immense line is to stretch across the waste which divides Siberia from the capital. Another will run deep into central Asia. But the execution of these magnificent designs must wait the restoration of Russian credit.

Among a people so little educated communication by writing is seldom resorted to. The Russians receive letters and post-cards at the annual rate of one for each of the population. Telegraphic messages are sent on the average of one to every twenty-two persons.

The territorial gains of Russia have proved financially a heavy loss. The government of Poland, of the Caucasus, of central Asia, forms a serious drain on the resources of the empire. There is no reason to suppose that the Russian government would willingly add to the burdens of the people by undertaking the rule of additional unremunerative provinces. Like England, she has had the cares of extended empire forced upon her by circumstances,* and it is not probable that she desires to increase the load. She has subjugated innumerable wandering tribes to whom law and industry were unknown. She has not bestowed upon them a high civilization—for they were not able to receive it, and she herself does not possess it; but to the extent of their capacity she is teaching them to be orderly and industrious. Wherever her arms have been carried, slavery has been abolished. Her teaching is always stern, often cruel. It is not in her nature to impart, nor in that of her subjects to receive, any other. Her influence has, however, beyond doubt, been beneficial to those who have been brought under its sway.

* Lord Northbrook, late governor-general of India, said "he believed that the extention of Russian territory had been brought about gradually (like our own) by force of circumstances, and that there had been no policy entered upon with the view of Russian extension in India."

CHAPTER VII.

TURKEY.

AT the beginning of the Christian era the Huns roamed over a vast reigion, now called Tartary, which stretched from the Caspian Sea eastward to the borders of China. They were exceptionally hideous even for savages. An ancient historian compares them to brutes set up awkwardly on their hind legs. Their eyes were small and deeply sunk in the head; their noses were flat; they had little hair and no beard. Some of their cotemporaries refused to acknowledge them as human, and abhorred them as the progeny of evil spirits and witches. No one, however, questioned their possession of great physical strength and energy, and their unsurpassed skill as horsemen. Their savage passion for war and their inexhaustible numbers made them the scourge of Europe as well as of Asia. Their neighbours of China built a great wall, fifteen hundred miles in length, to repel the inroads of the Huns. Nor did this defence avail them. They were obliged to purchase the tranquility of their frontier by a tribute paid to the savages who tormented them.

From time to time hords of these Tartar horsemen rode westward or southward into unknown regions to taste delight of battle and enrich themselves with the spoils of their victims. One such horde, followed in time by many others, found a settlement in Bokhara, a reigon spoken of with reason by the

Arab historian as "the most delightful of all places which God has created." But they did not enjoy this genial possession in quietness. Mohammed was then inspiring his Arabs with that fierce enthusiasm which was destined to carry their arms in triumph over half the world. The Turks, as they were now called, were invaded by the fiery Saracens and, after years of fighting, subdued. They were not driven away; they liven on for many generations as the servants of their conquerors, whose religion they speedily accepted.

Three or four centuries after their settlement in Bokhara, the Turks are found to have undergone a striking amelioration both in appearance and nature. They had lost the hideous aspect of their forefathers, and their reputation for courage and fidelity was such that they were employed as guards to the caliph. Gradually they rose to commands in the army, to offices in the palace, to governorships of provinces. Their savage impetuosity disappeared, and in its place there came something of the dignity and gravity and capacity of silence by which the Turk of our own day is characterized. In the eleventh century they were again masters of the fair region where they had served so long.

Rising thus under the discipline of centuries out of the primeval degradation, the Turks were at length ready to enter upon the career which was in store for them. They began to expand on every side. Eastward their conquests stretched far into the depths of Asia. Before the century closed they had taken Asia Minor and Syria from the Saracens, and possessed themselves of Jerusalem, whose sacred associations made it a rich prize to men of their faith. They were now perilously near Constantinople, and the timid emperors called aloud to the Christians of the West for protection against the heathens who seemed ready to overwhelm them. But the fall of the tottering empire was not yet at hand.

The possession of Jerusalem by unbelieving Saracen and

Turk, and the thrilling tales of cruelty inflicted upon pilgrims
to the Holy City, awakened passionate indignation in western
Christendom.   Were not devout travellers habitually stripped
of their possessions and often bereft of life?   Had not the
patriarch himself been dragged by the hair along the streets
and cast into a dungeon?   Was not the Church of the Resurrection constantly invaded by a misbelieving rabble and the
most solemn services of the church disturbed?   Europe roused
herself to chase the pagans from those sacred fields which they
had acquired so lawlessly and governed so ruthlessly.   For two
hundred years armed men from the west arrested and even
rolled back the tide of Asiatic conquest.   And then—but not
until two million of her sons had perished—Europe desisted
from the profitless task.   The Turkish hordes, constantly reinforced from the wilds of Asia, were left within easy striking
distance of the decaying Roman empire.   The catastrophe,
however, was not immediate.   It was not till the middle of the
fifteenth century that the turks seized Constantinople and
entered on full possession of the vast dominions which the
imperial city had ruled.

The progress of Turkish arms continued for many years
after Constantinople was taken.   The powers of south-eastern
Europe were unable to combine against the common foe.
Bitter religious strifes divided them.   Each met alone the
attack of the savage invaders; one after another they sank
under it.   In a few years Greece, mainland and island, had
fallen.   Servia, which had heretofore been a tributary principality, now sank into a province.   In a few years more Bosnia
and Albania were annexed.   The Crimea was wrested from
the Genoese.   While rival kings contended for the crown of
Hungary the conquering Turk availed himself of their weakness, and possessed a large portion of the kingdom.   Wallachia and Moldavia became vassal states, and paid ignominious
tribute to the unbelievers.   Egypt was added to the Ottoman

dominions; and a Turkish army besieged Vienna. The sultan possessed himself of spiritual as well as temporal sovereignty, and wielded the vast authority of the caliphate. Resistance to this terrible power seemed vain. The conquest of south-eastern Europe was complete, save where, on the shores of the Adriatic, the stubborn Montenegrins held their mountain fast-ness against the power of the Turks—beginning a heroic defence which was to reach its victorious close only after four centuries of almost incessant war.

But at length the spread of Ottoman dominion was arrested. In the year 1571 the fleet of Turkey met, in the great battle ot Lepanto, the united fleets of Venice and Spain, Genoa and the pope, and was destroyed. It was the first decisive defeat which the Turk had sustained in Europe, and it marks a turning-point in his career. Hitherto all had been success and rapid increase of power. Henceforth there is chiefly decay. The central government began to grow weaker and more op-pressive; its corruption became more extreme. Lands began to lie untilled; houses to be without inhabitants; population to diminish. Incessant war raged between Christian and Turk; and the Christians gained slowly back what they had lost. Hungary was rescued. Venice drove the Turks back on the mainland of Greece. The warlike Poles defeated them in many desperate battles. Above all, their strife began with Russia—an implacable foe, whose hatred would not be satis-fied without their utter ruin.

It was indeed a lordly heritage of which the Turks had made themselves masters. In extent it was more than three times the size of France. A delicious climate and a soil of wondrous fertility requite with opulence even the most primi-tive industry. Gold is found in the rocks and in the streams. Quicksilver is to be seen bubbling out of the ground. Iron, coal, salt, copper, and other mineral treasures, are profusely

26

abundant. A vast sea-board and a position enabling her to lay her hand alike on Europe, Asia, and Africa, endow Turkey with singular advantages for conducting lucrative commerce.

Amid the boundless wealth of these magnificent possessions the descendants of the ancient Huns encamped. They entered as conquerors, and as such they have remained. They never mingled, as the Normans did in England, with the people they subdued. They brought with them a religion of hatred and contempt, and they never ceased to regard with abhorrence all who refused to believe in their prophet. Christians do for the most part the work of the empire. The Armenians and Jews are its bankers; the Greeks are its merchants and its sailors; the subject races cultivate its fields. The conquering Turk—luxurious, indolent, execrably licentious—looks with scorn upon the Christian peasants by whose plunder he is maintained. He rouses himself, when occasion calls, to the business of war. When not thus engaged, his life is one of apathy and voluptuous repose. He is grave even to melancholy; listens patiently, speaks softly and with deliberation; will sit silent, like the friends of Job, for days together. The religion of the Turks forbids progress. The Koran fixes their civil and criminal law and many of the usages of daily life, excluding thus all possibilities of amelioration. Laws framed upon the simple requirements of Arab life in the seventh century still enfold in a grasp of iron the complex interests of a great modern state. The fine arts are not practised, for the Koran forbids representations of natural objects; medicine and surgery are scarcely known; anatomy is forbidden; with the sciences in general the barbarous Turk has never entered into any relations.

The religion of Mohammed discourages education. In the public schools which exist—few in number, and miserable in quality*—there are almost no school-books. The Koran con-

* Among the Bulgarian Christians there is a lively desire for education, and an effective educational system exists governed by a board popularly elected. A marked improvement in the educational condition of the Bulgarians has taken place during the last twenty years.

tains all that the ordinary Turk requires to know, and is the only book which he is taught to read. The women receive almost literally no education at all. Rich ladies purchase girls, and after bestowing some care upon their personal appearance sell them to rich men for wives.* Georgian girls are brought in rags and filth to Constantinople, and after a process of amelioration and adornment they too are sold. The highest in the land—even the sultans themselves—obtain wives in this manner. With mothers grossly ignorant and almost savage, and a religion which forbids change, there is no influence operating to rescue the Turks from their utter degradation.†

The Turks conduct the affairs of the people whom they conquered on the principles of a hostile military occupation rather than a government. The despotism of the sultan is absolute and unrestrained. All life and property belong to him, and the Christian population must vindicate by an annual payment of money their claim to the elementary privilege of living. When the sultan requires their property he can send and take it. The people have no defence in law, and, by the principles on which the government is founded, none in right. But the sultan is not by any means their worst enemy. Men purchase from him the privilege of collecting taxes, and having paid the purchase-money they are at liberty to inflict upon their victims such personal violence as may be deemed necessary to enforce the yielding up of their available means. Magistrates, judges, and government servants of every degree plunder at will for their own personal benefit. Every post, high and low, has been purchased by its holder, whose single aim in discharging its duties is to enrich himself at the expense of those over whom he has gained authority. Any trader who incurs the

* The wife of Reschid Pasha ordinarily kept about forty wives for sale, and earned large sums by the traffic.

† If the social condition of the Turks could be fully explained, the English people would shudder at the thought of maintaining the government of a horde of savages so unutterably debased. But that is impossible. It was truly said by Cobden that we must remain ignorant of the social condition of Turkey, because it is indescribable.

perilous suspicion of being rich, any proprietor of a good estate, may be put to death on a slight pretext, and his possessions seized. Any Turkish ruffian may with impunity assault or murder a Christian. A good Mohammedan regards it as his right and duty to kill a Christian when he has opportunity. The evidence of a Christian against a Turk is not received in a court of law. A Turk can legally steal Christian children and forcibly convert them to Islamism. The frightful principle of slave-owning law is practically in force in the Ottoman domin- ion—no Christian has any rights which a Turk is bound to respect. The only security of the people is to conceal their wealth and seem to be poor. Under the sway of the Turk the appearance of poverty is rarely deceptive.

The system of organized robbery which is known in Europe by the name of the Turkish government has changed into wilderness one of the fairest regions of the world. Popula- tion, in spite of the amazing wealth of the soil, is steadily declining, and has already sunk to less than one-third of its numbers under the Romans. So powerfully does the increas- ing desolation affect the mind, that recent travellers have expressed the extreme apprehension that the human race must become extinct in the Ottoman dominions. Enormous tracts which formerly supported in comfort a numerous population are now abandoned. The once populous land is covered with ruins, often hid from view by the rank vegetation of the fertile wilderness. Between Angora and Constantinople forty or fifty villages have become extinct during the present century. Towards Smyrna two hundred villages have been forsaken since the middle of last century. The Turkish population of Smyrna itself has declined in thirty years from eighty thousand inhabitants to forty-one thousand; that of Candia has sunk, during the present century, from fifty thousand to ten thousand. A traveller in the northern portions of the empire found, on a ride of seventy miles through what he regarded as an earthly paradise, not so much as a single inhabitant. Approaching Constantinople from the north, one rides almost to the gates of the city without any trace of a road through wild grass which reaches to the horse's girths. Nine-tenths of Mesopotamia lie unused by man. In the rich provinces of Wallachia and Moldavia only one-twentieth of the soil was cultivated. Never has the goodness of Providence been so utterly frustrated during long centuries by the vileness of man.

Russia has for ages looked with an eye of desire upon Constantinople and the Turkish sea-board. A prophecy of extreme antiquity foretells the ultimate accomplishment of her purposes. When or by whom it was first uttered no man knows. Eight centuries ago it might be read upon an equestrian statue, then very old, which had been brought to Constantinople from Antioch. It was believed for centuries before the invasion of the Turks; and the Turks themselves soon learned to look forward to its fulfilment. In Russia a powerful national sentiment regards the possession of Constantinople as a manifest destiny, and urges forward every measure which tends to accomplish it. The Emperor Alexander claimed that he himself was the only Russian who resisted the national desire to seize Turkey. The Emperor Nicholas stated that he did not wish Russia to possess Constantinople, but it was inevitable: as well, he said, strive to arrest a stream in its descent from the mountains. Russia has omitted no opportunity of aggravating the disorders of the Turkish empire, and thus of silently hastening its overthrow. During great part of the eighteenth century she contrived to involve the Turks in perpetual quarrel, and waged against them frequent and destructive wars.* And she would long ago, by open violence, have fulfilled the ancient prediction had not the jealousies of the other European powers peremptorily forbidden this aggrandizement.

* Since the beginning of that century Russia attacked Turkey on nine separate occasions.

Until lately, English statesmen have attached a high value to the maintenance of what was called a balance of power among European states. It is now generally acknowledged that any such arrangement is purely fanciful, and that any attempt to frame and uphold an artificial equipoise of forces is vain. But England fought many wars and shed oceans of human blood in this visionary enterprise. On her principles it was clear that the possession of Turkey would endow Russia with an undue and dangerous ascendency among European nations. Later on she entertained the belief that her own interests were specially involved. It was desirable that a weak power rather than a strong one should possess the eastern shores of the Mediterranean; otherwise free communication with India would be put in danger. Under the influence of these motives, it became the traditional aim of English foreign policy to preserve the Turkish government. England laboured, often by diplomacy, and sometimes even by arms, to uphold the most unjustifiable despotism which modern Europe ever endured. Her efforts have preserved to one million Turks* absolute power, brutally abused, over the lives and property of eight million men of different race, and for the most part of different religion. In maintaining the Turks, she has prolonged the misery of a nation and the desolation of vast tracts of fertile land capable of high usefulness to man. It is, beyond dispute, a singular infelicity that a great Christian state should feel herself impelled by any consideration of her own advantage to the performance of a task which involves consequences so lamentable.†

* Fifty years ago it was estimated that there were 2,700,000 Turks in Europe. That number has now dwindled to 1,150,000. The Eastern Question would, in course of ages, be helped to its solution by the extinction of the unwelcome intruders who have vexed Europe during the last four or five centuries.

† Sir Henry Elliot, the English ambassador to Turkey, defends the "hereditary policy" in a letter addressed to Lord Derby, dated 4th September, 1876: —"We have been upholding what we know to be a semi-civilized nation, liable under certain circumstances to be carried into fearful excesses; but the fact of this having just now been strikingly brought home to all of us " [by the Bulgarian massacres] "cannot be a suffi-

Once there occurred an important deviation from the established course of English policy. It arose, unexpectedly, during the war which the heroic little state of Greece waged for her independence of the Turks.

Turkish rule had been for ages intolerably bitter to the Greeks. During the eighteenth century insurrections had occurred under the fostering care of the Russian government. These were suppressed with barbarous severity, deepening constantly the hatred with which the tyrants were regarded. At length the Greeks burst into inextinguishable revolt. **1821 A. D.** For years they maintained a heroic and moderately successful resistance to their oppressors. Europe looked on with enthusiastic approval, but her governments long maintained a neutrility which was little in harmony with the wishes of her people. The turks butchered without mercy or sold into slavery all the captives who fell into their hands. So extreme was their cruelty that the population of Greece was diminished by one-half, and many portions of the country were changed into desert. At length, when the war had continued for nearly seven years, the English, French, and Russian governments agreed, by formal treaty, that it must now cease, **July 1827 A. D.** and that Turkey must be contented in the future with a tribute and a nominal sovereignty over Greece. The sultan indignantly refused to suffer the interference of foreign powers in his questions with revolted subjects. The allies intimated their purpose of compelling instant peace, and their fleets entered the Bay of Navarino to give effect to the decision which they announced. The Ottoman squadron, of superior strength, rode at anchor there under the guns of certain formidable batteries. The allied fleets passed quietly into the bay,

cient reason for abandoning a policy which is the only one that can be followed with due regard to our own interest." In other words, we are entitled to protect a horde of murderous savages because it appears to be for our advantage to do so. It is probable the judgment of posterity will not approve the wisdom which regards such a course as advantageous, any more than it will approve the mortality which feels at liberty to acquire advantages at such a price.

and dropped their anchors opposite the Turkish ships. On both sides every preparation for battle had been made, but there was yet no fixed intention to fight, and no war had been declared. A Turkish ship fired with musketry upon some English boats, and slew an officer bearing a flag of truce. One or two English ships returned the fire without orders. The battle, opened in this random way, soon raged along the whole line. For four hours the Turks fought bravely against enemies with whom, as it quickly appeared, they were utterly unable to cope. When the battle closed the Turkish fleet was extinct. Fifty-two ships and seven thousand men had perished.* Greece was free, and Europe rejoiced with a great joy over the discomfiture of the Mohammedan oppressor.

Oct. 20, 1827 A. D.

From the exasperations of this struggle there resulted instantly an invasion of Turkey by the Russians. The czar marched an army of one hundred and fifty thousand men to attack his ancient foe. The Turks offered an obstinate but fruitless resistance. The invaders defeated their armies, stormed their fortresses, forced the passes of the Balkans, and stood at length unopposed within eighty miles of Constantinople.

1829 A. D.

But here the western powers caught alarm. England and Austria hastened to interpose, lest the balance of power should be overthrown. Russia was invited to negotiate, and an English admiral was ready to seize her fleet if she had chosen to push her advantage further. But Russia had done enough for that time, and she consented to peace. The humble sultan assented with tears in his eyes to a treaty which despoiled him of territory, and laid upon his impoverished treasury burdensome pecuniary indemnities. Russian subjects resident in Turkey were exempted from the jurisdiction of Turkish authorities—

* The king, in his speech at the opening of Parliament, referred to the battle of Navarino as "an untoward event." The Duke of Wellington was then the head of the government, and no man had firmer faith than he in the necessity of Turkey to the political balance of Europe.

a provision which furnished inexhaustible opportunity for vexatious and humiliating interference. The virtual independence of the Servians, who had been for many years in arms against their oppressors, was finally secured at this time.

The process of decay now became more rapid. Egypt asserted her independence, stimulated thereto by the secret encouragement which Russia for her own purposes afforded. A great army was sent to reclaim the revolted vassal, but the Egyptians inflicted upon it a defeat from which there could be no recovery. A great fleet was despatched on the same errand. But the admiral, intent, like other Turkish officials, upon his own advantage, sailed to Alexandria, and handed over his ships to the enemy whom it was his duty to subdue. Egypt was from that day virtually independent.

1839
A. D.

It was hoped, after the Crimean war,* that the influence of the allies, to whom it owed so much, would lead the Turkish government into the path of reform, and make its continued existence tolerable by its neighbours. England demanded complete religious equality of Mohammedans and Christians, and the Turks, with grave courtesy, yielded immediate compliance. It was discovered afterwards that they did not construe the agreement as England did. But this difference need not concern us, as no attempt whatever was made to give effect to either construction. Various important reforms were promised, and large reduction in the profligate expenditure of the administration. No single promise then made was ever sought to be fulfilled. Our alliance with the Turks in the dangers and sarcrifices of a great war was naturally the origin of a friendly regard, and an unreasoning expectation that a better future was in store for them. These favourable impressions created an opportunity of which the Turks were not slow to avail themselves. Their government attempted to borrow money of the

* See Book II., Chapter vi.

English people. Unexpected success induced frequent renewal
of such applications. The honest earnings of credulous Englishmen were squandered on the filthy pleasures of Turkish
savages. The tempting interest promised to the earlier dupes
was paid from sums yielded by the later. Not till a debt of one
hundred and forty million had been incurred did the simple
Christians discover that they were being plundered by the
cunning misbelievers. So soon as it ceased to be possible for
them to borrow, the Turks began to apply to the enormous
debt which they had contracted the easy and comfortable process of repudiation.

While the English people were realizing the hopeles loss inflicted upon them, the Turkish difficulty once more became acute.
The Christians in Bosnia and the Herzegovina were
1875 driven to take up arms against their oppressors, and the
A. D. Turks proved unable to suppress the insurrection. The
great powers, anxious always to postpone the inevitable settlement, required that the Turks should pledge themselves to such
reforms as might be expected to satisfy the insurgents. Religious equiry was again demanded, and again promised. The
farming of taxes was to be discontinued. Táxes levied in the
revolted provinces were to be expended there. A commission,
composed of Mohammedans and Christians, were charged
with the execution of these reforms—the announcement of
which, it was vainly hoped, would disarm the revolted provinces, and restore tranquility.

The desired postponement was not gained. The overtures
of the embarrassed ard faithless Porte was unheeded by the
insurgents. And soon the disturbance was intensified by a
declaration of war by Servia, which professed to be moved by
sympathy with the revolted provinces to a course which
threatened to procure her own ruin.

April During the spring a rising of trivial importance oc-
1876 curred in Bulgaria. The Turks were urged by the
A. D. English government to be prompt in restoring order

throughout the disturbed territories. Bulgaria was chosen for the premeditated exhibition of Turkish vigour and Turkish justice. A force sufficient to overbear any possibility of resistance occupied the unhappy state, which was now the victim of atrocities scarcely paralleled in modern Europe. Christian villages were plundered and burned down. Their inhabitants, by thousands, were slaughtered without mercy. Women, little children, unoffending old men, perished under nameless torture. The dead lay in heaps in the churches, to which they had vainly fled for shelter, and the dogs tore their unburied flesh as they rotted by the wayside.

By the noble efforts of an English newspaper—the *Daily News*—details of these infamies reached London, and were revealed to the world. Unworthy attempts were made by the friends of the Turks—for even in England they had friends—to deny and then to soften the appalling facts. But these were frustrated without difficulty. The British people read in the Bulgarian atrocities the true character of the savage power which they had so long upheld. Their indignant horror made a sudden breach in the " hereditary policy " of the government, and for the time saved the nation from the shame of protecting the Turks against the vengeance which their iniquities had provoked.

The Emperor of Russia availed himself of the opportunity created by the revulsion of English sentiment. He proposed that Turkish misrule should be forcibly terminated, and intimated that if Europe failed to join him in this urgent work he was prepared to act independently. A vain attempt was made by a conference of the great powers to bring the disturber of the public peace to reason. The stubborn Turk would not yield to the counsel and entreaty of Europe. The great powers desisted from their efforts, and ceased to interpose between Turkey and the measureless calamities which impended. In due time Russia declared war, and moved her armies to the frontier.

Dec. 1876 A. D.

April 24. 1877 A. D.

Two great natural lines of defence—the Daunbe and the
Balkan Mountains—lie between Turkey and her assailant.
Efficiently held, these would have long delayed the Russian
advance, and could not have been forced without a large ex-
June 20, penditure of life. But the supine commander of the
1877   Turks allowed the river to be crossed without firing a
A. D. shot. The passes of the Balkans were not held more
firmly. The Shipka Pass was seized almost without fighting,
       and Russian troops in force occupied the norther parts
July 14, of Roumelia.

But now the Turks roused themselves from this fatal lethargy.
The weak old man who had led their armies to so little purpose was displaced, and successors were appointed on whom
was laid the obligation to immediate battle. The Russians,
scorning an enemy who seemed incapable of resistance, had
ventured too far, and lay exposed to the blows which an enterprising commander might direct against them. General Gourko
was driven back into the Balkans by a rapid concentration of
Turkish forces, and for a little it seemed as if he might be compelled to surrender. Osman Pasha led an army to Plevna, a
Roumelian town lying in a valley commanded by a series of
ridges on which hastily constructed intrenchments and redoubts.

For five months the interest of the contest centred in this
little town. The Turkish general was resolute, full of resource,
and utterly regardless of life. His soldiers, splendidly armed,
were brave, submissive, enduring. The Russians, impatient of
the obstacle, dashed themselves against Osman's earthworks,
and were slaughtered in thousands by the terrible musketry of
his soldiers. When the unexpected difficulty of the enterprise
was at length understood, General Todleben, who held Sebastopol against the English, was placed in command. Heavy
masses of troops were drawn around Plevna, and communication with the outside world was completely barred. Hunger
would, in time, quell the defence of the Turks. Osman en-

dured till Plevna was a charnel-house, filled with wounded and unburied dead. Then he attempted to break through the encircling lines. But his strength was gone. Surrounded and overmatched, he laid down his arms, after many hours' fighting. The flower of the Turkish army had perished or been made captive at Plevna, and it now became evident that the Turkish power to resist was approaching exhaustion.

Dec.
1877
A. D.

During all these months a Russian force had held a position in the Shipka Pass in spite of desperate efforts made by the Turks to dislodge them. A few weeks after the fall of Plevna three Rssian armies were led across the Balkans. The difficulty of the march was extreme. The roads were slippery with ice, often almost impassable from deep snow. Many men perished under the intense cold. But the Russians were now animated by a spirit before which difficulty vanished. They made their way into Roumelia, and striking on the rear of the Turkish army which guarded the outlet from the Shipka Pass, compelled its surrender. Twenty thousand men laid down their arms. The victorious Russians advanced quickly to Adrianople, and the vanquished Turks begged for terms of peace.

Jan.
1878
A. D.

Throughout the war the Turks abated nothing of the cruelty in which their race has always taken delight. They took no prisoners. All the Russians who fell into their hands were massacreed, often with torture which forbids description. When the fortune of war left them in possession of a battle-ground, they habitually murdered the wounded. The forbearance shown by the Russians under the provocation of these atrocities is worthy of the highest admiration. The Turkish wounded were cared for by the Russians as tenderly as their own. The Russian army acquitted itself nobly by courage endurance, and humanity.

It was a work of extreme difficulty to frame the new politi

cal adjustments which the overthrow of Turkey rendered necessary. The government of Lord Beaconsfield avowed the design of upholding in such degree as might be found possible the integrity and independence of Turkey. Happily for the subject populations of the Turk, the ruin was too complete to permit full success in this questionable enterprise. The terms to which Turkey was compelled to submit left her still in nominal possession of considerable territory, but involved her final extinction as a European power at no distant term. To the north of the Balkans, Bulgaria was erected into a principality, paying a tribute, but wholly exempt from Turkish control. To the south of the great mountain range, there was formed the province of Eastern Roumelia, nominally under the political authority of the sultan, but ruled by a Christian governor-general, and effectively protected against Turkish interference with her newly-conferred privilege of self administration. The independence which the Montenegrins had maintained by arms for four hundred years was now recognized, and some addition of territory given. Roumania and Servia received also a formal acknowledgment of their independence. Bosnia and Herzegovina were made over to Austria. Russia took back Bessarabia, of which she had been deprived in the time of her adversity twenty-three years ago, and Roumania was indemnified for the loss out of Turkish territory. Russia received also Batoum, Kars, and Ardahan in Asia. England accepted Cyprus in requital of her friendly offices, and guaranteed the safety of certain Turkish possessions in Asia—securing for herself certain rights to promote good government in these regions.

July 13, 1878 A. D.

When the war began the sultan ruled a European population of eight and a half million, or, if the tributary states are included, of over thirteen million. When the war closed the tributary states were finally broken off from the empire. Bulgaria, Bosnia, Herzegovina, and Cyprus had passed from under

Turkish dominion. Roumelia took the first step in a progress which must ultimately result in her emancipation. Of the vast European populatoins upon whom there fell, four or five centuries ago, the calamity of Turkish conquest, all excepting four million have at length obtained deliverance. Had not England forbidden, these too would have been rescued, and the chapter of European history which is so dark with the miseries of Turkish rule would have been finally closed.

CHAPTER VIII.

THE UNITED STATES OF AMERICA.

SINCE the closing period of the eighteenth century an experiment of the deepest interest to mankind had been in progress on the western shores of the Atlantic. Three million British subjects, dissatisfied with the rule of the parent country, had undertaken to govern themselves. They entertained no purposes of aggression, and being troubled with n ofear of their neighbours, they did not waste the national resources by the maintenance of fleets and armies. Having the development of a continent with its boundless resources to occupy them, they elected a career of peaceful industry. Europe still lay at the feet of a few great families; still squandered her substance in the maintenance of enormous multitudes of armed men; still baffled the industry of her toiling millions by the constant employment of these armed multitudes in devastating wars, flowing out of the ambition or self-will or offended pride of monarchs. The Americans were so bold as to undertake the conduct of their affairs on principles directly the reverse of those by which the world in all preceding ages had been guided.

The first twelve years of the century were spent by America in profound tranquility. She looked from afar with a serene neutrality upon the furious efforts which the European nations were making to compass the ruin of each other. She had not yet regained her old love and reverence for England; for her grievances were recent and her suffering had been deep. But Washington had urged a policy of peace with all the world, especially with England, and his wise counsels still bore fruit in the peaceful dispositions of the American people. The great European frenzy had nearly burned itself out, and America was still free from its influence.

But in process of time England and France, eagerly bent upon mutual harm, adopted measures by which the lucrative traffic heretofore enjoyed by the Americans was destroyed. American produce could no longer reach European markets; American ships lay in unprofitable idleness; grass grew upon the untrodden wharves of New York and Philadelphia. Moreover, the high-handed British enforced a hateful claim to search American ships and take away any sailors whom it might please them to suspect of being British subjects.

These grievances might have been peacefully redressed. Indeed, England withdrew the regulations which were injurious to American commerce, and proposed that the right of search should be dealt with in the way of friendly negotiation. But America was too angry to be reasonable. She was almost without an army. It was said of her, almost truly, that she had no fleet strong enough to lay siege to a British sloop-of-war. But she was resolute to try her strength in battle with England—a power which had a million men under arms, and commanded the sea with a fleet of a thousand armed ships.

June,
1812
A. D.

The Americans invaded Canada, but fared so badly in that undertaking that twice their incursions were closed by a surrender of all the troops engaged. At sea an unexpected gleam of good fortune brought compensation for these discouragements. Numerous engagements between single ships occurred, and in many of these, especially at the beginning of the war, the Americans were victorious. The British devised an attack upon Washington. That city is fifty miles from the sea-coast;

27

the force wh:ch could be sent against it was only three thousand five hundred men. But the Americans failed to protect their capital even from an invasion so little formidable as this. After routing with ease a superior American force, the British quietly entered the city; and as the Americans refused to ransom their public buildings, all these were most ungenerously destroyed. At New Orleans the Americans were able to exact a terrible revenge. Six thousand veterans, under Sir Edward Pakenham, fresh from the triumphs of the Peninsula, were rowed on shore from the English ships and advanced against the city. General Jackson had made for himself a strong position, with a deep wide ditch, crowned by a strong earthen wall running in front. The British pushed on under a murderous fire of grape-shot and musketry till they reached the American works. But there it was found that fascines to enable them to pass the ditch had been omitted in the preparations for the assault. The Americans, shooting in safety from their impregnable defences, inflicted fearful slaughter. The discomfitted Btitish retired, having lost in this wretched enterprise two thousand men. The American loss in killed and wounded was fourteen.

Jan. 8, 1815 A. D.

When all these things had been done and endured, there was found to exist on both sides a disposition which made it easy to restore peace. The American people were wearied of the sufferings which this senseless war entailed. England had never wished for the war, and was willing to close it; moreover, she might still need her troops to expend on the bloodier battle grounds of the Old World. A treaty of peace was concluded. The countries had fought for two years and a half about the right of search, but no mention was made of the grievance in which the war originated in the treaty by which it was terminated.

For the next fifty years the history of America is a record of peaceful industrial progress, without parallel in the annals of the human family. In the year 1860 the Americans made their decennial enumeration of the people and their possessions. The industrial greatness which the census revealed was an astonishment, not only to the rest of the world, but to America herself. The slow growth of the old European countries seemed absolute stagnation beside this swift multiplication of men, and of beasts, and of wealth in every form.

The three million colonists who had thrown off the British yoke had now increased to nearly thirty-two million. This great population was assisted in its toils by six million horses and two million working oxen. It owned eight million cows, fifteen million other cattle, twenty-two million sheep, and thirty-three million hogs. The products of the soil were enormous. The cotton crop of that year was close upon one million tons. Under the impulse of an insatiable European demand, it had more than doubled within the last ten years. The grain crop was twelve hundred million bushels. The tobacco crop had more than doubled in ten years, and was now five hundred million pounds. There were five thousand miles of canals, and thirty thousand miles of railroads,—twenty-two thousand of which were the creation of the preceding ten years. The textile manufactures of the country had reached the annual value of forty million sterling. America had provided for the education of her children by erecting one hundred and thirteen thousand schools and colleges, and employing one hundred and fifty thousand teachers. Her educational institutions enjoyed revenues amounting to nearly seven million sterling, and were attended by five and a half million pupils. Religious instruction was given in fifty-four thousand churches, in which there was accommodation for nineteen million hearers. The daily history of the world was supplied by four thousand newspapers, which circulated annually one thousand million copies.

The thirteen states had increased to thirty-four. The territory of the Union had been prodigiously enlarged. Louisiana had been purchased from Napoleon. Florida had been ceded by Spain. Texas and California had been acquired from Mexico by the sword. Time after time tribes of vagrant Indians yielded up their lands and enrolled themselves subjects of the great republic. The American people owned two thousand million acres of land, but as yet they had been able to make use of no more than one-fifth of this enormous heritage. The remainder lay unoccupied,—a vast reserve of wealth against the time when the nation should have need of it.

But there was a deadly taint on the industrial greatness of America. In her Southern states four million negroes were still held in slavery. In her Southern cities men and women were still sold by auction to the highest bidder. Slave-dealing was still followed as a trade in her capital. The breeding of slaves for Southern markets was still a source of gain in some of the border states. The cotton, the rice, the tobacco which formed so large a portion of her wealth were still raised by the enforced toil of the slave. A code of slave laws, the most wicked which the world has ever seen, guaranteed the subjection of the victims. As judicially expounded, this law gave to the black man no rights at all which the white man was under any obligation to respect.

At the period of the revolution, and for many years after, American feeling was adverse to slavery. The British parliament had continued to give every possible encouragement to the importation of slaves, in defiance of American remonstrance. So highly was this resented that, in the original draft of the Declaration of Independence, one of the charges brought against the king was his perverse support of the slave-trade. The wisest and best of the Americans—Washington, Jefferson, Hamilton—regarded slavery with horror. Nearly all Americans acknowledged the evils of the system, and desired its extinction.

But in process of years slavery became a source of vast profit to the slave-owner. Hitherto the grower of cotton had been vexatiously baffled by the difficulty of clearing away from the fibre the seeds which clung to it. So toilsome and, in consequence, so costly was the work that a man could not in a day prepare more than one pound of cotton for the spinner. But when the steam-engine and the spinning-frame came fully into use, there arose in England an urgent demand for copious supplies of cotton. An ingenious New England mechanic invented a machine which performed, at trifling cost, the indispensable task of removing the cotton seeds. Henceforth the growing of cotton became one of the most lucrative employments to which human labour could be applied. It was wealth to own a little plantation and a few slaves. England was insatiable in her craving for cotton. Unoccupied lands stretched far and wide around every man's holding. Every negro added to the planter's stock added directly and immediately to his wealth.

The man of the South became passionately attached to this gainful iniquity. They would listen to no remonstrance; they would permit no discussion. The enthusiast who within the limits of a Southern state ventured to condemn slavery did so at peril of his life, and hundreds of persons suffered death or mutilation for their untimely boldness. Gradually, as the gains of slave-owning swelled out, new sanctions enfolded the system of labour which yielded results so pleasant. Southern religion consecrated the traffic in human beings. The church taught that slavery was of divine appointment. The slave who fled from his owner was guilty of aggravated theft. The man who sought to overthrow slavery was a profane person fighting against God.

In the early days of the colonies slavery prevailed in the North. Even famous New England divines accepted thankfully, and with unharmed conscience, the gift of a negro servant. But in the North slavery scarcely survived the revolution.   Slave labour, void of intelligence and cheerful energy, as it ever must be, is profitable only where genial conditions of soil and climate make production easy and leave room for a thriftless husbandry. These conditions did not exist in the North.

But although the Northern states had ceased to employ slaves, they did not cease to approve of the continued use of slave labour in the South.   They participated in the gains of slavery.   The cotton-planter borrowed money at high interest from the Northern capitalist. He bought his goods in Northern markets. He sent his cotton to the North for sale.   The Northern merchants made money at his hands, and were in no haste to overthrow the peculiar institution with which their own personal relations were so agreeable.

At length there came an awakening of the Northern conscience on the subject of slavery. Like many of the great movements of opinion in America, it burst forth with startling suddenness.   On the 1st of January 1831 a journeyman printer, William Lloyd Garrison, published in Boston the first number of a paper devoted to the abolition of slavery. Little had hitherto been publicly spoken on the subject, but now the air was full of voices. An Anti-Slavery Society was formed, whose original membership numbered only twelve persons.   In three years there were two hundred anti-slavery societies.   In seven years more there were two thousand.   The abolitionists applied themselves with a fiery energy to the propagation of their beliefs.   They were devoured by a zeal which knew no bounds and permitted no respite.   The slave-owners, joyfully reaping large and easy gains from the labour of their bondmen, met with a deep, remorseless, murderous hatred the enthusiasts who sought the ruin of their institutions.   Their allies in the North lent them willing and appropriate support. In Boston a mob of well-dressed citizens forcibly suppressed a meeting of female abolitionists.   Philadelphia disgraced herself by riots in which negroes were slain and their houses burned down. Throughout the Northern states the meetings of abolitionists were habitually invaded and broken up, often with shameful violence.

For thirty years this contest raged. It became the grand absorbing question of American politics. It evoked hatreds of unparalleled intensity and bitterness. It drew a deep line of separation between the states which owned and those which did not own slaves. Politicians exhausted the resources of their ingenuity in devising concessions and compromises. Now the South was offered help in the recovery of her escaped slaves. Now large accessions of territory were gained that she might find room for the amplest extension of her cherished institution. But ever the hatred of the Northern people to slavery deepened. Ever the intolerable assault of the abolitionists became more vehement and daring. Ever the wrath of the slave-owners became more fierce and deadly. It was not a quarrel which moderation and forbearance would assuage. It was "an irrepressible conflict between opposing and enduring forces."

For the most part the presidents of the Union had been Southern by birth or by sentiment, and the South had thus enjoyed the advantages which a control of the executive government afforded. A new president fell to be chosen in 1860. The North, now fully roused, had determined that slavery should be shut out for ever from the Territories of the Union. The South claimed for slave-owners the right to settle in the Territories, carrying their slaves with them. The North was victorious, and Abraham Lincoln—from his youth an enemy to slavery—became president.

For the defeated slave-owners there appeared now to be only one resource. It was impossible to remain longer in a Union presided over by a man who had been avowedly thus elevated because of his abhorrence to slavery. Secession was the sole remaining alternative. The estimate formed in the South of the tie which bound the states to each other made it easy to fall back upon this solution of the difficulty.

From the very foundation of the American government there had been a conflict of opinion regarding the rights of the states which composed the Union. One party, fearing the evils which spring from the weakness of the governing power, sought protection from these in the close union of states under a strong government. Another party, impressed by the unhappy condition of the over-governed nations of the Old World, feared the creation of a government which might grow into a despotism. The aim of the one was to vest the largest possible measure of power in a central government; the aim of the other was to limit the powers accorded to the central government, and give the widest possible scope to the sovereignty of the individual states. These two sets of opinions continued to exist and to conflict irreconcilably. In the North the belief prevailed that America was a nation formed by the voluntary junction of states, and made indissoluble by their agreement that it should be so. In the South, on the other hand, it was maintained that each individual state retained her sovereign right to withdraw, at pleasure, from the Union.

Believing thus in their right, and holding that the Northern antipathy to slavery created a sufficient occasion for its exercise, the slave-owners entered promptly on the dark and bloody path of secession. South Carolina, always the least loyal of the states to the Union, led the way. Georgia, Alabama, Mississippi, Louisiana, and Florida followed her at once; Virginia, North Carolina, Tennessee, Arkansas, and Texas joined the revolted sisterhood a few months later. Eleven states, stretching over an area of a million square miles, and inhabited by six million whites and over three million negroes, thus declared that their connection with the Union had ceased, and formed themselves into a new association. Moreover, they intimated that they were prepared to

Dec. 20, 1860 A. D.

maintain by arms what they had done. The task which lay before the North was to bring these men and their territory forcibly back into the Union.

It was a task the enormous difficulty of which was at first imperfectly appreciated by the North. The Southern rising seemed to her nothing more than a gigantic riot, which she proposed to suppress in a few weeks. Inspired by this ill-founded confidence, her imperfectly disciplined troops were ordered to attack the Southern army, which lay at Manassas Junction in Virginia. The battle was bravely fought, and was approaching a victorious close, when it was turned into defeat and shameful rout by the arrival upon the field of Shuthern reinforcements.

July 21, 1861 A. D.

This success confirmed the Southern confidence in the superiority of their own military prowess, and raised to the highest pitch their hopes of final triumph. It also revealed to the people of the North the true character of the enterprise which they had undertaken. But it did not weaken their settled purpose that the work, gigantic as it now appeared, must be accomplished. Government called for volunteers, and the youth of the country, rich and poor alike, crowded into the ranks. Congress resolved that the suppression of the rebellion was a sacred duty, from the performance of which no disaster should discourage; to which they pledged the employment of every resource, national and individual.

The South was able to supply her people with food from her own resources. But her progress in manufacturing enterprise had been inconsiderable, and her supplies of arms and ammunition, of clothing, of medicines for her sick, had to come from abroad. Before she could pay for these necessary articles, her cotton and tobacco must find their way to foreign markets. To shut her in, so that no commercial intercourse with the world was possible, was to inflict a blow which must prove scarcely less than fatal. Four days after the first shot was fired, Mr.

Lincoln announced the blockade of all the rebel ports. The blockade was quickly made effective, and to the end of the war

it was rigorously maintained. New Orleans was brought with little difficulty back into the Union, and the rebels barred from intercourse with the world by the Gulf of Mexico. The possession of the Mississippi was an object of the highest importance to the North. Three of the revolted states—Louisiana, Texas, and Arkansas—lay to the westward of the great river. If the river-line were regained, these states would be entirely severed from the other members of the Confederacy, and no help conld pass from one to the other. The work was difficult, for the South had done her utmost to hold a communication so vital. Giadually the Federals possessed the Lower Mississippi, and extended their dominion northwords, till nothing remained to their enemies but the strong fortress of Vicksburg. General Grant, whose high military capacity had already signalized itself by many successful enterprises, besieged this last hope of the Confederacy in the west. It fell to his arms on the 4th July, 1863. Henceforth the Mississippi was firmly held by the Federal power, and the rebel territory was cut in two.

Meanwhile the war had been raging with divided success on the northern frontier of the Confederacy. The Southerners had chosen for their capital Richmond, the chief city of Virginia, situated on the James River, one hundred and thirty miles from Washington. To force a way to Richmond, and drive the rebel government from the home which it had audaciously set up, was an object dear to the northern heart. Two hundred thousand men destined for that enterprise lay on the Potomac. under General M'Clellan, by whom their equipment and discipline was carefully perfected. Between the Southern capital and that splendid army there interposed a greatly inferior Southern force commanded by General Lee. M'Clellan advanced till he was within a few miles of Richmond, and then his heart failed him, and without striking a blow he commenced to retreat. The rebels, with their weaker forces, pursued and attacked him. On each of the seven days of the retreat there was a battle, resulting for the most part in Federal success. But although often repulsed, Lee continued his pursuit till the Federals gained inglorious security beside their gunboats on the James River.

The exulting rebels, not-fearing an army thus conducted, passed northward, and threatened Washington itself. M'Clellan was summoned in haste for the defence of the capital. A bloody but indecisive battle was fought in Maryland. Lee, not finding himself sufficiently strong to prosecute his invasion, withdrew southwards, and M'Clellan resumed his accustomed inactivity. But a more energetic leadership was now urgently desired, and the president relieved M'Clellan of his command. *Nov. 1862 A. D.*

During the earlier period of the war the slave question was a cause of some embarrassment to the Northern government. This cruel war had been caused by slavery, and it was not unreasonable that the North, in self-defence, should suppress the system out of which evils so measureless had flowed. Escaped slaves sought in crowds the shelter of the Northern armies. These were loyal subjects, while their masters were in arms against the Union. Could the government recognize the right of the rebel to own the loyal man? But on the other hand, some of the slave states had remained loyal. Great care was needful that no step should be taken fitted to alienate or offend these states, and thus to hinder the restoration of the Union.

But American opinion, under the stern teaching of war, ripened quickly into the determination that as the slave system had taken the sword, it must perish by the sword. The president issued a proclamation, giving freedom to all slaves in those states which should still be in rebellion on New Year's day 1863. This proclamation *Sept. 1862 A.D.*

gave freedom to over three million slaves. It did not touch slavery in the loyal states, for there the president had no right to interfere. But all men well understood that it rendered slavery henceforth impossible on any portion of American territory. And so it quickly proved. Before the war closed, the states which had remained loyal, or which had been brought forcibly back to the Union, freed themselves by their own choice of the taint of this unhappy system. Slavery was now abolished, but there was no legal security against its restoration. To render this forever impossible, a clause was added to the Constitution, prohibiting slavery on American soil. Now indeed this evil system was finally extinct. This was the result which Providence had mercifully brought out of a rebellion whose avowed object it was to establish slavery more firmly and extend it more widely.

1865
A. D.

During the later years of the war the North exerted her giant strength to the utmost, in order to crush the stubborn defence of the revolted states. She had a million men under arms. She had six hundred ships-of-war. Her people supplied freely, although on terms whose severity patriotism did not appear to modify, the means of an enormous expenditure. Her own factories worked night and day to provide military stores; and their efforts were freely supplemented by the dockyards and foundries of Europe. Peaceful America was for the time the greatest military power of the world. Her soldiers had gained the skill of veterans. Among her generals men had been found worthy to direct the vast forces of the republic. Grant, Sherman, Thomas, Sheridan, in especial, had given evidence of their possession of high military capacity.

While these enormous powers were called into action for attack, it became obvious that the resources of the South for defence were radidly approaching exhaustion. Her isolation was almost complete. From time to time an adventurous ship stole into her harbours, and sold at excessive prices a welcome supply of arms and clothing. But these precarious supplies were wholly inadequate to the need. The South was in destitution of every article required for the prosecution of a great war. Her government was in utter poverty, having no better representative of money than a worthless paper currency, which was forced upon the reluctant acceptance of creditors. Her flag was unseen on the ocean, excepting where it was carried by two or three piratical vessels which preyed upon the commerce of the North. Her soldiers, forced into the ranks, freed themselves by desertion from a service which they knew to be hopeless.

And yet the skill with which these-failing resources were directed by General Lee sufficed to gain important advantages, and shed lustre over a doomed cause. In the third year of the war Lee repulsed with heavy loss every effort which was made in the direction of Richmond. So completely, for the time, had he established a supremacy over his assailants, that he crossed the Potomac and followed them into Pennsylvania. At the little town of Gettysburg the armies met and fought for three days. On the third day Lee gathered all his force for a decisive attack on the Federal position. He was repulsed with terrible slaughter. It was the most disastrous battle which he had ever fought, for in killed, wounded, and prisoners he lost one-half of the troops engaged. He retreated at once, and the war was never again carried into Northern territory. July 1863 A. D.

General Grant was now raised to the chief command of the Union forces, and was summoned eastward to direct a campaign which all men expected to be final. Lee, unable now to gather more than sixty thousand men around his standards, held a position in the Wilderness, a desolate region of northern Virginia, where he awaited the attack of his powerful antagonist. Grant, with a magnificent army of one hundred and twenty thousand veterans, crossed the Rapidan. Eight days of continuous fighting ensued. It was Lee's prac- May 8.

tice to throw up earthworks, which served to equalize the otherwise unequal strength of the combatants. When Grant found himself unable to force these defences, he passed south-ward by the flank of his enemy, compelling Lee constantly to retire to a new position. Frightful losses were sustained. In one week Grant lost thirty thousand men. The Southern losses were proportionately heavy. But Grant had ample re-sources from which to recruit his ranks, while Lee was irre-parably weakened.

Grant fought his way southwards until both armies stood twenty miles beyond Richmond, before the little town of Petersburg. This was the position chosen for the final conflict. It was the purpose of General Grant to straiten the supplies of his enemy by cutting the railroads which maintained his con-nection with the interior, and to wear down his strength by the continual attack of superior forces. The result was no longer doubtful. The Northern troops pressed on in full con-fidence of victory. General Lee had for some time looked upon the position of the Confederacy as desperate, and his soldiers, although they fought bravely, fought without hope.

The contest stretched over ten weary months. Earthworks were thrown up on either side so industriously, that in the end there were intrenchments forty miles in length. The outposts of the armies were within talking distance of each other. The Federals had boundless supplies brought by their ships to City Point, eleven miles away, and sent thence by a railroad to the camp; reinforcements came at the call of their general. The poor Confederates were habitually ill supplied with food. Every available man was already in the ranks; if men could have been found, there were no arms to give them. The strength of the Confederacy waned so steadily that Grant became anxious lest General Lee should take to flight and renew the war on other Mar. 29, fields. He prepared an attack with overwhelming num-1865 bers upon the enfeebled Southern lines. He stormed a A. D. fort in the centre of Lee's position, cutting his army in two, and making an immediate retreat inevitable. The rebel government fled from Richmond, and General Lee, a few days afterwards, laid down his arms. The North had triumphed. After four years of war the rebellion was quelled, and the authority of the Federal government was undisputed from Atlantic to Pacific, from the Great Lakes to the Gulf of Mexico.

The South had fought out the war to its bitter end, not ceasing from her resistance till the extremity of exhaustion compelled. She could make no terms; she lay wholly at the mercy of her conqueror. The great purposes for which she had striven so bravely had been rendered for ever unattainable. Slavery was extinguished. It was written in the blood of thousands of slaughtered men, so that the whole world could read that America was a nation, and not merely a temporary association whose existence was terminable at the pleasure of any of its members. The South accepted in good faith the decision of the sword.* The North, singularly merciful in her use of victory, inflicted no penalty on those whom she had defeated. It was her sole concern now "to bind up the nation's wounds, to cherish a just and lasting peace among ourselves and with all nations." But a great disaster was to interrupt and mutilate the performance of this blessed work.

Mr. Lincoln had been re-elected president, and entered upon his second term of office a few weeks before the close of the war. He was with the army when its final triumphs were gained, and he visited Richmond on the day of surrender, walking through the streets with his little boy in his hand. No heart in all the rejoicing land was more thankful and more glad than his. He occupied himself with measures for healing the nation's wounds. No thought of vengeance for the past was

---

* In 1868 General Lee said he could "promise for the Southern people that they will faithfully obey the constitution and laws of the United States, treat the negro with kindness and humanity, and fulfil every duty incumbent on peaceful citizens, loyal to the constitution of their country."

entertained. Security for the future was necessary, but it was to be sought for with all leniency and gentleness. Possessing as no man but Washington had ever done the confidence of the American people, Lincoln was pre-eminently fitted to soothe the humiliated South, and reunite the severed sisterhood of states. But the nation was to lose him when its need was at the greatest.

A few days after the fall of Richmond, Mr. Lincoln visited one of the Washington theatres. He went with some reluctance, moved by the consideration that the people expected him to go, and would be disappointed by his absence. As the play went on, a fanatical adherent of the fallen Confederacy, an actor called Booth, made his way stealthily into the president's box. He crept close up to Mr. Lincoln, and holding a pistol within a few inches, lodged a bullet deep in the brain. The president sat motionless, save that his head sank down upon his breast. He never regained consciousness, but lingered till morning, and then passed away.

April 14, 1865 A. D.

The restoration of order in the utterly disorganized South was a slow and difficult work. Eleven states were left without a legal state government, and their affairs were necessarily administered by the Federal executive. Unworthy persons obtained undue control, and in their eager and unscrupulous pursuit of personal advantage inflicted grievous wrongs upon the prostrated states. The finances of the South were in hopeless disorder. The debt contracted during the war was not burdensome; for the North ordained that it should not be recognized as a lawful obligation. But the temporary rulers of the South incurred fresh obligations, applying in large measure to their own purposes the loans which they were able to obtain. In some states the new debt thus incurred was repudiated; in others, no provision could be made for interest on the undisputed obligations of the state. The South was utterly wasted, and her recovery was unexpectedly slow.

The inevitable difficulties of reconstruction were gravely aggravated by a violent conflict of opinion between the president and Congress. Mr. Lincoln's successor was Andrew Johnson, a man of defective education, and of arbitrary, impracticable temper. Throughout the whole of his presidency the disputes which he unwisely kindled raged hotly, to the hindrance of those measures of restoration which the unhappy condition of the South so urgently craved. The Southern states did not immediately accede to the terms which the North imposed as the condition of their restoration to full political privilveges. In especial, their assent to the amendment of the Constitution, which raised the negro to the same political level with the white man, was long withheld. It was not till 1870 that President Grant was enabled to announce the fully completed restoration of the Union, which his own success in war had done so much to save.

The chosen career of the American people has been a career of peaceful industry. Contemplating from afar the bloody politics of Europe, they have wisely shunned the glories and the calamities of war. They have been able to satisfy themselves with the happier if more prosaic employment of subduing for the use of man the great continent which is their magnificent heritage.

When the war of the rebellion was over, the Northern states resumed with quickened energy their task of industrial development. Their growth was now more rapid than it had been at any previous period of their history. The population, which in 1860 was nearly thirty-two million, increased to thirty-eight million in 1870, and at the present rate of progress will, when the census of 1880 is taken, amount to nearly fifty million. America has now a more numerous population than any European state, excepting Russia; and she is growing with vastly greater rapidity. Immigration from Europe now,

28

as always before, helps to build up this mighty power. From free England and despotic Russia, from the sunshine of Italy and the eternal winters of Iceland, men crowd to her hospitable shores. During the ten years ending in 1870 she received four and a half million strangers, who came to make for themselves homes upon her soil. A large proportion of these sought the valley of the Mississippi, and the young states in that region doubled and even trebled their population within the ten years. The cities by which the agricultural products of the West pass eastward to the markets of the world increased with unparalleled rapidity. St. Louis rose from one hundred and sixty thousand to three hundred and ten thousand; her great rival Chicago from one hundred and nine thousand to two hundred and ninety-eight thousand. That this progress must long continue is to be anticipated from the fact that as yet scarcely more than one-fifth of the soil of America is under cultivation.

The amount of her surplus products which America can sell to other countries is growing with her population. In 1860 it was sixty million sterling; in 1870 it was ninety million; in 1878 it has risen to one hundred and forty million. Very different from this is the history of her imports. The Americans seek to be independent of supplies from abroad. A century ago, in the well-remembered words of Lord Chatham, they were not allowed to make so much as a nail for a horse's shoe. Their revenge has been the adoption of a policy of protective duties, under shelter of which all industries shall strike deep root at home, and ultimately enable the country to dispense with foreign supplies. The system has been maintained at enormous cost, but it is visibly serving the purpose intended. Year by year the imports of America diminish. Once she bought from England goods to the annual value of forty million sterling; now she takes scarcely twenty million. Formerly most of her iron and steel came from England; now her own boundless stores supply nearly all her wants. Formerly she took largely of our cotton manufactures; now she competes with us successfully in foreign markets.* America has one thousand cotton factories and three thousand woollen factories, giving employment to six hundred thousand persons. Her iron-works employ one hundred and thirty thousand persons, and her production of pig-iron is two million tons—about one-third that of Great Britain. She raises fifty million tons of coal annually, not greatly short of one-half the quantity raised in the United Kingdom.

Russia spends annually thirty million sterling upon the appliances of war, and two million upon the education of her people. America contents herself with a warlike expenditure of nine million, but the total income of her schools is eighteen million. In spite of this lavish expenditure, she has four and a half million citizens who cannot read. These are nearly all in the Southern states, whose educational condition has not yet recovered from the debasing influences of slavery. The native American of the Northern states is scarcely ever without education.

America has no established church, but spontaneous liberality has created an abundant provision for the religious instruction of her people. She has seventy-two thousand congregations, and twenty-two million worshippers can be accommodated in her religious edifices. The property owned by her denominations is valued at seventy million sterling. England is believed to have about thirty thousand places of worship. State support, largely supplemented as it is by private bounty, has thus

---

* Her exports of cotton goods rose during the years between 1868 and 1878 from rather less than one million sterling to about two and a half million. In manufactures of iron and steel her exports have doubled; manufactures of copper and brass have trebled; in manufactures of leather the increase is sixfold. British manufacturers who suffer from the diminution of American demand and the growth of American competition are still able to persuade themselves that these disagreeable circumstances are merely accidental and temporary results of depressed trade. There is no warrant for this expectation. The dependance of America upon the manufactures of Europe is steadily diminishing, and will continue to diminish until that country ceases to bear to us the endearing relationship of a customer, and is known to us only as our most formidable competitor.

done less for England than voluntary offerings have done for America.

Previous to the rebellion, American vessels carried four-fifths of the commerce of the country; but the extravagant duties and vexatious restrictions ignorantly imposed discouraged ship-building, and the Southern privateering led to an extensive transfer of American ships to foreign flags. For a number of years no effort was made to regain for American shipping the lost advantage. Only in 1872 an increase of tonnage began, and during the next three or four years the number of ships rose from twenty-nine thousand eight hundred and forty-eight to thirty-one thousand nine hundred and twenty-three, and the tonnage from four million one hundred and fifty thousand to four million five hundred and ninety-six thousand. All but four thousand are sail-ships.

Long ago America was a nation without debt and without other financial trouble than that which arose from a revenue larger than she was able to spend. She disposed of her excess by distributing it among the individual states, nominally in loan, but virtually in gift. But during the four years of war she ran up with unprecedented rapidity a debt of six hundred million pounds, most of it contracted on hard terms, for money was dear, and her credit was not good. But no sooner had the war ceased than the Americans addressed themselves to the task of paying their debt. They have reduced it now to about four hundred million, and have further materially diminished its burden by availing themselves of their improved credit to borrow on easier terms. Their army is only twenty-five thousand strong, and the warlike expenditure of the country is therefore light. The entire national expenditure, which has been for some years steadily diminishing, is only forty-seven million sterling, and nearly one-half of this is for interest on debt. America is the only great power in the world which does not consume the substance of her people by upholding huge military establishments in time of peace.

CHAPTER IX.

THE PAPACY.

OPENING from some of the most crowded thorough-fares of the city of London there are quiet lanes whose picturesque aspect tempts the foot of the inquiring stranger. A few steps conduct from the crowd and tumult of the street into a narrow court surrounded by buildings of great age. Over the scene there broods a quaint, antique repose. The muffled sound of the neighbour-ing street do not dispel, do not even disturb the deep calm which seems to have reigned here for centuries.

A contrast not less striking than this is experienced by the student of the nineteenth century when he turns to the inves-tigation of the Papacy. The splendid activities of the age have occupied his mind: its mechanical greatness, its humane dispo-sition to alleviate suffering, its vindication of individual rights, its eagerness to educate and elevate—all the gracious pheno-mena which compose the civilization of this wondrous time. He turns the page, and at once he breathes the air of buried centuries. The beliefs, the tendencies, the purposes of the Middle Ages are around him. The progress of man is repro-bated and forbidden as a thing offensive to Heaven. Eternal hostility to the civilization which is deemed the glory of the century is announced, with copious and energetic malediction, by the spiritual chief of two hundred million Christians.

In the early years of the century the Papacy endured no

small hardness at the cruel hands of Napoleon. Rome discerned an irreconcilable enemy in the French republic from the very dawn of that appalling phenomenon. The republic recognized an irreconcilable enemy in Rome, the natural ally of all despotism. Moved by his sympathies, the pope was about to put in execution appropriately hostile purposes. But Napoleon, with the malign promptitude which often characterizes the sons of Belial, interrupted his preparations. Utterly disregarding the sacred character of the pope, he marched on Rome. His holiness, taken at a disadvantage, hastened to conclude a treaty, in which he consented to appease the wrath of the youthful conqueror by a contribution of nearly a million sterling and one hundred of his best pictures. But, lured by deceptive indications of Austrian success, he quickly repudiated the treaty, and went out to battle against the French. Napoleon routed his troops, wrested from him many towns, and increased his exactions so mercilessly that the diamonds of his holiness had to be given up in payment. The French government of the day contemplated the overthrow of the pope's temporal sovereignty, and Napoleon gave willing furtherance to their designs. French troops seized Rome and plundered the sacred city. The pope—then a man of eighty-two—was sent by a toilsome land journey into France, where the old man died within a few days of his arrival. A republic was inaugurated in Rome, and for a time the patrimony of St. Peter was ruled by the profane.

A few years later Napoleon—now at the very pinnacle of greatness—seemed to relent towards the distressed head of the church. He was about to be crowned emperor, and he desired the pope to take part in the ceremony. His holiness, not insensible to the value of Napoleon's friendship, readily consented. The church rejoiced over the reconversion of erring France But these felicitations were of brief duration. Pius VII., presuming upon the sincerity of this

1796 A. D.

1798 A. D.

1804 A. D.

happy concord, applied to the emperor for restoration of certain portions of papal territory. The emperor would not listen to the request; the rights of the tiara, he alleged, were merely "humiliation and prayer," His Italian policy gave full effect to this principle. Rome was again occupied by French troops. The Roman states were formally united to France. Next morning after the lawless annexation was announced, the pope issued a bull, excommunicating this ravisher of sacred lands. The emperor was not slow to find a reply to the courageous pontiff. The palace of the Quirinal was forced by French soldiers, and the holy father, expecting instant death, was lead away into France. Napoleon had long desired to have the pope subject to his own control. He himself would have been head of the church, had that been possible; but the residence of the pope in France would yield results scarcely less important. Paris would become the capital of the Christian world. "I," said this marvelous dreamer of dreams, "would have directed the religious world as well as the political."

1809
A. D.

The states of the church were immediate gainers by this lawless transference of authority. Just laws were immediately enacted and inflexibly enforced. Assassination ceased in Rome; life and property enjoyed effective protection. Preparations were begun for draining the Pontine marshes. The monuments of ancient Rome were rescued from neglect and decay. The removal of the holy father marked the opening of a brief era of order and progress—of which his return marked the close.

The pope was held in custody for nearly five years. Latterly his place of detention was Fontainebleau, where he lived in absolute seclusion, deprived of the services of his usual advisers, and reduced to occupy himself with needlework. It was not till the disasters of the Moscow campaign broke his power that Napoleon sought to conciliate offended Christendom by terminating the captivity of the pope. Even then he hesitated. The

pope was suffered to begin his homeward journey, but was subjected to delays so numerous that his final deliverance was
1814 A. D. not accomplished until the abdication of the emperor had taken place. A little later he obtained from the Congress of Vienna the complete restitution of all the former possessions of the Holy See.

The Romans bestowed a cordial welcome on the returning pontiff; for the harshness of Napoleon's rule had offended them. For some years they bore silently the evils of papal government; but gradually the liberal spirit gained strength among them. Secret organizations overspread the patrimony of St. Peter, and sought to compass the overthrow of his successor. A series of abortive plots stimulated to incessant vigilance the zeal of the papal police. At length there came
1831 A. D. a rash but formidable insurrection. It originated in Modena, but quickly passed over to papal soil, and in a few days all the Romagna was in arms. The insurgents were within full view of St. Peter's. Unmoved by the sight of the hallowed edifice, they formerly decreed that the temporal sovereignty of the holy father was abolished. But the time had not yet come. An Austrian army scattered the patriots and restored order.

Gregory XVI. had been elected pope on the very day before the insurrection broke out, and he never lost the impression which its hateful incidents produced upon his mind. His official and personal antipathy to political change was extremely intensified. While yet his reign was only beginning, the great powers united in urging upon him that " great administrative and organic improvements " were necessary in his dominions. Russia and Austria were parties to this representation, and it may be reasonably inferred that methods of government which these states deemed faulty were seriously in need of amelioration. But Gregory was immovable. Every change seemed to him to favour liberalism—a thing hateful to God and to all good men. The fifteen years of his reign was one long struggle to repress the love of freedom which was gaining strength on every side. His difficulties increased as the years passed; but the old man was inflexible in his resolution to withstand the very beginnings of reform.

The political and social conditions under which the people of the Roman states then lived could not have been maintained anywhere in Christendom excepting by a government of priests. Only one-third of the soil was cultivated. The people were miserably poor. Employment was scarce and wages small. The country was overrun by brigands, whom government was powerless to restrain. The press was effectively bridled; literature and science was discouraged. Vaccination was not permitted. There was no education for the poor; and it was said that only one person in a thousand could read. Enterprise was repressed; men lived hopelessly in that degraded position to which they had been born. When certain capitalists proposed to organize steam navigation between Rome and the chief towns of the sea-coast, the papal government withdrew its consent after the ships were contracted for. The origin and perpetuation of these evils are sufficiently explained by the circumstance that there was in Rome one ecclesiastic for every ten families.

When death had silenced Pope Gregory's defence of the rank abuses which surrounded him, his vacant throne was occupied by Pius IX., a man who, under more favourable circumstances, would probably have lent his aid to the cause of progress and improvement.* His task as a temporal prince had fallen on evil times; but he did not for a moment forget the grave theological interests of which he was the guardian. He occupied himself about "the prerogatives of the mother of God," while secret societies undermined his throne and revolution thundered at his gates. The absolute sinlessness of the Virgin Mary had, until now, been a subject re-

1846
A. D.

* See Chapter v., Book III.

garding which loyal Catholics might without impropriety differ They had differed, and much controversy had ensued, not leading towards any satisfying result. The pope desired to terminate these uncertainties, to silence controvesy, to make it a wickedness for the faithful longer to question the immaculate purity of Mary. He inquired of the bishops in all parts 1849 of the world what were their opinions and their advice A. D. on this subject. The bishops were courtiers as well as ecclesiastics, and they replied in the terms which, as they perceived, would be acceptable. The holy father, solaced and encouraged by the support which he received, issued the bull "Ineffabilis" for the instruction of the faithful. It was 1854 a high day in Rome. A multitude of ecclesiastics past A. D. numbering walked in solemn procession. The pope, under deep emotion, crowned with a diadem the figure of the Madonna. And then he declared it to be a doctrine revealed by God that the Virgin Mary "from the first instant of her conception was preserved immaculate from all stain of original sin." He who hereafter disputed this newly disclosed truth "suffered shipwreck of the faith and incurred the penalties justly established against heresy."*

Ten years after Christendom was enriched by this weighty dogma, the pope celebrated the high anniversary by Dec. 8, publishing an encyclical letter for the guidance and encouragement of the faithful. Having offered some in-1864 structions concerning the approach of his people to the A. D. Virgin Mary, "the well-beloved mother of us all," whom the church had so highly honoured, and who had "destroyed all heresies throughout the world," the holy father proceeded to

---

* The church had brooded for many centuries over this question, and had suffered vast conflicts of opinion in her efforts to settle it. There were two great contending doctrines: the earliest was that of the Immaculate Nativity, which asserts that Mary was liberated from sin and born without it. Since the eleventh century this doctrine has been felt to be less and less adequate to explain the absolute sinlessness of Mary. The doctrine of the Immaculate Conception teaches that Mary was free from sin in the very first moment of her existence; and this having been deemed a more satisfactory solution of the problem than the other, has, as we see, been conclusively adopted.

compile a catalogue of eighty separate and distinct heresies over which he pronounced his solemn anathema. Thirty-seven of these pernicious tenets bore reference to such matters as pantheism, rationalism, and religious indifference; ten related to marriage; twenty were errors against the church; the balance were political heresies. Foremost among these was the detestable opinion that "the pope can and ought to become reconciled to progress, liberalism, and modern civilization." Equally offensive was the opinion that "civil liberty of worship and freedom of the press do not conduce to the corruption of morals." These poisonous opinions, and the erring persons who held them, were cursed by the holy father with all the vigour of execration for which Rome has ever been renowned. Moreover, the pope condemned with equal heartiness all societies for circulating the Scriptures, and all persons, not being members of the true church, who presumed to entertain any hope of eternal salvation for themselves or other misbelievers.

In this manner Rome defined her attitude to the nineteenth century. During fifty years a marvellously rich development had taken place in human affairs,—a marvellous progress in intelligence, in regulated freedom of thought and action, in inventions higly endowed with power to benefit man; and by necessary consequence a marvellous addition to the well-being of the human family. It behoved the church to express herself regarding these unprecedented circumstances. She opened her lips to curse them. She announced irreconcilable and eternal hostility to the spirit and impulses which are the peculiar glory of the age. She placed the stamp of her preference upon the imperfect development of an earlier time. She condemned Heaven's great law of progress,—of advancement from a lower level of cultivation and well-being to a higher,—and sought to lay enduring arrest upon its operation. Thus Rome broke finally with the nineteenth century, and declared her antagonism to all its maxims, its aims, its achievements. And the millions who owned her sway raised no protest, uttered no remonstrance. Nay, a few years after, their chiefs are found solemnly declaring that the man who was specially chargeable with this egregious folly was so amply blessed with divine guidance that error was to him impossible.

In 1868 the sorrows of the holy father had reached a measure of intensity which seemed to lift them above the possibility of augmentation. All Italy was now free and united, excepting the patrimony of St. Peter, which remained a little islet of despotism and misrule alone in a great sea of liberty and order. The French troops, whose bayonets had long upheld papal authority, had lowered their flag and marched out of Rome.* The Romans had risen against their father, and wicked persons had blown up with gunpowder the barracks in which his soldiers lodged. Garibaldi, "the evil genius of the Italian peninsula," had defeated his army. Austria had withdrawn from the church the control of her schools, and allowed freedom of the press and of worship—proceedings which the grieved pope condemned as "abominable." Italy made it too plain that she intended Rome to become, as of old, the capital of the kingdom. In the words of the pope himself, "Satan, his satellites and his sons, did not cease to set loose in the most horrible manner their fury against our divine religion, against us, and against the chair of St. Peter."

June 29, Fallen thus on evil times, his holiness summoned to
1868 his aid the princes of the church. "A horrible tempest"
A. D. was threatening society and religion, and a council was required to find and apply a remedy for the thickening miseries of the time.

Dec. 8, In obedience to his call the twentieth Ecumenical
1869 Council convened in Rome. Nearly eight hundred
A. D. priests, of whom the larger portion were bishops, arch-

---

* "Difficult and sorrowful are the times in which we live," said the pope, when the French withdrew and left him alone with his subjects.

bishops, and patriarchs, formed the august assembly. The distances from which they came illustrate impressively the widely extended authority of Rome. Toilsomely across Asiatic deserts, borne by swift Atlantic steamers, the soldiers of the church journeyed to her relief. The Patriarch of Babylon reminded men of the slow, unmoving societies of the East, and carried their thoughts back to the mysterious depths of unrecorded time which lie around the cradle of the human race. The Bishop of Chicago symbolized the fiery, unresting activities of the New World. The Archbishop of Westminster brought with him distasteful suggestions of London, where in a special sense "Satan hath his seat." Crowds of dignified ecclesiastics from Eastern lands dominated by the followers of the false prophet breathed gladly for a little space the congenial air of Rome, and approached with unbounded devotion the head of their church. There were archbishops bearing the names of those famous and fallen churches to which the Apostle John conveyed mysterious words of commendation and rebuke eighteen hundred years ago. Thirty nations were represented. From France, from Austria, from Spain, from South America vexed by perennial revolution, saintly men hastened to Rome to save religion and society from the calamity of liberty and progress. The pope had summoned all Christendom to his help. But there were differences not yet ready to be reconciled. The Greek Patriarch of Constantinople declared the convening of the council to be "vain and fruitless," and ungraciously returned the letter which conveyed the papal summons. Schismatical Russia would not even permit her Polish bishops to attend the council. Heretical Prussia declined the invitation. England, busied with matters which seemed to her more urgent, scarcely condescended to notice it. Bavaria actually sought to bring about a combination of governments which should prevent the council from being held.

The Council of the Vatican met in the great hall in the

Church of St. Peter. The holy father, clothed in white, snt upon a throne, with a golden mitre on his head, made specially for this high occasion. The bishops, too, were all in white; for it was the Feast of the Immaculate Conception. The white-robed bishops advanced in long procession, and one by one knelt down and kissed the knee of the white-robed father. The pope three times blessed his children, and then he addressed to them an opening exposition of the sorrows which they had come to heal.

The purpose of the council, as the pope himself comprehensively defined it, was "to supply a remedy for the many evils which disturbed the church and society." During the months which intervened between the summoning and the meeting of the council, there had been eager debate as to the special remedial measures which were appropriate to the crisis. Gradually from out the multitude of suggestions one rose pre-eminent, and engrossed the thought of the church. The personal infallibility of the pope ought to be asserted. The whole power of the church ought to be concentrated in the person of his holiness. The father of endangered Christendom ought to meet his enemies with an overawing claim to the prerogatives of divinity. The world, it was said, was worn out with vacillation and uncertainty. Its supreme need was to find assured truth, and a person qualified to proclaim the same. Let this need at last, after long centuries of waiting, be satisfied by the assurance that the pope is the inspired and unerring revealer of all truth.

It was no new device which the papal party now pressed upon the church. A powerful impulse has from the earliest period of her career driven Rome towards the establishment of absolute despotism. No sooner was her primacy acknowledged than her apologists began to assert the unlimited power of the pope. Somewhat later that claim was strengthened by the suggestion that it was impossible for the pope to err. Among the manifold controversies of the schoolmen in the twelfth and thirteenth centuries the dogma of Papal Infallibility is to be met with, and its vindicators grow bolder as the years pass on. During the century which preceded the Reformation—when the vices and errors of the Papacy became gigantic beyond human endurance—the doctrine of infallibility made rapid progress. For a time Rome was discredited by the great secession, and those who desired the increase of her authority were silenced. But the freedom of thought claimed by the Reformation was a thing too high for the enfeebled intellect of the Catholic nations. In the reaction which ensued, men sought refuge from the anxieties and responsibilities of inquiry in blind and passive obedience to authority. The order of the Jesuits, formed at this time, expressed truly, in its fundamental laws, the sentiment of the age. During the ensuing centuries, the inherent despotism of Rome advanced slowly but with unswerving tenacity to its coveted investiture with unlimited authority sanctioned by inability to err.* The revolutionary tempest which has raged around the church during the nineteenth century quickened the movement. Rome could not stay the departure of her temporal sovereignty,—could not prevent the governments of Europe from bestowing a constantly diminishing regard upon her wishes. There was all the greater need to assert loudly her supernatural pretensions. The claim to infallibility is the reply of Rome to the aggressive liberalism of the age.

It was known very early in the history of the council that an overwhelming majority of members proposed to save the church by conferring unlimited power upon her head. Only a small minority hesitated in presence of absolutism such as Christendom had never known before. Archbishop Manning, lately a Protestant, now more popish than the pope himself, was prominent among the champions of infallibility; as a French priest, the Bishop of Orleans was among its adversaries.

The council had much work laid out for it. It was arranged

---

* Centuries passed while the question was under discussion whether infallibility attached to the person or the office of the pope.

in four great sections, under the heads of Faith, Discipline, Affairs of the East, and Religious Orders. The fathers debated a multitude of topics. The manners and also the garments of the clergy, the catechism, the authority of the bishops over priests and of the pope over bishops, with other topics of sub-ordinate interest, occupied the meetings of five months. Witty fathers, if they were asked when the council would finish, replied by inquiring when it would begin. During all these months the question of infallibility had scarcely been named. It filled all minds; it was eagerly debated out of doors; manifold intrigues were framed by the promoters of the dogma. But as yet the council appeared to shun the supreme hour on whose decision the future of the church, for good or for evil, must depend. The excitement of approaching battle already stirred the pulses of the fathers. Already an unacceptable speech was received with "violent gestures." The saintly calm of the council hall had once been broken by a formidable uproar, which so agitated the sympathetic crowd without that the civil arm had to interpose in the interests of tranquillity. A certain Armenian vicar-general offended the pope by an act of imperfect obedience, whereupon the holy father ordered his arrest. The unruly ecclesiastic resisted the ministers of papal justice, and much scandal ensued from his audacious contumacy. But a still worse scandal arose from the action of the Turkish ambassador at Florence. That officious unbeliever, hearing of the incident hastened to Rome to offer to an Armenian Christian ecclesiastic of dignity the protection of his odious government against the universal father of Christendom!

But time soothed these agitations, and at length the arena was cleared for the great contest. The powers of the Vatican had been diligent in forwarding a cause which was peculiarly their own. The pope himself openly promoted the dogma; openly blessed its supporters; openly prayed for the illumination of its enemies. Public processions, prayers and masses, kindled the religious enthusiasm of the faithful. The authorities watched with anxious care the currents of opinion within the council. They circulated schemes for the enactment of infallibility, with the customary anathema on all unreasonable persons who hesitated to accept the same. They modified or silently dropped these proposals when they found that opinion was scarcely ripened up to the necessary point. They " strongly advised " the parish priests of Rome to sign an address in favour of infallibility, and their advice was accepted with unconcealed reluctance. With admirable strategic skill they guided the great measure onward to success.

The Bishop of Poitiers opened the debate in a long and ardent harangue. His purpose was to exalt the church by showing the superiority of St. Peter over St. Paul. As one conclusive evidence of that superiority, he dwelt upon the circumstance that Providence allowed Paul to be beheaded, but protected Peter from such a doom. The already convinced fathers seemed by their applause to accept the argument as satisfactory. *May 18, 1870 A. D.*

Henceforth the council gave itself to the absorbing controversy. The minority, which was held to number one hundred and fifty to two hundred fathers, fought with steady but despairing resolution. They foretold schisms and abjurations in the church as the consequence of this unhappy measure. An American bishop, nursed in democracy, stated that the scheme was repugnant to his countrymen, and would form an obstacle to the conversion of Protestants. The Bishop of Savannah denounced it as sacrilegious, at which statement a loud uproar burst from the angry majority. The eagerness to take part in the debate was excessive. One day seventy fathers inscribed their names as intending orators; another day the candidates numbered eighty; later on they rose to one hundred and eight. Speeches were strictly limited to twenty minutes, and a bell was provided to aid the president in the frequent necessity of

29

silencing orators who were diposed to transgress. At length
the majority became impatient of this inundation of
June 3, words, and by a sudden vote declared the general debate
1870
A. D. closed. Henceforth only the details of the measure
might be spoken to.

Displeased with this violence, a few of the liberal bishops
quitted the council and returned to their dioceses. The minority
was now held to number about one hundred and thirty. A
nearly unanimous vote was indispensable, and the strength of
the opposition gave much concern to the Vatican. All attempts
to divide or win over having failed, the Archbishop of Malines
suggested that the council should terminate the difficulty by
cursing the obstructive fathers, and driving them from the
church. It was said that the Archbishop of Westminster approved of this vigorous policy. But when it appeared that the
proposal would seriously divide the majority, more moderate
counsels prevailed.

All through the month of June the debate drew out its interminable length. July came with its burning heat, its pestilential airs from the marshes of the Campagna. The thermometer
stood at one hundred and fifteen degrees in the shade. The
fathers, all elderly men, drooped in the sickening heat, and
many of them—especially those accustomed to northern tem-
peratures—became ill. Some of them died. The opposition
besought the pope to adjourn the council. But the Vatican
would not be baffled, and the petition was refused. The
July 3. minority resolved to discontinue a vain resistance, and
the debate closed.

The council met in public to confirm what had already been
done at private meetings. There were present only five
July 18. hundred and thirty-five members, the minority being
wholly absent. Two votes were recorded against the measure.
One was given by an Italian, the other by the Bishop of Little
Rock in Arkansas. While the vote was being taken, thunder

pealed and lightning flashed around the fathers. · The enemies
of infallibility recognized the voice of divine indignation; its
friends were reminded of Sinai and the Ten Commandments.
The pope in a short speech acknowledged the greatness of the
dignity now assured to him. The monks, nuns, and other
religious persons who hovered around the doors of the hall
gave clamorous expression to the joy which this great victory
inspired. In the evening the public buildings and a few private houses were illuminated, but the city maintained an attitude of indifference. Sixty-three bishops protested formally
against the step which the council had taken. Next day the
official journal announced that the decision was unanimous,
with the exception of two votes.

The declaration of Papal Infallibility was delivered to the
church enveloped in malediction, the familiar drapery of papal
decrees. It solemnly anathematized the following persons:—
Those who deny that the blessed Apostle Peter was chief
of the apostles and head of the whole vissible church.
Those who deny that Peter had perpetual successors, or
that the Roman pontiffs are his successors.
Those who deny the supreme authority of the pope over all
churches and pastors in all parts of the world, not only in regard to faith and morals, but also in regard to discipline and
government.
Those who deny that the official decisions of the Roman
pontiff, on questions of faith and morals, are infallible, without
any consent of the church.

On the surface it seems merely an idle jest that five hundred
elderly gentlemen, after months of agitating debate, should
gravely declare another gentleman, also elderly and conspicuously erring, to be wholly incapable of error. But this view,
however just, does by no means exhaust the significance of the

transaction. The assertion of infallibility is a reiterated declaration of irreconcilable hostility against all enlightening
modern impulses. It is the assumption of power more despotic
than the world ever knew before, in order the better to give
effect to that hostility. Such a despotism, accepted by two
hundred million Christians, and animated by such a motive,
cannot be lightly regarded.

But it furnishes no ground of alarm. This vast and threatening aggression upon human liberty is, in truth, an evidence
of decay. It is a device of church officials, forced upon them
by the decline of faith among their people. The supporters
of infallibility were especially numerous in France and Italy,
where the power of the church is waning; in England and in
Eastern countries, where the faithful are a little band living
among enemies. The growing intelligence of Europe saps the
foundations of papal authority. Men who are learning to read
and reflect, and who have tasted the enlightening influences of
travel, cannot help an increasing alienation from a power which
abhors railways and the printing-press, and would gladly suppress freedom of thought if it could. Men used to self-government in state feel the yoke of absolute authority in church
becoming constantly more irksome. Priests, conscious of the
charge, flock to Rome and vainly strive to recall by the vote
of a council the diminishing supremacy of the church. It is
the only defensive measure that is possible for them. Once
Rome could prevent progress; now she can but curse it.

Rome has entered on a mortal contest with forces which are
universal, ineradicable, irresistible. She has undertaken to arrest and turn back the mightiest power upon the earth. She
has announced resistance to the laws of Providence—silent,
patient, but undeviating. Nothing less than shameful defeat
can result from such an enterprise. The nations which own
her sway cannot now be barred from increase of intelligence—
cannot therefore be prevented from contemning as ascertained

foolishness the counsels on whose behalf she asserts infallibility. If Rome is unable to reconcile herself to modern civilization, her decline and fall are inevitable.

Just as this great victory was gained, it became known to his holiness that France, "with a light heart," had declared war against Prussia. In quick succession there came ^{July 19,} 1870 tidings of unparalleled disaster to the "eldest son" of the A. D. church. The strong arm was broken which had so long maintained the patrimony of St. Peter against the encroachments of " Satan, his satellites and his sons." The holly father's extremity was Satan's opportunity. The Italian government sent an army to possess the ancient capital. The pope would not voluntarily relinquish any portion of the church's possessions, and a gentle cannonade was found to be necessary. The troops entered Rome by a breach which ^{Sept. 20} their artillery created. The people were invited to choose whether they would be ruled by the pope or the king. They were practically unanimous* in rejecting priestly government and joining themselves to their countrymen. The rights of the pope as the spiritual chief of a large body of Christians were scrupulously conserved. There was guaranted to him an income of nearly one hundred and fifty thousand pounds sterling. The Vatican — a palace with eleven thousand apartments—was assigned to him as a palace of residence. He was endowed with certain ecclesiastical buildings, as beseemed the establishment of a spiritual prince. His free exercise of his own proper sovereign functions was secured. But every shred of temporal sovereignty had now departed. On the closing day of the year Victor Emanuel entered Rome—once more the capital of united Italy.

Defeats came thick on the infallible pontiff, whose lofty pretensions the blinded nations treated with cruel disregard. His

---

* The numbers were one hundred and thirty-three thousand six hundred and eighty-one to one thousand five hundred and seven. Ever since, the Romans keep holiday on the anniversary of the plebiscite, in joyful commemoration of their great deliverance.

clergy, fired by the consciousness of a chief to whom error was impossible, went forth with quickened zeal to reclaim the allegiance of backsliding Europe. They pursued this arduous enterprise in Prussia as elsewhere. In that country the church enjoyed rights of inspection and superintendence of schools, and the priests used the opportunity with undue vigour for the purposes of proselytism. The work was full of peril,

March 1872 A. D. but to the servants of an infallible power fear was unknown. Prince Bismarck met their indiscreet zeal by a law which withdrew from the church and transferred to the state the supervision of all educational institutions and the appointment of all inspectors of schools. The Vatican highly resented this diminution of its prerogatives. Many hard words were lavished on the king, "the modern Diocletian," and Bismarck, "his bloodthirsty minister." The church necessarily regarded with disfavour the great revolution which had cast down France and consolidated Germany under a Protestant chief. She was not reluctant to wage war with the newly established order which was so hostile to her own principles and interests. The German clergy were soon in arms against the state, striving by every means to weaken the authority of the government and to conquer German for the pope. Prince Bismarck did not shrink from the inevitable contest.

July 1872 A. D. The Jesuits, whose mischievous political intrigue has been for centuries a standing menace to government, were expelled from the German empire. And then there was enacted in Prussia a code of laws for the regulation of eccesiastical affairs. Prussia endows a Catholic as well as a

1873 A. D. Protestant Church; and as the preists could not dispense with their incomes, they were well within reach of the arm of the state. Dr. Falck, the minister of public worship, introduced the new laws, which have since been called by his name. The aspirant to a clerical office must study theology for three years at a German state university, and must pass a state examination in science. The royal tribunal might forbid his appointment should his acquirements seem defective or his loyalty to the government doubtful. For offences against public order he might be dismissed from his office by the state authorities. Ecclesiastical discipline was not to be exercised excepting by German ecclesiastical authorities, and every punishment, excepting the most trivial, must be reported to the appropriate state officials. Intimidation of electors, an offence to which Romish ecclesiastics are prone, was punishable by fine or imprisonment. A Prussian who chose dissent might now free himself from his obligations of membership in the state churches by a simple declaration before the judge of his district. In all ecclesiastical causes the decision of the royal tribunal was final.

Rome denounced, as "impious and satanic," laws which curbed so sternly her injurious pretensions. The pope declared them void, and excommunicated all clergy who yielded obedience. But none the less for his objurgation were the laws enforced with a salutary vigour which all but extreme Romanists approved.

A year or two later another blow was struck by Prussia at ecclesiastical domination. Marriage was declared to be a mere civil contract. The church was at liberty to attach to it any religious ceremonial which she might deem appropriate, but her operations were no longer of legal significance. Nor was this defection confined to Prussia. In Italy, in Austria, and in France, marriage, ceasing to be a sacrament of the church, has become merely a civil contract. *Jan. 1875 A. D.*

Pio Nono survived for nearly eight years the loss of his temporal sovereignty. His closing years were full of trouble. From the windows of the Vatican he could see, on the Quirinal, the flag of that reprobate king who had stripped the church of her patrimony. He could see also a scarcely less offensive sight—the depot whence an English Bible Society supplied openly copies of the Scriptures to the Roman people. He never quitted the Vatican, and persisted in speaking of himself as a prisoner. He refused to accept the income which the Italian government offered, choosing that the dignity of his office should be upheld by the free contributions of the faithful. He had once before said of himself,—"I am weak; I have no resource upon earth; I tranquilize myself by confiding in God." At length, after lingering into extreme and burdensome age, he passed away.

1878
A. D.

CHAPTER X.

THE PROGRESS OF LIBERTY IN EUROPE.

THE French revolution—interrupted and abortive as it seemed—rendered forever impossible the continuance of the despotism which had heretofore governed Europe. Napoleon—himself one of the most extreme of despots—sowed revolutionary principles broadcast over Europe. His judicial code taught the equality of man before the law. His overthrow of multitudinous princes inculcated a lower estimate than had hitherto prevailed of the sanctity of crowned heads. His consolidation of the petty German states awakened the desire for a united Germany and paved the way for its accomplishment. His administration of Italy taught the excellence of unity and self-government—lessons which the people effectively learned and never forgot. He gave constitutional government for a time to Naples, Westphalia, and Spain. He weakened the temporal power of the pope; he dealt fatal blows at the immunities of the old feudal nobility. His rude assault shook to its foundation the whole fabric of privilege and unjust preference of one class over its fellows, and led the lower orders of the people to entertain new ideas regarding their own rights. Never before had influences so powerful been brought so widely into operation over vast multitudes of men. The results were quickly apparent. When Napoleon fell the desire for self-government had silently overspread Europe.* And the anxiety which dis-

* Napoleon himself was the first to appreciate the change. On his return from Elba he intimated that as the people wished for liberty and constitutional government he was ready to grant their wish.

457

tressed monarchs evinced to please their subjects, and thus gain their help against the arch-oppressor, began to disclose to the people the secret of their own strength.

To all this the Congress of Vienna was absolutely blind. A consciousness of irresistible military force possessed its members and pervaded all their decisions. It is told that when the King of Piedmont was restored to his throne he called for an old court almanac, and restored the ceremonial which formed so large a portion of its existence, in strict accordance with pre-revolutionary models. In a similar temper the congress reconstructed Europe. It regarded the revolution and all that flowed from it as a series of exceptional violences now happily suppressed. It aim was to restore to authority what revolution had torn away. Its concern was for the interests of princes. It dreamed not of the new forces which had been silently waxing strong underneath the tumult and confusion of universal war. The old world was reproduced, with only the trifling modifications which were plainly indispensable. When the great settlement was complete, all the interests of Europe were given over to the absolute control of a few families. Britain indeed enjoyed constitutional government, the privileges of which were confined to a very small class. France had received in gift from the restored Bourbon king a charter, according to which that monarch promised that he would conduct his government. Everywhere besides, the will of the king was the law of the European people. Everywhere the people desired and expected free institutions in fulfilment of promises which their sovereigns had made to them; everywhere these promises were violated. The struggle by which, during the succeeding half century, the nations of Europe vindicated their liberties and won back their inherent right of self-government is unsurpassed in interest, as the victory gained is unsurpassed in grandeur and beneficence.

The impulse which first broke a hollow and insincere tranquillity issued from the insurrectionary movements in South

America. The American possessions of Spain had risen against the despotism under which they had long suffered, and successfully asserted their independence. Their success kindled a democratic ardour in Spain herself. Some years before, while the French occupation still existed, the Spanish Cortes had adopted a constitution, of which universal suffrage and biennial parliaments were prominent features. When the exiled Bourbon king was sent back to his throne he hastened to subvert the constitution and restore congenial despotism. But now an insurrection burst out and overspread a large portion of the country. The king was obliged to yield, and the constitution of 1812 was proclaimed. The movement extended into Portugal on the one hand, into Naples and Piedmont on the other. Everywhere the insurgents demanded to be governed according to the Spanish constitution, and everywhere they gained for the time complete success. In England, in France, in Germany there were many evidences of popular sympathy with the liberals of the southern peninsulas; but the impulse was not yet of such strength as to result in the disturbance of public order.

_1820_
_A. D._

Across the Adriatic, Greece took encouragement from the energy of her neighbours to assert the liberty of which Turkish oppression defrauded her. Helped by Europe, she succeeded, and was enabled to establish herself as a free state. No other gain for liberty was secured at that time. The French Bourbons, with appropriately despotic sympathies, sent an army into Spain and silenced the demand for constitutional government. Austria performed the same congenial office in the Italian peninsula. The liberal agitations of the south were calmed by the slaughter of their authors.

But the interest which the Greek war of independence awakened throughout Europe was a powerful factor in dispelling political apathy. It was felt especially in France, where it hastened the revolution of July. The influences of that great outburst reached all the states of

_1830_
_A. D._

western Europe.   It turned men's minds everywhere to political thought and discussion.   It quickened the efforts of the
Swiss to overthrow the undue authority of the ruling families
in the cities; to gain equal rights for the rural districts; and
to consolidate the central government on a purely democratic
basis.   It roused the unhappy Poles to the revolt which was so
ruthlessly suppressed.   It strengthened in England the desire
for parliamentary reform.   In Italy it encouraged the subjects
of the pope to a rising which the Austrians easily trampled
down.   In Germany it kindled political excitement which led
to the very verge of insurrection.

The events of 1830 may be said to mark the complete political awakening of Europe.   For fifteen years the despotic
governments had been able, with little effort, to repress the
liberal tendencies of their people.   Now the conflict entered a
new phase.   The free spirit drew from the movements of this
year reinforcement so powerful that the task of despotism
became year by year more hopelessly difficult.   Secret associations of rapidly growing strength and determination overspread
Europe.*   On the surface prevailed the submissive calm which
absolute governments love; underneath, forces were mustering
which were destined ere long to trample absolutism in the dust.

Throughout the non-Germanic provinces of Austria a new
political life manifested itself.   The Hungarians and Slavs
began to dream of national independence, and a spirit of resistance to the existing order of things spread silently over the
empire.   The Germans, powerless against the bayonets of the
associated despots, cherished in secret a constantly growing
desire to be united and free.   Italy was a vast network of
political societies, in which, notwithstanding the energy of the
police, the insurrectionary spirit perfected its organization and
waited for its opportunity.   The people of Great Britain quelled
the obstinate resistance of their privileged class, and entered on

* See Note A. "Secret Societies."

possession of their right of self-government. The provinces of Turkey felt the universal impulse; Egypt and Syria sought to throw off the hateful yoke. France alone, under the corrupting influences of the citizen monarchy, seemed to enter upon a period of reaction; but this was apparent rather than real.

When in 1848 a French revolution flung out for the third time its terrible summons to the European people, it became at once evident how largely the cause of freedom had gained in strength. Liberalism could now venture everywhere to try conclusions in battle with the forces of absolutism. The Hungarians asserted their independence of Austria by well-organized military operations which rose to the dignity of a great war, and would have gained success but for the intervention of a foreign power. Italy had been able to lay a solid foundation for her long-desired unity. The Sardinians had obtained constitutional government, and their king was in some measure prepared to give expression to the national demand. Everywhere the Italian people rose in arms, and strove in regular and not extremely unequal battle to drive the Austrians out of the peninsula. The liberals of Vienna took possession of the capital, and maintained it for a time against the royal forces. In Prussia and the smaller German states the people exacted by force a temporary fulfilment of the broken promises which had been made thirty years before. France expelled her king and hastened back to republican government. Even English Chartism—then a mere reminiscecne of injustice which had ceased—was roused by the impulses of the time to an expiring effort in the direction of a wider liberty than was yet enjoyed.

In so far as their immediate object was concerned, all these efforts failed. A Russian army set up again the despotism which the patriots of Hungary had overthrown. In the Italian peninsula Austria restored such order as her government loved; at home she quelled with terrible slaughter the insurrection of her capital. In Prussia and the minor German states the governments found themselves strong enough to annul liberal concessions made in moments of weakness and fear. France relapsed into the degradations of the empire. In Britain—happier than any other European state—those who would have made a revolution without any sufficient basis of unredressed grievance were baffled by the contentment of the people with the institutions under which they lived.

Liberalism fell once more, crushed by the military strength which absolute governments commanded. But even in its fall it triumphed. A spirit now prevailed which it was impossible to resist. Despotism exists only by sufferance; it cannot continue when nations have determined that it shall cease. The absolute princes felt themselves now under restraint to make peace with their people by the grant of free institutions. In Prussia representative government was firmly established, although its exercise was modified by the power of the executive, to which the people submitted willingly, in the belief that thus only could the unity of Germany be reached. Austria consoled her people for the defeats of Magenta and Solferino by the gift of parliamentary government. Constitutional Sardinia absorbed one Italian state after another, until at length final success crowned the protracted struggle, and the peninsula formed one free and self-governing kingdom. Spain dismissed her queen, and organized a government based on universal suffrage. Great Britain widened the basis of her electorial system, and admitted her labouring classes to their just influence in the direction of public affairs. France —the birthplace of Continental liberty—was among the last to gain the privilege for herself. But the fall of the empire restored the self-government of which she had been robbed twenty years before; and she received ample compensation even for the horrors and humiliations of a shameful war.

1860 A. D.

1870

1868

1867–8 A. D.

1870 A. D.

Western Europe was now free and self-governing. The long and painful transition from government by a few individuals to government by the people was accomplished. Sixty years ago Europe was an aggregate of despotic powers, disposing at their own pleasure of the lives and property of their subjects, maintaining by systematic neglect the convenient ignorance which renders misgovernment easy and safe. To-day the men of western Europe govern themselves. Popular suffrage, more or less closely approaching universal, chooses the governing power, and by methods more or less effective dictates its policy.* One hundred and eighty million Europeans have risen from a degraded and ever dissatisfied vassalage to the rank of free and self-governing men; and one of their earliest concerns has been to provide the means of universal education.† The East has not taken her place in this mighty progress. Russia—only a semi-European power—retains her despotism, and relegates to a still distant future the revolution by which she must rise to an equality with her sister states.

Human history is a record of progress—a record of accumulating knowledge and increasing wisdom, of continual advancement from a lower to a higher platform of intelligence and well-being. Each generation passes on to the next the treasures which it inherited, beneficially modified by its own experience, enlarged by the fruits of all the victories which itself has gained. The rate of this progress, as the eye of man deciphers it, is irregular and even fitful. Now it seems to pause, and the years seem to repeat themselves unalterable. Now it bursts forth in sudden ameliorations, in the violent overthrow of evils which had been quietly endured for generations. But the stagnation is only apparent. All the while there is a silent accumulation of forces whose gathered power will, in

* See Note B. "The Electoral System of Europe."
† See Note C. "Education in Europe."

Heaven's own time, reveal itself to the terror and the joy of man.

The nineteenth century has witnessed progress rapid beyond all precedent, for it has witnessed the overthrow of the barriers which prevented progress. Never since the stream of human development received into its sluggish currents the mighty impulse communicated by the Christian religion has the condition of man experienced ameliorations so vast. Despotism thwarts and frustrates the forces by which providence has provided for the progress of man; liberty secures for these forces their natural scope and exercise. The nineteenth century has witnessed the fall of despotism and the establishment of liberty in the most influential nations of the world. It has vindicated for all succeeding ages the right of man to his own unimpeded development. It has not seen the redressing of all wrongs; nor indeed is that to be hoped for, because in the ever-shifting conditions of man's life the right of one century becomes frequently the wrong of the next. But it has seen all that the most ardent reformer can desire—the removal of artificial obstacles placed in the path of human progress by the selfishness and ignorance of the strong. The growth of man's well-being, rescued from the mischievous tampering of self-willed princes, is left now to the beneficent regulation of great providential laws.

NOTE A, PAGE 460.   SECRET SOCIETIES.

SECRET combination is the natural and necessary method of resistance resorted to by men whose just liberties are invaded by despotic power. Prussia furnishes a curious and perhaps unique example of a despotic monarchy forced by a despotism stronger than itself to seek defence in secret association. When Prussia lay crushed under the merciless tyranny of Napoleon, Baron Stein, the prime minister of the day, bethought him how he could rouse the German spirit and unite the country against the invader. He devised the Tugendbund, or League of Virtue (1807), which spread rapidly over the country, and soon numbered in its ranks the flower of the people, including the very highest rank. Its organization and discipline were perfect, its authority unbounded, although the source of that authority was veiled in the deepest secrecy. One of the motives by which Stein kindled to white-heat the enthusiasm of the people was the hope of representative institutions and a free press; but the king did not hesitate to violate his royal promise when its purpose was served. The Tugendbund contributed powerfully to the resurrection of German national life in 1813, and to the overthrow of Napoleon.

The Society of the Carbonari (whose authentic history goes no further back than to 1814) was an agent of inestimable value in the regeneration of Italy. In default of good government by those who had assumed the function of governing, this society instituted a code of civil and criminal law different from that of the state, and inflicted penalties for the infringement of its laws. Its aims were, however, political and not judicial. It overspread the country so entirely that in some districts the whole adult male population were in its membership. It was tempted by its strength into premature and unsuccessful assaults upon the despotisms which it hated. Many of its members fell in battle; many of its chiefs perished in the dungeon or on the scaffold. But its incessant activity weakened the power of despotism and nourished into constantly growing strength the spirit of freedom and unity among the Italian people.

Some years later, Guiseppe Mazzini, one of the most purely self-devoted of Italians, deeming that the efforts of the Carbonari were unsuccessful because ill-directed, founded a new society under the designation of Young Italy. The avowed aim of this society was revolution and the unity of Italy under republican institutions. It sought these results by means of education and insurrection. To the latter Mazzini resorted with a frequency whose wisdom may well be doubted; but it admits of no doubt that his labours helped the great cause and hastened the deliverance of Italy.

In Germany, in Austria, in Russia, in Poland, in Greece, in France, in Spain, the oppressed people combined in secret to overthrow methods of government which had become intolerable. When their purpose was attained by the establishment of representative institutions, there was no longer a necessity or a desire to continue this irregular form of political action. The European nations having now a decisive voice in the creation of governments, have no motive for seeking their destruction. 'Self-government has brought progress and contentment, and the secret

30

societies of western Europe have passed away or sunk into insignificance. Only under the great despotism of the east are intelligent men still compelled to plot secretly against their government. The Russian secret society of "Nihilists" has, during the last ten years, gained much strength even among the educated classes. The aim of a portion of its membership seems to be the universal overthrow of institutions political and social—the throne, the military system, the church, property, marriage. There will then remain "pure humanity," with all its possibilities of an improved future. How profoundly must the minds of thinking men be affected by existing evils before suggestions so wild can gain support! It is not, however, to be supposed that such views as these are entertained by the majority of Nihilists. The generally prevailing desire points to nothing more objectionable than the establishment in Russia of those free institutions which western Europe has now gained.

NOTE B, Page 463. THE ELECTORAL SYSTEMS OF EUROPE.

THE following outline of the electoral systems of European countries shows the measure of completeness with which the privilege of self-government has been secured:—

	Upper Chamber appointed by	Lower Chamber appointed by
FRANCE	One-fourth by Senate, three-fourths by citizens of twenty-one.	Citizens of the age of twenty-one.
BELGIUM	Citizens who pay £1, 15s. in direct taxes.	Citizens who pay £1, 15s. in direct taxes.
AUSTRIA	Partly by crown; partly hereditary.	Citizens of twenty-one with small property qualifications.
HUNGARY	Mainly hereditary.	Citizens of twenty-one paying 16s. in direct taxes.
PRUSSIA	Mainly crown.	Citizens of twenty-five, classed according to taxation.
GERMANY	The individual states.	Universal suffrage.
DENMARK	Partly by crown; mainly by citizens.	Citizens of thirty.
GREAT BRITAIN	Crown; and hereditary.	In towns, householders who pay poor-rates; in counties, tenants who pay rental of £12.
ITALY	Crown.	Citizens of twenty-five who pay £1, 12s. in direct taxes.
GREECE	[Single Chamber.]	Manhood suffrage.
PORTUGAL	Crown.	Citizens with income of £22.

NETHERLANDS...Provincial states.

Citizens who pay £1, 13s. in direct taxes.

RUSSIA ....[Absolute Monarchy.]
SPAIN ....Crown and corporations.

Electoral juntas.

SWITZERLAND ...The cantons.

Males of twenty.

NORWAY.........[Single Chamber.]

Citizens of twenty-five with property qualifications of £33.

SWEDEN .... Representatives of corporations, etc.

Natives of twenty-one with property qualifications of £56.

SERVIA ....Crown.

Males of twenty-one paying direct taxes.

ROUMANIA .... .All citizens of twenty-five who can read and write.

All citizens of twenty-five who can read and write.

NOTE C, PAGE 463. EDUCATION IN EUROPE.

THE following outline presents a summary of the educational arrangements of European countries:—

AUSTRIA-HUNGARY.—Compulsory, since 1849, between six and twelve years of age. Compulsion fully carried out only in Germanic portions of the empire. Supported by imperial and local taxation.

DENMARK.—Compulsory from seven to fourteen; poor children taught gratuitously.

BELGIUM.—No compulsory law; one-fifth of adult population unable to read.

FRANCE.—Supported and directed by government at a cost of £2,000,000. Thirty per cent of population above six unable to read.

GERMANY.—Compulsory, and almost universal. Supported by local rates, and governed locally. All the recruits of 1870 could read.

GREAT BRITAIN.—Compulsory. Expenditure of England and Wales, £3,915,441.

GREECE.—Nominally but not really compulsory. Only one third of grown men and one woman in fourteen able to read.

ITALY.—In 1864 only one-fifth of the people could read. Considerable progress has been made since. Government expends a million sterling, besides the confiscated monastic funds.

NETHERLANDS.—Compulsory since 1878; one in seven and a half at school; among rural population one-fourth of the men and one-third of the women unable to read.

PORTUGAL.—Nominally but not really compulsory; one in thirty-six at school.

SPAIN.—In 1860, three-fourths of population unable to read. In 1871, one in sixteen at school.

SWITZERLAND.—Compulsory. Attendance in Protestant cantons, one in five; in mixed cantons, one in seven; in Roman Catholic cantons, one in nine.

RUSSIA.—Government expends on education about £2,000,000; of this, only £350,000 on primary education. In 1870 only eleven per cent. of recruits could read; but this has improved since. In Finland the whole population can read.

www.ingramcontent.com/pod-product-compliance
Lightning Source LLC
LaVergne TN
LVHW012207040326
832903LV00003B/172